CADOGANguides

VIENNA, PRAGUE, BUDAPEST

*'Lovers of café life, lavish cakes, classical music, Baroque or
Gothic architecture, Art Nouveau, Jewish history or antiques
shopping will find something of interest in each; each has a
palimpsest of a castle whose layers tell the story of the city's past;
each has a labyrinthine warren of an old town at its heart,
with lanes and passages to wander in.'*

Mary-Ann Gallagher, Sadakat Kadri, Matthew Gardner

About the Guide

The full-colour introduction gives the authors' overview, together with suggested itineraries for each city to help you plan your trip.

Planning Your Trip starts with the basics of when to go, getting there and getting around, coupled with other useful information, including a section for disabled travellers.

Each of the three city chapters begins with a Practical A–Z section, providing all the essential information and contact details that you may need while you are away. The city sights follow, arranged in a loose touring order, and complemented with plenty of practical information on how to get around, where to eat and stay, as well as suggestions for day trips. Following the city chapters, you'll find a language and pronunciation guide.

The authors' top 'Don't Miss' ✪ sights are highlighted at the start of each chapter.

Although everything we list in this guide is personally recommended, our authors inevitably have their own favourite places to eat and stay. Whenever you see this Author's Choice ★ icon beside a listing, you will know that it is a little bit out of the ordinary.

Hotel Price Guide

	Vienna	Prague	Budapest
Luxury (€€€€)	over €250	over 5,000kč	over €180
Expensive (€€€)	€150–€250	3,500–5,000kč	€140–€180
Moderate (€€)	€100–€150	2,000–3,500kč	€80–€140
Inexpensive (€)	under €100	under 2,000kč	under €80

Restaurant Price Guide

	Vienna	Prague	Budapest
Luxury (€€€€)	over €60	over 1,500kč	over €50
Expensive (€€€)	€40–€60	1,000–1,500kč	€35–€50
Moderate (€€)	€25–€40	500–1,000kč	€20–€35
Inexpensive (€)	under €25	under 500kč	under €20

3rd edition published 2011

01 INTRODUCING VIENNA, PRAGUE AND BUDAPEST

Top: Prague's
distinctive castle
Above: Viennese
fountain detail

The great central European cities of Vienna, Prague and Budapest are often combined into a single trip. This is partly because of their physical proximity, and partly because of their shared histories and cultures, which make the experience of visiting them similar in some ways, and certainly worthwhile for comparison. Lovers of café life, lavish cakes, classical music, Baroque or Gothic architecture, Art Nouveau, Jewish history or antiques shopping will find something of interest in each; each has a palimpsest of a castle whose layers tell the story of the city's past; each has a labyrinthine warren of an old town at its heart, with lanes and passages to wander in.

Not surprisingly, however, each city has its own distinct character, supported by different languages that are a matter for fierce national pride even as they wholeheartedly enter today's Europe; and each is compact, with a modern, clean, efficient transport system that makes getting around easy for native and visitor alike. Many people visiting all three cities will find it easiest to book on a tour operator trip that conveys you between them (*see* p.25). However, their proximity to one another makes it easy for the independent traveller to fly to one of the three and take a train to the others. Many airlines offer single fares, so you can fly into one place and out of another.

Top Ten: Vienna

1 The most theatrical of Gothic cathedrals: **Stephansdom**, p.52

2 The **Hofburg**, a glittering Imperial residence, with museums, Sisi's apartments, and the Spanish Riding School, p.59

3 A treasure trove of world-class art at the **Museum of Fine Arts (Kunsthistoriches Museum)**, p.69

4 Cool white curves and Klimt's sensuous Beethoven frieze define the iconic **Secession Building**, p.75

5 Superb contemporary art, a children's museum, and terrace cafés at the fashionable **MuseumsQuartier**, p.76–7

6 Art, design, textiles and decorative arts at the eminently stylish **MAK**, p.80–81

7 A fairytale palace complete with gardens and the world's oldest zoo: **Schönbrunn**, p.83

8 Wild **woods, wine villages and _heurigen_** around the city, p.105

9 Celebrate Vienna's extraordinary musical heritage with a night at the opera house, **Staatsoper**, p.73

10 A princely residence, magnificent gardens, and a fabulous art collection at the **Belvedere**, p.79

Above: Stephansdom Cathedral
Right: Museum of Fine Arts (Kunsthistoriches Museum)

Vienna's Café Society

According to local legend, Vienna's first *kaffeehaus* was established in the 17th century by a Polish soldier called Kulczycki, who was given some sacks of mysterious beans as a reward for his heroic part in delivering Vienna from the Turks. Kulczycki's picture still adorns many a coffeehouse, which have remained an intrinsic part of Viennese life over three centuries. Café society reached its height around the turn of the 20th century, when artists and intellectuals were fermenting artistic revolution, and their spirit lives on in many of the city's glorious Habsburg-era cafés.

Above: Classic Viennese Coffeehouse

- The **Café Bräunerhof** famously offers its guests the biggest selection of newspapers and magazines in the city, p.100

- Sigmund Freud and Leon Trotsky were among the former patrons of the elegantly vaulted **Café Central**, p.101

- The *grande dame* of Viennese coffeehouses, **Demel** prides itself on its spectacular cakes and pastries, p.101.

- Mozart´s last public performance took place in the historic **Café Frauenhuber** in 1791, p.101.

- A classic literary café, **Café Griensteidl** has a sought-after terrace overlooking the grandest Hofburg entrance gate, p.101

- A low-lit mecca for local artists, the **Café Hawelka** is the place to try jam-filled *buchteln*, p.101

- The splendidly formal **Café Sacher** is the home of the Sacher Torte, p.101

- The deliciously retro **Café Prückel** is filled with 1950s-style furnishings, p.102

- Handsomely refurbished, the century-old **Café Landtmann** boasts a wonderful terrace near the Rathaus, p.101

- Proudly unchanged, the **Café Sperl** oozes early-20th-century charm with its chandeliers and burnished woodwork, p.102

Vienna, City of Music

Music is embedded into the very soul of Vienna. The city has inspired some of the world's greatest composers – among them Haydn, Mozart, Beethoven, Schubert, Johann Strauss and Mahler – and opera houses and concert halls continue to host world-class performers.

- Watch an opera at the splendid **Staatsoper**, where Mahler was conductor, p.73
- The composer's former home and garden have been converted into the delightful **Haydn Museum**, p.45
- Mozart wrote *The Marriage of Figaro* in the **Mozarthaus**, now a museum and small concert hall, p.54
- Learn more about the 20th-century composer and his legacy at the **Arnold Schönberg Center**, p.46
- Pay your respects to Beethoven, Schubert, Brahms, Johann Strauss and other composers buried in the **Central Cemetery (Zentralfriedhof)**, p.86
- Enjoy the perfect acoustics of the lavishly decorated **Musikverein**, p.103

Above: Staatsoper (Opera House)

- Conduct your own orchestra at the entertaining **Haus der Musik**, p.56
- Attend the Hofburg chapel on Sundays, to hear the **Vienna Boys' Choir** singing mass, p. 59
- Waltz the night away at one of Vienna's celebrated **balls**, p.103
- Visit the **Beethoven Museum** in the pretty town of Mödling, p.105

Itinerary: Essential Vienna

If you've only got a couple of days in the city, this whirlwind tour will ensure you don't miss Vienna's best attractions. Don't forget to book concert tickets in advance.

Day One

Breakfast: Gird yourself for a full day of sightseeing with fresh pastries and coffee at the sumptuous 19th-century **Café Central** on Herengasse.

Morning: Walk down Herengasse to **Michaelerplatz**, and admire the huge Baroque gate into the **Hofburg** on your right. Peek in to **Michaelerskirche** for a glimpse of the mummified corpses of long-dead aristocrats in the crypt. Then stroll down **Kohlmarkt**, enjoying the window shopping, and turn right onto **Graben**, which has more fancy boutiques. Pause at the Baroque **Plague Column**, then continue walking until you reach **Stephansplatz**. Spend an hour exploring **Stephansdom** – don't miss the incredible views from the top of the towers. Keeping walking east until you reach Stubenring, part of the 19th-century ring road which encloses the city's old quarter.

Lunch: Stop for a traditional lunch at the **Café Prükel**, or, for something more contemporary, cross the street to the fashionable **Österreicher im MAK** in the Museum of Applied Arts.

Afternoon: Jump on a **tram** heading west, which will give you time to take in some of the splendid neoclassical edifices on the Ringstrasse, and jump off at the **Museum of Fine Arts**. This is one of the world's finest art museums, with an outstanding collection of antiquities, paintings, and sculpture. There is too much to see on a single visit, so consider concentrating on highlights such as the German, Dutch and Flemish collection. After the museum, take a breather at one of the cafés in the nearby **MuseumsQuartier**, a stunning contemporary cultural complex which has become a fashionable hang-out for Viennese hipsters.

Dinner: Try out one of Vienna's hot new restaurants, such as award-winning chef Christian Petz's latest offering **Holy Moly!**, a stylish yet casual eaterie on a boat on the Donaukanal. Or you could splash out on the award-winning cuisine at **Le Loft**, with stunning views over the entire city. Both restaurants also double as bars, and both are ideal for post-prandial drinks.

Day Two

Breakfast: Tuck into a couple of *buchteln* (sweet jam dumplings) at the **Café Hawelka**, opened in 1939 and still going strong.

Top: Stephansdom Cathedral
Middle: Graben Street
Bottom: Museum of Fine Arts (Kunsthistoriches Museum)

Above: Vienna Riesenrad (Ferris Wheel) Below: Staatsoper (Opera House)

Morning: Dedicate the morning to the **Imperial Palace**. First visit the Imperial Chapel; if you're here on a Sunday, and book months in advance, you could see a performance by the world-famous **Vienna Boys' Choir**. Then admire the magnificent collection of jewel-studded crowns and imperial robes at the **Secular and Ecclesiastical Treasuries**. Finally, hit the **Imperial Apartments**, which contain a special exhibit dedicated to the Empress Sisi.

Lunch: After such a busy morning, it's time to relax. Head down to the colourful **Naschmarkt**, the city's celebrated open-air food market. Choose lunch from one of the myriad stalls – you'll find everything from Turkish to Vietnamese – or make for the **Café Amacord** to enjoy traditional Viennese fare.

Afternoon: Spend the afternoon at the **Prater**, a stunning expanse of verdant lawns and huge, shady trees. Take a whirl on the Riesenrad, or ferris wheel, immortalised in the film of *The Third Man*.

Evening: Dress up in your best finery and take in an opera (book tickets well in advance) at the opulent **Staatsoper**.

Dinner: Enjoy a romantic dinner, out on the cobblestoned terrace if possible, at **Zum Finsteren Stern**.

Top Ten: Prague

1 **Old Town Square**: the Grimm Brothers in stone, p.143
2 **St Vitus's Cathedral**: 14th-century Gothic magnificence, p.161
3 **Funicular up Petřín Hill**: heart-melting views and magical walks, p.186
4 **Charles Bridge**: the city's jugular vein, p.139
5 **St Nicholas' Church**: Baroque propaganda at its sensual best, p.175
6 **Old-New Synagogue** and **Old Jewish Cemetery**: the heart of the old ghetto, p.155
7 Coffee, strudel and schnapps at either the **Café Imperial**, **Café Slavia**, or **Café Louvre**, p.198
8 **Municipal House**: Art Nouveau splendour, p.149
9 **Wenceslas Square**: the modern hub of the capital, p.180
10 **Pedaloes**, **rowboats** or an island of your choice, p.180

Below:
Charles Bridge and
the Vltava River

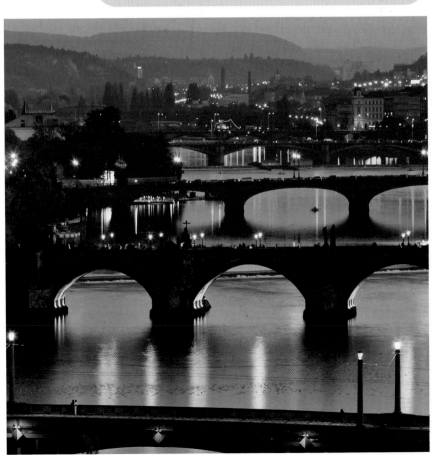

Prague's Baroque Beauty

The defeat of Protestantism during the Thirty Years War saw Prague all but rebuilt by the monks and carpet-baggers of the Counter Reformation, and no better preserve of the Baroque now exists in northern Europe. Façades undulate, statuary swoons, and light plays tricks across the capital, in the churches, palaces and shrines of Catholicism triumphant; and its streets routinely echo to the sound of fugues and choral works that were composed here three centuries ago.

- Intoxicating confusion at the **Church of St Nicholas**, p.175
- The Philosophical Hall Library at **Strahov Monastery**, p.172
- Stucco reliefs, Baroque altars and an opulent tomb at **St James's Church**, p.149
- Iberian mysticism at the **Loreta**, p.170
- Nerve-centre of the Czech Counter-Reformation, **Clementinum**, p.142
- Elegant terraces of the secluded **Vrtba Gardens**, p.177
- The Bambino di Praga at the **Church of Our Lady of Victory**, p.179
- An idyllic summer retreat, the **Waldstein Palace**, p.134

Below, left: Cupola, Church of St Nicholas
Bottom, left: Vrtba Gardens
Below, right: Baroque Façade, Church of St Nicholas

Romantic Prague

Prague's dreamy spires, ancient bridge and castle in the air make for a backdrop against which the improbable is imminent, and impossibilities can seem real. Amidst so tangible a magic, the aimless stroll, the riverboat cruise and the candlelit dinner are elevated from cliché to novelty – making the city the perfect place to bring romance, or find it for the first time.

- A **funicular** ride to the top of Petřín Hill, p.186
- A walk along the water southwards from the **Charles Bridge** , p.139
- A sunset stroll through the **castle** grounds, p.166
- The cobbled lanes of **Nový Svět**, p.170
- A drink at the **Municipal House**, p.149
- A meal at the **Pálffy Palác**, p.195, **U Modré Kachničky**, p.195 or **Cihelná**, p.196
- Padlocks by the waterwheel, near the **John Lennon Wall**, p. 180

Below, left: Love Padlocks near John Lennon Wall Below, right: Charles Bridge Bottom, left: Funicular Bottom, right: Old Town Square

01 Introduction | Romantic Prague

Itinerary: Prague

Prague is a labyrinth of the senses. Wherever you turn, you're confronted by come-hither tunnels, curling lanes and the distant sound of music. Secluded gardens peep through doorways, bells chime and unseen organists practise in empty churches. It doesn't always feel so dreamy, but if you pack your senses of adventure and humour, a visit is an unforgettable jaunt into a city where history is in the making – and a thousand years have already been made. The city is well suited to ambling, but if you have a hunger for sensation and ruthless organisational skills, you can conquer the Czech capital and have the photos to prove it in as little as three days. Use the following itineraries as a guide, and expand as time allows.

Day 1: Catch the ubiquitous **number 22 tram** from Národní street across the river, up the hairpin hill bends, and five minutes further to **Pohořelec**. Find the **Strahov monastery**, and then walk via the **Loreta shrine** and Nový Svět to Prague Castle. Visit **St Vitus' Cathedral**, the **Vladislav Hall** and **Golden Lane**. Retrace your steps to the castle's main gate, and walk down Nerudova street into Malá Strana. Take in the splendour of **St Nicholas' church** and head for the **Charles Bridge**. Raise a glass at a riverside café on **Kampa Island** below.

Day 2: Start at the foot of **Wenceslas Square**, and follow Melantrichova street until you reach the **Old Town Hall**. Loiter until the turn of the hour to watch the striking of its **Astronomical Clock**, then cross the square and walk along swish **Pařizská** street to the **Old-New Synagogue** and neighbouring **Jewish cemetery** (both closed on Saturdays). Return to the square, and take in the twin towers of the **Týn Church** and before finding the splendid Baroque interior of **St James' Church**. Finish up in the magnificent Art Nouveau café at **Municipal House**, or walk down Hybernská street to the almost as splendid Café Imperial.

Day 3: Dawdle around the hushed streets of the eastern Old Town, around **St Agnes' Convent**, and then cross to the opposite side of the Old Town Square and wander towards the **Charles Bridge**. Karlova street leads there directly, but negotiating a few of the lanes to its south will take you a route that is all but bound to be both emptier and prettier. Cross the bridge, and make for one of the several pretty gardens to be found in Malá Strana: either those at the **Vrtba Gardens** or **Waldstein Palace** (both April–Oct only), or the **Vojan Park**.

Top: Astronomical Clock
Middle: Detail, Old Town Square
Above: St Vitus' Cathedral

Top Ten: Budapest

1. Enjoy perfect views over the Danube from the **Fishermen's Bastion**, p.243
2. Admire the towers, murals and ecclesiastical treasures at the ancient **Matthias Church**, p.241
3. A superb collection of European art and antiquities gathered under a graceful neoclassical roof at the **Museum of Fine Arts**, p.274
4. Cross the 19th-century **Chain Bridge**, one of the city's most prominent landmarks, p.249
5. Attend an opera, concert or ballet at the extravagantly decorated **Hungarian State Opera**, p.274
6. Climb up to the great dome of **St Stephen's Basilica** for splendid views, p.256
7. Walk up **Gellért Hill** and gaze out across the city from the Monument, p.245
8. Soak in the thermal waters of the gilded Art Nouveau **Széchenyi Baths**, p.282
9. Stroll around the Jewish Quarter and visit the vast **Great Synagogue**, p.285
10. Relax by the riverside on the verdant **Margaret Island**, p.264

Top: Matthias Church
Above : St Stephen's Basilica
Below: Fishermen's Bastion

01 Introduction | Top Ten: Budapest

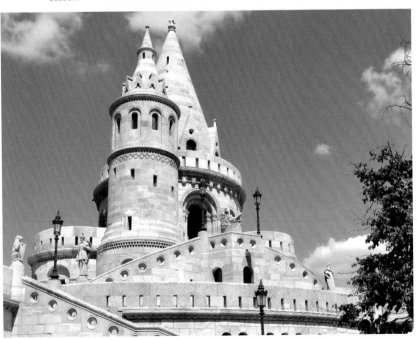

Budapest: Off the Beaten Track

Once you've got Budapest's blockbuster attractions under your belt, consider exploring some of its quieter corners, among them secret gardens, silent cemeteries, and off-beat museums.

- Enjoy a concert in a graceful Art Nouveau villa surrounded by gardens at the **Béla Bartók Memorial House**, p.290
- Pick your way through the shady paths and admire the lavish tombs at the **Farkasréti Cemetery**, p.291
- Escape the city hubbub and head for the verdant **Buda Hills** p.289
- Gawp at the gigantic sculptures at a unique retirement home for communist artworks, the **Statue Park**, p.291
- Admire the lavish **Tomb of Gül Baba**, a Turkish dervish who is credited with introducing the rose to Budapest, p.254
- Learn about Continental Europe's first underground railway at the curious **Underground Railway Museum**, p.266
- A lesson in Hungarian architectural styles, the picturesque **Vajdahunyad castle** overlooks a lake and leafy gardens in City Park, p.281
- Pick up some unusual crafts or contemporary fashion at the **Hungarian Design Market (WAMP)**, p.295

Above: Communist-era Sculpture, Statue Park
Right: Vajdahunyad Castle

Budapest: City of Spas

The Romans were the first to enjoy the thermal springs in Budapest, but it was the Turks who institutionalised the city's famous bath culture in the 16th and 17th centuries. Bubbling beneath the Hungarian capital are 118 hot springs, which can be enjoyed at more than a dozen public baths.

- Europe's largest thermal compex, the **Széchenyi Baths** are built in gorgeously gilded neo-Baroque style. Join the chess-players in the outdoor pools, and admire the lavish fountains, p.282
- Part of an elegant, Belle Époque-style hotel, the smart **Gellért Baths** are opulently decorated, p.246
- For an authentic experience, visit the **Lukács Baths**, frequented by more Hungarians than tourists. They occupy an elegant neoclassical complex, with a lovely outdoor pool, p.253
- The **Rudas Baths** retain an Turkish-style octagonal pool and cupola and are famous for the summer parties, p.249
- The atmospheric **Király Baths** have a 16th-century Ottoman pool under an original dome, p.253
- On Margaret Island, the baths at **Palatinus Strand** are particularly good for families with young children, p.265
- First built under the Turks, the **Rácz Baths** have been thoroughly modernised and have been incorporated into a glossy new spa hotel, see p.248

Below, left: Cupola, Széchenyi Baths
Below, right: Chess-players, Széchenyi Baths

Itinerary: Budapest

This one-day walking tour provides an introduction to the city's highlights, from the world-famous view over the Danube from the Fisherman's Bastion to the richly decorated interior of the Matthias Church. It culminates with a dip in the Art Nouveau-style Géllert baths – perfect therapy for footsore visitors.

Breakfast: Start with breakfast on the pavement terrace at Müvész, on the grand 19th-century boulevard **Andrássy Út**.

Morning: Stroll down grand **Andrássy Út**, admiring the elegant neoclassical buildings, glossy shops, and the **State Opera House**. Turn up Bajcsy-Zsilinsky Út to reach the huge neo-Baroque swirls of **St Stephen's Basilica**. Make the climb to the dome to enjoy wonderful views.

Lunch: Stop for lunch on the terrace at **Lugas Étterem**, or grab some picnic supplies and head south to the verdant square **Erzsébet tér**, where locals sprawl on the grass in summer.

Afternoon: Walk east towards the river and the **Chain Bridge**, the first permanent bridge to link Buda and Pest. Soak in the extraordinary views along the Danube, with the castle crowning Buda to the east and the glittering **Parliament Building** dominating the riverbank to the west. Take the **Sikló**, the funicular, for the short ride up Buda's slopes. Visit the **Budapest History Museum**, which occupies a section of the vast **Royal Palace**. Amble through Buda's atmospheric streets until you reach the **Matthias Temple**: visit the richly decorated interior if building works allow. Then make for the **Fishermen's Bastion** to take in the panoramic views. The Várbusz (shuttle bus) will bring you down the hill, where you can take a tram along the riverbank to the magnificent **Géllert Baths**.

Dinner: Tuck into Hungarian specialities at elegant **Kárpátia**, or try more contemporary fare at **21 Restaurant** in Buda. Follow dinner with post-prandial drinks on one of the terrace cafés on Liszt Ferenc tér.

Top: Chain Bridge
Above: St Stephen's Basilica
Right: Parliament Building

CONTENTS

About the Authors

Mary-Ann Gallagher (Vienna) has written, and contributed to, more than a dozen Cadogan guides, and her travels have taken her everywhere from Japanese hill villages to glossy European capitals. She's currently resident in Barcelona, and continues to write regularly for newspapers, magazines and guidebook publishers.

Sadakat Kadri (Prague) studied history and law at Cambridge and Harvard, and is a qualified New York attorney and practising London barrister. He has been a regular visitor to Prague since the early 1990s, when he wrote the original, expanded version of this guide. He is a past winner of the *Spectator*/Shiva Naipaul Memorial Prize for travel writing, and is the author of two books: *The Trial: A History from Socrates to O.J. Simpson* (2005) and *Heaven on Earth: A Journey through Sharia Law* (2011).

Matthew Gardner (Budapest) is an unrepentant hedonist who loves travel almost as much as football, jazz, food and Shiraz. Though raised in outer London, he lives in a remote valley in Western Canada with his wife Alison, their two children, two dogs, one cat and occasional itinerant packrats.

Planning Your Trip

O2

Entry Formalities

Passports and Visas

All three countries are EU members. For a list of their embassies, *see* their individual **Practical A–Z** chapters.

Vienna and **Prague**: UK and Irish citizens need a valid passport; visas are not required and visitors may stay for an unlimited period provided their passports remain in date. US and Canadian citizens need a valid passport: visas are not required for US and Canadian citizens staying less than 90 days; visas are needed for a stay exceeding 90 days.

Budapest: UK citizens need a valid passport, and can stay for up to three months without a visa; visas are required for longer stays. US, Canadian and Irish citizens need a valid passport, and visas for a stay exceeding 90 days. All visitors staying more than 30 days must register with the police or local government office within 48hrs of arrival.

Customs

Those from other EU countries do not have to declare goods imported into or exported from Austria, Hungary or the Czech Republic for personal use if they have paid duty on them in the country of origin. In theory, you can bring as much as you like, provided you can prove the purchase is for your own use. In practice, Customs will be more likely to ask questions if you buy in bulk.

Travellers from the USA are allowed to take home, duty-free, goods to the value of $800, including 250 cigarettes or 50 cigars, plus one litre of alcohol. For more information, call the US Customs Service.

UK Customs, **t** 0845 010 9000, *www.hmrc.gov.uk*.

US Customs, **t** 1 877 CBP 5511, *www.cbp.gov*; see the pamphlet *Know Before You Go*.

Disabled Travellers

For information about organizations in Austria, the Czech Republic and Hungary, and for specific details about facilities in these countries, *see* the individual **Practical A–Z** chapters.

Disability Organizations

UK

RADAR (Royal Association for Disability and Rehabilitation), Unit 12, City Forum, 250 City Rd, London EC1V 8AF, **t** (020) 7250 3222, *www. radar.org.uk (open Mon–Fri 10–4)*.

RNIB (Royal National Institute for the Blind), 105 Judd St, London WC1H 9NE, **t** (020) 7388 1266, *www.rnib.org.uk*.

Tourism For All, *c/o* Vitalise, Shap Road Industrial Estate, Kendal, Cumbria LA9 6AZ, **t** 0845 124 9971, *www.tourismforall.org.uk*.

USA and Canada

American Foundation for the Blind, 11 Penn Plaza, Suite 300, New York, NY 10001, **t** (212) 502 7600, **t** 800 232 5463, *www.afb.org*.

Mobility International USA, 132 East Broadway, Suite 343, Eugene, OR 97401, **t** (541) 343 1284, *www.miusa.org*.

SATH (Society for Accessible Travel and Hospitality), 347 5th Ave, Suite 605, New York, NY 10016, **t** (212) 447 1928, *www.sath.org*.

Health and Insurance

EU citizens are entitled to emergency health care through reciprocal healthcare agreements. You will need a European Health Insurance Card (EHIC), available free from the UK's Department of Health at *www.ehic.org.uk* or by phone on **t** 0845 606 2030.

In practice, getting refunds for medical treatment is a time-consuming and painfully bureaucratic process, and visitors (both from the EU and other countries) are advised to take out travel insurance which covers health emergencies. *See* each city's **Practical A–Z** chapter for further details.

Getting There

Many people visiting all three cities will find it easiest to book on a tour operator trip that conveys you between them (*see* p.25). However, their proximity to one another makes it easy for the independent traveller to fly to one of the three and take a train to the others. Many airlines offer single fares, so you can fly into one place and out of another.

By Air

All three cities have a nearby airport; Vienna has two, if you include Bratislava (60km/40miles east). Thanks to no-frills airlines in the UK, prices are competitive. Budget flights are usually cheaper if booked early and online – last-minute bookings are not much less expensive than flights by major carriers. Flights tend to be cheapest in November and February. Shop around and book as far ahead as possible.

In the UK, for flights and price comparisons on the Internet, see *www.skyscanner.net*, *www.whichbudget.com*, and *www.kayak.com*. For other websites, *see* box on p.22.

From North America, it's marginally easier to find flights to Prague than to Budapest or Vienna; however, most will involve a stopover in another European city. It can often be cheapest to fly to London and then pick up a flight with one of the European low-cost airlines. *See* box below.

Airline Carriers

UK and Ireland

Aer Lingus, t 0818 365044 (Ireland), **t** 0871 718 2020 (UK and Northern Ireland), *www.aerlingus.com*. Direct flights from Dublin to Prague, and Dublin to Vienna.

Air Berlin, t 0871 5000 737, *www.airberlin.com*. To Vienna from London Stansted (usually via another German airport).

Austrian Airlines, t 0870 1 24 26 25, *www.austrian.com*. To Vienna from London Heathrow. To Budapest via Vienna.

British Airways (BA), t 0844 493 0787, *www.ba.com*. To Vienna from London Heathrow, Birmingham and Manchester. To Prague from London Heathrow and Dublin. To Budapest from London Heathrow.

British Midland (bmi), t 0844 8484 888, *www.flybmi.com*. To Vienna from London Heathrow.

bmibaby, t 0905 8282828, *www.bmibaby.com*. To Prague from Birmingham, Cardiff, Manchester and East Midlands.

ČSA Czech Airlines, t (020) 7365 9189, *www.czech airlines.com*. The national carrier abandoned all UK-Czech services in late 2010; keep an eye on its website to see if it recovers its nerve.

easyJet, t 0871 244 2366, *www.easyjet.com*. To Prague from London Gatwick and London Stansted. To Budapest from Bristol, London Gatwick. To Vienna from London Gatwick.

Jet 2, t 0870 737 8282, *www.jet2.com*. To Prague from Manchester, Newcastle, Edinburgh and Leeds-Bradford. To Budapest from Edinburgh and Manchester.

German Wings, t 0906 294 1918, *www.germanwings.com*. To Vienna from Dublin, Manchester and London Stansted. To Prague from London Stansted. (Most flights require a change at Cologne.)

Malév Hungarian Airlines, t 0844 482 2360 (UK), **t** (01) 844 7371 (Ireland), *www.malev.com*.

To Budapest from London Gatwick, London Heathrow and Dublin. To Prague (and on to Budapest) from Edinburgh, Birmingham, Glasgow and Manchester.

Ryanair, t 0871 246 0000 (UK), **t** 0818 30 30 30 (Ireland), *www.ryanair.com*. Flies from Bristol, Birmingham, Dublin, Edinburgh, London Stansted to Bratislava, which is linked to Vienna by a shuttle bus (around 90mins) or by train from the city centre. Ryanair also flies from London Stansted to Graz (90 miles from Vienna – about 2½hrs by car or 1hr by train).

Wizz Air, t 0906 959 0002 (UK), **t** (01) 550 475 970 (Ireland), *http://wizzair.com*. To Budapest and Prague from London Luton.

USA and Canada

Air Canada, Canada and USA **t** 1 888 247 2262, *www.aircanada.com*. Flies (in conjunction with United Airlines or Lufthansa) direct to Vienna from Toronto. To Prague via London, Vienna and Frankfurt. To Budapest via Frankfurt.

American Airlines, t 800 433 7300, **t** 1 800 543 1586 (TDD) *www.aa.com*. To Prague, Vienna and Budapest via London (code-shares with BA).

Austrian Airlines, USA **t** 800 843 0002, Canada **t** 888 817 4444, *www.austrian.com*. Direct to Vienna from New York (JFK), Washington DC and Toronto. To Budapest and Prague via Vienna.

British Airways, t 800 AIRWAYS, **t** 800 247 9297, *www.ba.com*. To Prague, Vienna and Budapest via London and other European cities.

ČSA Czech Airlines, t 800 223 2365, *www.czechairlines.com*. To Prague direct from New York (JFK), with connections from Boston, Chicago, Los Angeles, Washington and several other North American cities.

Delta, USA and Canada **t** 800 221 1212, **t** 800 831 4488 (TDD), *www.delta.com*. To Prague directly from New York (JFK and Newark) and via Amsterdam, Brussels, Helsinki, Paris, Riga and Vienna. Flights from New York (JFK) to Budapest and Vienna via Paris.

Malév Hungarian Airlines, USA and Canada **t** 1 235 3888, *www.malev. com*. Belt-tightening has forced Malév to suspend its own trans-atlantic flights, but it still operates flights from New York (JFK), Chicago and Toronto through its code-sharing partner American Airlines.

Swiss Air, USA and Canada **t** 1 877 359 7947, *www.swiss.com*. To Prague, Vienna and Budapest from New York (JFK) via Zurich.

United Airlines, **t** 800 538 2929, **t** 800 323 0170 (TDD), *www.united.com*. Direct to Vienna from New York (JFK) and Washington DC; indirect to Vienna and Prague via Amsterdan and other European cities. To Budapest via Frankfurt.

Discounts, Students and Special Deals

UK and Ireland

Students with ID cards are eligible for considerable reductions, not only on some flights but also on trains and admission fees to museums, concerts and more. Agencies specializing in student and youth travel can supply ISICs (International Student Identity Cards). Check **websites** including: *www.travellersweb.com*; *www.cheapflights.com*; *www.last minute.com*; *www.expedia.co.uk*; *www.skydeals.co.uk*; *www. aboutflights.co.uk*; *www.travelocity. co.uk*.

Budget Travel, 29 Lower Abbey St, Dublin 1, **t** (01) 435 0024, *www.budgettravel.ie*.

Club Travel, 30 Lower Abbey St, Dublin 1, **t** (01) 500 5586 within Eire, *www.clubtravel.ie*.

STA, 33 Bedford St, London WC2E 9ED, **t** 08701 600 599, *www.statravel.co.uk*. With 47 branches throughout the UK (and more than 450 around the world).

Trailfinders, 194 Kensington High St, London W8, **t** (020) 7937 1234, *www.trailfinders.com*.

United Travel, 2 Old Dublin Rd, Stillorgan, County Dublin, **t** (01) 215 9300, *www.united travel.ie*.

USA and Canada

If you're resilient, flexible and/or youthful and prepared to shop around for budget deals or even courier flights, you'll find some good bargains. Numerous travel clubs and agencies also specialize in discount fares, but they may require you to pay an annual membership fee.

The best deals are almost always available online, particularly if you book well in advance. Check the small print, particularly 'administration fees', before booking.

Useful **websites** include: *ww.skyscanner.com*; *www.momondo.com*; *www.justfares.com*; *www.flyaow.com*; *www.air-fare.com*; *www.cheapflights.com*; *www.expedia.com*; *www.travelocity.com*; *www.orbitz. com*; *www.priceline.com* (bid for low-cost airline tickets and hotels); *www.smartertravel.com*; *www.sidestep.com*.

Last Minute Travel Club, USA/Canada **t** 800 442 0568, *www.lastminutetravel.com*. Last-minute flight deals, hotels, special car rental rates in Europe, and Europass train tickets.

STA, **t** 800 781 4040, *www.statravel.com*. Eighteen stores across the USA with branches at most universities and at 30 3rd Ave, New York, NY 10003, **t** (212) 473 6100.

TFI, 1270 Broadway Suite 409, New York, NY 10001, **t** 800 745 8000, *http://tfitours.com*. Low-cost negotiated fares, with discounts of up to 80% on advertised fares.

Travel Cuts, 187 College St, Toronto, Ontario, ON M5T 1P7, **t** 800 592 CUTS (2887) or **t** 800 592 CUTS (2887) from the USA, *www.travelcuts.com*. Canada's largest student travel specialists, with branches in most provinces, plus several branches in the USA, including Seattle, San Francisco and San Diego.

Student Universe (*www.studentuniverse.com*) which offers flights, rail passes, ISIC cards, and hostel-booking services.

By Train

You can take the train all the way from London; the connections are complicated and you should always book ahead. Reservations usually open 90 days in advance, although Eurostar tickets can be booked up to four months in advance. Fares can be comparable with budget airlines if you are flexible with your timings, and book as early as possible. Have a look at the website *www.seat61.com* (see also below) for advice on routes and how to book.

For **London St Pancras–Prague**, there are two main options, the first taking Eurostar, sleeper and EuroCity trains via Brussels and Cologne. The journey takes 21hrs: travel by Eurostar from London Waterloo to Brussels in the afternoon, then take the ICE high-speed line to Cologne, where you can pick up the City Night Line sleeper. This arrives at Prague Holešovice station the next morning at 9.28am. The second and slightly slower option (journey time 24 hours) is to travel by Eurostar to Paris, change stations, then take the overnight sleeper to Berlin. Take he morning train to Prague, which arrives at about 3.30pm.

For **London St Pancras–Vienna**, the best option is to take a mid-afternoon Eurostar to Brussels, then the ICE high-speed train to Cologne, where you can connect with a comfortable sleeper train along the Rhine Valley to Vienna. The journey takes 21hrs. Alternatively, take an early afternoon Eurostar to Paris Gare du Nord, change to the Gare de l'Est, and take the City Night Line overnight hotel train to Munich. A RailJet train departs Munich at 9.28am, arriving in Vienna at lunchtime.

For **London St Pancras–Budapest**, the journey takes 24hrs: take the Eurostar to Paris Gare du Nord, go to the Gare de l'Est, and take the high speed TGV to Munich. A sleeper departs Budapest at 11.40pm. Alternatively you could take the Brussels–Cologne–Vienna route (see above): from Vienna it takes just under 2½ hours to Budapest.

Train Operators, Booking Agencies and Other Websites

Deutsche Bahn UK, **t** 08718 80 80 66, *www. bahn.de*; trains to Austria via Brussels and Germany. The very useful website features timetables for all journeys within Europe, and is available in English.

Eurostar, **t** 08432 186 186, *www.eurostar.com*.

Ffestiniog Travel, **t** 01766 772030, *http://ffestiniogtravel.com*. Organises escorted rail holidays across Europe.

Rail Europe: UK: British Columbia House, 1 Lower Regent St, London SW1 4XT, **t** 08448 484 064, *www.raileurope.co.uk*. Canada and USA: **t** 800 622 8600 (USA), **t** 1 800 361 7245 (Canada), *www.raileurope.com*.

Trains Europe, **t** 0871 700 7722, *www. trainseurope.co.uk*.

The Man in Seat Sixty-One, *www.seat61.com*. Excellent website featuring lyrical descriptions and meticulously researched details on every conceivable aspect of train travel. Superb resource for rail travellers.

Rail Passes

If you're planning to travel extensively within Europe, it may be worth investing in a rail pass. But, with intercity train tickets starting as low as €36 (from Vienna to Budapest, for example), you will need to travel very frequently to take advantage of the various rail passes. **EU citizens and anyone resident in the EU for at least six months** is elegible to purchase an **InterRail pass**, available either as global passes (valid for unlimited travel in up to 30 countries excluding the country of purchase) or one-country passes (for travel within a single nation). The **InterRail Global Flexi** offers unlimited travel in up to 30 countries: choose from passes offering five days' travel within a 10-day period, or 10 days within a 22-day period. Prices range from £230 for five days of standard class travel within 10 days to £495 for 10 days of first class travel in a 22-day period. The **InterRail Global Continuous** pass enables you to travel for 15 or 22 consecutive days or a whole month: prices start at £362 for 15 days' consecutive travel in standard class, to £823 for one month of consecutive travel in first class. Discounts are available for children (4–11), youths (12–25), and seniors (60+). Note that supplements are required for some trains, particularly sleeper trains.

One-country passes are available, offering 3, 4, 6 or 8 days of unlimited travel within a one-month period, but they are only useful if you intend to travel extensively and intensively. Standard class fares in Austria range from £155 (3 days) to £267 (8 days); Hungary £66 (3 days) to £128 (8 days); Czech Republic £66 (3 days) to £128 (8 days). First class fares are also available.

In **North America**, you can select from a wide range of rail passes. The most useful is probably the **Central Europe Triangle Pass** which includes single fares between Vienna, Budapest, Prague and back to Vienna for $146 (adult, standard class). The **Eurail Austria-Czech Republic** or **Austria-Hungary** passes provide unlimited first-class travel within Austria and the Czech Republic or Hungary for 4, 5, 6, 7, 8, 9, or 10 days within a two-month period (travel days may be used consecutively or non-consecutively). They cost between $262–475, with discounts for children. Saver fares are available on most North American rail passes for groups of between 2 and 5 travellers.

Other rail passes to consider include the **European East Pass**, for unlimited train travel

Rail Passes

For UK/Europe Residents

www.raileurope.co.uk. UK's biggest European rail specialist, with an online booking service.

www.internationalrail.com. Huge range of international train passes and related services.

www.europeanrail.com, t (020) 7619 1083. Rail passes, timetables, rail tours.

www.seat61.com/Railpass.htm. Extensive information on every kind of rail pass.

For USA/Canada Residents

www.raileurope.com, USA t 800 622 8600.

www.raileurope.ca, Canada t 800 361 RAIL.

www.railpass.com. Online booking service for rail passes.

www.eurorailways.com, t (954) 323 8389: rail passes, rail 'n' drive passes, senior and youth passes, car rental, air tickets.

www.europrail.net, t 888 667 9734.

in Poland, the Czech Republic, Slovakia, Austria and Hungary; the **Global Pass**, for unlimited travel in more than 20 countries (including Austria, Hungary and the Czech Republic); the **Eurail Select Pass**, for travel in 3, 4 or 5 bordering countries connected by train or ship; and the **EurailDrive Pass**, which combines rail travel with two days of car rental.

By Train between the Three Cities

There are frequent direct train connections between all three cities. The following fares are for pre-booked, flexible and refundable tickets. Non-flexible tickets bought directly at the train stations can be cheaper, except for tickets purchased on the day of travel. It's usually worth paying a small supplement to reserve a seat.

Prague to Budapest is 329 miles/530km; the journey takes around 7hrs, or 9hrs overnight, and costs from £35 one-way or £70 return. Up to four trains a day leave from Prague hl.n. (main station) or Prague Holešovice for Budapest Nyugati pu and Budapest Keleti pu, and vice versa.

Vienna to Prague is 183 miles/300 km; the journey by train takes 4½hrs or 7hrs overnight and costs from £30 one way or £60 return. Up to five trains a day leave from Vienna Südbahnhof for Prague hl.n. and Prague Holešovice, and vice versa.

Budapest to Vienna is 151 miles/243km; the journey takes just under 3hrs and costs around £36 one way or £70 return. Up to four trains a day leave from Budapest Keleti pu for Vienna, and vice versa.

You can book tickets via the Rail Europe or Deutsche Bahn websites a maximum of 90 days ahead. To check timetables, *see* Deutsche Bahn, *www.bahn.de*, or for travel from Vienna *see www.oebb.at/en/*.

Austria rail information, *www.oebb.at*.

Czech rail information, *http://www.cd.cz/en*.

Hungary international rail information, *www.mav-start.hu*.

By Coach

Travelling by coach is tiring and, thanks to the budget airlines, no longer much of a bargain. Still, for students and at peak holiday periods, coach travel can sometimes offer a cheap alternative. It takes 23hrs on **Eurolines** to Vienna, and return tickets booked 7 days in advance cost £82. It takes 19–21hrs to Prague, costing from £54 return. It takes 25–27hrs to Budapest (usually with a change in Vienna), costing from £85 return.

An excellent cost-cutting option for travelling between cities is a **Busabout** pass, allowing flexible travel on coaches used exclusively by independent travellers. Choose from fixed itineraries (North, South or Western Loop) or go for a flexipass which allows a fixed number of journeys on the Busabout network. Prices vary depending on the number of stops. Buses run from May to October. Eurolines also offer a pass (*www.eurolines-pass.com*) ranging from 15, 30 to 60 days; prices vary according to season.

Busabout, t 0845 026 7514, *www.busabout.com*.

Eurolines, t 08717 818 181, *www.eurolines.co.uk*

By Car

Driving to Prague, Vienna or Budapest is no picnic: it takes almost two days of solid driving via Belgium and Germany. Drivers will need to ensure that they have proof of ownership of the car, or a letter from the owner giving permission to drive the car (smuggling of stolen cars is a common crime). All vehicles must be roadworthy, registered and insured, at least third party; you'll need a 'green card' international insurance form (not obligatory but highly recommended). UK and the Republic of Ireland driving licences with photo are accepted. Canadian and American drivers may need an IDP.

Crossing the Channel is cheapest by ferry from Dover, quickest via the Channel Tunnel. For ferries, check out *www.directferries.co.uk*.

Eurotunnel, t 08443 35 35 35, *www. euro tunnel.com*. Operates the shuttle through the Channel Tunnel, Folkestone to Calais.

DFDS Ferries, t (020) 8127 8303, *www. dfdsseaways.com*. Dover to Dunkirk.

P&O Ferries, t 08716 642 121, *www.poferries. com*. Dover to Calais; Hull to Rotterdam or Zeebrugge.

Seafrance, t 0871 423 7119, *www.seafrance. co.uk*. Dover to Calais.

Belgian and German motorways are free but you must buy a **pass** for Austrian, Czech and most Hungarian motorways, available at border crossings, post offices and petrol stations, valid for 10 days, a month or a year.

Motoring organizations can provide more information on routes and petrol prices.

AAA (USA), **t** 800 222 1234, *www.aaa.com*.

AA (UK), **t** 08706 000 371, *www.theaa.com*.

RAC (UK), **t** 08705 722 722, *www.rac.co.uk*.

Moto Europa (Europe), *www.ideamerge. com/motoeuropa*. Driving-abroad website.

You could also consider **hiring a car** when you get there. Car hire firms are also listed under the three cities in this book. It's often

Car Hire

UK

Avis, t 08445 810 147, *www.avis.co.uk*.

Budget, t 0844 544 3470, *www.budget.com*.

easyCar, *www.easycar.com* (web only).

Europcar, t 0870 607 5000, *www.europcar.com*.

Hertz, t 08708 448 844, *www.hertz.co.uk*.

Thrifty, t (01494) 751500, *www.thrifty.co.uk*.

USA and Canada

Auto Europe, t 888 223 5555, *www. autoeurope.com*.

Avis Rent a Car, (USA) **t** 800 331 1212, (Canada) **t** 800 879 2847, *www.avis.com*.

Europe by Car, t 800 223 1516, *www.ebctravel.com*.

Europcar, t 877 940 6900, *www.europcar.com*.

Hertz, (USA) **t** 800 654 3131, **t** 800 654 2280 (TTD), *www.hertz.com*.

cheaper to book through car hire companies in your own country before you go, or look into fly-drive package deals. For an instant online price comparison, log on to *www. autosabroad.com*, **t** 08700 66 77 88.

By Hydrofoil

From May to October, hydrofoil services are operated along the Danube between Vienna and Budapest via Bratislava. Contact **Mahart PassNave** (*www. mahartpassnave.hu*) in Budapest or DDSG (*www.ddsg-blue-danube.at, see* also p.89) in Vienna. Fares are around €110 return or €90 one-way, and €85 with reductions for children (those under 2 travel free, half price for children aged 2–14) and students with ISIC cards.

Tour Operators and Special-interest Holidays

From the UK

Abercrombie & Kent, A&K Travel Boutique, Lower Ground Floor, Harrods, 87–135 Brompton Rd, London SW1X 7XL **t** 0845 618 2000, *www.abercrombiekent.co.uk*. Luxurious city breaks in each of the three capitals.

Ace Cultural Tours, Babraham, Cambridge, CB22 3AP, **t** (01223) 835 055, *www.acestudytours.co.uk*. In-depth cultural tours led by writers or art and architectural historians. Currently offering art

tours of Vienna and Budapest, an opera tour and a royal tour of Prague.

Archers Direct, t 0844 573 4806, *www.archers direct.co.uk*. Organised holidays by plane and coach, visiting all three capitals.

Brompton Travel, 3 Hinchley Way, Hinchley Wood, Esher, Surrey KT10 0BD, **t** (020) 8398 4071, *www.bromptontravel.co.uk*. Opera tours to all three cities covering entire opera seasons.

Čedok, *www.cedok.com*. Former Czech national tourist agency and a reliable source of information on city breaks in Prague.

Contiki Travels, t +41 (0)22 929 9216, *www. contiki.com*. Coach tours for 18–35-year-olds.

Cox and Kings, 6th Floor, 30 Millbank, London SW1P 4EE, **t** (020) 7873 5000, *www. coxandkings.co.uk*. Luxurious city breaks in all three cities and Danube cruises.

Heritage Group Travel, 12 Charlotte St, Bath BA1 2NE, **t** (01225) 466620, *www.grouptravel.co.uk*. Tailor-made tours (art, history, architecture, garden design, including exclusive visits to museums).

Kirker Holidays, 4 Waterloo Court, Theed Street, London SE1 8ST, **t** (020) 7593 1899, *www.kirker holidays.com*. Short trips to Prague, Vienna and Budapest; cultural tours, opera tours, luxury tours and tailor-made holidays.

Leger Holidays, **t** 0844 504 6251, *www.leger.co. uk*. A range of air/coach tours to all three cities.

Martin Randall, 10 Barley Mow Passage, London W4 4GF, **t** (020) 8742 3355, *www.martinrandall. com*. Superb small group cultural tours led by lecturers: includes the Danube Festival of Song and the Budapest Spring Music Festival as well as themed visits toVienna and Budapest.

Orient Express, **t** (020) 7960 0500, *www.orient-express.com*. From Venice to London, stopping off for two nights at Prague or Budapest (one of several possible combinations).

Page and Moy, Compass House, Rockingham Rd, Market Harborough, Leicestershire, LE16 7QD, **t** 0844 567 6633, *www.pageandmoy. com*. Escorted tours with sightseeing, concerts, cruises, excursions. Also offer a a Grand Rail Journey tour.

Prospect Cultural Tours, 79 William Street, Herne Bay, Kent CT6 5NR, **t** (01227) 743307, *www.prospecttours.com*. Musical and cultural tours, including opera and ballet. Danube cruises too.

Titan Hitours, **t** 0800 988 5823, *www.titanhi tours. co.uk*. Escorted city tours, multi-centre coach tours and combined cruises and tours.

Travel for the Arts, 12–15 Hanger Green, London W5 3EL, **t** (020) 8799 8350, *www.travelforthearts. co.uk*. Tailor-made opera tours and weekends in each of the three capitals.

Travelsphere, Compass House, Rockingham Road, Market Harborough, Leics LE16 7QD, **t** 0844 567 9966, *www.travelsphere.co.uk*. Wide choice of coach tours and short breaks.

United Travel, 12 Clonkeen Rd, Deansgrange, Blackrock, Co. Dublin, **t** (01) 219 0600, *www.unitedtravel.ie*. City breaks in Prague, Budapest and Vienna.

Voyages Jules Verne, 21 Dorset Square, London, NW1 6QG, **t** 0845 166 7003, *www.vjv.co.uk*. Special tours: the Habsburgs, along the Elbe, Vienna, Budapest and Bratislava. Cruises along the Danube.

WA Shearings, Miry Lane, Wigan WN3 4AG, **t** 0844 824 6351, *www.washearings.com*. Coach, air and rail tours for the mature traveller. They offer a Historic Capitals of the Danube tour, and a Danube Symphony Cruise, among others.

In the USA and Canada

Check *www.affordabletours.com*, **t** 1-800 935 2620, for thousands of discounted escorted tours by established operators including Contiki, Globus, Trafalgar, etc.

Abercrombie and Kent, 1520 Kensington Road, Oak Brook, IL 60523, **t** 800 554 7016, *www. abercrombiekent.com*. The 10-day 'Tale of Three Cities' features a guest speaker, behind-the-scenes tours of Budapest and Prague opera houses, a private concert, and top dining and hotels. The 'Storybook Adventure' is geared towards families.

Dailey-Thorp Travel, PO Box 670, Big Horn, Wyoming, WY 82833, **t** 800 998 4677, *www. daileythorp.com*. Luxury escorted tour to opera houses: current tour to Prague, but Budapest and Vienna have featured in other years.

Europe Train Tours, **t** 877 929 7245, *www. vacationsbyrail.com*. Escorted and non-escorted train journeys and tours.

Globus, **t** 866 755 8581, *www.globusjourneys. com*. An 11-day tour of Vienna, Budapest and Prague travelling by hydrofoil and train.

Go Ahead Tours, 1 Education St, Cambridge, MA 02141, **t** 1-800 590 1170, *www.goaheadvacations. com*. A reasonably priced 11-day tour of the three capitals, as well as a Danube cruise, and individual city breaks.

Go-Today.com, **t** 1-800 227 3235, *www.go-today. com*. Several holidays featuring all three cities.

Kesher Kosher Tours, 347 Fifth Ave, Suite 706, New York, NY 10016, **t** (212) 481 3721, **t** 800 847 0700, *www.keshertours.com*. A 12-day Jewish heritage tour taking in Vienna, Budapest and Prague.

International Curtain Call, 3313 Patricia Ave, Los Angeles, CA 90064, **t** (310) 204 4934, *www.icc operatours.com*. Opera tours focusing on the Vienna and Prague Festivals.

Maupintour, 2690 Weston Rd, Ste. 200, Weston, FL 33331, **t** 800 255 4266, *www.maupin tour.com*. Luxury tours to the three Imperial cities, plus a Danube cruise.

Trafalgar Tours, **t** (866) 544 4434, *www. trafalgartours. com*. Ten-day tours to all three cities.

Worldwide Classroom, PO Box 1166, Milwaukee, WI 53201, **t** (414) 224 3476, *www.worldwide.edu*. Language schools and university exchanges.

Austria:
Practical A–Z

03

Climate and When to Go

Austria has mild summers and cold winters, with temperatures dropping considerably the higher you go. The city is perhaps best visited from April to October, when the weather is pleasantly warm, but cosy cafés and a wealth of excellent museums and sights provide the perfect refuge from the cold if you choose to come in winter. Christmas markets and the famous ball season in Vienna draw plenty of visitors in December and January.

If you are travelling further afield, note that resorts in rural areas have two distinct seasons: a summer season for those interested in hiking, fishing or other outdoor activities, and a winter season when skiing and snowboarding take over. Transport is often reduced, and many hotels and restaurants may close during the quiet periods (April–May and Oct–Nov) in these regions.

Disabled Travellers

For Vienna, go to www.vienna.info and click on 'Hotels and Travel Info', then 'Accessible Vienna', where you will find an array of pdfs for downloading, with information on hotels, transport, restaurants, cinemas and theatres and sightseeing, all regularly updated.

Buses and trams are mostly equipped with low floors for wheelchair users, and most metro stations can be accessed by lift.

Driving

You need a special pass (called a 'vignette') to drive on Austrian motorways. These are available at post offices and larger petrol stations and are valid for 10 days, two months or one year. A 10-day pass currently costs €7.90. You will be fined if you are caught driving without this pass.

More information (in English and German only) at www.vignette.at.

Electricity

The current used in Austria is 220v, which is fine for British appliances (240v). Visitors from North America, with 110v appliances, will need to use a transformer.

Plugs have two pins in Austria, but adaptors are readily available in department stores or shops selling electrical goods.

Embassies and Consulates

In Vienna

UK: Jauresgasse 12, t (01) 716130, www.britishembassy.at.

USA: Boltzmanngasse 16, t (01) 31339-0, http://austria.usembassy.gov/index.html.

Canada: Laurenzerberg 2, t (01) 531 38 3000, www.canadainternational.gc.ca.

Australia: Mattiellistrasse 2–4, t (01) 506 740, www.austria.embassy.gov.au.

Austrian Embassies Abroad

UK: 18 Belgrave Mews West, London SW1X 8HU, t (020) 7344 3250, www.bmeia.gv.at/botschaft/london.html.

USA: 3524 International Court NW, Washington DC, t (202) 895 6700, www.austria.org.

Canada: 445 Wilbrod St, Ottowa, K1N 6M7, t (613) 789 1444, www.bmeia.gv.at/en/embassy/ottawa.html.

Australia: 12 Talbot St, Forrest, ACT 2603, Canberra, t (02) 6295 1533, www.bmeia.gv.at/botschaft/canberra.html.

Health and Emergencies

Local **pharmacies** are well-equipped to deal with minor ailments, and are usually open Mon–Fri 8–12 and 2–6, Sat 8–12. Lists of duty pharmacies and 24hr pharmacies are posted outside all pharmacies. In an emergency head for the nearest Ambulanz (emergency room) at any hospital.

The helpful **Vienna Medical Association Service for Foreign Patients**, 1 Weihburggasse

Emergency Numbers

t 112 (pan-European emergency number, for all services)
t 122 (fire brigade)
t 133 (police)
t 144 (ambulance)
t 120 (motorway breakdown)

10/12, *www.aekwien.at*, **t** (01) 5150 1213,
24hr hotline **t** (01) 513 95 95 (*U1, U3 to Stephansplatz*), open Mon–Wed 8–4,
Thurs–Fri 8–6, can provide information on English-speaking doctors and local hospitals.

Money

Austria's unit of currency is the **euro**, available in coins (1, 2, 5, 10, 20 and 50 cents, and 1 and 2 euros) and notes (5, 10, 20, 50, 100, 200 and 500).

ATMs (*bankomats*) are found on virtually every street corner, and almost all accept foreign credit cards and have instructions in English. Some central banks also have automatic money-changing machines which accept foreign banknotes. Banks usually offer a better rate of exchange than the various *bureaux de change* clustered in the city centre, although it is often cheaper to withdraw money using your credit card from an ATM (check rates before you leave home).

Banks are usually open Mon–Fri 8–12.30 and 1.30–3, until 5.30 on Thurs, although some city centre banks don't close at lunchtimes.

Credit cards and all major **travellers' cheques** are widely accepted, although you might have trouble at some of the smaller and more old-fashioned establishments.

National Holidays

The following are all public holidays, when many places will be closed.

1 Jan New Year's Day
6 Jan Epiphany
Easter Sunday
Easter Monday
1 May Labour Day
Whit Monday (6th Mon after Easter Sun)
Ascension Day (6th Thurs after Easter Sun)
2 June Corpus Christi
15 Aug *Maria Himmelfahrt* (Assumption)
26 Oct National Holiday
1 Nov *Allerheiligen*
8 Dec *Maria Empfängnis* (Immaculate Conception)
25 Dec Christmas Day
26 Dec *Stefanitag* (Boxing Day)

Post and Post Offices (*Post- und Telegrafen*)

Post offices (the central office is at Fleischmarkt 19, *see* p.89) have yellow signs, and the postboxes are also yellow. Those with an orange strip have weekend post collections. Postcards and letters (up to 20g) sent to destinations within Europe will take 3–4 days and cost 65 cents; those sent outside Europe take around 4–5 days and stamps are €1.40.

More information can be found at *www.post.at* (some information in English).

Stamps can also be bought from newsagents, and most post offices have stamp-vending machines.

Price Categories

The hotels and restaurants in this section of the guide have been grouped into price categories according to the following rates.

Hotels

Average price for a double room with bath/ shower in high season:

Luxury	€€€€	over €250
Expensive	€€€	€150–250
Moderate	€€	€100–150
Inexpensive	€	under €100

Restaurants

Prices for a three-course meal for one person with wine:

Luxury	€€€€	over €60
Expensive	€€€	€40–60
Moderate	€€	€25–40
Inexpensive	€	under €25

Telephones

There are plenty of public telephones scattered around, most of which have instructions in English. All accept **phonecards** (available from post offices or newsagents), and some also accept **credit cards**.

Post offices have phone booths, which are usually cheaper for long-distance calls. Rates are high, but are cheaper after 6pm on weekdays and all day at weekends.

To **call abroad** from Austria, dial **t** oo plus the country code (1 for the USA and Canada, 44 for the UK, 353 for Ireland, 61 for Australia, and 64 for New Zealand).

For **directory enquiries** relating to Austria or the EU call **t** 11 88 77, or **international directory enquiries** on **t** 0900 11 88 77 (both usually have English-speaking operators).

The **international country code** for Austria is **t** (00) 43, and the **city code** for Vienna is 01, which you don't need to dial from within the city. Drop the first 0 of the city code if phoning Vienna from abroad.

Phone numbers vary in length, and some of them include direct dial extensions, which are tacked on to the end of the main number, sometimes with a dash, sometimes not.

Time

Austria is on Central European Time, which is one hour ahead of GMT. Clocks go forward one hour on the last Sunday of March, and go back on the last Sunday of October.

Tipping

In restaurants, add about 10% to the bill, or round it up to the nearest euro in cheaper places. Taxis usually expect around 10%.

Hotel porters usually expect a euro for each piece of baggage, and give a little something to hotel cleaning staff (in the smarter hotels at least) and anyone else who provides a service.

Toilets

There are public toilets scattered around the city centre, many of which are open 24 hours. Those with attendants usually charge 50 cents.

Underground (U-Bahn) stations also have toilets, in varying states of cleanliness.

Tourist Information

The website ***www.austriatourism.com*** has local sites for most countries; start on the home page and then choose your country of origin.

UK: 3rd Floor, 9-11 Richmond Buildings, London W1, **t** (020) 7440 3830; brochures and holiday information, **t** 0845 101 1818

USA: PO Box 1142, New York, NY 10108-1142, **t** (212) 944 6880.

Canada: 2 Bloor St East, Suite 3330, Toronto, ON M4W 1A8, **t** (416) 967 3381.

Austria: Vienna

Vienna, long the glittering capital of a vast empire, oozes Imperial magnificence: from its opulent palaces and glorious gardens to the equestrian ballets at the Spanish Riding School, the city gorgeously evokes the splendour of the Habsburg court during the Baroque age.

04

Don't miss

⭐ **Gothic theatricality**
Stephansdom **p.51**

⭐ **Secular and ecclesiastical treasures**
The Imperial Palace **p.59**

⭐ **A night at the opera**
Opera House **p.73**

⭐ **Magnificent Flemish paintings**
Museum of Fine Arts **p.69**

⭐ **Baroque magnificence**
Schönbrunn Palace **p.83**

See map overleaf

Vienna

Don't miss

1. Stephansdom **p.51**
2. The Imperial Palace **p.59**
3. Opera House **p.73**
4. Museum of Fine Arts **p.69**
5. Schönbrunn Palace *off map* **p.83**

The streets of Vienna are paved with culture, the streets of other cities with asphalt.

Karl Kraus (Austrian writer, 1874–1936)

The Habsburgs have been gone for almost a century, but they left behind their splendid art collections and priceless jewels in extraordinary, world-class museums – as well as their hearts and entrails in the city's macabre catacombs and burial crypts.

As Habsburg influence began to wane in the mid-19th century, the increasingly powerful burghers of Vienna were flaunting their wealth by erecting the showcase monuments that still line the Ringstrasse. In the lavish new Opera House, they whirled to the strains of Strauss waltzes as far-flung territories were shorn from the Empire. *Fin-de-siècle* Vienna was explosive: its coffee houses brimmed with writers, artists and philosophers; the Secessionists, led by Gustav Klimt, had electrified the art world; and Jugendstil architecture was blooming across the city. The decadent, hothouse atmosphere of turn-of-the-20th-century Vienna has long vanished, but its memory is still evoked in the city's legendary coffee houses, or when a street musician breaks into a poignant waltz.

The 20th century was a whole different story: two world wars and their aftermath put an end to the party. The last Habsburg emperor abdicated in 1918, when the Republic of Austria was declared, and the Reds took over the capital. Red Vienna erected the vast public housing projects that still stand on the fringes of the city, but Austria was on its knees. Rich neighbouring Germany seemed to provide the only solution, and in 1938 Hitler declared the incorporation of Austria into the German Reich from a balcony of the former Imperial palace. The once-thriving Jewish community was virtually wiped out, and the city was destroyed by bombs. After a decade of Allied Occupation, Vienna began to repair its monuments and its relationship with the rest of Europe. But the country has found it difficult to shake off its reputation for xenophobia and anti-Semitism. Immigration and the economy remain the two most contentious political issues in Austria, which has seen – as elsewhere in Europe – a resurgence in right-wing politics. The fiercely anti-immigrant FPÖ (Freedom Party of Austria) led by Heinz-Christian Strache made significant gains in Vienna's local elections in 2010, taking almost a quarter of the vote.

For decades, Vienna has clung to the splendour and romance of its Imperial heritage. The first major sign that things were changing was the erection of Hans Hollein's curving glass-and-

Addresses in Vienna

Vienna is divided into 23 numbered districts or *Bezirke*. Addresses are commonly prefixed with a number indicating the district, and the street number follows the street name (for example, 1 Dorotheergasse 11 means No.11 Dorotheergasse, in the 1st District). The Innere Stadt (Inner City) is the 1st district, with the other districts spiralling outwards from here. Postcodes incorporate the district number, so the postcode for the 1st district is A-1010, and for the 15th district it's A-1150, etc.

Getting to Vienna

Many airlines fly direct to Vienna from London and other UK airports, and from the USA and Canada (*see* **Planning Your Trip**, pp.21–2). You can also travel by train or coach, *see* pp.22–3.

Getting from the Airport

Vienna international **airport**, Flughafen Wien-Schwechat, **t** (01) 7007 222 33, *www.viennaairport.com*, is 20km southeast of the city. There are three **bus** services to the city centre: one for Schwedenplatz, one for UNO City, and another for the train stations at Südtiroler Platz, Südbahnhof and Westbahnhof. They leave every 30mins (4am–11.30pm) and cost €7 (timetables are available on the airport website).

A faster option is the **city–airport train** (the 'CAT'), which departs at least every half-hour for Wien-Mitte station between 5.38am and 11.08pm (journey time 16mins) and costs €10 (single); *www.cityairporttrain.at*. There is also an S-Bahn (commuter train), line S7, to Wien Nord, Mitte and Rennweg stations, which costs €3.60 (single) and departs approximately every 30mins betweeen 4.54am and 12.18am.

There is a **taxi** rank outside the arrivals hall. Journeys to the city centre cost €25–35.

steel Haas Haus right opposite the Viennese holy-of-holies, the Stephansdom cathedral. Baroque riding stables have been glamorously converted into one of the world's largest cultural complexes, with a string of excellent museums and a wealth of cafés where fashionable Viennese hipsters lounge on terraces in summer. The Albertina has had a futuristic new makeover and the city's culinary scene has never been so creative. The palaces, cafés and opera houses still provide Vienna with its alluring old world charm, but the recent injection of 21st-century confidence and optimism has given the city a welcome new dynamism.

History

Romans and Babenburgs

Vienna began humbly, with a small Celtic settlement on the banks of the Danube. In the 1st century BC the **Romans** established the garrison town of Vindobona (you can still see some remnants under the Hoher Markt, *see* p.59), but it was merely an outpost of the provincial capital at Carnuntum, about 25 miles west. Continually beset by attacks from troublesome German and Hungarian tribes, the exhausted Romans finally withdrew and handed over the settlement to the Huns in the 4th century.

It wasn't until the 10th century, when the **Babenburg dukes** acquired the territory, that the town began to expand. The name Wenia, which would transmute into **Wien** (Vienna), came into use during the 9th century, and the town became an important trading centre thanks to its strategic location at the crossroads between East and West. In 1156, **Heinrich II 'Josomirgott'** (who acquired his nickname from his favourite oath, 'So help me God!') moved his court to Vienna and, under his successors, **Leopold V** and **Leopold VI**, the town flourished economically and culturally.

Getting around Vienna

You can get information, plans and tickets for the U-Bahn, tram and bus systems at the transport information offices located at U-Bahn stations across the city, including Stephansplatz, Karlsplatz, Volkstheater and Westbahnhof (*open Mon–Fri 6.30am–6.30pm, Sat–Sun 6.30am–4pm*).

Also *see www.wienerlinien.at*, or call the helpline, **t** (01) 7909-100.

Tickets

Tickets, available from ticket machines at tram and bus stops and in U-Bahn stations, or at newsagents (*Tabak Trafik*), are valid for all forms of public transport. A single ticket costs €1.80 (unless you buy from onboard machines on the bus or tram, when it will cost €2.20); a 24hr-ticket costs €5.70 and offers unlimited use of the public transport for 24 hours; a 72hr-ticket is €13.60; and an 8-day Climate ticket or Streifenkarte (which can be shared – just date-stamp a strip for each person using it) costs €28.80 (note that the travelling days don't have to be consecutive). Other passes include weekly, monthly and student passes (visit the information offices). The Vienna Card (*see* p.88) includes free public transport. Children under 6 travel free.

By U-Bahn

Vienna has a clean, efficient and inexpensive underground metro system which is easy to use. There are five colour-coded numbered lines (U1, U2, U3, U4, and U6), and plans are available in all U-Bahn ticket offices. Date-stamp your ticket in the orange machines at the entrance to the underground before getting on the train. *See* p.336 for a map. Trains run all night on Saturday and Sunday.

By Tram (Strassenbahn)

Vienna's older trams – snub-nosed, rickety and endearingly old-fashioned – are gradually being replaced by a sleek, 21st-century version designed by Porsche. The excellent tram system doesn't penetrate the old city, but is useful for getting around the surrounding neighbourhoods.

Trams 1 and 2, which circle the Ringstrasse around the old city, are the most useful for visitors, but tram stops have maps showing the vast network of lines. Date-stamp your ticket in the machines by the doors. You can also take the Ring Tour, a special tourist tram which circles the Ringstrasse and provides an audiovisual commentary on the main sights (*see* p.89).

In the mid-13th century, **Freidrich II**, who had no heir, fell in battle against the Magyars, ending three centuries of Babenburg rule, and **Ottokar II** of Bohemia took advantage of the power vacuum to take possession of Vienna. To cement his position, he married Friedrich's widow, and sought election to the vacant German throne. But the Electors were wary of his ambition and increasing power, and chose the little-known **Count Rudolf of Habsburg** as King-Emperor in 1273, under the mistaken assumption that he would be easier to control.

The Rise of the Habsburg Dynasty

However, Rudolf easily matched Ottokar for boldness, cunning and ambition: the Bishop of Basel, hearing of his elevation, is said to have muttered wryly, 'Sit fast, Lord God, or Rudolf will occupy thy throne.' By 1276, Rudolf had taken Vienna from Ottokar, starting more than six centuries of Habsburg rule. His son, known as **Albrecht the One-Eyed** owing to a disfiguring battle injury, was as power-hungry as his father, but his cruelty angered the Viennese, who revolted in the late 13th century. The 14th century began badly, with plagues of locusts that ravaged the surrounding countryside and the arrival of the **Black Death**, which decimated Vienna's population. Things improved

By Bus

Most places on a visitor's itinerary will be served by metro or tram but, for those that aren't, there are buses. Bus stops have useful bus maps and you should date-stamp your ticket in the machines by the doors.

Night buses run every 30mins from around 12.30am to 5am, and the standard public transport tickets are valid.

By Taxi

Vienna's taxis have a 'taxi' sign on the roof, illuminated when they are free. They can be found at numerous taxi ranks (but not hailed on the street), or call **t** (01) 40100 or **t** (01) 60160. Fares are reasonable (a short trip in the centre costs between €10 and €12), but more expensive after 10pm and at weekends, and there are supplements for luggage. A small tip is expected.

By Car

A car is virtually useless in Vienna's city centre, and parking can be hard to find. Public transport is clean, efficient and inexpensive. However, your own transport can be very useful for visiting sights outside the centre. That said, Austria's national public transport system is excellent, and most places are easily accessible by train or bus.

There are several car hire offices at the airport, with branches in the city centre.

Avis, t (01) 7007 32700 (airport), **t** (01) 587 6241 (city centre), *www.avis.com*.
Budget, t (01) 7007 32711, **t** (01) 714 6565 (city centre), *www.budget.com*.
Europcar, t (01) 7007 32699 (airport), **t** (01) 714 6717 (city centre), *www.europcar.com*.
Hertz, t (01) 7007 32661 (airport), **t** (01) 512 8677 (city centre), *www.hertz.com*.

On Foot

The old heart of Vienna is perfect for strolling – small and compact with cobbled alleys and secret passages beckoning at every turn. The Ringstrasse and access to the many attractions just off it are plagued by traffic, but most of the main sights are within easy walking distance of each other.

For walking tours arranged by the tourist office, *see* p.89.

under **Rudolf IV, 'the Founder'**, who expanded what would become the Stephansdom cathedral and established Vienna's university.

In 1438, **Albrecht V** was elected Holy Roman Emperor, a title which would become virtually synonymous with the Habsburgs for almost four hundred years. A year later, Albrecht was killed fighting against the Ottomans (who would remain a thorn in the side of the Habsburg rulers until the late 17th century). The accession of Albrecht's grandson, **Maximilian I** (1493–1519), marked the beginning of a Golden Age in the fortunes of both the Habsburgs and Vienna, which was developing into a major European city with a strong reputation for learning and the arts. Through the astute marriages and dynastic alliances that always characterized the Habsburg dynasty, Maximilian managed to acquire vast swaths of land, including Burgundy, Flanders, Bohemia and much of Spain, including the rich Spanish territories of South America. His grandson, **Charles V** (1519–58), acceded to an empire on which the 'sun never set', although he ceded the Austrian possessions to his brother, Ferdinand, in 1521.

The **Ottomans** continued to batter at the gates of Vienna and in 1529 laid siege to the city. Ottoman victory seemed assured, and yet the besieging forces – mystifyingly – withdrew back to Hungary. Vienna's defences were immediately reinforced. The Ottomans were not the only problem facing the Viennese: the **Reformation** pitted Catholics against Protestants, and tensions regularly erupted into conflict. The **Jewish community** also suffered: restrictions on the owning of property and the plying of certain trades were imposed, and all Jews were required to identify themselves with a yellow ring. Although more than three-quarters of the population was Protestant, the Habsburg rulers vigorously championed the Catholic faith by persecuting 'heretics' and inviting the Jesuits, zealous leaders of the **Counter-Reformation**, to the city in 1551. Churches and monasteries proliferated, the University and other major institutions were purged of Protestantism, and laws were passed ensuring that only Catholics could become burghers of the city.

Baroque Vienna

Despite the simmering religious tensions, Vienna was blossoming into a major centre of the arts, particularly under **Leopold I** (1658–1705), who was determined to outshine his cousin Louis XIV of France. Vienna saw more than four hundred theatrical spectacles under his reign, many featuring the emperor himself, who was a gifted composer and performer (his extraordinary ugliness, the talk of courts across Europe, proved no impediment). Painting, architecture, music and dance flourished, and a slew of new theatres were established. Patron of the arts he may have been, but Leopold was also a religious bigot. The Habsburgs had thrown their considerable weight behind the cause of the Counter-Reformation, and the establishment of the Imperial Burial Vault in the Capuchin church (Kaisergruft; *see* p.55) was a flamboyant outward symbol of their commitment to the cause. In 1699, Leopold, who harboured all kinds of ludicrous notions about the Jews (including that they were responsible for his wife's failure to conceive), expelled them from their enclave in what is now the 2nd District, stripped them of their property (which was given to Christians) and renamed the area Leopoldstadt. But, although Jews and Protestants were persecuted, the threat of Islam was perceived as even more dangerous. In a famous sermon, court preacher Abraham a Sancta Clara answered his own question, 'What is a Turk?' with a list of blistering insults that began with, 'He is a replica of the Anti-Christ.' In 1683, the Ottomans besieged the city for the last time. Leopold fled, but the Viennese held out for two months, and were finally saved by the arrival of relief forces led by the Polish king. Victory was claimed by Leopold on his return, and the city gates were festooned with inscriptions celebrating Austria's triumph 'with the help of Jesus Christ'. With the restoration of peace, Vienna began a building spree, particularly under **Karl VI** (1711–40), who commissioned the beautiful Court Library (Hofbibliotek; *see* p.59), the Winter Riding School (*see* p.63), and the Karlskirche (*see* p.74) among many other landmark edifices.

The Golden Years

Karl VI had no male heir, but under the terms of the Pragmatic Sanction of 1713 his daughter, **Maria Theresia** (1748–80), inherited the throne. Despite the wars that ravaged Europe during the 18th century, Austria under Maria Theresia would enjoy hitherto unimagined peace and affluence. The young queen – who bore 16 children – astutely characterized herself as 'Mother of the Nation' and was adored by her people, whom she treated with a bossy familiarity, much as she dealt with her own children (her daughter Marie-Antoinette once wrote, 'I love the Empress, but I am afraid of her.'). She shrewdly surrounded herself with capable advisors, and ushered in a new, enlightened period of government. When her adored husband **Franz Stephan** died in 1765, she ruled jointly with her son, **Josef II** (1765–90), who would take her enlightened reforms further, although his earnest, well-meaning manner failed to captivate the Viennese. Josef II worked ceaselessly: he abolished serfdom, reduced censorship, introduced an administrative system to carry out the reforms, and curtailed the power of the nobility, as well as opening up Imperial parks, including the Prater (*see* p.87) to the people. Probably his greatest legacy was the institution of **freedom of worship**, to Protestants and Orthodox Christians in 1781 and to Jews in 1782.

The 19th Century

Josef II was succeeded briefly by his son, **Leopold II**, who died after reigning for only two years. By the time **Franz II** came to the throne in 1792, revolution was sweeping Europe, and his great-aunt, Marie-Antoinette, was guillotined in Paris the following year. A decade later, **Napoleon** was sweeping across the continent and his armies occupied Vienna in 1805 and again in 1809. In 1804, Napoleon declared himself Emperor, and Franz II retaliated by declaring himself Emperor of Austria, although this new title made little difference to his beleaguered land in the face of Napoleon's incursions. The following year, he was forced to relinquish the title of Emperor of the Holy Roman Empire, and great swaths of Austrian territories, including the Low Countries and parts of Italy, were ceded to the French. Napoleon was finally defeated in 1814, and the allied powers (Austria, Britain, Russia and Prussia among others) came for the **Congress of Vienna** to discuss how Europe should be carved up in the wake of Napoleon's fall. Franz II's gifted chief minister **Clemenz Metternich** ensured that Austria emerged from the Congress with substantial territories, but the enormous cost of hosting and entertaining the foreign representatives – more than 50,000 florins – was wrung from the protesting populace in the form of taxes. But the end of the wars brought relative prosperity, and Vienna was to enjoy thirty years of relative peace and stability. This, however, was largely achieved through the repressive government of Franz II and Metternich, whose secret police ensured that any lingering revolutionary fervour was immediately quashed. The city's population exploded, as peasants driven from the war-ravaged countryside poured into Vienna to seek work at the newly industrialized factories that were springing up. Their living conditions were squalid, and there was at least one major cholera epidemic. In 1835, **Ferdinand I**, who suffered from epilepsy, ascended to the throne, shored up by a **Great Council** which counted Metternich among its members.

1848 was the year of **revolution** across Europe: the French king was deposed and revolutionary fervour once again swept the continent. Vienna was no exception: simmering discontent from the poor and the politically frustrated middle classes finally boiled over in March of that year. Metternich, who was hated by the people, was forced to flee (apparently disguised as a washerwoman), and the remaining ministers were forced to grant some concessions including a new constitution and the lifting of the repressive censorship laws which had long stifled artistic and intellectual life. In October, the Habsburg family including **Ferdinand I** (who acceded to the throne in 1835) abandoned the Hofburg and made for a new, temporary home in Moravia, as troops were massed around the city under Marshal Windischgraetz. The city was finally subdued, but more than 2,000 Viennese were killed and another 2,000 were arrested.

In the new post-Revolution Habsburg order, Ferdinand I was forced to abdicate by senior family members in favour of his 18-year-old nephew, **Franz Josef** (1848–1916), who would rule for 68 years. Once the ringleaders of the Revolution had been executed, his next task was to bring the rebellious Hungarians, who refused to recognize his legitimacy, to heel. This was finally achieved in 1867, with the *Ausgleich* (**Compromise**) with Hungary, which established dual monarchy. Franz Josef was crowned King of Hungary, and the Hungarians were granted their own parliament with responsibility for everything except defence and foreign affairs. Peace may have been made with the Hungarians, but the increasing demands of the myriad other ethnic groups that came under Austrian rule would remain a thorn in the side of the emperor throughout his long reign.

In Vienna, the last decades of the 19th century were marked by a building frenzy which began with the destruction of the city walls in 1857. The broad boulevard of the Ringstrasse, which still circles the old city, was constructed and lined with resplendent museums and theatres (*see* 'Art and Architecture', p.47) which ranked with some of the finest in Europe. Financially, the city was thriving, although there were some major upsets, including a terrible crash in 1873 which bankrupted over one hundred banks and companies. The anti-Semitism that had long smouldered in the city was fanned again by rumours that the crash was engineered by Jewish financiers – an opinion loudly expressed by **Karl Lueger**. Leader of the Christian Social Party and mayor of the city from 1897, he was virulently anti-Semitic but his exposure of corruption within the upper echelons of the government and his socialist policies made him hugely popular with the Viennese (although Franz Josef, unhappy with his anti-Jewish stance, blocked his election three times before finally bowing to public opinion). In response to these attacks, **Theodor Herzl** developed his highly controversial ideas for a Jewish state, arguing that Jews were not safe in Central Europe. This notion outraged the Viennese Jews, but sowed the seed for the eventual creation of Israel. Vast numbers of immigrants, particularly Czechs and Jews from the eastern borders of the Empire, increased tensions further. Despite this ugly backdrop, the artistic and intellectual creativity in *fin-de-siècle* Vienna was extraordinary: Gustav Mahler was presiding over the Staatsoper; Klimt had led the Secession movement away from the turgid Eclecticism of the Künstlerhaus; and Freud published *On the Interpretation of Dreams* and coined the term 'psychoanalysis'.

The Early 20th Century: Red Vienna

The farthest-flung corners of the Empire were clamouring for independence as Austria entered the 20th century. In 1908, Austria annexed Bosnia-Herzegovina, a disastrous move which almost completely destroyed relations with the Slavs. In 1914, Archduke **Franz Ferdinand** was assassinated in Sarajevo. The Austrians declared war, without consulting their powerful neighbours, triggering a chain of events that culminated in the outbreak of the **First World War**. Franz Josef died in 1916, and was succeeded by **Karl I**, whose clandestine and unsuccessful attempt to sue for peace with the western powers in 1917 was humiliatingly made public the following year. When the war finally ended, Karl I was forced to resign the throne, although he refused to offically abdicate. He, his family and their entourage packed their bags and left the Hofburg, never to return. The Austrian Empire was in shreds, shorn of all its non-German-speaking territories, and its population decimated.

The **Republic of German Austria** was declared in 1918. The people were starving and desperate, and saw annexation by Germany as their only hope, but this was firmly denied by the Allied powers, who refused to countenance a more powerful Germany. In 1919, the Social Democrats (founded in the 1880s by the Prague-born Jew **Viktor Adler**) swept to power in the Vienna City Council, and the city gained its nickname '***Rotes Wien***', meaning 'Red Vienna'. The rest of Lower Austria was dominated by the conservative Christian Socials, which caused considerable tension, but, when Vienna became a *Bundesland* (Federal Province) in its own right, the Social Democrats embarked on a staggeringly ambitious social programme which (among many other social and cultural initiatives) saw the creation of new housing and the development of the welfare system. However, tensions between the Church-backed Christian Socials who held the balance of power in the national government and the Social Democrats who controlled Vienna grew throughout the 1920s, flaring into armed conflict on several occasions (both parties had private armies).

The worldwide economic depression of the 1930s exacerbated the situation, and in 1934 a three-day battle between the two forces ended Social Democrat rule in the city. Meanwhile, Adolf Hitler had won an absolute majority in the German parliament, and began to put pressure on Austria by insisting on the appointment of Nazis to key Austrian political posts. The Austrian Chancellor, Kurt Schuschnigg, decided to hold a plebiscite, believing that the country would vote against the **Anschluss** (Union) with Germany, but Hitler was enraged by this and insisted on Schuschnigg's resignation. Schuschnigg's replacement, the Nazi Seys-Inquart, immediately invited German troops across the border, ostensibly to prevent civil war. Hitler followed, and was greeted by a rapturous crowd on the Heldenplatz.

The Jews were hounded mercilessly, and on the infamous night of 9 November 1938 ('*Kristallnacht*'), synagogues, prayer houses, homes and businesses across the city were torched, and tens of thousands sent to concentration camps. During the **Second World War**, the city was repeatedly bombed, and few of its monuments were spared. Finally, the Soviets reached the city in the spring of 1945 and it was declared independent again on 27 April 1945.

Post-war Vienna

Post-war Vienna was divided into four zones, each controlled by one of the occupying powers. The occupation dragged on until 1955, when the Allied forces finally withdrew and the **Austrian State Treaty** was ratified. During the Cold War years, Vienna, as capital of a neutral country bordering the Warsaw Pact countries, was chosen for high-level political and diplomatic discussions, including the meetings between Kennedy and Khrushchev in 1961 and between Carter and Brezhnev in 1979. Austria established a free trade treaty with the European Economic Community (now the **European Union**) in 1972, and applied for full membership in July 1989. The country formally joined the European Union in 1995. Scandal rocked the country in 1986, when it was revealed that newly elected president **Kurt Waldheim** had served in a German Wehrmacht unit implicated in war crimes. He was shunned by most of the international community, and Austria was put on a watch list. Waldheim did not run for office again, and was replaced in 1992 by **Thomas Klestil**. In 1998, the Austrians raised their international standing once again by promising to restore artworks belonging to Jewish families who had fled the city in 1938. Unfortunately, this noble gesture was soon overshadowed by another political scandal: in 2000 the far-right **Freedom Party** (FPÖ) under the xenophobic **Jörg Haider** formed a coalition government with the conservative **People's Party** (ÖVP) led by **Wolfgang Schuessel**. The international community responded by freezing all high-level diplomatic contacts and briefly imposed sanctions. Protest against the new government erupted across the city, with marches and demonstrations on the Heldenplatz and elsewhere. In the fiercely fought 2002 elections the ÖVP had its biggest electoral success, but they still had too few votes to form a government alone. Once again, a coalition was formed with the FPÖ – although without Haider, who had become embroiled in political scandal and was forced to withdraw. Haider formed the Bündnis Zukunft Österreich (BZÖ, meaning Alliance for the Future of Austria) party, which won 4 per cent of the vote in the 2006 elections. Haider was killed in a car crash in 2008, sparking a host of conspiracy theories. In 2008, the Social Democrats and the Austrian People's Party formed a 'grand coalition', after a poor showing for both parties in elections ensured that neither could rule with a majority. Each declared that they wouldn't share power with either the FPÖ and BZÖ, which had, however, attracted more than 25% of the vote between them.

The economic global crisis has seen an explosion in support for right-wing political parties throughout Europe, including Austria. In the increasingly tense Austrian political arena, immigration and asylum issues remain political hot potatoes.

Art and Architecture

Early Vienna

The Romans left nothing interesting behind when they abandoned their small garrison town in the 5th century: the **Vienna History Museum** (*see* p.75) contains a few pot shards and coins, and there are minor ruins (featuring little more than heating conduits, and the sparse walls of the guardhouse) thinly scattered around the city, most notably under the **Hoher Markt** (*see* p.59). The origins of the great cathedral of **Stephansdom** are still shadowy: the oldest surviving section of the present building, the massive Giant's Doorway, dates back to the first half of the 12th century, but recent excavations have unearthed what may be the ruins of a pagan temple erected on the site several centuries earlier. The church contains beautiful examples of Gothic craftsmanship, including the celebrated **Pilgram's Pulpit** (*see* p.51). The city's other great landmark, the vast **Hofburg** palace (*see* p.59), also contains a medieval kernel, the Alte Burg (old fortress), although little is visible today underneath the embellishments and extensions of succeeding centuries. The web of crooked streets splintering east of Stephansdom are the hub of the medieval city (even Stephansdom, now the literal and spiritual heart of modern Vienna, once stood outside the old city walls), and still retain their appealingly haphazard medieval aspect. Here you'll find the simple Gothic church of St Rupert (**Rupertskirche**), originally founded in 711 but first documented in 1161, its sturdy tower peering above the huddled rooftops. The 14th-century **Minoritenkirche** (on Minoritenplatz) is altogether grander, although the tip of its tower was blown off during a Turkish bombardment and replaced with a curious pointy cap. The **Augustinerkirche** (where the Habsburg hearts are gruesomely stored in their silver urns) also dates from the 14th century (*see* p.64), and the 13th-century church of **Maria am Gestade** contains some delicate Gothic tracery.

One of the most recent and poignant discoveries in Vienna are the sparse remains of a 15th-century **synagogue** (*see* p.58), now buried beneath Judenplatz but accessible through the Judenplatz Museum. Close by, the oldest secular frescoes in the city, the **Neidhart Frescoes** (*see* p.58), are jolly depictions of popular scenes, painted around 1400. The **Medieval Treasury** (in the Lower Belvedere, *see* p.79) displays fine altarpieces and statuary from the 14th and 15th centuries, including the extraordinary Altar of Znaim.

Baroque Vienna

With the Turks battering at the gates of Vienna during much of the 16th and 17th centuries, the city was more concerned with defences than art and the city boasts little Renaissance architecture. However, once the Turks were finally defeated, extravagant Baroque palaces and buildings began to bloom across the city. The sumptuous **Belvedere Palace** (*see* p.78), the Imperial lodge at **Schönbrunn** (*see* p.83), the magnificent **Karlskirche** (*see* p.74), and the dazzling **Prunksaal** and **Winter Riding School** (both in the Hofburg, *see* p.59), are among the most spectacular of the new constructions, many designed by the indefatigable Johann Bernhard Fischer von Erlach.

The decorative arts flourished (there's an excellent collection of furniture and ceramics at **MAK**, *see* pp.80–81) and both the **Kunsthistorisches Museum** (*see* p.69) and the **Lower Belvedere** contain fine 18th-century statuary and paintings in their Baroque collections. The Imperial Apartments at Schönbrunn, a whirl of gilt, marble and crystal, eloquently convey the wealth and extravagance of Baroque Vienna.

The Habsburgs staunchly allied themselves with the Counter-Reformation, and lavish new churches – the **Jesuitenkirche**, the **Franziskanerkirche** and **Peterskirche** among them – were erected, their statue-festooned façades and dazzling interiors a magnificent testament to the wealth and power of the Catholic Church, and a deliberate rejection of the stark simplicity promoted by the Protestants. Equally florid public statuary, such as the **Plague Column** (Pestsäule) in Graben (*see* p.56), and the **Marriage Fountain** (Vermählungsbrunnen) in Hoher Markt (*see* p.59), were also designed to convey the twin spiritual threats of Protestantism and Islam.

Music in Vienna

Vienna resonates with music. Since the late 18th century, some of the world's greatest musicians and composers have flourished here, and the city is liberally strewn with monuments to titans of the musical world, from Mozart to Mahler. The following short list of celebrated musicians associated with the city incorporates details of memorials, museums and burial places.

The young **Franz Josef Haydn** (1732–1809) first came to Vienna aged eight, and was a choirboy at Stephansdom. Under the patronage of the wealthy Esterházy family (*see* Eisenstadt, p.111), he would become one of the most creative and influential composers in the history of music. The Haydn Museum (6 Haydngasse 19, **t** (01) 596 1307, *www.museum.vienna.at*) is where he lived for the last years of his life, and created some of his most celebrated works, including *The Creation* and *The Seasons*.

Wolfgang Amadeus Mozart (1756–91), child prodigy, and later friend and admirer of Haydn, was born in Salzburg but regularly performed for the Imperial family in Vienna. He moved to the city in 1781, and was engaged as court composer in 1787, a year after the presentation of *The Marriage of Figaro*, his most successful work. His unconventional beliefs made him unpopular at court, and he died a pauper in 1791. He was buried (like all non-aristocratic Viennese of the period) in an unmarked grave in St Marx Cemetery (*see* p.87), where a memorial has been erected. You can also visit his home, the Figarohaus (*see* p.54).

Ludwig van Beethoven (1770–1827) was born in Germany, but came to Vienna in the mid-1790s where he was taught by Haydn and created his most enduring works. Notoriously restless, he moved 69 times in 30 years, and three of his former residences are memorials to the great composer. These include the Pasqualati House (1 Mölker Bastei 8, **t** (01) 535 8905); the Heiligenstadt Testament House (19 Probusgasse 6, **t** (01) 370 5408), and the Eroica House (19 Döbliner Hauptstrasse 92, **t** (01) 369 1424). Although his music initially failed to capture a popular audience, his funeral was attended by more than 10,000 people. His body was removed to the Central Cemetery (*see* p.86) in 1899, where it remains a place of pilgrimage. There's also a small museum dedicated to his life and work at Baden (*see* p.106), where he regularly spent his summers.

Franz Peter Schubert (1797–1828) was born in Vienna (Schubert birthplace, 9 Nussdorferstrasse 54, **t** (01) 317 3601, *www.wienmuseum.at*) and produced an extraordinary number of intensely lyrical works in his short life. It was only after his death that his music began to attract widespread recognition and his body, like Beethoven's, was transferred to the Central Cemetery (*see* p.86) in 1899. Schubert's last residence (4 Kettenbrückengasse, **t** (01) 581 6730, *www.wienmuseum.at*) is also a small museum.

The Viennese waltzes that still haunt the city streets are the legacy of the extraordinary Strauss family. **Johann Strauss II** (1825–99), known as 'The Waltz King', composed almost 400 waltzes, as well as the celebrated operetta *Die Fledermaus*, but his father **Johann Strauss I** (1804–49) had already composed the Radetsky March, and brothers **Josef** (1827–70) and **Eduard** (1835–1916) made their own contributions to this quintessentially Viennese musical style. They are all buried in the Central Cemetery, *see* p.86.

German-born **Johannes Brahms** (1833–97) made his home in Vienna from 1868, where he took several positions as a choral and orchestral conductor and performed as a soloist. His songs (which often incorporated popular musical styles), symphonies and concertos were enormously popular in late 19th-century Vienna. He is also buried in the Central Cemetery.

If the music of Brahms responded to the *Zeitgeist* of pleasure-loving Vienna at the end of the 19th century, his contemporary, the devout **Anton Brückner** (1824–96), was its antithesis. Brückner's sublime, elegiac symphonies, deeply influenced by Wagner and Beethoven, earned him the nickname 'God's musician'. There are no major memorials to this composer in Vienna, who is buried near Linz.

Gustav Mahler (1860–1911) studied at the Vienna Conservatory of Music, and later became director of the Staatsoper (*see* p.73), where he is commemorated with a memorial plaque. As a conductor, Mahler gained his greatest fame with opera, but his creative energies were directed towards symphony and song. He was forced to undergo Christian baptism to take the post of director, but anti-Semitism dogged his career in Vienna and he eventually left for the United States. He was laid to rest in an austere Jugendstil tomb designed by Josef Hoffmann in Grinzing Cemetery (Grinzinger Friedhof) in the 19th district.

While director of the Staatsoper, Mahler championed young composers including **Arnold Schönberg** (1874–1951), who fled Nazi persecution and emigrated to the United States in 1933. Among Schönberg's early pupils were **Anton van Webern** (1883–1945) and **Alban Berg** (1885–1935), who both developed Schönberg's ground-breaking twelve-tone composition technique. Schönberg is remembered in Vienna's Arnold Schönberg Center (3 Zaunergasse 1–3, **t** (01) 712 1888, *www.schoenberg.at*), a music school and archive dedicated to his life and work.

19th-century Vienna

After the defeat of Napoleon in 1814, Vienna enjoyed a period of peace and affluence. However, the upper middle classes found themselves excluded from the political process under the restrictive rule of Emperor Franz II and Chancellor Metternich. As a result, they began to look to their homes to provide a showcase for their newly acquired wealth, and domestic architecture and the decorative arts flourished. The elegant, simple lines which characterized this style of furniture and design became known as **Biedermeier** ('Bieder' means plain and 'Meier' was a common surname, but the name came from a popular German cartoon of the age depicting smug *nouveau riche* burghers). The movement was deliberately anti-French, and rejected the lavish ornamentation of the earlier French Empire style. Despite the matter-of-fact name, the costly materials and fine craftsmanship meant that only the very wealthy could afford to commission the new designs. There is a wealth of Biedermeier design at MAK, and the rather dull idealized versions of upper class domestic life that characterized the painting and sculpture of the period can be found at the Upper Belvedere and at the Kunsthistorisches Museum. The **birthplace of Franz Schubert** (*see* 'Music', above) boasts an elegant Biedermeier courtyard.

In 1857, the walls which had contained the old city for centuries were finally demolished. In their place, a grand circular boulevard, the **Ringstrasse**, grew up, lined with a slew of lavish museums, theatres and public buildings. By now, architectural fashion had swung away from the elegant simplicity of the Biedermeier age towards monumental Eclectic Historicism. From the lavish neo-Renaissance Kunsthistorisches Museum to the Greek Revival **Parlament** and the spiky towers of the neo-Gothic Rathaus, late 19th-century architects like **Gottfried Semper** (responsible for the Staatsoper) and **Karl von Hasenauer** (who worked on the **Kunsthistorisches Museum**) plundered myriad historical periods for their inspiration. The fine arts followed the same course, with massive canvases depicting major historical events, and can be seen in the collection of 19th-century art in the Upper Belvedere as well as at the Kunsthistorisches Museum.

As the 19th century drew to a close, a new and dynamic aesthetic was emerging in Vienna's artistic community: in 1897, Gustav Klimt, Josef Hofmann, Josef Maria Olbrich and Kolo Moser withdrew from the conservative Society of Artists at the Künstlerhaus and formed the **Association of Visual Artists Secession**. The Secessionists vehemently rejected the turgid, backward-looking values of the Historicists, and the rigid traditionalism of the art establishment in favour of an idealized, quasi-religious quest for beauty which emphasized the natural and functional. It was the specifically Viennese expression of the Jugendstil movement, and the stunning **Secession Building** (*see* p.75) was a physical embodiment of their beliefs, which eschewed elaborate ornament and embraced modern techniques and materials. Viennese Secessionism owed more to the restrained forms of architects like Charles Rennie Mackintosh (whose work was featured in an enormously successful exhibition in 1902) than to the flowing curves of French Art Nouveau, and its main exponent in the capital was **Otto Wagner** (1841–1918). His delicate buildings (which include the frothy pavilions created for the new underground network on Karlsplatz, *see* p.74) emphasized the use of new materials like concrete and iron, and were exquisitely decorated with floral motifs and gilding. Wagner would later dispense with ornamentation altogether as his work moved towards Modernism, most notably in the remarkable **Post Office Savings Bank** (near MAK, at Georg-Coch-Platz 2).

04 **Austria: Vienna** | Art and Architecture

Early 20th-century Vienna

Gustav Klimt (1862–1918) is the most celebrated Austrian artist of the late 19th and early 20th centuries: his early work was in the Historicist tradition (you can see his early mural decorations on the staircase of the Kunsthistorisches Museum), but his mature works are characterized by a highly decorative style which reached its apotheosis with the famous *Kiss* (in the Upper Belvedere). The haunting *Beethoven Frieze* is on view in the basement of the Secession Building. Klimt and the other leaders of the Secession movement were determined to open up the inward-looking art world of Vienna, and mounted major exhibitions dedicated to the Symbolists, Impressionists and other international art movements, which deeply affected young Viennese artists. **Egon Schiele** (1890–1918), a student at the Vienna Academy of Fine Art, was greatly influenced by Klimt's ornamental elegance but his paintings are imbued with a dramatic Expressionist intensity and made bold new use of colour. There's a superb collection of his work at the Leopold Museum, *see* p.76. Other key innovators in the early years of Austrian Expressionism were **Richard Gerstl** (1883–1908), **Oskar Kokoschka** (1886–1980) and **Herbert Boeckl** (1894–1966).

The Secessionists believed in the *Gesamtkunstwerk* (total work of art), and every detail, from the façade to the light fittings, was subject to the same rigorous principles of design. In 1903, the architect **Josef Hoffmann** and designer **Kolo Moser** took this theory to its logical conclusion and formed the **Wiener Werkstätte** (Vienna Workshops), an arts and crafts co-operative which produced everything from furniture to postage stamps (a gallery at MAK illustrates the extraordinary variety of their output). Not everyone approved of this approach, and detractors included architect **Adolf Loos** (1870–1933), who championed a simple, functional approach to interiors rather than the lavish, hand-crafted décor of the Secessionists. Loos, whose writings (particularly *Ornament and Crime*, published in 1908) attracted more fame during his lifetime than his buildings, believed that the absence of decoration generated spiritual power, and sought to purge his buildings of all ornament. The **Loos Haus** is the most representative of his works in the city centre, and its uncompromising severity famously got him in trouble with the Emperor (*see* pp.57–8). One of the earliest Modernists, Loos' rigorous pursuit of pure forms was a model for later architects.

After the First World War, Vienna became increasingly politicized, and new buildings reflected the principles of the ruling Social Democrat Party. The enormous **Karl Marx Hof**, a huge public housing complex containing 1600 apartments, was built between 1927–30 and reflected the ideals of 'Red Vienna'. In the years

Austrian Food and Drink

Vienna, like most major capitals, has a wide range of restaurants serving everything from sturdy local dishes to chic fusion cuisine (although the latter is a relative newcomer to Vienna's culinary scene). The traditional *Beisln* – simple inn-like places – have been going upmarket in recent years and, in the best, classic Austrian recipes have been given a new lease of life. This reflects what's happening to Viennese palates: food, a long-ignored facet of Austrian culture, is now sexy, and the city's gourmets have an ever-growing number of excellent restaurants.

Traditional Austrian cooking is simple and hearty, and always good for keeping out the cold: meat features heavily, particularly pork and veal, along with game, goose and duck in winter. The classic dish is *Wiener Schnitzel*, a breaded veal escalope, and delicious soups, like *Leberknödelsuppe* (a herby beef broth with dumplings) are also common. An excellent local dish which appears on menus in winter is *Martinigansl*, roast goose served with red cabbage and potato dumplings. Another favourite is Hungarian goulash, well seasoned with paprika, or local variations made with potatoes or frankfurters. For a quick snack, the city is liberally sprinkled with *Würstelstands*, simple outdoor booths selling hot sausages (best eaten doused in mustard). In late spring, try the delicious fresh asparagus, and in summer, juicy fruits like local strawberries and apricots are piled high at market stands. In autumn, the Viennese collect pungent wild mushrooms, particularly chanterelle and porcini mushrooms, which are delicious simply sautéed.

Vienna's fabulous **cafés** are legendary, many oozing *fin-de-siècle* grandeur, and all serving a dazzling array of cakes and pastries. The most famous is the *Sacher-Torte*, a moist chocolate cake with an apricot filling hidden beneath a thick chocolate topping: the Hotel Sacher and the fancy *pâtisserie* Demel both claim the original recipe (although when these claims led to the courts, it was the Hotel Sacher that was finally granted rights to the term 'the original *Sacher-Torte*').

The pause for afternoon coffee and cake is called the *Jause*. Don't miss sweet delights like the delectable *Topfenknödel*, dumplings made of curd cheese with a crispy, nutty coating which come served with a fruit compote, the delicately spiced apple strudel, or the rich, chocolatey *Mohr im Hemd*, a steamed pudding with a thick chocolate sauce and vanilla-scented cream.

Viennese coffee is taken very, very seriously: the most common is the *melange*, a coffee with milk, but if you want it black, ask for a *Schwarzer*. With whipped cream and rum, it's a *Fiaker*, and with an egg yolk and brandy, it's a *Kaisermelange*. Strong, syrupy Turkish coffee, made in a special long-handled copper pot, is also common.

Vienna is almost completely circled by **vineyards**, many with restaurants to sample the new vintages along with simple (and, in some cases, more elaborate) Austrian specialities. A visit to a local *Heurige* is a pleasure that shouldn't be missed (*see* p.100). The most famous local grape is the grüner veltliner, which produces a fruity white wine, but there are also some excellent rieslings and pinot blancs. Red wines are generally soft and fruity, but there are some robust reds made with the blaufränkisch grape.

leading up to the Second World War, the city was to lose many of its most promising artists and architects, with thousands more incarcerated or exterminated under the Nazi regime. The city suffered terribly during bombardments, when many of its most beautiful buildings were damaged or destroyed. Many have been restored, but some are lost for ever.

Modern Vienna

From the late 1950s, a group of architects known collectively as the '**Austrian Phenomenon**' (which included Hans Hollein, Walter Pichler and groups such as HausRucker Co, Coop Himmelb(l)au and Missing Link) began to attract international attention with their visionary projects and installations, usually small-scale and often temporary (the Architekturzentrum, p.77, regularly hosts exhibitions featuring their work). At the same time, the **Viennese Actionists**, among them Günter Bros, Otto Muehl and Hermann Nitsch (*see* Museum Moderner Kunst/MUMOK, p.77), sought to shatter traditional conceptions of art with their violent and shocking public performances (Hermann Nitsch, for example, regularly enacted fake crucifixions). Art met architecture in the colourful, playful paintings and buildings designed by **Friedensreich Hundertwasser** (1928–2000), who famously declared himself an 'enemy of the straight line' (*see* Hundertwasserhaus, p.87, and KunstHausWien, p.87). Hundertwasser fans should make the trek out to the city's rubbish incinerator (the Fernwärme, 9 Spittelauer Lande 45), topped with his trademark gilded onion dome, which he strikingly remodelled in 1989. In 1995 **Hans Hollein** was commissioned to create a new building opposite the venerable Stephansdom, but his glassy modern Haas Haus (*see* p.53) caused a furore with many Viennese, who felt it had no place on the square. The most successful contemporary architecture in the city has taken older buildings and remodelled them, such as the Baroque Imperial Riding Stables which were expanded in 2001 to create one of Europe's largest cultural complexes, the **MuseumsQuartier** (*see* pp.76–7). The city's newest landmark is the Sofitel Stephansdom Hotel (*see* p.95), designed by Pritzker Prize-winning architect **Jean Nouvel**.

Around the City

Innere Stadt (Inner City)

The historic core of Vienna is a compact maze of narrow passages and cobbled squares, where ancient churches, Baroque mansions and modern shopping streets jostle cheek-by-jowl. It's dominated by the glittering tiled roof and jagged spires of Stephansdom, Vienna's magnificent Gothic cathedral, which is both the literal and metaphorical heart of the city. A great swath of the old city centre is taken up by the Hofburg or Imperial Palace, a sprawling complex built over 800 years, which is home to the celebrated Winter Riding School, the spectacular Secular and Sacred Treasury, and the Imperial apartments once inhabited by Franz Josef and Empress Sisi. Horse-drawn carriages clatter romantically across the cobbles, and coffee houses beckon cosily from every street corner.

Stephansdom

⑰ Stephansdom
*1 Stephansplatz,
t (01) 51552 3530,
call t (01) 51552 3767 for
info on guided visits,
www.stephans
kirche.at; open daily
6am–10pm; guided
tours 10am, 3pm, 7pm,
tours in English 3.45pm
(April–Oct only); adm
for guided tours and
audioguide, free to a
restricted area near
main door, free for
mass; much of the
cathedral is roped off
and can only be visited
with the purchase of an
audioguide; see the
website for information
on concerts*

Cathedral roof
*roof walks June–Sept
Sat, 7pm ; adm*

The spiky towers and steeple of St Stephen's Cathedral soar theatrically above the huddled streets of the Inner City, much as they have for almost 800 years. The original church was begun in the 12th century, but gained its colossal proportions in 1359 when Rudolf IV of Habsburg ordered its complete reconstruction in the Gothic style and had it raised to the status of cathedral. Friedrich III enlarged it further a century later, making Stephansdom one of the largest and most magnificent cathedrals in Europe – and the Habsburg name, as the ambitious rulers intended, was on everyone's lips. Rudolf IV, Friedrich III and other prominent members of the Imperial family are interred here, and the cathedral's shimmering tiled roof, added in the early 19th century, depicts the double-headed eagle, symbol of the Habsburg dynasty. The **roof** was badly damaged by bombs during the Second World War, but meticulous post-war restoration ensured that its magnificent gold and green chevron design glitters beautifully once again. These bombs were just the latest in a long line of attacks (twice by the Turks, again by Napoleonic armies) that damaged but failed to destroy the cathedral, and its remarkable endurance has earned it a special place in Viennese hearts, who call one tower *Steffl*, 'little Stephen'.

The main entrance is through the '**Giant's Doorway**', one of the few surviving sections of the original Romanesque church. No one really knows how it got its intriguing name, but it is said that early builders discovered some enormous mammoth bones and believed they belonged to giants. The '**Heathen Towers**' that flank the imposing portal date back to the late 13th century, and are a reminder of a pagan shrine which was believed to have existed here long before the cathedral's construction. To the right of the doorway, the letters 'O5', the symbol of the Austrian Resistance (capital O and the 5th letter, E, the first two letters of Oesterreich), were carved into the stone in 1945. The symbol is now protected behind a glass panel, after it was repeatedly coated in chalk to make it stand out whenever Kurt Waldheim, former Austrian president and Nazi collaborator, attended Mass. On the left of the doorway, a worn alcove was used to measure the size of a loaf of bread by medieval customers who suspected they'd been diddled by local bakers.

The vast, dim interior, with its lofty vaulted ceiling and ranks of slender columns, is crammed with masterpieces of Gothic craftsmanship. The most celebrated is the beautiful **Pilgram's Pulpit** (1515), carved with such delicacy that the stone appears as insubstantial as foam. A staircase winds around the pillar to the main pulpit, with a rank of salamanders and toads (good and evil) creeping up the balustrade towards a perfectly wrought dog, yapping furiously at the intruders. Portraits of the four Fathers of the Church (Augustine, Ambrose, Gregory and Jerome) are sculpted with astonishing naturalism, and Anton Pilgram himself (the master craftsman who created the pulpit) peers out of a window below to admire his handiwork. (He pops up again, in another self-portrait, beneath the corbel of the original organ in the north aisle.)

To the right of the main entrance, a stone canopy protects the 17th-century icon of the *Pötschen Madonna*, which supposedly wept tears during the Battle of Zenta against the Turks in 1697, and assured victory to the Habsburg armies under Prince Eugene of Savoy. The prince's elaborate tomb is tucked away behind a massive grille in the **Tirna Chapel** off the north aisle. There are several other miraculous statues, including the 14th-century *Servant's Madonna* in the south aisle, which apparently proved a wrongly accused maid innocent of thievery, and the **Lord of Tooth Ache**, now in a small chamber of the north aisle, which once stood in the graveyard and is claimed to have stricken non-believers with toothache.

The black marble **High Altar** is dark and gloomy, with overblown Baroque sculpture and a grisly depiction of the martyrdom of St Stephen. To the left, is the exquisite *Wiener Neustadt* altarpiece, with painted panels that open out to reveal scenes of the life of the Virgin Mary, which was commissioned in 1447 by Friedrich III. Friedrich himself is buried in an opulent red marble **tomb** on the other side of the High Altar, thickly encrusted with sculpted saints, fabulous creatures and inscribed with his famously enigmatic 'AEIOU' motto. This acronym was emblazoned everywhere during the Emperor's lifetime, but it wasn't until just before his death that Friedrich finally revealed its meaning: *Alles Erdreich Ist Österreich Untertan* ('The whole world is subject to Austria'). The **Donor's Tomb**, topped with effigies of Rudolf IV and his wife Catherine of Luxembourg, sits close to the High Altar, but their remains are actually buried in the catacombs.

North Tower and Pummerin
open Nov–Mar 8.30–5; April–Oct 8.30–5.30; July–Aug 8.30–6; adm

Off the north aisle, a lift swoops up to the **North Tower**, which was originally meant to be as tall as the main steeple, or South Tower, but which remained unfinished – the mundane explanation is that the builders ran out of funds and that the Gothic style had gone out of fashion, but the more romantic tale has it that work was stopped after a young architect threw himself off the tower because of an unrequited love affair. Now capped with a copper dome, it houses the huge **Pummerin** ('Boomer') bell, originally made from melted-down cannons taken from the Turks after they were defeated in 1683. The original *Pummerin* plummeted through the roof in 1945, and the present bell – even larger than the first –

South Tower
open daily 9–5.30;
adm (restricted views
owing to construction
at the time of writing)

was made from its remains and dates from 1952. The **South Tower**, or steeple, fondly known as '*Steffl*', can also be climbed. If you make it up the 343 steps, you'll be rewarded with spectacular views across the old city rooftops from a tiny platform (once the watchman's lookout).

Catacombs
guided visits only,
every 15–30mins;
Mon–Sat 10–11.30 and
1.30–4, Sun and hols
1.30–4.30; adm

Further down the north aisle, is the entrance to the **Catacombs** (Katakomben), which contain the remains of the principal members of the Habsburg family. The earlier rulers were left intact, but by the 17th century Habsburg burial customs had been formalized in macabre fashion: their hearts were presented to the Augustinerkirche (*see* p.64), and their entrails (considered the seat of the emotions) were given to the Stephansdom. What was left was entombed in elaborate sarcophagi in the Kapuzinerkirche (*see* p.55). After vigorous and antiseptic renovations in the 1960s, the Stephansdom catacombs are at first disappointingly lacking in Gothic creepiness, but then the small chamber housing the bronze urns of Imperial entrails gives way to the 18th-century tunnels and chambers piled high with the bones and skulls of more than 16,000 cadavers.

Cathedral and Diocesan Museum
1 Stephansplatz 6,
t (01) 512 52 3569,
www. dommuseum.at;
open Tues–Sat
10–5; adm

The cathedral treasures are kept on display in the **Cathedral and Diocesan Museum** (Erzbischöfliches Dom- und Diözesanmuseum), up a narrow staircase in a Baroque townhouse on the northern side of the square. There are ranks of 14th- and 15th-century saints (including one bizarre Madonna whose cloak opens to reveal God the Father being worshipped by a crowd of saints), several paintings, including two by Luis Cranach, and a delicate 16th-century *Pietà* by Luís Morales. There is a host of ornamental church plate, mainly from the 16th century, and the burnished gold burial cloth of Duke Rudolf IV 'The Founder', who first enlarged the cathedral and established Vienna's prestigious university. A 14th-century painting of the duke is believed to be the oldest portrait in Western Europe. The most valuable treasures are kept in a low-lit chamber, and include a jewel-studded 16th-century reliquary containing the bones of St Leopold, some exquisitely illuminated manuscripts, and a richly embroidered cassock.

Stephansplatz and Around

Haas Haus
U-Bahn to
Stephansplatz

Opposite the Giant's Doorway of the Stephansdom, the curving steel-and-glass **Haas Haus** (Stephansplatz 12), by celebrated architect Hans Hollein, was erected in 1990 amid huge controversy – 'carbuncle' was the least offensive of the descriptions it elicited. If traditionalists were appalled by its proximity to Stephansdom, enthusiasts of contemporary architecture were disappointed by its blandness. It now contains a luxury hotel (*see* p.93), and the bars and restaurants on the upper floors, all with beautiful views of Stephansdom, are among the most sought-after in the city.

Virgilkapelle
Stephansplatz U-Bahn,
www.wienmuseum.at,
t (01) 505 8747;
open Tues–Sun 10–1
and 2–6; adm

Underneath the square (access through the U-Bahn station), seek out the **Virgilkapelle**, a minuscule Gothic chapel with vestiges of mural decoration. Probably built in the mid-13th century, it later served as the tomb for a wealthy family of merchants.

The narrow, medieval lanes (such as delightful Grünangergasse) to the east of Stephansplatz are perfect for an aimless stroll, each corner throwing up a delightful cobbled courtyard, or carved Renaissance doorway. **Blutgasse** – 'Blood Street' – is one of the prettiest, despite its grim name. According to local legend, a group of Knights Templars were attacked with such viciousness here in 1312 that the street flowed with blood. Look out for the charming courtyard at No.3. **Singerstrasse** is also crammed with noble mansions, many still bearing elaborate stone carvings, as well as the elegant little church, the **Deutschordenskirche**. This was commissioned by the Brotherhood of Teutonic Knights, an ancient order established during 12th-century crusades and still active. The church was originally Gothic, but it's hard to discern beneath the flurry of Baroque gilding which was added later. Many knights of the order have been buried here, and you can still make out their armorial bearings on the upper walls. The Order's **treasury** (Schatzkammer; through the courtyard and up the staircase) occpuies just five rooms, but contains an eclectic collection spanning almost nine centuries and encompassing everything from medals, seals and coins to weapons, reliquaries and jewels. Look out for the curious Welcome Cups in Room 2, including one in the form of a dog (made for a member of the Hund family) and another in the form of a stag sporting bright orange coral antlers. The collection of weaponry includes intricately decorated Persian and Turkish swords and sabres, studded with jewels and covered in delicate gold filigree. Room 4 contains some strange devices for self-mortification, including a deceptively handsome 17th-century scourge.

Deutschordens-kirche
1 Singerstrasse 7,
t (01) 512 1065; open
daily 7–6; free; treasury
open Tues, Thurs and
Sat 10–12, Wed and Fri
3–5, closed Sun and
Mon; adm

Domgasse (stroll up Blutgasse from Singerstrasse) is another elegant street, with graceful cobbled courtyards and palaces adorned with swirling Baroque façades. Mozart lived with his young wife Constanze and their son at No.5 between 1784 and 1787, now known as the **Mozarthaus** or the **Figarohaus**, and is said to have spent some of his happiest and most productive years here. He created some of his greatest works during this period, including *The Marriage of Figaro*, after which the building is named. Unfortunately, as Mozart died impoverished, the museum contains no original objects from the period and, despite extensive and expensive refurbishment, the museum may be a disappointment to all but true aficionados. An audioguide recounts the composer's life as visitors wander around his former apartment, now filled

Mozarthaus/
Figarohaus
1 Domgasse 5,
t (01) 512 17 91-70,
www.mozarthaus
vienna.at; open
daily 10–8; adm exp,
joint tickets with the
Haus der Musik
available

with reproductions of portraits, letters, annotated sheet music and some curious contermporary art installations.

Kärntnerstrasse, a broad, pedestrianized thoroughfare, sweeps down from Stephansplatz to the Staatsoper, and is the main shopping street of central Vienna. What it lacks in charm it makes up for in buzz and bustle – almost every major chain store, from H&M to EMI, is represented here. When shopping palls, you can stop for cocktails at the sleek American Bar, designed by Adolf Loos, or sink into a plush velvet bench at the venerable Café Frauenhuber, Vienna's oldest coffeehouse and said to be Mozart's favourite (off Kärntnerstrasse at Himmelpfortgasse 6).

Just west of Kärntnerstrasse (walk down Marco d'Aviano Gasse) the small Neuer Markt square contains one of Vienna's most popular sights: the **Imperial Burial Vault** (Kaisergruft). In 1618, the church of the Capuchins was selected as the last burial place of the Habsburg rulers – at least, what was left of them after their hearts were taken to Augustinerkirche and their entrails to Stephansdom. By choosing the **Kapuzinerkirche**, the church of the zealous and ascetic Capuchin Order, the Habsburgs under Ferdinand III (the first Habsburg Emperor to be buried here, in 1633) proclaimed themselves at the forefront of the Counter-Reformation. The modern entrance is to the right of the church, and a blank modern passage leads down to the vaults. All Habsburgs have the right to be buried here, and a wall in the first and oldest chamber is filled with the tiny tombs of a dozen Habsburg children. Ranks of incredibly elaborate Imperial tombs follow, of which possibly the most opulent is that of Karl VI (1685–1740), surmounted with grimacing skulls and etched with a gory battle scene. The next chamber contains the famous double tomb of the redoubtable Maria Theresia (1717–80) and Franz Stephan (1708–65). Maria Theresia was heartbroken at the death of her husband: she insisted on sewing his shroud, preserved his apartments in the Hofburg palace just as he had left them, and seriously considered entering a convent. The tomb she had designed for them both is an enormous, frilly affair, which stands over three metres high and is thickly covered in rococo flounces. It's topped with effigies of the royal couple looking deliciously like a pair of lovers disturbed in a rumpled bed. Next to this Baroque extravagance is the pointedly plain and unadorned coffin of their eldest son, Josef II (1741–90), whose rule was characterized by earnest, well-meaning reforms but who – unlike his domineering mother – failed to win the hearts of the people. The Neue Graft (New Vault) is dark and chilly, with a curious jagged modern roof. Napoleon's second wife, the Habsburg princess Marie Louise, lies here, along with Maximilian I, whose brief rule as Emperor of Mexico was cut short when he was tried and shot by his subjects in 1867. The following vault, with

Imperial Burial Vault
1 Neuer Markt/ Tegetthoffstrasse 2, t (01) 512 68 99, www. kaisergruft.at; open daily 10–6

04

Austria: Vienna | Innere Stadt (Inner City)

elegant Secession detailing, contains the coffins of Franz Josef I (1830–1916) and his wife Elisabeth of Bavaria (1854– 98), better known as Sisi, both covered with drapes and always surrounded by a sea of fresh flowers. Franz Josef, mild, kind and hard-working, was greatly loved and admired by his people, and Sisi's unconventional life (see p.62) and dramatic death at the hands of an assassin are legendary. Near their coffins lies the tomb of their son, the Crown Prince Rupert, who committed suicide in 1889 (see pp.105–106). The final vault contains the tomb of Empress Zita, who died in exile in 1989 and was buried here with elaborate pomp and ceremony. She was the wife of the last Austrian emperor, Karl I, who died and was buried in Madeira in 1922, but is commemorated here with a bust.

On the other side of Kärntnerstrasse (take Krugerstrasse), you'll reach one of the city's newest and most high-tech museums, the fantastic **Haus der Musik**, a vast emporium of sound housed in an elegant former palace. Most of the excellent exhibits are interactive – you can compose your own waltz, or conduct the Vienna Philharmonic. The futuristic second-floor Sonosphere throbs with the sound of the heartbeat in the womb, or myriad sounds from beneath the oceans. A series of galleries is dedicated to Austria's major composers – Schubert, Beethoven, Mozart, Haydn, Strauss and Mahler – and you can catch a re-run of the New Year's Day Vienna Philharmonic concerts. The top-floor café has fabulous views over the rooftops to Stephansdom.

Haus der Musik
*1 Seilerstätte 30,
t (01) 513 48 50,
www.hdm.at; open
daily 10–10; adm;
guided tours for
children aged 6–12
(German only) available*

West of Stephansplatz

The **Graben** leads west of Stephansplatz. Although the name translates as 'ditches' (after a moat which lay outside the old city walls), this street is one of the most chi-chi in central Vienna, lined with expensive boutiques (many bearing the royal appointment device 'k.u.k', denoting *kaiserlich und königlich*, or 'imperial and royal'). It's dominated by an elaborate Baroque pillar dazzling after a recent refurbishment, in the centre, covered in puffs of angels, which was commissioned by Emperor Leopold I after the city was delivered from the plague in 1679: the **Plague Column** (Pestsäule) was designed by the Jesuits and features the Plague, in the guise of an old crone, being killed off by an angel, while the emperor, resplendent in a wig, prays earnestly. The subliminal message, incorporated by the canny Jesuits, was the deliverance of the city from the twin spiritual plagues of the infidel Turks and Protestant-ism. Among the regal early 19th-century buildings which line the Graben, look out for No.13 (now the upmarket men's tailor Knize) designed by Loos, and the **Ankerhaus**, at No.10, designed by Otto Wagner. Austria's hottest contemporary architect, Hans Hollein, designed the shop front at No.26.

Leading off Graben, smart **Dorotheergasse** reeks of old money, with its elegant antique shops and legendary auction house, the **Dorotheum** (*see* 'Shopping', p.90).

Jewish Museum of the City of Vienna
1 Dorotheergasse 11, t (01) 535 04 31, www. jmw.at; closed for renovation until end 2011/early 2012

The Palais Eskeles at No.11 is now home to the fascinating **Jewish Museum of the City of Vienna** (Jüdisches Museum der Stadt Wien), which outlines the history of the Jewish community in the city through imaginative permanent and temporary exhibitions. At the time of writing, the palace is closed while extensive refurbishment takes place, but the exhibits should be back in place by the end of 2011 or early 2012. At the end of the 19th century, the Jewish community was flourishing in Vienna, and had become the third-largest in Europe. A Jewish Museum, Europe's first, was founded in 1895 but forcibly closed by the Nazis on the eve of the Second World War. The visit begins on the top floor with a stark reminder of the pogrom of November 1938, the infamous *Kristallnacht* ('Crystal Night'), when synagogues and prayer houses were torched, thousands of Austrian Jews arrested and many sent to Dachau. Ranks of glass cabinets are crammed with charred and blackened Torah crowns, lamps, plates and other ritual objects saved from the fires. The first and second floors house temporary exhibitions dedicated to different aspects of Jewish life in the city. On the ground floor, the glassed-over courtyard has become an attractive, light-filled auditorium. The whitewashed walls are studded with stamped block prints by the American artist Nancy Spero depicting a medieval matzoh bakery and the smoky ruins of a synagogue in the wake of the Nazi destruction. Dedicated to 'Remembrance and Renewal', they try to capture the fragmentary nature of memory. A glass cabinet spanning an entire wall contains valuable ritual objects collected by Max Berger, whose family were wiped out by the Nazis.

Even snootier than Graben, adjoining **Kohlmarkt** is lined with top international fashion boutiques, but it's most famous for the legendary *Konditorei* **Demel** (*see* 'Cafés', p.101). In opulent 19th-century surroundings, ladies-who-lunch and footsore tourists from the nearby Hofburg gather over sublime, frothy cakes and cream-topped hot chocolate. Adolf Loos designed the sleek Modernist portal of the **Manz bookstore** at No.12, and Otto Wagner's student, Max Fabiani, was responsible for the elegant **Artaria Haus** (now home to the Freydt & Bernt map shop) at No.9.

Kohlmarkt opens up on to **Michaelerplatz**, overlooked by one of the grandest gateways to the Hofburg Palace (*see* p.59). This pompous neo-Baroque archway is thickly covered with heavy-handed sculptures, and was begun in the 1720s but only completed in the 1890s. In stark contrast, the **Loos Haus**, facing it across the square, is resolutely unadorned. Designed by Adolf Loos for the prestigious men's tailor's Goldman and Salatsch, it was built between 1909 and 1911 and caused a furore while still in the planning stages. The Imperial family apparently despised the 'house without eyebrows', a reflection of Loos' decision not to add the customary Viennese window boxes, and planning permission was only finally given once he promised to add some. Roman ruins have been discovered at the centre of the square, and are partly visible from a viewing platform, but there's not much to see. The **Michaelerkirche** was once the Imperial church and gives the square its name. It was originally built in the 13th century, but the interior is overwhelmingly Baroque, and an extravagant neoclassical façade was tacked on in 1792. A small fee grants admission to the small, macabre crypt, where the desiccated remnants of former parishioners, many still handsomely (if now rather tattily) dressed, can be glimpsed in their open coffins.

Michaelerkirche
open daily 6.30–6; adm

Heading back down Kohlmarkt, the street name changes to Tuchlauben. At No.19 (buzz the first-floor bell for admission) the **Neidhart Frescoes** are the oldest secular frescoes in Vienna, discovered by chance during building work in 1979. They were commissioned around 1400 by a wealthy cloth merchant, and illustrate the stories of Neidhart von Ruental, a 12th-century aristocratic minstrel, depicting rosy-cheeked figures dancing, playing ball games and pelting each other with snowballs.

Neidhart Frescoes
t (01) 535 9065, www. wienmuseum.at; open Tues–Sun 10–1 and 2–6, adm

Narrow Schultergasse winds from Tuchlauben to the **Judenplatz**, dominated by Rachel Whiteread's *Memorial to Austrian Holocaust Victims*, a large, boxy concrete sculpture reminiscent of a library with locked doors and shelves full of books facing the wrong way. This represents the truncated lives of the 65,000 Austrian Jews who were killed by the Nazis. The **Judenplatz Museum** (Museum Judenplatz Wien) opened in 2000, and is dedicated to the history of medieval Jewish Vienna. In a stark, uncompromisingly modern space, visitors are given special headphones which are linked to sensitive computer screens giving futuristic audio-visual descriptions of medieval Jewish Viennese life. Traditional exhibits are limited to a few stones, and a model of the city around 1420. A subterranean passage leads to the sparse ruins of the **medieval synagogue**, the oldest in the city, where it is just possible to trace the original outlines of the walls, with a small section of tiled floor, and the barely visible mound of the bimah, the special platform from which the Torah is read. The combined ticket also allows admission to the only Jewish **synagogue** to survive the fires of *Kristallnacht*. This elegant Biedermeier construction dates from 1824 and is now Vienna's main synagogue.

Judenplatz Museum
1 Judenplatz 8, t (01) 535 0431, www.jmw.at; open Sun–Fri 10–6, Thurs 10–8; adm, combined ticket with Jewish Museum and synagogue available

Synagogue
a 10min walk from the Judenplatz at 1 Seitenstettengasse 4, admission by guided visit only, held on Mon and Thurs at 11.30am and 2pm; bring ID

On the other side of Tuchlauben, you'll find **Hoher Markt**, Vienna's oldest square. It's now an unappealing car park, surrounded by banal buildings from the 1960s and 70s, but endowed with a very good *Würstelstand*. At the centre, the flamboyant Baroque **Marriage Fountain** (Vermählungsbrunnen) with its sickly-sweet depiction of the marriage of Mary and Joseph by the High Priest, is a reminder of the square's former glory. At the northern end of the square, a delightful and extravagantly gilded Jugendstil **clock** on the Anker insurance building draws a crowd each day at noon, when twelve little figures from Viennese history shuffle across the clock-face to the accompaniment of tinny organ music. If you miss the noon performance, you can catch at least one figure strutting its stuff every hour. Beneath the Hoher Markt, scant **remains of Roman Vindobona**, dating from around AD 1, have been discovered (Römische Ruinen unter dem Hohen Markt), and interesting displays recount life in the former Roman garrison.

Roman Vindobona
t (01) 535 5606, www. wienmuseum.at; open Tues–Sun 9–1 and 2–5; adm

The Imperial Palace (Hofburg)

The spectacular Imperial Palace which dominates the Inner City is a sprawling, confusing maze, built over more than six centuries in a dizzying array of architectural styles. The earliest fortress was built here in 1275 by Ottokar II of Bohemia, a protective bastion designed to withstand attacks from the Ottomans and the Hungarians. In the mid-16th century it became the official residence of the Habsburg rulers under Ferdinand I (1503–64), who remodelled the **Alte Burg** (Old Castle) in the Renaissance style, beginning a trend which was continued with increasing relish under succeeding rulers. Most chose to build new apartments in the latest fashions, rather than take over those of their predecessors, with the result that the palace grew in all directions – a wing added here, a courtyard there – with a complete disregard for uniformity. The most extravagant builder was Karl VI (1711–40), whose additions include the sumptuous Hofbibliotek, or **Court Library**, while the **gardens** (the Volksgarten and the Burggarten) were laid out in the 19th century. It now contains more than 2,600 rooms, 19 courtyards and 18 wings – but even this wasn't enough, and, right up until the abdication of Karl I in 1918, plans were under way for yet more building work. Now one wing contains the apartments of the Austrian president, and the rest has been converted into a string of museums dedicated to everything from weaponry to Esperanto.

For a taste of the magnificent Habsburg lifestyle, you can visit the Imperial apartments, or gaze at the jewels in the glittering Treasury, but the two most celebrated attractions of the Hofburg Palace remain the delicate ballets performed by the Lipizzaner horses at the Spanish Riding School, and the Vienna Boys' Choir, who sing Sunday Mass at the Burgkapelle (chapel). Tickets for either of these are notoriously hard to come by, so organize them months in advance if possible.

㉒ Imperial Palace
www.hofburg.wien. info; U-Bahn to Stephansplatz, Herrengasse or Volkstheater; tram 46, 49, 48A to Dr Karl-Renner Ring; tram D, J, 1, 2, 57A to Burgring

Negotiating the confusing layout of the palace is difficult, but the attractions are generally arranged around four access points: the Burgkapelle and the Schatzkammer are on the **Schweizerhof** (Swiss Courtyard); the entrance to the Kaiserappartements is on the **In der Burg** courtyard; the Spanish Riding School is on **Josefsplatz**, along with the Prunksaal (in the National Library); and the collection of museums held in the Neue Burg is accessed from **Heldenplatz** (Heroes' Square).

The oldest surviving part of the palace complex is the **Schweizerhof**, a courtyard dominated by a handsome 16th-century blue and red Renaissance archway dedicated to the Swiss guards who attended Empress Maria Theresia. A staircase leads up to the Gothic **Imperial Chapel**, the Burgkapelle, built in the mid-15th century and much restored since, although the lofty Gothic vaults and some statues have survived. The world-famous **Vienna Boys' Choir** sings Sunday Mass here, an unforgettable experience, but tickets should be booked months in advance if possible.

The dimly lit chambers of the **Secular and Ecclesiastical Treasuries** (Weltliche und Geistliche Schatzkammer) contain a dazzling array of jewel-studded crowns, Imperial robes and regalia and magnificent religious objects, attesting to the extraordinary wealth and power of the Habsburg dynasty over 800 years. One of the first and most magnificent exhibits is the late 16th-century crown of Emperor Rudolf II, sparkling with emeralds, rubies and sapphires and encrusted with pearls. There's also a gorgeous selection of coronation robes, including a brilliant blue velvet mantle edged with ermine, commissioned in 1838. Tiny christening garments belonging to the princes and princesses (who were baptised on the day of their birth according to Imperial custom) are laid out complete with miniature lace-edged caps, and (in a lugubrious touch) a cabinet in the same gallery contains the hefty keys to the 139 Habsburg coffins in the Kaisergruft. In Room 5, a huge, overblown cradle, groaning with allegorical figures, was donated by the City of Paris to Napoleon (who married Marie Louise of Austria in 1810) on the occasion of the birth of their son, quickly proclaimed King of Rome by the proud father. The Habsburg family took their private jewel collection with them into exile in 1918, but the state jewels they left behind are spectacular: among them are brilliant gems carved into extraordinary forms, such as the enormous 17th-century emerald which has been hollowed out to contain potions; diamond-studded ceremonial swords; and a glowing ruby set in enamel. Room 8 contains two of the most important treasures in the entire collection: a lustrous agate bowl, once believed to be the Holy Grail, which was made around the 4th century AD in Constantinople, and the so-called 'Unicorn's Horn', in fact a narwhal (a kind of whale) tusk more than

Imperial Chapel
*1 Schweizerhof, **t** (01) 533 99 27; guided tours only Mon–Thurs 11–3, Fri 11–1; adm*

Vienna Boys' Choir
*Sun at 9.15am Jan–June and mid-Sept–end Dec; reservations hmk@aon.at, or **t** (01) 533 99 27*

Secular and Ecclesiastical Treasuries
*entrance below the Burgkapelle, **t** (01) 525 24 448, www.khm.at; open Wed–Mon 10–6; adm, English audioguide*

two metres long. Rooms 9–12 exhibit the treasures of the Holy Roman Empire, including the magnificent 10th-century Byzantine crown, the 8th-century Holy Lance which contains a nail said to have come from the cross on which Christ was crucified, and faded coronation robes, exquisitely embroidered on silk, dating back over a thousand years. Room 12 contains a huge collection of gory reliquaries, mostly gathered by Karl IV of Bohemia, with the desiccated bones, hair and fingernails of scores of saints presented in costly caskets.

The Ecclesiastical Treasures are laid out in elaborate cabinets of burnished wood and gilt. There are shimmering crucifixes, sumptuously embroidered vestments glittering with gold and silver thread, medieval altarpieces, silver reliquaries and religious sculpture. Look out for a golden copy of the Column of the Virgin Mary encrusted with precious stones in Room 1, and the beautifully embroidered Pouch of King Stephen of Hungary, the oldest piece in the collection, which dates back to the late 11th century (Room 2). There's a spectacular and much-venerated reliquary in Room IV, studded with enormous gems, which supposedly contains one of the nails used to crucify Christ.

Walk through the Swiss Gate to the grand **In der Burg** courtyard, where you'll see the entrance to the **Imperial Apartments** (Kaiserappartements). The Apartments are surprisingly dull, but they have been pepped up for visitors with the addition of the **Sisi Museum**, dedicated to the Empress Sisi (*see* box, p.62), and the **Silberkammer** (Silver Collection), a dazzling display of Imperial silver, porcelain, glass and linen.

Visits begin with the Silver Collection, where visitors can admire an 18th-century Sèvres dining service, and a staggering 30m-long gilded bronze centrepiece and candelabrum from the turn of the 19th century. One of the most remarkable exhibits is a beautiful dinner service with a bold, brightly design featuring flowers, birds and insects, which was commissioned by Sisi for Franz Josef's hunting lodge. Continue upstairs for the Sisi Museum, dedicated to Elizabeth of Bavaria, whose unconventional life and tragic death (often compared with that of Princess Diana) continue to fascinate millions. These galleries contain a collection of personal mementoes, fleshed out with flashy displays and gossipy information panels. There are copies of her ballgowns, quotations from her letters and poetry, a reconstruction of the palatial Imperial rail car in which she travelled, and photographs of the grieving crowds who attended her funeral in 1898. Her obsession with her appearance made Sisi one of the earliest fitness freaks, and some of her massive collection of gym equipment is also here. The highlight is perhaps the dagger with which Italian anarchist

Imperial Apartments/Sisi Museum/ Silberkammer
t (01) 533 75 70, www. hofburg-wien.at; open Sept–June daily 10–5.30, last admission 4.30; July-Aug daily 10–6, last admission 5.30; closed Tues; adm

Sisi, the Reluctant Empress

Elisabeth of Bavaria, better known as Sisi, was never meant to be Empress of Austria. Franz Josef's mother, the indomitable Archduchess Sophie (whose own marriage had been arranged according to Habsburg custom), had picked out Sisi's elder sister, Hélène, and arranged for the pair to meet in the spa town of Bad Ischl. But the young prince was instantly smitten with 16-year-old Sisi, and the pair were engaged within three days. Their whirlwind romance captured the hearts of everyone in the empire, and the demand for souvenirs commemorating their engagement and marriage was insatiable. But, despite appearances, the relationship quickly fell into difficulties. While Franz Josef adored Sisi, his new wife was quickly disillusioned with court life. She fought bitterly with her strong-willed mother-in-law, chafed under Franz Josef's overly protective affection, and found the constraints of the Habsburg court unbearable. She was devoted to her children – Sophie, Gisela, Rupert and Marie Valerie – but she never fully recovered from the death of Sophie aged only two. In 1860 she spent several months in Madeira, ostensibly for health reasons, although the Imperial physician could find nothing wrong with her. She had barely returned to court when she set off again, this time to Crete. Her absences grew longer – she would leave for months or even years, sailing around the Mediterranean, reading, writing poetry and painting – and Franz Josef, who remained dazzled by her until the day he died, indulged her every whim. She was obsessed with her appearance, particularly the luxuriant ankle-length hair which had so captivated her husband, and refused to be photographed or painted after the age of 40. She was particularly concerned about her weight (which she never allowed to top 50kg, though she was 5ft 7ins tall), and had gyms installed in all the Imperial residences. In 1867, Hungary's historic rights were restored with the *Ausgleich* (Compromise) and Sisi developed an obsession with all things Magyar, learning the language and engaging Hungarian servants. While this made her enormously popular with the Hungarians, the Viennese deeply resented her sentiments. Tragedy struck in 1889, when Crown Prince Rupert committed suicide in mysterious circumstances in Mayerling (*see* p.106) and Sisi withdrew completely. She wore black until her untimely death in 1898, when she was assassinated by an Italian anarchist on Lake Geneva.

Luigi Lucheni killed her, a surprisingly small and apparently innocuous sliver of steel.

Beyond the Sisi Museum, the Imperial Apartments where the Empress and her uxorious husband Franz Josef I lived have been preserved virtually intact. Although this section of the palace was built in the 18th century, they are mostly decorated in the flamboyant style of the 19th century, with red brocade walls, plenty of swirling gilt, and enormous chandeliers. Franz Josef gave audiences twice a week to his subjects: all were welcome (much to the annoyance of the Austrian aristocracy), but they were required to wear either uniform, a dark dress with a train, or national costume, displayed here on mannequins. The emperor was a stickler for form, and once famously berated an officer at the dinner table for not having the requisite number of buttons on his uniform sleeves, a dereliction he considered 'monstrous'. One corner of the audience chamber is dominated by a vast golden ceramic stove, one of several throughout the palace, which were tended by a team of Imperial Stove Stokers – once a specific job in the palace. Beyond the audience chamber is a conference room, decorated in pale eau-de-nil brocade, and behind it is Franz Josef's study, which is more personal and interesting than the other *salons*. Franz Josef, who took the Habsburg creed of 'First Servant' very seriously, was astonishingly industrious: after a cold bath and a frugal breakfast, he was at his desk by 3.30 every morning. The room is still filled with photographs of his children and grandchildren, and the famous portrait of his 'Angel Sisi', her long hair falling to her waist, sits directly opposite his desk. After Sisi withdrew to her own apartments (the emperor had to ring a bell if he wanted to enter), he slept on a simple iron bedstead in a modest room adjoining his study. The Smoking Room, off a large *salon* used for family visits, is now dedicated to Franz Josef's younger brother, Maximilian, who accepted the crown of Mexico (against his brother's advice), but was tried and executed by revolutionaries in 1867. Next come Sisi's apartments, beginning with her extravagantly decorated bedroom and drawing room, as well as the tiny Bergl chamber, beautifully decorated with dreamy tropical friezes. Her obsessive concern for her appearance is reflected in the lavish bathroom and a fitness room crammed with equipment. A long series of empty *salons* follows, which were famously used by the Tsar of Russia during the Congress of Russia in 1814–5, and are known as the Alexander Apartments. These culminate with the Dining Room, where the table has been set for a family dinner. Even in this intimate setting, it was impossible to escape court ceremony which dictated exactly how the table should be laid on such an occasion.

The next swath of the Hofburg's attractions are off **Josefsplatz**, dominated by a pompous equestrian monument to Emperor Josef II. This square is home to the Hofburg's most celebrated attraction, the **Spanish Riding School** (Spanische Hofreitschule). Entering the Baroque **Winter Riding School** is like stepping inside a wedding cake: creamy stuccowork swirls across the ceiling, hung with massive chandeliers, and makes frothy puffs around the entrance arches. The origins of the legendary Spanish Riding School date back to the end of the 16th century, when the elegant horses were first bred from Spanish, Italian and North African stallions at the Imperial Stud in Lipizzaner, near Trieste. It was Emperor Karl VI (1685–1740), born and brought up in Spain, who gave it its current form and commissioned the lavish Winter Riding School from Josef Emanuel Fischer von Erlach (who also created the Prunksaal). The graceful manoeuvres performed today date back to this period, although they are based on steps developed during the Renaissance by cavalrymen who needed nimble mounts in battle. An equestrian portrait of the emperor hangs over the entrance to the ring, and the riders salute it by raising their hats as they enter. There are two galleries, where lucky spectators who booked their tickets well in advance can view the beautiful Lipizzaner horses perform their intricate ballets. The horses are born dark, but gradually whiten, and the finest animals begin their rigorous

Spanish Riding School

1 Josefsplatz 1, t (01) 533 90 31, www.srs.at; performances and morning work Feb–June and end Aug–beginning Nov; programme on website, or available in a booklet from the tourist office; adm exp

training at the age of three. They are trained to perform extraordinary moves like the Courbette, in which the horse bounds kangaroo-like on its back legs, and the Capriole, a balletic leap in which the back legs are kicked out. Tickets to performances are very expensive, but it's possible to see the horses **rehearsing** their moves during the morning training sessions for a relatively reasonable fee. These are for committed fans only, as they can be dull, but just watching the horses being led across from their stables to the Winter Riding School is a romantic sight. The Lipizzaner Museum, which once stood across the road, has closed down, but you can pick up books, gifts and DVDs at the shop in the visitor centre.

Back on Josefsplatz proper, the **Austrian National Library** (Nationalbibliothek) contains the dazzling **Hall of State** (Prunksaal), the largest Baroque library in Europe, a giddy whirl of columns, gilt, statuary and heavily allegorical frescoes. The work of Johann Bernhard Fischer von Erlach, who also designed the Karlskirche, it's one of the masterpieces of the late 18th century. Frescoes span each archway, but the hall is dominated by a huge domed allegory depicting the Apotheosis of Karl IV, painted by Daniel Gran. Delicate spiral staircases twirl up gracefully between the gilded wooden shelves, which contain more than two and a half million leather-covered books, including the 15,000-volume personal collection belonging to Prince Eugene of Savoy, much fêted hero of the Turkish campaign around the turn of the 18th century. There are several statues and busts, including one of Karl VI, who commissioned the hall, and a small but extraordinary **Papyrus Museum**. The magnificent globes in the Prunksaal are just a harbinger of what's to come in the absorbing **Globe Museum** in the Palais Mollard at Herrengase 9. Also in the Palais Mollard is the **Esperanto Museum**, which offers an overview of this and other 'planned languages'.

Overlooking Josefsplatz, the 14th-century **Augustinerkirche** is one of the oldest surviving churches in Vienna, although its stone walls have been plastered over in an ugly institutional grey. The lofty, vaulted interior is dominated by Antonio Canova's sentimental memorial to Maria Theresia's favourite daughter, Maria Christina, which was commissioned by her husband in 1805. Weeping angels and distraught mourners cluster around the entrance to the tomb, although Maria Christina is actually buried in the Imperial burial vault in the Kapuzinerkirche. But dead Habsburgs are still the main draw in this church: while their bodies lie in the Imperial vault and their entrails in Stephansdom, their hearts are arranged in silver caskets in the tiny **Loreto Chapel** to the right of the main altar. The church is famous for the Sunday **masses by Haydn and Schubert**, but get there early to be sure of a place.

Rehearsals
€12 on the day at Gate No.2, on Josefsplatz or in advance from the visitor centre at Michaelerplatz 1

Hall of State
Josefsplatz 1, t (01) 534 10 394, www.onb.ac.at; open Tues, Wed and Fri–Sun 10–6, Thurs 10–9; adm

Papyrus Museum
www.onb.ac.at, t (01) 534 10 420; open Tues, Wed and Fri–Sun 10–6, Thurs 10–9; adm

Globe Museum
www.onb.ac.at, t (01) 534 10 710; open Tues, Wed and Fri–Sun 10–6, Thurs 10–9; adm

Esperanto Museum
www.onb.ac.at, t (01) 534 10 730; open Tues, Wed and Fri–Sun 10–6, Thurs 10–9; adm

Augustinerkirche
1 Augustinerstrasse 3; t (01) 533 7099, www.hochamt.at; open daily 8–5; free, adm to Loreto Chapel, which is only open by prior appt and after Sunday Mass; **Haydn and Schubert masses** *at 11am, except July and Aug when special performances are held*

Albertina

1 Albertinaplatz 3, t (01) 534 830, www. albertina.at; open Thurs–Tues 10–6, Wed 10–9; adm

Augustinerstrasse leads to the **Albertina**, located in the southern wing of the Hofburg palace. It gets its name from Duke Albert of Sachsen-Teschen, who married Maria Theresia's favourite daughter, Maria Christina, and thereby came into a fortune. He was able to fund his passion for art with Habsburg money, and founded this extraordinary collection in 1768, when he was given a thousand artworks from the Genoese art expert and ambassador to Austria, Comte Durasso. By the time of the duke's death in 1822, the collection comprised some 14,000 drawings and around 200,000 graphic art prints: now, the holdings include almost 70,000 drawings and over a million graphic prints, with works by Raphael, Dürer, Leonardo da Vinci, Michelangelo, Rembrandt, Picasso, Matisse, Schiele and Klimt among others. These have recently been augmented by the superb Batliner Collection, which contains key works from international modern art movements, including French Impressionism, Post-Impressionism and Fauvism – none of which have historically been well-represented in the Austrian capital until now. About a hundred paintings from the collection, including works by Cézanne, Monet and Picasso, now form the hub of a new permanent exhibition which traces the development from Impressionism to modern art. They are complemented by the smaller Forberg collection, which is particularly strong on works from German Expressionism and the Russian avant-garde. The vast graphic art, architectural and photographic holdings, however, are usually shown in temporary exhibitions which focus on a particular artist or theme. Those with a penchant for Imperial interior design can visit the **Imperial Apartments**, which have been painstakingly restored to look much as they would have in 1822, and include a dazzling 100m-long ballroom and a Wedgwood Chamber that boasts some of the oldest English porcelain reliefs.

Austrian Theatre Museum

Lobkowitzplatz 2, t (01) 525 240, www.theater museum.at; open Tues–Sun 10–6; adm

It's worth taking a brief detour behind the Albertina to find the Lobkowitz Palace, which now contains the **Austrian Theatre Museum** (Österreichisches Theatermuseum). Behind the sumptuous Baroque façade is a huge collection of costumes, stage props, photographs and some stunning Art Nouveau stick puppets.

Wiggle back through the palace courtyards to emerge onto **Heldenplatz** (Heroes' Square), where the splendid curve of the **Neue Burg** (New Castle) was built between 1881–1913 under Emperor Franz Josef I. It was part of an ambitious plan for a Kaiser Forum (Emperor's Forum), which was originally intended to be the crowning glory of the development of the Ringstrasse, but the breathtakingly grandiose plans were never fully realized. At the turn of the 20th century, the Habsburg Empire was unravelling as its diverse peoples – Hungarians, Czechs, Slovaks, Poles, Slovenes and Croats – demanded their independence, and this florid piece of bombast served only to paper over the cracks. Just five years after

Neue Burg museums
t (01) 525 240, www.khm.at; all museums open Wed–Mon 10–6; adm (single adm ticket for all three collections)

the completion of the Neue Burg, the last Habsburg Emperor (Karl I) abdicated and went into exile. The Neue Burg made the history books again in 1938, when Adolf Hitler proclaimed the incorporation of Austria into the Third Reich (the *Anschluss*) from one of its balconies. Now the castle houses several **museums**, all accessible with a single ticket.

The interior of the Neue Burg is every bit as florid and pompous as the exterior, with monumental staircases, ranks of marble columns and elaborate stucco ceilings providing a splendid backdrop to the museums' collections. The **Collection of Arms and Armour** (Hofjagd- und Rüstkammer) is vast and surprisingly engrossing, with prancing horses decked out in full jousting gear, fanciful costume armour which would have been worn at court rather than on the battlefield (including a set with strange duck-shaped feet which was commissioned for a wedding), and a whole gallery dedicated to exquisitely decorated Turkish armour and weaponry. There's a set of tiny child's dress armour, created for the future Charles V, and some extraordinary horse armour, including a beautifully embossed set commissioned by Friedrich III, in which a dragon seems to erupt from the saddle.

The **Collection of Ancient Musical Instruments** (Sammlung alter Musikinstrumente) is altogether more soothing – quite literally, as the audioguide provides a gentle musical background to the exhibits. It's another enormous collection, spreading across several vast galleries and encompassing one of the most remarkable collections of Renaissance instruments in the world. Exhibits range from prehistoric rattles and early chimes and bells, to glowing 17th- and 18th-century violas, cellos and violins, and elegant pianos. Some of the most curious pieces include a strange double guitar made in Paris in the late 15th century, and a late Gothic bass lute which is absolutely unique. There's also a glass harmonica, in which the bowls are set humming when touched with damp fingers (making a sound like that produced by running a wet finger around a wine glass). Mozart even wrote for this instrument, which has a surprisingly delicate sound (you can hear a piece on the audioguide).

The lower galleries contain the archaeological fragments discovered at Ephesus, one of the most important cities of Classical Antiquity and site of the Temple of Artemis, once of the Seven Wonders of the World. Almost nothing remains of the temple, but a model of the monumental altar is dotted with a few surviving sculptures, including the delicate torso of an Amazon (who were said to amputate a breast to fight better, although this figure survives intact). The most striking exhibit is the massive Parthian Monument, a series of exquisitely wrought relief panels which may have been part of an altar. They were erected to commemorate the

Roman victory over the Parthians, and are considered the finest such monument in Asia Minor. An earlier frieze of a cavalry battle celebrates a Greek victory over the Galaceans, and is one of the earliest known depictions of a historic battle in the world.

Ethnographical Museum
open Wed–Mon 10–6; adm

The **Ethnographical Museum** (Museum für Völkerkunder) has a separate admission fee. It is housed in what was originally intended to be the Imperial guest house, and has a separate entrance on the Heldenplatz. Its holdings span every continent, and the enjoyably diverse and curious collection has all kinds of oddities, including some fetching fashion made from reeds in rural Japan, or from seal intestine in the Arctic. The star of the Africa section is the striking series of bronze sculptures from Benin, but the most famous piece in the whole collection is the 16th-century feathered head-dress which belonged to the Aztec king Montezuma, who was stoned to death by his own people for failing to resist the Spanish conquistadors. It is under restoration at the time of writing, and not all the galleries are open.

Behind the Ethnographical Museum is the leafy expanse of the **Burggarten**, laid out in 1819 as a private retreat for members of the Imperial family, and now popular with picnicking locals. It's scattered with busts, including those of Mozart, Goethe and Emperor Franz Josef I. A graceful Jugendstil greenhouse, built in 1901, now contains the **Butterfly House** (Schmetterling Haus), where visitors are surrounded by huge tropical butterflies fluttering freely amid the palm trees.

Butterfly House
Burggarten, t (01) 533 8570, www. schmetterling haus.at; open April–Oct daily 10–4,45, Sat–Sun 10–6.15; Nov–Mar daily 10–3.45 ; adm

Around the Ringstrasse

When the city walls were finally demolished in 1857, work began on this spectacular circular boulevard, designed to outshine anything Paris or London had to offer. It was soon lined with some of Vienna's most emblematic buildings – the legendary Opera House (Staatsoper), the magnificent Fine Arts Museum (Kunsthistorisches Museum), and the National Theatre among them – which cemented Vienna's reputation as a leading centre of the arts. Nearby, the pure lines of the beautiful Secession Building highlights the revolution which the Viennese art world underwent at the turn of the 20th century (*see* p.47). The sublime Baroque palace of the Belvedere displays Austrian art from the last millennium, and the fashionable new MuseumsQuartier shows the most exciting 20th-century and contemporary Austrian art.

The Rathaus and Around

City Hall
1 Friedrich-Schmidt-Platz 1, www.wien.gv.at/english/ cityhall/tours.htm; free guided tours (in German only) 1pm Mon, Wed, Fri except when in session and hols

The spiky, neo-Gothic **City Hall** (Rathaus) was built between 1872 and 1883 to replace the rambling old Rathaus on Schwedenplatz. It symbolizes the wealth and influence of the burghers, and its position opposite the Hofburg was no accident: the Imperial court was left in no doubt as to who really held the reins of power. The design deliberately echoes the Hôtel de Ville in Brussels, another city built on the wealth of its burghers, and the architect, Friedrich Schmidt, drew heavily on the Flemish Gothic style. The courtyards are open to the public, but the lavish interior can only be visited by guided tour. Right at the top of the clocktower in the main façade, a statue of a knight in armour brandishing a lance known as the 'Rathausman' gazes out across the city. Outdoor film performances take place in summer, and the square is flooded and frozen in winter to create a popular ice rink.

Parliament building

Dr Karl-Renner-Ring 3, t (01) 401 100, www. parlament.gv.at; guided tours (in German and English) except when in session and hols, mid-July–mid-Sept Mon–Fri 10, 12, 1, 2, 3, 4, Sat 10, 11, 12, 1; mid-Sept–mid-July Mon–Thurs 11, 2, 3, 4; Fri 11, 1, 2, 3, 4; Sat 11, 12, 1, 2, 3, 4; free

It might come as a bit of a shock to see a Greek temple on the Ringstrasse, but the **Parliament building** does a very good imitation. The Danish-born architect, Theophil von Hansen, studied in Athens and was deeply influenced by classical Greek architecture. A pediment frieze above the columned portico depicts Franz Josef I begrudgingly granting the 17 peoples of the nation a limited constitution, and graceful caryatids, modelled on those of the Erechtheion on the Acropolis, support the porticoes along the flanks of the building. The whole complex is liberally strewn with marble sculptures, busts and chariots, and an enormous statue of Pallas Athene, Goddess of Wisdom, rises seductively above the fountain which dominates the main square. The Parlament was bombed during the Second World War and took almost a decade to rebuild. Restoration work, begun in 1990, is still continuing (much of the main square is a building site), but you can visit the interior on one of the free guided tours.

National Theatre

1 D. Karl-Lueger-Ring 2, t (01) 514 44 4140, www. burgtheater.at; guided tours in German, other languages on prior request, Mon–Sat 3pm, Sun and hols 11am; July and Aug daily at 2pm and 3pm

Across the Ringstrasse from the venerable political institutions is the city's most prestigious theatre, the **National Theatre** (Burgtheater). It's housed in another of the grand Ringstrasse buildings, erected in 1888, only for it to be discovered that there was no view of the stage from much of the auditorium and that the acoustics were appalling. The problems were fixed, but the theatre suffered serious bomb damage during the Second World War, although extensive restoration has returned it to its former opulence. The original Burgtheater was created by Maria Theresia in 1741, but it was Josef II who raised it to the status of a national theatre in 1776. It may be one of the most celebrated theatres in Europe, but it has refused to rest on its laurels, and continues to stage some of the most exciting and innovative performances in the German-speaking world.

Volksgarten

entrances on Heldenplatz and Dr Karl-Renner-Ring; open winter daily 6am–8pm, summer daily 6am–10pm

Next to the Burgtheater, the **Volksgarten**, once the preferred strolling ground of Vienna's aristocrats, is now a welcome stretch of green on the hectic Ringstrasse. Manicured gardens unfold elegantly, and the statue of the Empress Sisi remains a pilgrimage site for her legions of fans.

Museum of Fine Arts (Kunsthistorisches Museum)

⭐ **Museum of Fine Arts**

1 Maria-Theresien-Platz, t 525 24 0, www.khm.at; **Hauptgebäude** *(Main Building) open Tues, Wed and Fri–Sun 10–6, Thurs 10–9; closed Mon exc June–Aug;* **Kunstkammer** *(Chamber of Art) closed for restoration until end 2012/early 2013.*

The vast, grandiose Kunsthistorisches Museum, across the Ringstrasse from the Hofburg, contains one of the finest and largest art collections in Europe, the legacy of several Habsburg rulers and spanning every corner of their once-vast empire. Built in overblown neo-Renaissance style at the end of the 19th century, the museum bristles with marble columns, statuary and gilded murals (some by Gustav Klimt), and the spectacular central staircase is dominated by Antonio Canova's enormous, powerful sculpture of Theseus defeating the Centaur, commissioned by Napoleon. The overwhelming setting and the sheer size of the collection may leave you breathless before you've even begun: this is definitely a museum to see in bite-sized chunks. When museum fever sets in, you can retire to the elegant (if overpriced) restaurant and café under the lofty cupola.

The collection is divided into several parts, which share the same ticket: the **Ground Floor** contains the **Collection of Greek and Roman Antiquities**, the **Egyptian and Near Eastern Collection**, and the **Chamber of Arts and Curiosities** (Kunstkammer, closed for restoration at the time of writing). The **First Floor** houses the **Picture Gallery** (Gemäldegalerie), which is what everyone mainly comes to see: to the right (the West Wing) is the collection of Italian, Spanish and French paintings, and to the left (the East Wing) is the German, Dutch and Flemish collection. The galleries are rather confusing: a connecting series of inner galleries in both wings are numbered with Roman numerals, while a second, outer ring of smaller rooms are given standard numbers. A floor plan (available at the information desk at the entrance) is essential.

The **Second Floor** is devoted to the **Coin Cabinet** and the **Vermayen cartoons** for a series of tapestries, which depict Charles V's campaign in Tunis in 1535.

Gemäldegalerie East Wing: German, Dutch and Flemish Collection

Dominating **Room IX** is full of luscious Classical deities, courtesy of the Flemish painter Bartolomeus Sprange (1546–1611) who was court painter to Maximilian II and Rudolf II. **Room X** is easily the most popular gallery in the entire museum, with a spectacular and virtually unrivalled collection of the works of Pieter Brueghel the Elder, including a sublime series of paintings depicting the seasons which mark the apotheosis of 16th-century landscape composition. There are three of the original six paintings here: *The Gloomy Day*, *The Return of the Herd*, and the celebrated *Hunters in the Snow*, in which you can almost hear the crunch of the tired hunters' boots. Also here are the *Peasant Wedding* and *Peasant Dance*, full of colour, vigour and movement, yet strangely joyless –

Brueghel gained his nickname 'The Peasant Painter' with the first of these, but he never sentimentalized the subjects of his paintings, nor forgot the hardship of their daily lives. Off Room IX, in **Room 14**, look for Roger Van der Weyden's exquisite triptych of *The Crucifixion* (c.1440), and in **Room 15** you'll find a panel from a small altarpiece by Bosch, depicting Christ carrying the Cross through a jeering, prodding crowd, and a charming depiction of a small child with a toy. **Rooms XI and XII** have monumental Baroque canvases by Jordaens and Snyders, and **Rooms XIII and XIV** are devoted to Van Dyck and Rubens. The museum has a huge collection of the latter's works, mainly panels from altarpieces, including a masterful series from the Ildefonso Altar painted towards the end of his life. There's also an intimate portrait (*The Little Fur*) of his second wife, Hélène Fourment, whom he married at the age of 53 when she was only 16. It echoes Titian's *Mädchen im Pelz* (*see* below), which Rubens admired greatly. The gallery adjoining Room XIII, **Room 20**, has Rubens' sketches for larger paintings, including a frightening *Head of Medusa* in murky blues and greens.

Room XV contains a fine collection of German paintings from the Danube School, including Dürer's tender and startlingly intimate *Virgin and Child with a Pear*, and a vivid *Adoration of the Trinity* from the Landauer Altar. There's a gory *Crucifixion* by Lucas Cranach the Elder, with a battered Christ coughing up blood, and several versions of *Judith with the Head of Holofernes*, a theme he clearly found deeply seductive. Also here is Bernhard Striegel's idealized portrait of the family of Maximilian I, which, although commissioned for the emperor's private use, is clearly intended to emphasize the far-reaching dynastic alliances of the Habsburg family: his much-loved wife and son appear (although they were both dead when it was painted), along with his young grandson whom he had never even seen.

Room 18 contains portraits by Hans Holbein, court painter to Henry VIII, including a demure portrait of Lady Jane Seymour, and an unforgivingly realistic portrait of the king's personal physican, Dr John Chambers, clearly worn out by the demands of his capricious sovereign. The most curious paintings in **Room 19** are the surreal works of Arcimboldo, who served three emperors but was a particular favourite at the court of Rudolf II. (Rudolf enjoyed Arcimboldo's quirky portraits formed of inanimate objects so much that he commissioned a whole series, one of every member of his court including the cook.) Here, Arcimboldo's evocations of the seasons and the elements (two of each survive, *Summer* and *Winter*, and *Fire* and *Water*) are formed of all manner of strange objects, from starfish to rifles. **Room 22** contains a charming, domestic scene by Pieter de Hooch of a woman suckling her baby by an open fire, and Vermeer's magnificent *The Artist's Studio*, one of his most important works.

Gemäldegalerie West Wing: Italian, Spanish and French Collection

This collection begins with a bang with a whole room full of the works of Titian, court painter to Karl V, including a blazing, dramatic *Ecce Homo* and a seductive portrait of a woman semi-clad in fur (*Mädchen im Pelz*). There are more Italian Mannerists in **Rooms II and III**, with a vivid *Judith with the Head of Holofernes* by Veronese, and Tintoretto's exquisite, light-drenched *Susannah Bathing*. **Room 4** contains Raphael's serene *Madonna im Grünen*, and Pietro Perugino's moving painting of the Virgin surrounded by children, which has just emerged from restoration and glows. There's a sensuous *Jupiter and Io* by Correggio in **Room 3**, in which the nymph abandons herself voluptuously to Jupiter in the form of a grey cloud. **Room V** contains Caravaggio's masterpiece *Madonna of the Rosary Feast*, sharp, shadowy and unsettling, and in **Room VII** you can see huge views of Vienna and the Imperial palaces by Bernardo Belloto, commissioned by Maria Theresia. Belloto was trained by his uncle, Canaletto, whose influence is clearly apparent. Look out for the fabulous Habsburg portraits by Velázquez in **Room 10**, including one of Philip IV with the characteristic Habsburg overbite, and another of Charles III, who was spectacularly ugly.

Chamber of Art and Curiosities (Kunstkammer)

The collection is quirkier than its name suggests, and includes all kinds of curiosities acquired by Rudolf II and Archduke Ferdinand, for their *Kunstkammern*, or Chambers of Art and Marvels. Among the sculptures are several handsome bronzes by Giambologna, busts of the Imperial family, including a pensive *Charles V* by Leone Leoni (1555), and Gregor Erhart's oddly unsettling *Allegory of Vanity*, in which a beautiful youthful couple are contrasted with a hideous old crone. The shimmering colours of the paintwork have been attributed to Hans Holbein the Elder. Among the oddities are a 16th-century musical clock in the shape of a galleon in full sail, and a clockwork globe designed to demonstrate the cosmos. George Roll presented two such globes to Rudolf II and his brother, Archduke Ernst, but when the Emperor's globe broke he had Roll thrown in prison for he 'had presented him with foul fish'. There are playing cards and games boards, a table decoration made with 'Adders' Tongues' (actually sharks' teeth) which were believed to neutralize poisons, and a tankard made from Unicorn Horn (really a whale tusk) which is studded with precious jewels. Among the beautiful tapestries is a handsome 18th-century hanging from the Gobelins factory in Paris, which recreates Raphael's frescoes for the Vatican. Perhaps the best known exhibit is the sumptuous Cellini salt cellar, richly gilded and enamelled, which was stolen in 2003 and only recovered three years later.

Collection of Greek and Roman Antiquities

These galleries are stuffed full of ancient treasures, from Etruscan art and vases to ancient Greek and Cypriot sculpture. The main gallery resembles a Roman villa, complete with a vast mosaic of Theseus and the Minotaur, and several busts. Also here is an extraordinary horde of 9th-century gold plate and vessels, discovered in 1799 in Romania.

Egyptian and Near Eastern Collection

The entrance to these galleries, in the West Wing on the ground floor, is guarded by two solemn statues of the Egyptian goddess Sekhmet, a sphinx-like creature with a leonine face.

Room 1 contains ancient sarcophagi, a single mummy tightly wrapped in papyrus leaves, mummy cases covered with symbols and hieroglyphs, mummified animals, and canopic jars which contained the entrails removed during the mummification process. **Room 2** contains the reconstructed tomb chapel of Ka-ni-nisut, which dates back five millennia, and **Room 4** is filled with mummies and enormous sarcophagi. **Room 5** has scores of Egyptian *Books of the Dead*, the papyrus scrolls containing instructions for life in the hereafter which were placed in ancient tombs, along with more elaborately decorated sarcophagi and mummies. There is a whole menagerie of fantastical gods, found in tombs, along with votive figures and amulets, and a beautiful, lapus-lazuli-blue ceramic hippopotamus. These were often found in Middle Kingdom tombs and denoted a favourite of the king, who granted hippopotamus-hunting rights to his most beloved courtiers.

Coin Cabinet

One of the largest and most comprehensive coin collections in the world, on the second floor, this contains early coins from Ancient Greece and Rome, Egyptian, Celtic and Byzantine currency, and a vast array of medieval and Renaissance coins. **Rooms 2 and 3** are dedicated to 19th- and 20th-century medals, including one cast to commemorate the birth of Napoleon's son.

Natural History Museum

*1 Maria-Theresien-Platz, **t** (01) 521 77, www.nhm-wien.ac.at; open Thurs–Mon 10–6, Wed 10–9; adm; **roof tours** Wed and Sat at 5 and 6.30, Sun at 2 and 4 (tour in English on Sun at 3pm); adm*

Natural History Museum (Naturhistorisches Museum)

Erected at the same time as the Kunsthistorisches Museum across the square, Vienna's Natural History Museum is equally sumptuous, and was conceived as a scientific complement to the artistic treasures held in the Museum of Fine Arts. In the mid-18th century, Emperor Franz Stephen I acquired what was then the world's largest and most celebrated natural history collection from a Florentine scholar, and these objects form the nucleus of the current holdings. Little has changed since the museum opened in 1889, and the elegant wooden cabinets are crammed with every imaginable stuffed creature from around the world, many displayed in delightfully old-fashioned dioramas.

The dinosaur skeletons in **Rooms IV and V** on the upper ground floor are the big draw, and include a spectacular 17-million-year-old tusked mammoth-like creature excavated in the Czech Republic, and the well-preserved skeleton of the Austrian rhino. On the first floor, you enter **Room XXXIV** through the enormous lower jawbone of a whale, and the gallery itself is almost filled by a huge, floating whale skeleton. There's also a model of the sea cow, a gentle, cumbersome creature which was discovered in the Pacific by shipwrecked sailors in 1741, who passed on the news to hide-hunters. By 1768, the harmless sea cow was extinct. The skeleton of the most famous extinct species, the dodo, can also be found here (in **Room XXXI**), one of the most complete in the world. In the last room on this floor, you can see Honzo, the beer-swilling, cigarette-smoking, fight-picking chimpanzee who lived in the Vienna zoo in the 1950s. The ground floor contains the enormous mineral collection, and **Room IV** boasts opulent Jugendstil decoration with wispy nymphs erupting from the walls. It's a suitably gorgeous setting for the **Gem Collection**, of which the highlight is the 'Bouquet of Gems', which Maria Theresia apparently gave to her husband Franz Stephan over breakfast, and which contains a staggering 3,000 precious stones, mainly diamonds. For giddy views over the city, take the **roof tour** (note that tours in English are held on Sundays at 3pm).

Staatsoper to Karlsplatz

① Opera House
1 Opernring 2, **t** (01) 514 44 2606, www.wiener-staatsoper.at; guided visits available; adm; but check times posted under the arcades on the Kärntnerstrasse side of the Opera House; for booking information, see 'Entertainment', p.103

Vienna's extravagant **Opera House** (Staatsoper) was the first of the grand buildings along the Ringstrasse to be completed, and opened with a performance of Mozart's *Don Giovanni* in 1869. Built in a heavy-handed neo-Renaissance style, complete with loggias to shelter carriages, the splendid main entrance is topped with bronze statues depicting Heroism, Drama, Fantasy, Humour and Love. The interior is even more opulent, and the glittering marble, gilt and profusion of allegorical frescoes provide a spectacular backdrop for the annual Vienna Opera Ball, one of the most exclusive balls on the Viennese social calendar. The main auditorium suffered extensive damage during the Second World War but has been restored with all the latest technological equipment, losing much of its original flamboyance in the process. Still, there are enough grand staircases and opulent salons to flounce around for a visit to the Opera to remain a heady and romantic experience. And if you can't get tickets, all is not lost: on warm summer nights, performances are broadcast live on to a huge screen on the adjacent square.

Kärntnerstrasse leads to **Karlsplatz**, once an elegant park on the fringe of the Ringstrasse, but which has been mercilessly chopped up and hemmed in by busy roads which often require steely nerves to cross. Once a definite no-go area at night, it's being remodelled, with new gardens and the ultra-trendy **Kunsthalle Wien Project Space**, a glassy outpost of the Kunsthalle in the MuseumsQuartier (see p.77). It shows excellent temporary exhibitions, but the main draw is the fabulous terrace café (see p.104). Almost lost in the whirl of traffic, a pair of frothy **Secessionist pavilions** were erected by Otto Wagner in 1898–9 for Karlsplatz underground station, although they have long lost their original function. Wagner used a metal frame with marble slabs to create the pavilions, which are delicately decorated with gold detailing and wrought-iron flourishes. They were almost demolished in the 1960s, but were reconstructed here after students protested, and one has become a café, while the other contains a small exhibition describing their construction.

Secessionist pavilions
1, Karlsplatz
t (01) 505 87 47-85177,
www.wienmuseum.at;
open April–Oct
Tues–Sun 10–6

Künstlerhaus
1 Karlsplatz 5, t (01)
587 9663, www.k-
haus.at; open
Tues–Wed and Fri 10–6,
Thurs 10–9; adm

Across the busy main road, the **Künstlerhaus**, a florid late 19th-century building, is home to Vienna's Society of Artists, against whom the Secessionists rebelled in 1897. It has shed its stuffy reputation, and hosts dynamic, resolutely modern temporary art exhibitions as well as showing the work of its members. Next door is the equally opulent **Musikverein**, doyenne of Vienna's classical music scene.

Karlskirche
4 Karlsplatz,
www.karlskirche.at;
open Mon–Sat 9–12.30
and 1–6, Sun 1–6; last
lift up to the dome
5.30; adm

The lofty **Karlskirche** dominates the southern (and more salubrious) end of Karlsplatz. One of the most extravagant expressions of European Baroque, it was commissioned by Emperor Karl VI in thanks for Vienna's delivery from the plague in 1713. Johann Bernhard Fischer von Erlach began work on the church in 1714, and it was completed by his son around 1739. The church was dedicated to St Charles Borromeo, the 16th-century Archbishop of Milan who worked tirelessly for plague victims in his city. His statue floats above the main entrance, which is carved with grim scenes of Viennese suffering during the plague. Two slender towers, reminiscent of minarets, flank the main portal, each topped with an elegant dome. The towers were inspired by Trajan's Column in Rome, and are decorated with a spiralling series of reliefs describing the life of St Charles Borromeo. But it was no accident that the saint shared a name with the emperor, and the heavy symbolism on the towers and throughout the church can also be read as a glorification of the Habsburg dynasty. The interior is surprisingly airy, and a lift up to the ethereal dome allows close-up views of Johann Michael Rottmayer's vast fresco depicting *The Apotheosis of St Charles*. The church is beautifully reflected in a shallow ornamental pond, with a strange sculpture by Henry Moore which looks like an eyeball. The pool is a favourite with Viennese dogs, who come to chase sticks and cool off in summer.

Vienna History Museum

4 Karlsplatz, t (01) 505 87 47-0, www.wien museum.at; open Tues–Sun 9–6; adm

A blank modern building across the square from the Karlskirche contains the **Vienna History Museum** (Wien Museum), which documents the city's history from prehistoric times until the 20th century. A series of models, one on each floor (each corresponds to a particular period), show the development of the city over the centuries. On the ground floor, fragments of Roman pots, statuary and tools rub shoulders with medieval religious sculpture and the remains of the original stained-glass windows of Stephansdom, which depict the stoning of St Stephen. There are some curious funerary helmets, decorated with enormous figures – dragons, angels, lions – which would have signified the religion and status of the deceased and been buried with them. On the first floor, which covers the 16th–18th centuries, Vienna's transformation from a city at war to an affluent and peaceful capital is charted with the aid of maps, paintings, armour, gilded house signs and fancy wigs. The top floor is the most rewarding, and contains a reconstructed interior designed by Adolf Loos, an exquisite chair inlaid with mother-of-pearl designed by Otto Wagner, and fascinating photographs of the major buildings erected at the turn of the 20th century. But the real highlight is the collection of early 20th-century art, including several pieces by Klimt (paintings of the interior of the Opera House which were carried out before he abandoned the solemn Historicism of his contemporaries, as well as later works) and some bleak portraits by Egon Schiele.

Secession Building

1 Friedrichstrasse 12, t (01) 587 5307, www. secession.at; open Tues, Wed and Fri–Sun 10–6, Thurs 10–8; adm

At the other end of Karlsplatz, stranded between major roads, you can't miss the glistening golden dome of the beautiful **Secession Building**. In 1897, a group of young artists, including Gustav Klimt, Josef Hoffmann, Josef Maria Olbrich and Kolo Moser, withdrew from the conservative Society of Artists at the Künstlerhaus and formed the Association of Visual Artists Secession (*see* p.47). They built this elegant, sparkling white building (completed in 1898) as a physical embodiment of the new movement's fundamental tenets, which were encapsulated in its very structure. Rejecting the weighty historicism of their predecessors, they emblazoned their motto over the main entrance: *Der Zeit ihre Kunst, der Kunst ihre Freiheit* ('To the Age its Art, to Art its Freedom'). The Secessionists viewed art as mystical, even sacred, and Olbrich's original designs describe it as a 'Temple of Art'. References to sacred temples abound, from the inscription *Ver Sacrum* ('Holy Spring') on the façade to the stylized laurel trees which flank the doorway, which are themselves echoed in the glittering golden cupola of interlocking laurel leaves. Above the main entrance, the snakes of the *aegis* of Pallas Athene are entwined around masks representing the three arts (painting, architecture and sculpture). The spaces are deliberately divided into the ornamental entrance area and the purely functional galleries – sleek, white, unadorned. The building was unlike anything ever seen in Vienna and critics lambasted it as 'a cross between a greenhouse and a blast furnace', 'a temple for bullfrogs' and even 'a bastard begot of temple and warehouse'. The original building was completely destroyed in 1945, when the retreating German army torched it, but it was finally renovated in 1980 and remains one of the most exquisite buildings in the city. Unfortunately, it's now stranded between busy main roads, which make it impossible to see as a whole without taking your life in your hands and standing in the middle of swirling traffic.

Contemporary exhibitions are held in the main galleries, and the association runs interesting tours and lecture programmes. Bizarrely, the only permanent exhibit was intended to be temporary: Klimt's unearthly *Beethoven Frieze*, painted for the 9th exhibition of the Viennese Secessionists in 1902. It was supposed to be destroyed after the exhibition, but luckily it was bought by a collector, and finally acquired by the Austrian government, who placed it here in a specially built gallery. The 34m-long frieze takes Richard Wagner's interpretation of Beethoven's *Ninth Symphony* as its inspiration, from the 'Yearning for Happiness' to its eventual fulfilment through the arts. Dreamy nymphs sway across the early panels, meeting terrifying monsters and wild-eyed gorgons along the way, finally discovering poetry, music and the arts and culminating in an erotic embrace amid a choir of angels on the final panel.

MuseumsQuartier

MuseumsQuartier
U-Bahn to MuseumsQuartier;
information office
open daily 10–7,
www.mqw.at

Leopold Museum
t 525 70, www. leopoldmuseum.org; open Wed, Thurs and Sat–Mon 10–7, Fri 10–9; closed Tues; guided tours in German on Sat and Sun at 3; adm

The former Imperial riding stables, designed by the indefatigable Johann Fischer von Erlach at the end of the 18th century, were in 2001 dramatically and expensively converted into the Museums-Quartier, one of the world's largest cultural complexes. Bold contemporary buildings have been slotted into the spacious central courtyard, now called the **Museumplatz**, which is full of terrace cafés where Vienna's young and fashionable come to lounge on summer weekends. There's an **information office-cum-shop** at the main entrance, which is a good first port-of-call to find out what's on when – the complex hosts several one-off events to complement the offerings of its array of cultural institutions.

The pale, gleaming cube inserted into the main square of the MuseumsQuartier houses the **Leopold Museum**, with a superb collection of the works of Austrian expressionist Egon Schiele.

The collection was amassed by Rudolf Leopold in the 1950s, and now comprises more than 5,000 works. The second floor is dedicated to Schiele, but there is plenty of art by other late 19th-century and 20th-century Expressionist and Modernist artists, including pieces by Klimt, Gerstl and Kokoschka.

Jutting out at an awkward angle on the other side of Museumsplatz is the unrelentingly contemporary **Museum of Modern Art** (Museum Moderner Kunst) known as **MUMOK**, a sleek, if forbidding, slate-grey block. It's a slightly oppressive space, with lots of steel and smoky glass but almost no natural light, but it does have an excellent collection spanning most of the major 20th-century art movements. Many of the holdings can be seen as part of changing themed exhibitions (usually on the top three floors), but some highlights are on permanent view, and cover everything from Pop Art (of which there's an excellent selection) to Arte Povera. The basement is devoted to Viennese Actionism, a deliberately provocative performance art movement whose proponents (Günter Bros, Otto Muehl and Hermann Nitsch among others) outdid each other with a succession of shocking public displays – blood, offal and faeces feature heavily. They were active during the 1960s, and sought to change the world and challenge 'bourgeois' conceptions of art through their shocking performances. The **café**, with a summer courtyard, provides a welcome respite from the blood and gore.

The former Winter Riding School of the Imperial stables has been converted into a vast, contemporary exhibition space and performance hall, the **Kunsthalle Wien**. It has an excellent, audience-grabbing programme of temporary exhibitions, which draw on Austrian and international artists, and remains deservedly one of the most popular art institutions in the city.

The **Architecture Centre** (Architekturzentrum Wien) is an archive and exhibition space, with an excellent permanent display detailing the major developments in architecture around the world, neatly complemented by thematic changing exhibitions. They also run architecture-themed walking tours around the city, usually held on Sundays.

The **Zoom Children's Museum** (ZOOM Kindermuseum) is a must for kids, who will be having too much fun to mind the language barrier. Vienna's dedicated children's museum runs hugely popular workshops for kids of all ages. There's an ocean-themed space for babies and toddlers, while older children can mess about with video cameras and sound recordings in the ZoomLab. Note that you have to pre-book sessions in advance, particularly for weekend visits.

MUMOK
t 525 00, www. mumok.at; open Tues, Wed and Fri–Sun 10–6, Thurs 10–9; closed Mon; adm

Kunsthalle Wien
t 521 89 33, www. kunsthallewien.at; open Fri–Wed 10–7, Thurs 10–10; adm

Architecture Centre
t 521 89 33, www.azw.at; open Thurs–Tues 10–7, Wed 10–9; adm

Zoom Children's Museum
t 4000 84500, www. kindermuseum.at; open Mon–Fri 8.30–5, Sat–Sun 10–5.30; adm

Belvedere Palace and Botanic Gardens

The glorious Baroque Belvedere Palace was built by Johann Lukas von Hildebrandt, arch-rival of Fischer von Erlach, for Prince Eugene of Savoy, the most celebrated military general of his day. Once the Turks were subdued and the War of Succession finally came to an end, Vienna was struck with building fever and began to expand beyond the old city walls. The elegant Lower Belvedere, a summer palace, was built first in 1714–16, and surrounded with expansive landscaped gardens. However, the prince required something even grander and more prestigious and commissioned the magnificent Upper Belvedere in 1721 – which functioned essentially as an extravagant party pavilion for Prince Eugene's spectacular firework shows and other festivities. The palaces are linked by graceful formal **gardens**, designed in the French style by Dominique Girard, and liberally strewn with fountains and statuary. Some years after the prince's death, the palaces were eventually sold to Maria Theresia in 1752, when they became known as the Belvedere. Emperor Josef II moved the Imperial Art Gallery here, and opened the grounds to the public as a pleasure garden. The art collection was rehoused when the Kunsthistorisches Museum was built, and the palace became the residence of Archduke Franz Ferdinand.

Palace gardens
open daily 6am–dusk

Both palaces were severely damaged during the Second World War, but were immaculately restored and now contain the **Austrian Gallery collection**: most of the artworks, including a stunning collection of works by Klimt, Schiele and Kokoschka, are displayed in the Upper Belvedere, while the Lower Belvedere hosts temporary exhibitions in its sumptuouous Baroque salons. There's a small gallery of medieval painting and sculpture in the former stables.

Lower Belvedere
3 Rennweg 6,
t (01) 795 570;
open Tues–Thurs 10–6;
Wed 10–9; adm

One wing of Prince Eugene's first palace, the **Lower Belvedere** (Unteres Belvedere), now hosts temporary exhibitions, which are usually excellent. The other wing, to the right of the entrance, contains some of the most opulent marble-and-gilt salons. The **Hall of Grotesques** (now the shop) is thickly covered with mythical beasts, dragons and Sphinxes among others, and allegories of the four seasons and four elements stretch across the ceiling. Another marble gallery follows, specially commissioned to house the prince's collection of classical statuary acquired from Herculaneum, and off it is the glittering **Cabinet of Gold**, in which every surface gleams with gold and mirrors. The centrepiece of the Lower Belvedere (in the middle of the temporary exhibition galleries) is the lavish **Marble Hall**, a double-decker extravaganza of red marble walls, white marble angels and *trompe l'œil* frescoes, with depictions of triumphs from the Prince's legendary military career. These culminate in a vast ceiling fresco in which the prince is transformed into Apollo. At the centre of the chamber is Georg

Raphael Donner's lead sculpture from the fountain in the Neuer Markt, in which four river deities are grouped around 'Providentia', in a flattering allegory praising the city of Vienna's good government.

A covered passage leads to the **Orangerie,** now used for temporary exhibitions, which has beautiful views over the gardens. Nearby, in the former **stables** (Prunkstall), you'll find the **Medieval Treasury.** The scalloped troughs, vaulted ceilings and pretty stucco horses' heads have been retained, providing a charming setting for a collection of 12th- to 15th-century paintings and sculpture. These include stylized crucifixes, golden altarpieces and ranks of statues of the Madonna and Child. Among the best pieces are an atmospheric *Crucifixion* (1450) by the Master of Leufen, a *Madonna* by the Master of Heiligenblut, and several excellent altarpieces including a fine triptych commissioned by Albrecht V. There are some brutal scenes from the Passion from the Salzburg painter Rueland Frueaf the Elder, and several pieces from the accomplished Michael Pacher, who was clearly influenced by Flemish and northern Italian art and strove to achieve perspective.

In the **Upper Belvedere** (Oberes Belvedere), a vast stone staircase guarded by a fleet of chubby cherubs affords stunning views of the ornamental lake and gardens, and leads to the palace's most extravagant chamber, the Marble Hall. The red marble panels and Baroque frescoes by Carlo Carlone have been beautifully restored and the chamber enjoys breathtaking views over Vienna, dominated by the spire of Stephansdom. To see the collection chronologically, start with the Baroque and medieval masterpieces on the ground floor. There are 13th- and 14th-century Viennese sculptures, including a charming one of St Elisabeth, in the former summer drawing room, which preserves its delicate frescoes. A dainty pavilion contains a pair of exquisite paintings (*Flight to Egypt* and *Mary as a Temple Virgin*) by the Master of Mondsee. The Baroque galleries contain domestic and courtly scenes by Franz Christoph Janneck from the first half of the 18th century, followed by monumental landscape and genre scenes, and an array of ecstatic late Baroque religious paintings. One gallery is filled with a host of extraordinary busts, caught grimacing, leering, sobbing, laughing, which were character studies by Franz Xaver Messerschmidt. Head up to the second floor for the early 19th-century and Biedermeier collection, with handsome portraits including Gérard's depiction of the Viennese banker Moritz Christian Fries, and massive, idealized landscapes. The Biedermeier period is represented with cosy family scenes of wealthy burghers, plenty of still lifes, and sentimental peasant scenes, which were very popular during the period.

Medieval Treasury (Stables)
open 10–12; same adm as for permanent collection

Upper Belvedere
3 Prinz-Eugen-Strasse 27, t (01) 795 570, www. belvedere.at; open Tues–Sun 10–6; closed Mon; adm; combined ticket to all the Belvedere collections available; guided tours or audioguide, short talks in English Fri–Sun 11.30am

The most famous paintings in the Belvedere are the first floor, where the late 19th-century collection includes several fine views of Vienna, such as Carl Kuger's smoky *Arrival of a Train at Westbahnhof*, and a throng of sentimentalized portraits. There is a wonderful self-portrait by Gustave Courbet, *The Wounded Man*, who had just been separated from his lover, and several scenes depicting the newly built Ringstrasse. The collection picks up steam with some Impressionist gems, including Renoir's dewy *Bather with Loose Blonde Hair* and *After the Bath*, and Van Gogh's clear, luminous *Plain at Auvers*, painted only weeks before his death. Carl Moll's *Dusk* is hauntingly lovely, and hangs close to two works by Munch: *Men in the Sea*, bright, joyful and confident, and a wonderful *Seascape* which features the Nordic midnight sun. An entire gallery is dedicated to works by Klimt, including an early portrait of a sour-faced miss in a pink, frilly dress. Also here is the real star of the Belvedere: Klimt's famous *Kiss*. This was virtually the last of his golden paintings, which had been inspired by Italian mosaics, and his later work is bolder, more colourful and entirely free of elaborate gilding. Just off the next gallery, take a peek into the extravagantly Baroque double-storey chapel, built so that the prince could attend mass from the gallery. The following galleries are devoted to the Viennese Expressionists, and include a whole several works by Egon Schiele, including the characteristically grim *Death and Girl*, and a sublime, pearly autumnal scene, with bare trees silhouetted against a rosy sky. Oscar Kokoschka's deliberately provocative paintings include the gory *Still Life with Dead Mutton*, a gleaming sheep's head paired with a blood-red tomato.

Work off museum fatigue in the **gardens**, where you can stroll under the gaze of inscrutable Sphinxes, and admire the fountains.

Botanical Gardens
*main entrance
Rennweg 14, t (01) 4277
54100; open daily
9am–dusk*

The palace gardens link with Vienna's extensive **Botanical Gardens** created by Maria Theresia in 1754 for the cultivation of medicinal plants. They were expanded and given their current form in the 19th century, and are now part of Vienna University's Botanical Institute. The tranquil, extensive gardens and shady paths are a welcome relief from the hubbub of the city, and perfect for a picnic lunch.

MAK

MAK
*1 Stubenring 5, t (01) 711
36248, www.mak.at;
open Wed–Sun 10–6;
Tues 10–12; closed Mon;
guided tour in English
Sun 12pm, special events
Tues nights; adm, free Sat*

The **Austrian Museum of Applied Arts and Contemporary Art**, better known simply as MAK, may be housed in a monumental, 19th-century Ringstrasse building, but its displays are anything but stuffy: in 1993, the curators invited celebrated artists to redesign the exhibition halls and the results (while sometimes annoyingly pretentious) have been a huge success. Add to that a fantastic shop full of stylish goodies and an excellent café, and it's easy to see why MAK has become the fashionistas' museum of choice.

The exhibits are laid out chronologically, beginning with the **Romanesque, Gothic and Renaissance galleries**, which contain sumptuously embroidered liturgical vestments, covered with fabulous creatures, which are among the finest pieces in the museum's textile collection. There are Spanish and Italian inlaid cabinets and chests from the 15th and 16th centuries. The **Baroque gallery** is suitably monumental, and contains the painstakingly recreated early 18th-century **Dubsky Porcelain Room**, which came from the Dubsky Palace in the Czech Republic and gets its name from the heavy use of ceramics on every surface – including the chandeliers. The delicate Far Eastern porcelain which had recently been introduced was much in fashion, and the Oriental theme is echoed in the huge tapestries. This is a good introduction to the **Orient** gallery, which contains one of the finest collection of Oriental carpets in the world. The **19th-century galleries** begin with monumental cabinets, intricate glassware, and lavish dinner services including one commissioned by Napoleon on the occasion of the birth of his son, the Duc de Reichstadt. In the following gallery, there's a selection of exquisite Oriental rugs and fabrics, including a unique 16th-century silk rug from Egypt, The most ingenious and enchanting presentation is in the **Historicism, Jugendstil, Art Deco room**, where the chair collection (arranged by Barbara Bloom) is beautifully back-lit and visible in silhouette through white screens, the forms emerging like shadow-puppets, enabling visitors to see the changing styles across the years.

Upstairs, a gallery is dedicated to the **Wiener Werkstätte** (Vienna Workshops), an arts and crafts co-operative founded in 1903 by architect Josef Hoffmann and designer Kolo Moser. They actively promoted design in all its forms, from the humble (ashtrays and postage stamps) to the classic (furniture and ceramics). There's an astonishing array of pieces here, from cigarette boxes to a gorgeous silver and ebony tea service studded with coral. The main highlight of the **Art Nouveau and Art Deco gallery** is a series of drawings by Klimt for a nine-panelled frieze, commissioned for the Palais Stoclet in Brussels, but look out for an elegant writing cabinet by Mackintosh, and a luminous collection of vivid Bohemian glass. Photographs and models of major modern and contemporary buildings introduce a gallery dedicated to **20th- and 21st-century architecture**, which includes Kiesler's curious *Endless House* (1959), a curvaceous concrete sphere on pillars, and Libeskind's design for the Jewish Museum in Berlin. From here, stairs lead up to a loft-like space with spiky examples of contemporary art. Don't miss the spectacular and über-fashionable café-restaurant (*see* p.98).

Stadtpark
open 24 hours

The perfect antidote to museum overload, the **Stadtpark** stretches leafily to the south of MAK. The main entrance is flanked

04 | Austria: Vienna | Around the Ringstrasse

by a pair of Jugendstil columns, and small pavilions and statues of musical greats from Schubert to Strauss are scattered across the lawns.

Outside the Centre

Strung out around the edge of the city centre are a host of sights, from the Baroque pomp and splendour of the Imperial lodge in Schönbrunn to the dreamy expanse of the Prater gardens. Linger in Freud's consulting room, or check out the gruesome anatomical models in the Josephinum; go boating on the Danube, or take in the city views on the Reisenbad, the ferris wheel immortalized in the film *The Third Man*.

Sigmund Freud Museum

Sigmund Freud Museum

*9 Berggasse 19, **t** (01) 319 1596, www.freud-museum.at; open May–Oct daily 9–6;, Nov–April daily 9–5; adm; audioguide; guided tours by appt, email fuehrungen@ freud-museum.at; tram D to Schlickgasse, tram 37, 38, 40, 41 to Schwarzspanierstrasse, or bus 40A to Berggasse*

Tucked away in this leafy, residential district, the Sigmund Freud Museum is discreetly signposted and hard to find (take the stairs up from the entrance hall). Freud lived, practised and studied here from 1891 until the Nazis forced him to emigrate in 1938, and in 1971 it was opened as a museum by his daughter Anna.

The waiting room is the only room which has been restored to look just as it did in Freud's time, and the rest of the apartment is now a modern exhibition space and study centre. One small room contains multilingual video screens showing black and white films of the Freud family, narrated by Anna, and there's a temporary exhibition gallery and a reference library.

The waiting room contains a cabinet of antiques and curiosities, and the walls are lined with diplomas, certificates and photographs, including one of the participants of the International Psychoanalytical Congress in Weimar in 1911. The consulting room contains copies of early photographs and documents, from the young Sigmund's school report (in which his 'moral conduct' is praised as 'exemplary') to the romantic letters exchanged between Freud and his fiancée, Martha Bernays. (In one he describes the effects of cocaine on German soldiers' endurance, and announces his intention to give it a go.) The former study contains excerpts from his books, more photographs including one of Jung, and a few personal trinkets such as his hat and cane. There are deeply disturbing photographs depicting the burning of Freud's books in Vienna in 1933, and another of Hitler addressing a vast throng of rapt Viennese in May 1931.

Josephinum

Josephinum

*9 Währinger Strasse 25, **t** (01) 4277 63401; open Mon–Fri 9–3 and first Sat of each month 10–2; adm; tram 37, 38, 40, 41 to Schwarzspanierstrasse*

In 1785, Josef II established the Josephinum as an institute for military surgery after seeing at first hand the crude techniques employed on the battlefield. The Institute was closed in the late

19th century, and now contains a small museum of medical history with cabinets full of alarming ancient instruments and gory diagrams. The main draw is a series of 18th-century anatomical models, commissioned by Josef II around 1780 and built in Florence. The eerily realistic wax figures expose the heart, brain, lungs and other internal organs, and are displayed in the original rosewood cabinets. In the centre of all this lies the strange **Mediceische Venus**, a Barbie-like creature, complete with pearl necklace and fluffy hair, smiling above her gaping chest cavity.

Liechtenstein Museum

The summer palace of the Princes of Liechtenstein is a charming Baroque confection surrounded by gardens. The Gartenpalais was commissioned by Prince Johann Adam Andreas von Liechtenstein (1657–1712), who was an avid art collector and a generous patron. The palace has been beautifully restored, and its stuccoed halls now hold a substantial part of Liechenstein's painting collection, as well as a superb array of bronzes, porcelain and furnishings. The permanent collection includes works by Rubens, van Dyck, Lucas Cranach, Raphael, Rembrandt, van Ruysdael and Hamilton, which are complemented by temporary exhibitions. Looking right at home amid the splendour is the 18th-century ebony and gilt Badminton Cabinet, purchased in 2004 for £19 million, making it the world's most expensive piece of furniture. One of the loveliest ways to spend a Sunday afternoon is to attend a concert in the magnificent Hercules Hall, with its fine frescoes and oil paintings, then follow it up with a stroll through the immaculate gardens, and perhaps coffee and cake in the garden restaurant.

Schönbrunn

Schönbrunn, an enormous, frilly Baroque palace on the southwestern outskirts of Vienna, was the summer residence of the Imperial family. The original hunting lodge was destroyed by the Turks in 1683, and a replacement was commissioned from Johann Fischer von Erlach in 1695. He planned a gigantic palace on a fabulous scale, one which would outshine Versailles, but finally the Imperial family were forced to make do with a mere 1,441 rooms in the final design by Nikolaus Pacassi. The palace was completed under Maria Theresia in the mid-18th century, and became the empress's favourite residence. It's possible to tour the extravagant interior, but be warned that Schönbrunn Palace is one of the biggest attractions in the whole of Austria, and the experience can be daunting: tour buses disgorge endless streams of visitors, and the tour of the apartments is a slow shuffle through the crowds. It's possible to escape the hordes in the beautiful gardens, which extend for miles and are scattered with

Leichtenstein Museum
Fürstengasse 1, t (01) 319 57 67 252, www.liechtenstein museum.at; open Fri–Tues 10–5; adm; Sunday concerts at 11 and 3; tram D or bus 40A to Bauernfeldplatz; gardens open 7.15am–8.30pm

✪ Schönbrunn
13 Schönbrunner Schloss Strasse 47, t (01) 811 13239, www. schoenbrunn.at; Imperial Tour (22 rooms in the palace, including the 19th-century apartments), Grand Tour (40 rooms, including the ornate 18th-century audience rooms), Sisi Pass (Grand Tour plus adm to the Imperial Apartments and the Sisi Museum in the Hofburg (see p.61) and the Imperial Furniture Collection's permanent exhibition of 'Sisi in the movies'), Schönbrunn Winter Pass (Grand Tour, Viena Zoo, Desert Experience, Palm House and Carriage Museum, Nov–Mar); transport: U-Bahn to Schönbrunn, tram 10, 58, bus 10a to Schloss Schönbrunn

other attractions including a puzzling maze and labyrinth, an exotic 19th-century palm house, the splendid Imperial carriage museum, and a zoo.

Imperial Apartments

Imperial Apartments
open Nov–Mar daily 8.30–4.30; April–June and Sept–Oct daily 8.30–5; July–Aug daily 8.30–6; tickets are marked with entrance time; adm exp

The tour of the palace begins in the West Wing with the humdrum **apartments** belonging to Franz Josef and Sisi. In the main audience chamber, a stuffy, walnut-panelled hall, the dutiful emperor would receive up to a hundred people in a morning, and the adjoining waiting room was kitted out with a billiard table for bored petitioners. Franz Josef's office is next, followed by his spartan bedroom which contains the simple iron bedstead on which he died in 1916. Sisi's dressing room had plenty of space for her endless array of beauty products, and connects with the marital bedroom – where the empress is said to have kept her new husband waiting for two days after her wedding day before finally succumbing. Passing through a lavish neo-rococo **reception room**, decked out in white and gold silk, there's a family **dining room**, with portraits of Maria Theresia's daughters, including the young Marie-Antoinette who was famously guillotined during the French Revolution. The **Mirror Room** was used for family concerts, including one given by the six-year-old Mozart and his sister, and legend has it that the child prodigy smothered the empress with kisses – no doubt a tale put about to enhance her reputation as 'Mother of the Empire'. The magnificent **Great Gallery** was used for balls, including during the Congress of Vienna in 1815 ('the congress danced but didn't advance'), and is a whirl of gilded stucco, crystal chandeliers (which held 70 candles each before the introduction of electricity) and enormous frescoes praising the Habsburg reign. Maria Theresia and her husband Franz Stephan are enthroned in the centre of the enormous ceiling fresco, and the hall was used for a celebrated meeting between Kennedy and Khrushchev in 1961. There is a pair of exquisite circular chambers off the **Small Gallery**, extravagantly decorated in the popular late Baroque Orientalist style with glossy lacquer panels and porcelain, and used by the Empress Maria Theresia for secret meetings with her advisers. The **Carousel Room**, in which the indomitable empress appears riding a Lipizzaner at the Winter Riding School in 1743, and the **Ceremonial Hall**, with a vast painting of Josef II's wedding to Isabella of Palma, follow, and mark the culmination of the Grand Tour.

If you've opted for the Imperial Tour, the best is yet to come: the following salons are the most opulent of the entire palace. The **Blue Chinese Salon**, covered in delicately hand-painted wallpaper inset with pretty panels, is where negotiations were held that finally led to Karl I's abdication in November 1918 – to the outrage of his wife, the Empress Zita, who said. 'A sovereign can never abdicate...never, never, never. I would rather fall here at your side.' Nearby is the **Napoleon Room**, which was originally Maria Theresia's bedroom but was taken over by the diminutive Frenchman after his marriage to the Princess Marie Louise. Maria Theresia's pale blue and green study is covered with graceful drawings and a medallion of her favourite daughter, Maria Christina, and leads into the splendid, if overwhelming, **Millions Room**, covered in fabulously expensive, rare rosewood panelling inset with Indo-Persian etchings. In the **bedroom**, the only surviving State Bed, built for the marriage of Maria Theresia and Franz Stephan, is barely discernible under the weight of its ornate decoration and richly embroidered hangings. The final rooms were used by Archduke Franz Karl, father of Franz Josef: more lavish than his son's plain quarters, they are still a disappointment after the eye-popping Baroque extravagance of Maria Theresia's apartments and are now filled with Habsburg family portraits.

Carriage Museum (Wagenburg) and Department of Court Uniforms

Carriage Museum and Department of Court Uniforms
t (01) 525 240, www.khm.at; open May–Oct daily 9–6; Nov–April 10–4; adm

The former stables now house the Imperial Coach Museum, where glittering Baroque carriages and sleighs, monumental funerary carriages and sleek early automobiles eloquently convey the dazzling opulence of the Habsburg court. Possibly the most lavish is the Grand Carosse, an Imperial carriage built around 1763 but used right up till 1916: oozing gilded flourishes, its windows are made of Venetian glass, and painted allegorical panels praise the sovereign's virtues. There's a sleek two-seater sleigh with a natty leopardskin interior, and a special hunting carriage made for Prince Leopold of Bourbon-Salerno, specially fitted with a revolving seat so that the plump prince could turn and take his shot. There are some wonderful children's carriages, every bit as opulent as the full-size versions, including an extravagant one built for Napoleon's son, the King of Rome, which was pulled by two specially trained merino sheep. A grim, black 19th-century funerary carriage was most recently used for the burial of the former Empress Zita in 1989. Just one of the Imperial court's fleet of automobiles, designed by Gräf and Stift, has survived, and still bears the Imperial Crown instead of a licence plate. Although the Department of Court Uniforms is off-limits to the public, it regularly hosts exhibitions of items from its collection.

Schlösspark

Schlösspark
open daily 10am–dusk
Gloriette
access above the café, open April–June and Sept daily 9–6; July and Aug 9–7; Oct 9–5; adm

Schönbrunn's gorgeous gardens stretch for miles, formally laid out in the French style in the 18th century, and scattered with statues and fountains. For fabulous views over the whole park, make for the **Gloriette**, a huge, florid victory arch surmounted

Maze and labyrinth
same opening times as Gloriette; adm

Vienna Zoo
t (01) 877 9294-0, www. zoovienna.at; open Nov–Jan daily 9–4.30; Feb daily 9–5; Mar and Oct daily 9–5.30; April daily 9–6; May–Sept daily 9–6.30; adm

Palm House
open daily May–Sept 9.30–5.30; Oct–April 9.30–4.30; adm

with the Imperial eagle, which was erected in 1775. Kids will enjoy the **maze** and **labyrinth**, near the exuberant Baroque Neptune fountain.

A huge swath of the park is taken up with the **Vienna Zoo** (Tiergarten), successor to Franz Stephan's Imperial Menagerie, which still contains some of the original Baroque cages. It's the oldest zoo in the world (the 240-year-old Kaiserglöckerl bell still sounds at closing time), and houses more than 750 species, including pandas, elephants and lions. Little Fu Hu, a baby panda born in late 2010, remains a huge attraction.

Near the entrance to the zoo, the 19th-century **Palm House** (Palmenhaus) is a graceful wrought-iron and glass pavilion based on the famous greenhouses of Kew, with luxuriant palms flourishing in the tropical heat.

Museum of Military History (Heeresgeschichtliches Museum)

Museum of Military History
3 Arsenal, Objekt 18, t 79 5610, www.hgm. or.at; open Sat–Thurs 9–5; closed Fri; adm; U-Bahn Südtirolerplatz, tram D, O, 18 to Süd-bahnhof or Fasangasse, bus 69A to Arsenal

Behind the Belvedere palaces, and to the east of Südbahnhof, stands the forbidding military Arsenal, built to curb unrest after revolution erupted across Europe in 1848. The entrance area is dominated by statues of famous generals, and the rear courtyard is crammed with tanks and other military vehicles.

The first floor contains booty from the Turkish campaigns, including a tent belonging to the Grand Vizier. On the ground floor, there's a fine collection of uniforms (the Austrian army won a prize for most elegant uniform at the 1900 Paris Exhibition), and a fascinating display on the shocking assassination of Archduke Franz Ferdinand in Sarajevo on 28 June 1914, which precipitated the events leading up the First World War. Among the exhibits is the car in which the archduke and his wife were shot, and the sofa on which he bled to death.

Central Cemetery (Zentralfriedhof)

Central Cemetery
11 Simmeringer Hauptstrasse 234, t 760 41; open winter 8am–dusk, summer 7am–dusk; tram 6, 71 to Zentralfriedhof

This vast cemetery, one of the largest in Europe, was opened in 1875, and contains more than 2.5 million graves and memorials. The plan, available at the entrance, is essential. The **Tombs of Honour** are grouped in section 32A, and include a memorial to Mozart (whose remains are lost in a mass paupers' grave in the Friedhof St Marxer, *see* box above right), and the graves of Beethoven and Schubert, who were disinterred and reburied here in 1899, Brahms, along with most of the Strauss family. The most atmospheric section is the huge Jewish area, with its crumbling, overgrown graves, many horrifically desecrated in the pre-war years. Behind the church are graves belonging to members of the Austrian Resistance, and the Soviet soldiers who died during the liberation of Vienna.

Death in Vienna

The Viennese take death very seriously: to see the full pomp and ceremony that attend burials, visit the **Burial Museum** (Bestattungsmuseum; *4 Goldegasse 19, t 50 195; open by appointment only Mon–Fri 12–3*). The **Zentralfriedhof** is the biggest and best known, but you can make a pilgrimage to the tombs of some of Vienna's most illustrious citizens in the following other graveyards:

St Marx Cemetery (Friedhof St Marxer; *3 Leberstrasse 6–8; tram 18, 71 to St Marx, or bus 74A to Hofmannsthalgasse; open 7am–dusk*). Tucked away in a bleak district bounded by motorways, this tree-lined 18th-century cemetery is where Mozart was buried in a pauper's grave in 1791.

Heitzinger Cemetery (Heitzinger Friedhof; *13 Maxingstrasse 15; U-Bahn Heitzinger*). The most atmospheric cemetery in Vienna, with the graves of Gustav Klimt, Otto Wagner, Franz Gillparzer and Katharina Schratt, actress and mistress of Franz Josef. It's close to Schönbrunn Palace.

Hundertwasserhaus

Hundert-wasserhaus
on the corner of Löwengasse with Kegelgasse; closed to the public; U-Bahn, tram to Landstrasse or Hetzgasse

Slap bang in the middle of an otherwise unremarkable residential street, architect Friedensreich Hundertwasser's playful, multi-coloured apartment building (1985) appears to have been transported from another planet. Hundertwasser was an enemy of the straight line, and there isn't one in sight – even the floors undulate dreamily. Trees and shrubs peer down from the communal roof terrace, and onion domes appear to float above the roof. The flats are private and not open to the public, but Hundertwasser's equally quirky shopping complex, the Kalke Village, is just across the street. Here, you can pick up all kinds of tacky memorabilia or have a drink in the (wobbly-floored) café. Committed fans of Hundertwasser can head around the corner to the fairytale **KunstHausWien**, another wacky blend of styles and bold colours. Inside are galleries displaying his paintings, temporary modern art exhibitions and a café.

KunstHausWien
3 Untere Weissgerberstrasse 13, t (01) 712 0495, www.kunsthaus wien.at; open daily 10–7; guided tours Sun and hols 12 and 3; adm

The Prater

The Prater
U-Bahn, tram 5, 21, O to Praterstern

This fabulous stretch of green parkland has been the city's most celebrated playground since Josef II opened it to the public in 1766. The chestnut-shaded avenue of the Hauptallee extends for 5km through the centre of the park and is a long-standing favourite for a Sunday stroll. The **Volksprater funfair**, at the northwest end, is the most popular section of the park, dominated by the giant Riesenrad or **ferris wheel**, immortalized in *The Third Man*. The Riesenrad was built over a century ago, and continues to make its panoramic, if sedate, journey high above the treetops.

Volksprater funfair
open daily 10am–11pm

Ferris wheel
www.wienerriesenrad.at; open daily May–Sept 9am–12am, Mar–April and Oct 10–10; Nov–Feb 10–8; adm

The Old Danube and Donauinsel

Alte Donau
U-Bahn Alte Donau

After centuries of unpredictable flooding, the Viennese finally dug a new, deep causeway for the Danube river at the end of the 19th century, which now runs a smooth, dead-straight course across the northeast of the city. A single undulation remains of its original course, known as the **Alte Donau** (Old Danube). This curving crook of water is prettily fringed with weeping willows and bathing areas, and there's a smattering of restaurants and bars. It's the best place for sailing and other watersports, with plenty of boat-hire locations.

The **Donauinsel** is an island caught between the Danube river and the Danube Canal, and is lined with little beaches and shady picnic areas. The wide paths make it good for biking and roller skating (there's a rental place next to the Donauinsel U-Bahn station). A tacky but fun collection of bars and restaurants are clustered next to the U-Bahn stop, popular on summer nights.

Stift Klosterneuburg

Stift Klosterneuburg
t (02) 243 411 214, www.stift-kloster neuburg.at; open daily 10–12 and 1.30–4.30; adm; guided tours (call in advance to arrange an English tour); S-Bahn from Franz-Josefs-Bahnhof to Klosterneuburg-Keyerling

Set high above the River Danube, 12km from the centre of Vienna, this massive fortified abbey was built in the 12th century to house the last remains of St Leopold. The saint, originally a margrave of the Babenburg dynasty, was later boldly, if entirely unconvincingly, claimed by the Habsburgs, and the abbey became an important pilgrimage location. Karl VI, who was obsessed with his ancestry, determined to expand the original complex in the 18th century, envisaging a massive complex on the scale of the Escorial near Madrid. Although the abbey was unfinished at his death in 1740, enough Baroque finery survives to give visitors a sense of what it might have looked like had Karl VI lived to complete it.

The abbey is now most famous for the celebrated 12th-century **Verduner Altar**, housed in a chapel off the main church. This magnificent winged altarpiece is one of the most extraordinary examples of medieval craftsmanship, and is made up of 51 scenes from the Bible, each exquisitely wrought in enamel. Look out too for the astonishing **pipe organ**, one of the finest surviving Baroque organs in Europe, which was finally restored in the 1990s after suffering terrible bomb damage during the Second World War. The abbey has also long been known for its **wines**, which you can taste (and buy) in the brick-vaulted *vinothek*.

(i) **Vienna** >
Wien Tourismus: 1 Albertinaplatz, t (01) 24 555, www.vienna.info; open daily 9–7; U1, U2, U4 to Karlsplatz

Youth Information Service (Jugendinfo): 1 Babenbergerstrasse 1, www.jugendinfowien. at; open Mon–Sat 12–7

Austrian Tourism Office: 4 Margaretenstrasse 1, t (01) 588 660, www.austria.info

Tourist Information in Vienna

The helpful staff at the main tourist office (**Wien Tourismus**) have lots of glossy maps and leaflets, offer a hotel-booking service, a ticketing service for major (and many minor) venues, a *bureau de change*, and sell the **Vienna Card** (a discount pass, *see* below). There are smaller branches at the airport and at the Westbahnhof train station.

There's also a special **youth information service** (note that it doesn't provide general tourist info).

For information on visiting other areas of Austria, contact the **Austrian Tourism Office**, *www.austria.info*.

Vienna Card

The Vienna Card offers discounts of between 10% and 35% at museums and attractions, shops and restaurants plus 72hrs' unlimited use of public transport. It costs €18.50, and can be bought at the tourist information office, online at *www.vienna.info*, at main train stations, some hotels, or by credit card on **t** (01) 798 44 00-148. Each card allows you to take a child under 15 along for free on public transport.

Guided Tours

The tourist office produces a monthly booklet listing the various **walking tours** offered by official guides in Vienna, also posted on the website. Themes include Jewish Vienna, Art Nouveau Vienna, Vienna in the footsteps of *The Third Man*, Freud's Vienna, Red Vienna, and the Homes of Mozart, Beethoven and Schubert. Tours usually last 1½–2hrs, and cost €11 (€10 with the Vienna Card), or €6 for under-18s. Visit *www.wienguide.at* for more information, or call **t** (01) 489 96 74.

Vienna Segway Tours/Pedal Power, **t** (01) 1 729 72 34, *www.segway-vienna.at*, run 3-hour **Segway tours** of the main sights of the city, starting at the Staatsoper (€70 per person). They also rent out bikes (from the Prater office at Ausstellungsstrasse 3) and operate bike tours; see *www.pedalpower.at* for details.

Year-round **boat excursions** along the Danube and the Danube Canal are offered by **DDSG Shipping Co.**, Handelskai 265, **t** (01) 588 80, *www.ddsg-blue-danube.at*.

The **Vienna Sightseeing Bus** makes a tour of the city's main sights, and is a 'Hop-on Hop-off' service with multilingual audioguides. Tickets are available for 1, 2 or 24hrs, and prices start at €13. The starting point is outside the Staatsoper. Info from **Vienna Sightseeing**, 14 Graf Starhemberggasse 25, **t** (01) 712 46 83, *www.viennasightseeing.at*. For a bus tour with a difference, try the **Oldtimer Bus Tours**: a historic bus navigates the main monuments in an hour-long tour of the city. Tours are run from May to October and cost from €19. More info at *www. oldtimertours.at*.

You can make a tour of the Ringstrasse on a classic Viennese tram, with multilingual commentary. The **Ring Tour**, **t** (01) 7909-121, *www.wienerlinien.at*, departs daily from Schwedenplatz (first tram of the day departs from Staatsoper) and costs €7 for a single circuit, or €9 for 24 hours unlimited use.

Horse-drawn carriages (*fiaker*) clatter around the cobbled streets and are available from outside Stephansdom and the Hofburg. Prices are fixed, and should cost approx €40 for a 20min tour of the city, or €65 for a 40min tour, but agree the terms before you get in.

Services in Vienna

Internet Access

There are plenty of places to get online in Vienna, with free Internet access offered everywhere from fast food joints to venerable cafés. Check out the website *www.freewave.at/en* for a regularly updated list of hotspots in Vienna. Most hotels and guesthouses now offer WiFi facilities to guests, and some also make computer terminals available. If you're travelling without a laptop or a smartphone, try **Bignet** (Hoher Markt 8, **t** (01) 533 2939) or **Surfland** (Krugerstrasse 10, **t** (01) 512 77 01), which have computer terminals, phones, and fax, scanning and printing services. The arty and attractive **Künstlerhaus Café** (Karlsplatz 5, **t** (01) 587 96 63 19, *www.k-haus.at/kino/netcafe/*) has about half a dozen terminals.

Post Offices

The main post office is at Fleischmarkt 19, **t** 0800 100 100 (*U-Bahn to Schwedenplatz, open daily 24hrs*), with several branches (including at Westbahnhof and Südbahnhof train stations) scattered around the city.

Festivals and Events in Vienna

31 Dec and 1 Jan: New Year's Eve concerts by the Vienna Philharmonic at the Musikverein (*see* p.103); Beethoven's Ninth Symphony at the Konzerthaus (*see* p.103).

6 Jan–Ash Wed: *Fasching* (Carnival). All kinds of events, including lavish balls (the most glamorous is the Opera Ball, held the last Thursday before Shrove Tuesday), and the traditional meal of *Heringschmaus* (herring and pickled fish) on Ash Wednesday.

Jan (usually 2nd and 3rd weeks): *Resonanzen*, a festival of medieval music held at the Konzerthaus.

Late Feb–mid-Mar: Dance Festival, classic and contemporary dance at various venues across the city.

Mar: Easter Market at the Freytung, with arts and crafts and traditional foods.

April–May: *Frühlingsfestival*, a festival of classical music, hosted in alternate years by either the Musikverein (*www.musikverein.at*) or the Konzerthaus (*www.konzerthaus.at*).

1 May: *Tag der Arbeit*, Labour Day, is marked with parades and processions on the Rathausplatz and Ringstrasse; *Maifest*, concerts and funfairs in the Prater.

Mid-May–mid-June: Vienna *Festwochen*, excellent festival of the performing arts at venues across the city. Info at t (01) 589 22 22, *www.festwochen.at*.

June–July: *Jazzfest Wien*, city-wide jazz festival, with concerts held in venues across the city, *www.viennajazz.org*.

July–Aug: Free concerts in the parks; hugely popular outdoor film screenings (free) in front of the Rathausplatz and in the Augarten Park (*www.kino untersternen.at*).

Oct: *Viennale*. Long-established international film festival, *www.viennale.at*.

Nov: *Wien Modern* – the Konzerthaus hosts this excellent festival of contemporary music, *www.konzert haus.at*.

Dec: Christmas markets (*Christkindl-märkte*) spring up across the city, including the Rathausplatz, Karlplatz, Schönbrunn and Spittelberg, with arts and crafts, traditional food and drink, and lots of special activities for children.

Shopping in Vienna

Traditional Viennese and Austrian specialities include cut glass, embroidered lace, typical Austrian clothes like dirndls and *lederhosen*, the ubiquitous chocolate 'Mozart Balls' from Salzburg and a wonderful range of cakes including the celebrated *Sacher-Torte* (which can be expensively packed up and even posted by the Hotel Sacher shop, *see* p.93).

The main shopping streets are **Kärntnerstrasse** (1st district) and **Mariahilferstrasse** (6th district), with department stores, all the major fashion chains (including H&M, Zara, Mango and Benetton), and a couple of shopping malls. Off Mariahilferstrasse is **Lindengasse**, known for its small fashion boutiques. Along **Graben** and **Kohlmarkt** (both 1st district), you'll find chichi designer fashion (Chanel, Louis Vuitton, etc.), and the fancy *pâtisserie*-cum-café Demel (*see* 'Cafés', p.101). **Dorotheergasse** and **Josef-städter Strasse** (both 1st district) are lined with smart antique dealers. The narrow streets and passages of the **old town** are wonderful for a stroll, with tiny shops selling everything from religious objects to slick designer household goods.

Many of the **museum shops** are excellent, especially the original, contemporary household goods, accessories and *objets d'art* on sale at the MAK shop (*see* p.80) and the MuseumsQuartier shop (*see* p.76).

Shops are usually **open** from Monday to Saturday from 9 or 10am to 6 or 7pm, although most are closed by 5 or 6pm on Saturdays. Few shops are open late, and even fewer are open on Sundays.

Antiques and Interior Design

Dorotheum, 1 Dorotheergasse 17, t 515 600, *www.dorotheum.com*. Set up as a pawn shop more than 200 years ago, this is now the oldest and most prestigious auction house in Central Europe.

Stilwerk Design Centre, 1 Praterstrasse 1, t (01) 890 4030, *www.stilwerk.at*. Jean Nouvel's stunning tower is home to a collection of superb interior and design shops. Several major brands are represented in 28 stores. Post-shopping, head to the bar, **Le Loft**, on the 18th floor (*see* p.95).

Books and Maps

Freytag & Berndt, 1 Kohlmarkt 9, t (01) 533 86 85, *www.freytagberndt.at*. An enormous range of maps and travel books in several different languages are on offer at the renowned map-makers' flagship store.

Shakespeare and Co., 1 Sterngasse 2, t (01) 535 50 53, *www.shakespeare. co.at*. This friendly little shop has a good range of books in English, including a small travel section, plenty of books on Vienna, and lots of English-language teaching materials. They also sell some second-hand books, and host readings and other events.

Department Stores and Malls

Gasometer, 11 Guglgasse, *www.gaso meter.at*. A stunning architectural *tour de force*, this shopping centre (and apartment complex) is housed in four former gas containers. Unfortunately the shopping doesn't live up to the dramatic setting, with the usual very ordinary chain stores, a supermarket, bars and cafés and a cinema. *U-Bahn Gasometer*.

Ringstrassen Gallerien, 1 Kärntner Ring 11–13, *www.ringstrassen-galerien.at*. An upmarket shopping centre spread over two adjoining buildings, with expensive boutiques (Armani, Christian Dior, Calvin Klein among them), plus a good supermarket, and lots of cafés and restaurants. *Open Mon–Sat 7.30am–10pm, shops open Mon–Fri 10–7, Sat until 6pm*.

Steffl, 1 Kärntnerstrasse 19, t (01) 514 310, *www.kaufhaus-steffl.at*. This convenient department store has several floors of fashion, an electrical goods department (if you need a plug adaptor in a hurry), and a panoramic bar on the top floor.

Fashion and Accessories

Humanic, 1 Kärntnerstrasse 1, t (01) 413 89 22, *www.humanic.at*. This chain of shoe stores has all kinds of styles for men, women and children, from the practical to the funky. Several branches across the city.

Pregenzer, 4 Schleifmuhlgasse 4, t (01) 586 5758, *www.pregenzer.com*. The best fashion boutique in Vienna, this boasts some of the most interesting (yet highly wearable) designer fashions for men and women in town. It's one of very few places in Vienna that can compete with the boutiques in fashion capitals like London and New York. Great accessories too.

Loden-Plankl, 1 Michaelerplatz 6, t 533 80 32, *www.loden-plankl.at*. One of the oldest and most famous stores dedicated to traditional Austrian clothing, this sells a full range of dirndls, *lederhosen*, and feathered hats.

Food and Drink

Altmann & Kühne, 1 Graben 30, t (01) 533 09 27. A divine little shop selling exquisite hand-made chocolates in pretty boxes. They're expensive, but worth every penny.

Bäckerei Grimm, 1 Kurrentgasse 10, t (01) 533 13 84. It's worth making a trip to this excellent bakery for the smell alone – although once inside you won't be able to resist purchasing one of their delicious loaves. *Open Mon–Fri 7am–6.30pm, Sat 8am–1pm*.

Meinl am Graben, 1 Graben 19, t 532 33 34, *www.meinl.com*. Vienna's premier gourmet supermarket, with three floors stocked with all kinds of delicious produce, and an excellent restaurant (*see* 'Eating Out', p.97) upstairs. *Open Mon–Fri 8–8, Sat 8.30–8*.

Zum Schwarzen Kameel, 1 Bogner-gasse 5, t (01) 533 81 25, *www.kameel. at*. The classic restaurant (*see* p.98) has an excellent deli and wine shop, with all kinds of delectable goodies from Austria and abroad. *Open Mon–Sat 9am–9pm*.

Glass and Porcelain

Augarten Wien, Spiegelgasse 3, t (01) 512 14 94, *www.augarten.at*. Augarten has been making porcelain for three centuries, and you can admire their delicate white figurines and tableware in the new flagship store.

J&L Lobmeyr, 1 Kärntnerstrasse 26, t (01) 512 05 08, *www.lobmeyr.com*. If you've admired the cut-glass chandeliers at the Vienna Opera House, you can pick some up at this world-famous store. As well as exquisite glassware, there's also a small museum and a selection of porcelain.

Swarovski, 1 Graben 15, t (01) 324 0000. This enormous store aims to make shopping a sensory experience, with its crystal-encrusted products displayed on several floors in artist-designed spaces.

Kids' Stuff

Dohnal, 1 Neubaugasse 8, **t** (01) 512 73 11. Austrian children's clothing and international designer fashions along with prams, cots and other essentials.

Kober, 1 Graben 14–15, **t** (01) 533 60 18, *www.kobertoys.com*. This famous toy emporium has the latest electronic gadgets, a huge range of train sets, and sturdy wooden toys and Steiff teddies for younger children.

Markets

Naschmarkt, 4 Naschmarkt. The city's famous open-air food market is a fabulous riot of colour and smells, with all kinds of stalls selling wonderfully fresh produce. *Open Mon–Fri 6am–6.30pm, Sat 6am–2pm*.

Kettenbrückengasse (5th district): Saturday flea market.

Kunst und Antikmarkt, Donaukanal-Promenade. Art, antiques, bric-a-brac and plain old junk are laid out in heaps at this summer market by the Danube Canal. *Open May–Sept Sat 2–8, Sun 10–8. U-Bahn to Schwedenplatz*.

Music

Arcadia, 1 Kärntnerstrasse 40, **t** (01) 513 95 68, *www.arcadia.at*. Arcadia (in the State Opera House) has an excellent selection of classical recordings, which often (but not always) feature Austrian performers. As you might expect, opera features prominently.

EMI, 1 Kärntnerstrasse 30, **t** (01) 512 36 75. This massive emporium of music stocks a huge selection of classical and pop CDs.

Sports and Activities in Vienna

Football

Hanappi Stadium, 14 Keisslergasse 6, **t** (01) 914 55 19, *www.skrapid.at*. This stadium is home to Rapid Vienna, the biggest Austrian team. (The national team play at the huge **Ernst Happel Stadium**, 2 Meierstrasse 7, **t** (01) 728 0854, *www.oefb.at*).

Franz Horr Stadium, 10 Fischhofgasse 10–12, **t** (01) 710 4528, *www.fk-austria.at*. The home of Rapid Vienna's only rivals, Austria Memphis.

Ice-skating

Eislaufanlage Engelmann, Syringgasse 6–8, **t** (01) 405 14 25. A popular outdoor ice-rink. *Open late Oct–Mar*.

Rathausplatz, 1 Rathausplatz. The square in front of the City Hall becomes an outdoor ice-rink in winter. *Open late Jan–early Mar*.

Wiener Eislaufverein, 3 Lothringerstrasse 22, **t** (01) 713 63530. Another good outdoor ice-rink. *Open late Oct–Mar*.

Horse-Racing

Freudenau Prater, 2 Freudenau 65, **t** (01) 728 95 17. Flat-racing is held at the eastern end of the Prater from spring to autumn.

Krieau Stadium, 2 Nordportalstrasse 247, **t** (01) 728 00 46. An elegant trotting stadium, built in 1913, which hosts international trotting races from September to June.

Skiing

Many Vienna-based travel agencies offer one-day ski packages, including transport and lift-pass. These usually head for the slopes at Semmering (about 60 miles/90km from the city). For more info, contact Semmering tourist office, **t** (02664) 20025, *www.semmering.at*, or look at *www.tiscover.com/noe-sued*.

Swimming

Krapfenwaldbad, 19 Krapfenwaldgasse 65–73, **t** (01) 320 1501. Perhaps the loveliest of Vienna's many outdoor municipal swimming pools (the tourist office has a complete list), with original 1920s fittings and beautiful views over the city. *Open May–Sept*.

Donauinsel (*see* p.88). The Danube canal is lined with beaches.

Watersports

To mess about in boats, head for the Alte Donau (*see* p.87), where there are sailing schools and boat-rental outlets.

Where to Stay in Vienna

Vienna t (01) –

Vienna offers a wide range of accommodation, from aristocratic palaces and opulent 19th-century hotels to family-run *pensions* and youth hostels. It's surprisingly expensive to stay in this city, and many hotels are often busy with tour groups. The tourist office has a hotel booking service, and can provide lists of rooms available in private houses (usually outside the centre, but inexpensive and quiet). Check websites for special deals, particularly at the chain hotels and those geared towards business travellers. Prices include breakfast at most hotels, but it's worth checking before you arrive. Within the Inner City is more expensive; prices drop outside the Ringstrasse.

Innere Stadt

Ambassador, 1 Neuer Markt, **t** 961610, *www.ambassador.at* (€€€€). This regal, five-star hotel is crammed with gilt, marble pillars, chandeliers and statues. Popular with visiting dignitaries, the rooms are formal and elegant, with heavy drapes and sturdy dark wooden furniture, and the finest have adjoining sitting rooms.

★ **Hollmann Beletage** >>

Astoria, 1 Kärntnergasse 32–4, **t** 515 770, *www.austria-trend.at* (€€€€). This is a classic old-fashioned hotel, which still manages to ooze turn-of-the-20th-century opulence while its facilities are bang up-to-date. The spacious rooms are well equipped, and there's a smart restaurant and bar.

Do & Co Hotel, Stephansplatz 12, **t** 24 188, *www.doco.com* (€€€€). Located in the iconic Haas Haus, right opposite the cathedral, this is the city's hottest new designer hotel (opened in 2006). Rooms are kitted out with every 21st-century luxury and breakfast is served in the spectacular glass dome.

★ **Hotel Sacher** >

Hotel Sacher, 1 Philharmonikerstrasse 4, **t** 514 560, *www.sacher.com* (€€€€). The *grande dame* of the Viennese hotel scene boasts splendid rooms filled with extraordinary art and antiques, a luxurious spa, a fabulous restaurant (where Emperor Franz Josef once tucked into his daily *Tafelspitz* – boiled beef), and a legendary café (*see* p.101). The hotel is justly famous for the magnificent service offered by its staff. To push the boat out, book one of their stunning suites.

Kaiserin Elisabeth, 1 Weihburgasse 3, **t** 51526, *www.kaiserinelisabeth.at* (€€€€). This delightful hotel retains much of its grandiose 19th-century opulence, and guests are greeted with a swirl of velvet and glittering crystal in the lobby. The rooms are equally plush, and most have been sympathetically modernized.

König von Ungarn, 1 Schulerstrasse 10, **t** 515 84, *www.kvu.at* (€€€€). The framed signatures of famous guests line the walls at this charming, good-value hotel which shares the same 16th-century building as the Figaro-haus (*see* p.54). Passages lead to the bedrooms, all individually decorated with a tasteful mixture of traditional and modern styles, plus there's a wonderful glassy atrium to relax in, and a good restaurant in the vaulted cellar. Unsurprisingly, this is one of the most sought-after hotels in the city and you'll need to book well in advance.

Hollmann Beletage, 1 Köllnerhofgasse 6, **t** 961 1960, *www.hollmann-beletage.at* (€€€). This chic boutique hotel is set in a handsome 19th-century townhouse, but the 25 rooms are individually decorated with crisp, contemporary furnishings. Prices vary according to room size (M, L, or XL). Other amenities include a small spa and even a small screening room (where *The Third Man*, unsurprisingly, is a favourite) and the fabulous breakfasts are the best in town. Its laid-back style makes it a favourite with celebs travelling incognito.

Wandl, 1 Petersplatz 9, **t** 534 550, *www.hotel-wandl.com* (€€€). This slightly ramshackle, family-run hotel has been going for almost two centuries, and the venerable old building still has hints of its former grandeur. Rooms vary widely; some boast original fittings while others are much plainer, but most are spacious and have polished wooden floors.

Nossek, 1 Graben 17, **t** 5337 0410, *www. pension-nossek.at* (€€€–€€). This modest, family-run hotel offers attractive rooms (the best have balconies overlooking the chic boutiques of the Graben), with basic bathrooms, but otherwise tastefully furnished with Persian rugs and antiques.

Pension Pertschy, 1 Habsburgergasse 5, **t** 534 49 49, *www.pertschy.com* (€€). The Pertschy is an excellent modestly priced choice in a prime location off the swish Graben. The building has seen better days, but it overlooks a stone courtyard and most of the (smallish) rooms have been newly renovated in a slightly flashy faux-Baroque style. A couple have retained attractive period touches like old-fashioned ceramic heaters, and there's a cosy, wood-panelled breakfast room.

★ **Pension Suzanne** >

Pension Suzanne, 1 Walfischgasse 4, **t** 513 25 07, *www.pension-suzanne.at* (€€). Possibly the best city-centre budget option, the simple little Suzanne is always booked out months in advance. Tucked away in unprepossessing surroundings just off Kärntnerstrasse, its old-fashioned, charming rooms, some with little kitchenettes, get friendly service from the Strafinger family. The best rooms look out on to the street – interior rooms face a dowdy courtyard. They also let apartments.

Zur Wiener Staatsoper, 1 Krugerstrasse 11, **t** 513 12 74, *www.zurwienerstaats oper.at* (€€). Tucked down a pedestrian street off Kärntnerstrasse, this family-run hotel is squeezed into a tall, narrow 19th-century townhouse. The rooms are smallish, but good value for the location, and in summer breakfast is served out on the terrace.

Hotel Orient, 1 Tiefer Graben 30, **t** 533 73 07, *www.hotelorient.at* (€). Taking the Japanese 'love hotels' as inspiration, the Orient has themed rooms and suites available by the hour, or by the night. *Fin-de-siècle* detailing and brisk service ensure that it's all more tongue-in-cheek than tacky.

Pension Riedl, Georg-Coch-Platz 3, **t** 512 7919, *www.pensionriedl.at* (€). A simple little *pension* near Wagner's Postparkasse building with just a handful of rooms (with and without bathrooms). Accommodation is basic but spotless, the location is perfect, and the charismatic owner (Maria) will make your stay as special as she can (including providing breakfast in the rooms at no extra cost). There's also an apartment, ideal for families, available to rent.

Schweizer Pension Solderer, 1 Heinrichgasse 2, **t** 533 81 56, *www. schweizerpension.com* (€). A pristine little *pension*, this offers budget rooms with or without bathrooms. An organic breakfast is included in the price. This is a non-smoking *pension*. Cash only.

Around the Ringstrasse

Bristol, 1 Kärntner Ring 1, **t** 515 160, *www.starwoodhotels.com* (€€€€). Possibly the most luxurious hotel in the city, the Bristol is a Viennese institution, and the interior is a glorious whirl of gilt, polished marble and glittering crystal. There's a splendidly formal restaurant, an elegant drawing room for afternoon tea, and the gorgeous rooms and suites are kitted out with every imaginable creature comfort.

Das Triest, 4 Wiedner Hauptsrasse 12, **t** 589 180, *www.dastriest.at* (€€€€). This sleekly designed modern hotel (Terence Conran did the interior decoration) is slotted behind an elegant old façade. With its pared-down minimalism and light-filled public spaces, it's the antithesis of most of Vienna's traditional luxury accommodation. The top-floor suites have private roof gardens, and there's an elegant Italian restaurant and glossy cocktail bar.

Imperial, 1 Kärntner Ring 16, **t** 501 100, *www.luxurycollection.com/imperial* (€€€€). The Imperial combines the best of traditional Vienna with crisp modern design in its sumptuous and spacious rooms, which are filled with heavy drapes and crystal chandeliers yet boast huge, modern bathrooms. There's a beauty centre and fitness room, and service is polished and attentive.

Marriott Hotel, 1 Parkring 12a, **t** 515 180, *www.marriott.com* (€€€€). This huge, glassy hotel has a superb location, and offers every imaginable comfort (including indoor pool, sauna and gym) yet remains rather soulless. There is a plant-filled atrium with waterfalls and fairy lights, which has plenty of shops and cafés. Exterior rooms look out over rooftops and the nearby Stadtpark, but can be noisy.

Le Méridien, 1 Opernring 13, **t** 588 900, *http://vienna.lemeridien.com* (€€€€). Near the Opera House, with a historic façade hiding minimalist modern 'design' style, all glass and cool colours. Pool, fitness centre, restaurant and bar, and the rooms all have hi-tech flat-screen TVs and Internet access.

Palais Hansen Kempinski, *www.kempinski.com*. The neo-Renaissance Palais Hansen, built in 1873, is currently being converted into a luxury hotel by the Kempinski brand. It is slated to open in 2012.

⭐ Sofitel Vienna Stephansdom >

Sofitel Vienna Stephansdom, 2 Praterstrasse 1, **t** 906 160, *www.sofitel.com* (€€€€). The city's newest, glossiest, most high-tech hotel is set in Jean Nouvel's landmark glassy tower by the Danube canal. The best rooms and suites have views across the old city to the spires of Stephansdom, and the many amenities include a fabulous spa, and a magnificent restaurant-bar **Le Loft** with painted ceilings and astonishing views from enormous windows.

Hotel am Schubertring, 1 Schubertring 11, **t** 717 020, *www.schubertring.at* (€€€–€€). Housed in a graceful Jugendstil building, this is a charming hotel filled with Art Nouveau-style lamps, murals and furniture. The rooms are spacious and comfortable, and the staff are welcoming and attentive. Room rates drop considerably during the winter months. Some of the suites boast kitchenettes.

Josefshof, 8 Josefsgasse 4–6, **t** 40419, *www.josefshof.com* (€€€–€€). This pretty 19th-century hotel is painted a sunny primrose-yellow, and has a delightful little garden courtyard. Now part of the Mercure chain, the rooms are comfortable but rather bland. Apartments are also available.

⭐ Das Tyrol >>

Hotel-Mercure Secession, 6 Getreide-markt 5, **t** 588 380 (€€). A modern, glassy hotel in the Mercure chain, this is geared towards business clientele, but offers crisp, newly renovated rooms at reasonable prices. Look out for special weekend deals. Breakfast is extra.

Hotel Baltic, 9 Skodagasse 15, **t** 405 62660 (€). A faded, but still charming, *pension* located in a battered Jugendstil building. Most of the rooms are spacious, all are crammed with a rickety mix of antique and 70s furniture, and the best have balconies. Bathrooms are old-fashioned, but it is still a great deal for its location. Note that the Baltic operates a cash-only policy.

Quisisana, 6 Windmühlgasse 6, **t** 587 33 41, *www.quisisana-wien.co.at* (€). The Quisiana is a good-value budget choice, offering spartan but adequate rooms with and without bathrooms. It's close to the centre and the buzzy shopping street of Mariahilfer Strasse.

Pension Wild, 8 Langegasse 10, **t** 406 51 74, *www.pension-wild.com* (€). Run by the Wild family, a deservedly popular *pension* which books up far in advance. The rooms are spartan, but pristine, and the owners are utterly charming. It's located close to the MuseumsQuartier, a short walk to the Ringstrasse.

Further Afield

Mercure Grand Biedermeier, 3 Landstrasser Hauptstrasse 28, **t** 716 710, *www.mercure.com* (€€€). Charmingly set around a cobbled Biedermeier passage courtyard, this elegant hotel offers spacious and blissfully quiet rooms prettily decorated in traditional Viennese style. It's just a short walk from the Belvedere palaces and the Ringstrasse, but, if you can't tear yourself away, there's also a traditional restaurant, coffee house and wine cellar. It's part of the Mercure chain.

Das Tyrol, 6 Mariahilferstrasse **t** 587 5415, *www.das-tyrol.at* (€€€). Just behind the MuseumsQuartier on a popular shopping street, this welcoming little hotel provides an enchanting retreat from the city hubbub. Original contemporary art is scattered around the hotel, and the 30 rooms, suites and studios feature thoughtful extras such as a Nespresso machine. A copious buffet breakfast is served, and staff are charming.

Alla Lenz, 7 Halbagasse 3–5, **t** 523 69 89, *www.allalenz.com* (€€). This family-run, rather upmarket *pension* offers all kinds of unexpected extras, including a sun terrace and small swimming pool. They also have bikes for rent, and there's a computer in the lobby for guest use.

⭐ Altstadt >

Altstadt Vienna, 7 Kirchengasse 41, **t** 522 66 66, *www.altstadt.at* (€€). This delightful hotel offers handsome rooms and suites, each individually decorated (the Matteo Thun Design Rooms are spectacular), and many with superb views over the city. Service is personal and friendly, and there are buses to the city centre. They also have well-appointed apartments with kitchenettes.

Altwienerhof, 15 Herklotzgasse 6, **t** 892 60 00, *www.altwienerhof.at* (€€). This lovely family-run hotel near the Schönbrunn palace offers a range of simple rooms and more luxurious suites set around a pretty cobbled Biedermeier courtyard. Wine enthusiasts should also try the Vinothek, where tastings are held regularly.

Baronesse My Secret Home, 6 Langegasse 61, **t** 512 83 30, *www.secrethomes.at* (€€). In the elegant Josefstadt district, which is packed with great restaurants, shops, and bars, this is a good-value guesthouse with immaculate, if slightly old-fashioned, rooms set around traditional courtyards. Excellent service includes a list of the day's events provided each morning at breakfast.

⭐ Spiess & Spiess >

Spiess & Spiess, 3 Hainburgerstrasse 19, **t** 714 8505, *www.spiess-vienna.at* (€€). An utterly delightful guesthouse with nine spacious and elegantly furnished suites, most with a/c and all with WiFi and cable TV. The family owners are dedicated to making visitors as comfortable as possible. There's a small supplement for rooms overlooking the gardens. Delicious breakfasts are served in the garden room. Book well in advance.

Hotel Pension Franz, 9 Währinger-strasse 12, **t** 310 40 40, *www. hotelpensionfranz.at* (€). Packed with weathered Baroque flummery, this is an excellent choice right opposite the imposing Votivkirche (the best rooms overlook the church). It's crammed with battered furniture, including lots of antiques; although it's been decades since any modernization took place, it's still an excellent budget choice. Rooms vary widely in size and comforts – check them out in advance if possible.

Pensión Kraml, 6 Brauergasse 5, **t** 587 85 88, *www.pensionkraml.at* (€). This is a charming family-run guesthouse in a quiet location just off the buzzy shopping street of Mariahilferstrasse. The traditional Viennese house is set around a courtyard, and the spotless rooms come with or without bathrooms. There is also an apartment, which is perfect for families.

Student Residences (*Saisonhotels*)

Between July and September, student residences around the city rent out rooms and apartments. Reserve well in advance.

Academia Hotels, **t** 401 76 55, *www.academiahotels.at*.

All You Need Hotels, **t** 512 74 93, *www.allyouneedhotels.at*.

Apartment Rental

There are dozens of companies offering apartments for rent in Vienna. These are generally better value than hotels, and are particularly good for families, or anyone staying for a week or more. As with hotels, prices drop outside the Innere Stadt.

Haus 1, 5 Kettenbrückengasse 1, *www.hauseins.com*. Easily the best apartment service in town, this is run by a delightful Anglo-Austrian couple. All five apartments are beautifully furnished – four in chic, contemporary style and one with traditional Viennese elegance. All have flat-screen TVs, computers with broadband, and DVD players. Thoughtful extras include the greeting gift of sparkling wine and chocolates, and the extra-fluffy towels in the bathrooms. They are perfectly located near the fabulous Naschmarkt and are well served by local transport. Highly recommended.

Sacher Apartments, 1 Rotenturmstrasse 1, **t** 533 32 38, *www.pensionsacher.at*. Slap bang in the city centre, these affordable apartments have little in the way of charm but plenty of mod-cons, and an unbeatable location.

Vienna Apartments, **t** 664 414 38 48 (mobile), *http://vienna.apartments.at*. A very friendly, helpful family-run business with an excellent website which allows you to see the various properties available. Most are outside the centre, but all are close to public transport.

Eating Out in Vienna

Vienna t (01) –
Innere Stadt

Do & Co, 6th floor, Haas-Haus, 1 Stephansplatz 12, **t** 535 39 69, *www.doco.com* (€€€€). The most famous restaurant in the Haas-Haus building, this serves elaborate and award-winning international cuisine to a well-heeled crowd who come to admire each other and the stunning views of the Stephansdom. *Booking essential.*

fabios, 1 Tuchlauben 6, **t** 532 22 22, *www.fabios.at* (€€€€–€€€). Ultra-sty lish fabios produces some of the finest and most imaginative Italian cuisine in Vienna. The seafood is particularly good – beautifully fresh and exquisitely prepared, and it's worth saving room for the melt-in-the-mouth desserts. *Book well in advance.*

Meinl am Graben, 1 Graben 19, **t** 532 33 34 (€€€€–€€€). This relaxed restaurant above the excellent Meinl gourmet supermarket (*see* 'Shopping', p.91) serves some of the best cuisine in the city. You'll find beautifully prepared food using the freshest ingredients accompanied by a fabulous selection of wines. The best tables have cushioned benches set into the

windows, and offer great views of the Graben. *Open till 12am; closed Sun.*

Novelli, 1 Bräunerstrasse 11, **t** 513 42 00, *www.novelli.at* (€€€). This fine Italian restaurant has won numerous awards, including a Michelin star, for its elegant Mediterranean cuisine. The stylish décor and a plant-filled summer terrace have ensured its enduring popularity. At the top end of this price category. *Closed Sun.*

Cantinetta Antinori, 1 Jasormigottstrasse 3–5, **t** 533 77 22, *www.antinori.it* (€€€). One of the chicest Italian restaurants in the city, this serves delicious, ultra-fresh cuisine in a flamboyant red setting lit with chandeliers. Sister restaurant to the Antinori brothers' celebrated Florentine establishment (there are a handful of others scattered around Europe), it serves the excellent range of family-produced Chianti wines.

Do & Co Albertina, 1 Albertinaplatz 1, **t** 532 96 69, *www.doco.com* (€€€). The indefatigable team behind Do & Co are also responsible for the elegant Viennese and fusion cuisine at this designer restaurant in the beautifully restored Albertina (*see* p.65).

Kiang, 1 Rotgasse 8, **t** 533 08 56, *www.kiang.at* (€€). One of the pioneers of Asian fusion cuisine in Vienna, Kiang has been serving up spicy delights in a dramatically modern setting for two decades. There are now three Kiang restaurants around town, plus a takeaway service. *Open daily.*

Palmenhaus, 1 Burggarten, **t** 533 10 33, *www.palmenhaus.at* (€€). This glorious Jugendstil palmhouse has been spectacularly converted into a bar-cum-brasserie, where you can dine amid the foliage on Mediterranean fare accompanied by an excellent selection of wines. In summer, there's an outdoor barbecue and the celebrated terrace is packed all year round. Unfortunately, prices reflect the setting rather than the quality of the food.

Wiebels Wirtshaus, 1 Kumpfgasse 2, **t** 512 39 86, *www.wiebel.at* (€€). This old-fashioned Viennese eaterie serves some of the best traditional dishes in the city, including delicious game in season. The wine list features the finest Austrian wines, and the service is impeccable. There's a summer terrace. Booking advised. *Closed Sun.*

Yohm, 1 Petersplatz 1, **t** 533 29 00, *www.yohm.at* (€€). A trendy Asian restaurant popular with Vienna's fashionable youth, Yohm serves fabulous, delicately spiced fusion cuisine in a vibrant setting. Huge picture windows overlook the elegant Baroque Peterskirche.

Zum Schwarzen Kameel, 1 Bogner-gasse 5, **t** 533 81 25, *www.kameel.at* (€€). A stunningly beautiful Jugendstil restaurant, 'The Black Camel' dining room is formal and elegant, serving spectacularly good Austrian fare. There's also a pavement terrace. *Closed Sun.*

Zum Finsteren Stern 2, 1 Sterngasse 2, **t** 535 81 52 (€€). In the cool, cream-painted, vaulted cellar of the 16th-century Palais Collato, you'll find a imaginative Viennese and European cuisine, prepared according to what's in season. Book early for a table on the cobbled passage, perfect for a romantic summer meal. *Closed Mon–Sat lunch and all day Sun.*

⭐ **Österreicher im MAK** >>

Wrenkh, 1 Bauernmarkt 10, **t** 533 15 26, *www.wrenkh.at* (€€–€). Christian Wrenkh's flagship restaurant is glassy and modern, and the (mostly) vegetarian cuisine is inspired and generally delicious. Some organic meat and fish dishes have been added to the once strictly veggie menu.

Bodega Marqués, 1 Parisergasse 1, **t** 533 91 70, *www.bodegamarques.at* (€). This cool, vaulted cellar tapas bar offers a delicious range of Spanish tapas made with fresh and authentic ingredients, accompanied by an excellent – and lengthy – wine list. Unsurprisingly, it's always packed. *Closed Sun.*

⭐ **Holy Moly** >>

Fino, 1 Tuchlauben 7, **t** 535 28 88, *www.fino.at* (€). A super-stylish wine bar, serving a range of delicious morsels to accompany the huge wine list, which showcases the best of Austrian wines. They do a good fixed price lunch menu for around €10 and there's a popular terrace. Perfect after you've been shopping around the Graben. *Closed Sun.*

Hoher Markt sausage stand, 1 Hoher Markt, no tel (€). There are dozens of *Würstelstanden* all around the city, but this one is a classic with the post-bar crowd thanks to its central location and late (or should that be early...) opening hours. *Open daily 7am–4am.*

Kern-Beisl, 1 Kleeblattgasse 4, **t** 533 91 88, *www.kern-beisl.at* (€). This delightful, crowded and atmospheric *Beisl* serves up draught beers and sturdy Austrian dishes to a mixed group of budget-minded locals, business people and students. Cash only. *Closed Sat and Sun.*

Around the Ringstrasse

Steirereck, Meierei im Stadtpark, **t** 713 31 68, *www.steirereck.at* (€€€€). One of the most lauded restaurants in Vienna, this is beautifully set in the Stadtpark. The menu reinvents classic Austrian dishes with spectacular success, and they are presented with aplomb by the theatrical staff. The outstanding food is accompanied by an equally stellar wine list. It also offers a more affordable lunchtime menu. *Closed Sat and Sun.*

Österreicher im MAK, 1 Stubenring 3–5, **t** 714 01 21, *www.oesterreicher immak.at*. The stunning contemporary restaurant at the Museum of Applied Arts (MAK, *see* pp.80–81) is one of the best in the city, with outstanding modern Austrian cuisine accompanied by fine wines. It's also a good place to drop in for a glass of wine accompanied by some tapas-style snacks. *Open till 2am; closed Mon.*

Holy Moly, Danube canal between Urania and Schwedenplatz, **t** 699 151 307 50 (mobile), *www.badeschiff.at* (€€). Viennese super-chef Christian Petz, formerly of the Palais Coburg, is behind this enticing dining option which is set in a boat on the Danube canal. With its slick white-painted interior and unusual menu of seafood alongside Petz's signature offal dishes, this has become a favourite with style mavens and gourmets alike. After hours, the action continues below deck in the trendy club. *Book ahead.*

Indochine 21, 1 Stubenring 18, **t** 513 76 60, *www.indochine.at* (€€€). Lazy paddle fans, potted palms and dazzling yellow walls provide a sleek backdrop for the delicious French-Vietnamese cuisine at this fashionable restaurant. The adjoining bar is a good place for a cocktail, too.

Gasthaus Wild, 3 Radetzkyplatz 1, **t** 920 94 77 (€€). One of the best of the new breed of neo-*Beisln* which have sprung up in Vienna over the past few years, the Wild serves authentic Austrian recipes prepared with the finest local ingredients. *Restaurant closed Mon.*

Xpedit Kiosk, 4 Schleifmühlgasse 7 , **t** 585 4077, *www.xpedit.net* (€). Vienna's sausage stands are a city institution, but this indoor kiosk takes the classic banger-in-a-bun and turns it into designer fare. With unusual sausages, a range of breads, and exotic flavours (the Thai version and the currywurst are standouts) this has become a mecca for local hipsters with discerning palates. It's open until 3.30am on Fri and Sat. *Closed Sun.*

Further Afield

Steirer Stub'n, 5 Wiedner Hauptstrasse 111, **t** 544 43 49, *www.steirerstubn.at* (€€€). A firm favourite with Viennese gourmets, you'll find delicious Austrian cuisine at this traditional restaurant, where classic recipes are not tampered with but prepared with ultra-fresh seasonal ingredients. Austrian wines are available by the glass, and the service is impeccable.

(★) Skopik & Lohn >

Skopik & Lohn, 2 Leopoldsgasse 1, **t** 219 89 77, *www.skopikundlohn.at* (€€€–€€). A chic designer take on the traditional Viennese *beisl*, this features graffiti-style black swirls on the creamy vaulted ceilings and a seasonally based menu of contemporary French and Austrian dishes. Simple but excellent, the cuisine is prepared with the best local produce. The restaurant is always buzzy, and attracts a glamorous crowd of actors, musicians and writers. *Closed lunch Mon–Sat, and all day Sun.*

Grünspan Biergaststätte,Ottakringer Strasse 266, **t** 480 57 30, *www. gruenspan.at* (€€). A big, friendly beer garden, great if you're travelling with kids, this serves local specialities best

sampled with jugs of their own brewed beers.

Stadtwirt, 3 Untere Viaduktgasse, **t** 713 38 28, *www.stadtwirt.at* (€€). Great Austrian food, prepared without fuss and served up in hearty portions. Fancier recipes have crept on to the menu, but you are best off sticking to the Viennese staples. Big, bustling and unpretentious, it's usually packed out. Reserve in advance.

Zu ebener Erde und erster Stock, 7 Burggasse 13, **t** 523 62 54, *www. zu-ebener-erde-und-erster-stock.at* (€€). This traditional pub in a Biedermeier building in the pretty Spittelburg quarter has a charming restaurant on the first floor, where you can dine on award-winning Austrian fare under the beams. There's a little summer terrace too. *Closed Sat lunch, Sun and Mon.*

Café Anzengruber, 4 Schleifmühlgasse 19, **t** 587 8297. A legendary *gasthaus*, this opened in the 1940s long before the neighbourhood had gentrified: now it's a stalwart of the arty Freihaus quarter, and a lively spot for artists and gallery owners. The *Wiener Schnitzel* is excellent. *Closed Sun, and lunch on Mon.*

Café Florianihof, 8 Florianigasse 45, **t** 402 48 42, *www.florianihof.at* (€). Light streams in through the huge windows at this appealing café-restaurant. It serves delicious breakfasts as well as a more extensive brasserie-style menu, and you can linger over newspapers.

Das Möbel, 7 Burggasse 10, **t** 924 38 34, *www.dasmoebel.at* (€). This bright funky café does reasonable breakfasts, cakes and snacks – and if you like the décor you can buy it, as the café functions as a gallery for young furniture designers. It's also a good place to come for a drink in the evenings. Brunch is served too.

Ra'mien, 6 Gumpendorfer Strasse 9, **t** 585 47 98, *www.ramien.at* (€). With fabulous, perfectly spiced Asian food upstairs and DJs and cocktails in the cool-but-kitsch bar downstairs, it's easy to see why Ra'mien is one of the hottest restaurants in town. Prices go up a category in the evenings. *Open*

Tues–Sun 11am–12am, bar open till 2am, until 4am Thurs–Sat; closed Mon.

Tunnel, 8 Florianigasse 39, **t** 947 57 20, *www.tunnel-vienna-live.at* (€). A big student favourite, the Tunnel is a spacious, wood-panelled pub with simple dishes – pizza, pasta, couscous, all in big portions – along with good breakfasts on the menu. There's often live music in the evenings.

Ubl, 4 Pressgasse 26, **t** 587 64 37 (€). A classic Viennese Beisl, with authentic 1920s décor and wood panelling, the Ubl offers tasty Austrian dishes, including stews and Schnitzel, at very reasonable prices. *No credit cards.*

Heurigen

The wine-growing areas which ring Vienna are famous for their *Heurigen*, traditional taverns selling local wines. According to custom, *Heurigen* serve the new vintage, or *Heuriger*, wines (after a year, they become *Alte* wines) from their own wineries, usually accompanied by a buffet of hot and cold snacks. Some traditions, such as the custom of hanging a pine branch over the door, survive, but many *Heurigen* have developed over the years to become much slicker establishments, open year-round and geared towards tourists. It's worth seeking out the surviving old-style places which can't accommodate large tour groups, and enjoy the beautiful views from their outdoor terraces in peace. Always call in advance to check opening times, or contact the tourist information office for a full list.

Heuriger Göbel, 21 Stammersdorfer Kellergasse 151, **t** 294 84 20. This elegant, glassy *Heuriger* was designed by architect Hans-Peter Göbel, whose wines are among the best produced in Vienna.

Hirt, 19 Eiserhandgasse 16, **t** 318 96 41. A delightful rustic little *Heuriger* which serves simple snacks on two panoramic terraces.

Reinprecht, 19 Cobenzlgasse 22, **t** 320 14 710, *www.weingut-reinprecht.at*. One of the largest of the *Heurigen* in Grinzing, the Reinprecht is set in a handsome former monastery. It's enormously popular with tourist

★ **Weingut Am Reisenberg >>**

groups, but the menu is more substantial than most.

Sirbu, 19 Kahlenberger Strasse 210, **t** 320 59 28. This traditional spot offers fabulous views from its wooden terrace overlooking the vines, along with all the popular *Heuriger* snacks at the buffet.

Wiengut Heuriger Wieninger, 21 Stammersdorfer Strasse 78, **t** 292 41 06, *www.heuriger-wieninger.at*. Franz Wieninger produces some of the top Viennese wines, available to taste along with a delicious selection of traditional dishes.

Weingut Am Reisenberg, Oberer Reisenbergweg 15, **t** 320 9393, *www.weingutamreisenberg.at*. This Grinzing *Heuriger* stands out for its setting on a hilltop with exceptional views across the entire city below. The traditional Austrian fare is served out on the summer terrace.

Cafés and Coffee Houses in Vienna

Innere Stadt

Aida, 1 Stock-im-Eisen-Platz 2, **t** 512 29 77, *www.aida.at*. The much-loved chain of Aida café-*pâtisseries* are famous for its sublimely kitsch 1950s styling and low prices. The coffee is by no means the best in town, but the cakes are good and the people-watching – Aida attracts all kinds – is fabulous. Look out for the trademark hot pink neon sign on other branches throughout the city. The first floor of this branch has great views.

Café Alt Wien, 1 Bäckerstrasse 9, **t** 512 52 22. This dimly lit café is almost completely papered over with posters, and is best in winter, when it feels cosy rather than gloomy. Better for evening drinks than coffee, when curious characters provide plenty of entertaining people-watching opportunities. *Open Mon–Thurs 10am–2am, Fri–Sat 10am–4am; closed Sun.*

Café Bräunerhof, 1 Stallburggasse 2, **t** 512 38 93. One of the loveliest, if least flamboyant, and most authentic of Vienna's coffee houses, the Bräunerhof has faded Jugendstil décor, time-mellowed walls and wood-panelled seating areas. Linger over the coffee and delicious cakes, or tuck into old-fashioned Viennese specialities for lunch. On Saturday afternoons, a string trio provide the background music. *Open Mon–Fri 8am–9pm, Sat 8am–7pm; closed Sun.*

Café Central, 1 Herrengasse 1, **t** 533 37 64 26. Inextricably linked with giants of the literary and artistic world at the turn of the 20th century, the Café Central reopened its doors in 1986. Some of its original fittings have been preserved intact, but it's largely the preserve of tourists nowadays. *Open Mon–Sat 8am–10pm, Sun 10am–6pm.*

Café de l'Europe, 1 Graben 31, **t** 532 14 69. This café has suffered unsympathetic remodelling in recent years, but it remains a classic on the chic Graben. The upstairs tea room has wonderful views. *Open till 12am.*

Café Frauenhuber, 1 Himmelpfortgasse 6, **t** 512 83 83. This is the oldest continually operating café in Vienna, with an opulent interior of plush red banquettes and crystal chandeliers. Nowadays it's popular with shoppers and tourists alike and is always full. *Open daily 8am–11pm.*

Café Griensteidl, 1 Michaelerplatz 2, **t** 535 26 92. The original Griensteidl café was a legendary meeting place for writers, architects and artists at the end of the 19th century, but it was demolished in 1897. This new version was opened in 1990, and has a perfect people-watching terrace on the vast Michaelerplatz. Perhaps inevitably, given its location at the meeting point of the chic Kohlmarkt shopping street and the Hofburg palace, it's always packed with tourists.

Café Hawelka, 1 Dorotheergasse 6, **t** 512 82 30, *www.hawelka.at*. This famous, old-fashioned coffee house was long renowned as a meeting place for intellectuals and artists. Nowadays, the arty crowd have moved on, but the Hawelka remains a much-loved institution. Sadly, Josefine Hawelka died in early 2005, but venerable Leopold still greets guests from his seat near the door. *Closed Sun lunch and Tues.*

Café Kleines, 1 Franziskerplatz 3. This sweet, old-fashioned coffee house is tucked away on a pretty square where tables are laid out in summer. Simple, charming and as tiny as the name suggests, it attracts a laid-back crowd of thespians and artists. Good for lunch, drinks and lazy afternoons.

Café de Provinz, 8 Maria-Treu-Gasse 3, **t** 944 22 72, *www.cafederprovinz.at*. A relaxed, arty hangout with ochre-painted walls and wooden furnishings, this charming Provençal-style crêperie and café is famous for brunch. Organic ingredients are used wherever possible. Free WiFi.

Café Sacher, 1 Philharmonikerstrasse 4, **t** 514 560, *www.sacher.com*. A bastion of tradition and place of sweet temptation, elegant origin of Sacher-Torte. Try the chocolate Sacher liqueur with a hint of apricot.

Demel, 1 Kohlmarkt 14, **t** 535 171, *www.demel.at*. Demel and the Hotel Sacher claim to be the only establishments with the authentic recipe for *Sacher-Torte*. You can do a taste test here – although you will be tempted by the whole fabulous array of exquisite *pâtisserie* on offer. This is perhaps the grandest Konditorei in the city, with prices to match. *Open daily 10am–7pm.*

Segafredo, 1 Graben 29, **t** 533 50 25. This sleek red and black café is still the place to see and be seen, with Vienna's most self-consciously beautiful people posing on the terrace. One of the best cups of coffee in town.

Triolaa, 1 Bognergasse 4, **t** 533 84 90, *www.triolaawien.at*. This popular café-restaurant offers cool minimalist design to go with the good coffee, and delicious Italian-influenced food. *Closed Sun.*

Around the Ringstrasse

Café Landtmann, 1 Dr Karl-Lueger-Ring 4, **t** 241 000, *www.cafe-wien.at*. Once a favourite haunt of Sigmund Freud, the Landtmann remains one of Vienna's foremost classic coffee houses, with a grand interior, and formal service. It's popular with politicians from the nearby Rathaus, along with actors from the Burgtheater, who add to the feel of a smart gentleman's club. *Open daily 8am–12am.*

⭐ Café Kleines >

Café Phil, 6 Gumpendorferstrasse 10–12, **t** 581 04 89, *www.phil.info*. A contemporary bookshop and café near the MuseumsQuartier, this attracts local hipsters for its cool soundtrack, free WiFi, and laid-back atmosphere.

Café Prückel, 1 Stubenring 24, **t** 512 61 15, *www.prueckel.at*. This huge, light-filled café sits right opposite MAK and is popular with local artists and designers, plus a hardcore crowd of regular bridge players who huddle in a back room. The original turn-of-the-20th-century building has completely overhauled, when the cool, retro 1950s-style banquettes were added. It's the perfect spot to linger with the newspapers after a hard morning's sightseeing.

Halle, 7 Museumsplatz 1, **t** 523 70 01, *www.diehalle.at*. One of the most fashionable café-restaurants in the heart of the MuseumsQuartier, the light, bright, ultra-modern Halle serves good coffee and snacks to a crowd of arty regulars. Posing on the so-called 'Spanish Steps' is *de rigueur*.

Further Afield

Café Sperl, 6 Gumpendorfer Strasse 11, **t** 586 41 58, *www.cafesperl.at*. This giant on the Vienna coffee house scene has appeared in countless films, thanks to its beautifully untouched, if now rather threadbare, original décor. A visit is still a theatrical experience, with its plush velvet booths and tuxedoed waiters.

Café Westend, 7 Mariahilfer Strasse 128, **t** 523 31 83. This old-fashioned coffee house, complete with marble-topped tables and enormous chandeliers, is perfect for a break from shopping along Mariahilfer Strasse, or if you have time to kill at the Westbahnhof train station.

High Tea, 4 Paniglgasse 17, **t** 504 15 08, *www.hightea.at*. A relaxed, laid-back mixture of shop, tea room and café, this is furnished with a mixture of flea-market finds and cool modern details. There's a wide range of teas to choose from, plus excellent light meals and snacks. *Closed Sat eve and Sun.*

Entertainment in Vienna

The weekly *Falter* magazine (in German) has the most comprehensive listings section and is available at news stands throughout the city. The monthly *Wien Magazin*, available free from the tourist office, has listings for theatre, opera and cinema with some information in English. The tourist office and many hotels (particularly at the top end of the scale) have ticketing services, but it's usually best to buy directly from the box offices and avoid hefty commissions. **Austria Ticket Online**, *www.ticketonline.at*, **t** 188 088, sells tickets for major theatres and opera houses, plus the biggest pop and rock concerts and sports events. Tickets for the major theatres and opera houses usually go on sale one month before the date of performance and are available through the **Österreichischer Bundestheaterkassen**, 1 Hanuschgasse 3, **t** 514 44 7880, or online at *www.burgtheater.at*. The **Wien-Ticket Pavilion**, next to the Staatsoper (*open daily 10am–7pm*), has tickets for all venues and its commission rates are reasonable compared to many of the ludicrously priced agencies around the city.

Theatre and Dance

Burgtheater (National Theatre), 1 Dr Karl-Lueger-Ring 2, **t** (01) 514 44 4140, *www.burgtheater.at*. This magnificent 19th-century theatre (*see* p.68) is Austria's most prestigious, with an internationally recognized ensemble of actors. The Burgtheater also manages the **Akademietheater**, 3 Lisztstrasse 1, *www.burgtheater.at*, which is a more intimate space for classical theatre.

English Theatre, 8 Josefsgasse 12, **t** (01) 402 12 600, *www.englishtheatre.at*. Established in the 1960s; its performances regularly feature famous actors and directors.

Josefstadt Theater, 6 Josefstädter Strasse 26, **t** (01) 42700, *www.josefstadt.org*. This delightful theatre in the Josefstadt district was established in 1788, and Beethoven composed and conducted his overture *The Consecration of the House* for its reopening in 1822 after major renovation. It currently hosts traditional performances of drama, comedies and occasional musicals. The Josefstadt also manages the **Kammerspiele**, 1 Rotenturmstrasse 20, a smaller space which offers a similar programme.

International Theatre, 9 Porzellangasse 8, **t** (01) 319 62 72, *www.international theatre.at*. Another English-language theatre.

Kabarett Simpl, 1 Wollzeile 36, **t** (01) 512 47 42, *www.simpl.at*. Fluent German-speakers will enjoy the satirical Kabaretts, a long Viennese tradition.

Tanzquartier Wien, **t** (01) 581 35 91, *www. tqw.at*. Vienna's biggest dance-space, with studios and performance halls, offers excellent contemporary dance. It's located in the Museums-Quartier complex (*see* p.76).

Volkstheater, 7 Neustiftgasse 1, **t** (01) 52111 *www.volkstheater.at*. Another grand institution in Vienna, this venerable 19th-century theatre performs classical drama.

Opera, Ballet and Classical Music

Konzerthaus, Lothringerstrasse 20, **t** (01) 242 002, *www.konzerthaus.at*. An extravagant Ringstrasse building, the Konzerthaus offers a programme which isn't afraid to stray from purely classical music (although this features prominently), and has a newer hall largely dedicated to contemporary music. It hosts, or co-hosts, several prestigious music festivals, including the *Frühlingsfestival* (classical music) and *Wien Modern*, Vienna's best festival of modern music.

Musikverein, Karlsplatz 6, **t** (01) 505 81 90, *www.musikverein.at*. Another flamboyant Ringstrasse edifice, the Musikverein is the setting for the annual New Year's Day concerts performed by the Vienna Phil-harmonic. Resolutely traditional, it is famous for its amazing acoustics.

Staatsoper, 1 Opernring 2, **t** (01) 514 442 250, *www.wiener-staatsoper.at*. Vienna's legendary opera house (*see* p.73) provides an opulent setting for some of the finest opera perform-ances in the world. It's also the home of the Staatsoper Ballet.

Wiener Volksoper, 9 Währinger Strasse 78, **t** (01) 514 443 670, *www.volksoper.at*. Traditionally, the Volksoper hosted performances of light opera, but this is now fleshed out with opera and ballet. It's easier to get tickets for the Volksoper than for the Staatsoper, even though many of the singers perform at both.

Wiener Kammeroper, 1 Fleischmarkt 24, **t** (01) 512 01 00-77, *www.wiener kammeroper.at*. A Jugendstil gem is the permanent home of this opera company, which has performances on a smaller scale and includes many less well-known operas in its repertoire.

Cinemas

Burg, 1 Opernring 19, **t** (01) 587 84 06, *www. burgkino.at*. This cinema shows a combination of Hollywood blockbusters and cult classics (in the original language with subtitles), and famously screens *The Third Man* (in English) most Friday and Saturday nights (check times in *Falter*).

English Cinema Haydn, 6 Mariahilfer Strasse, **t** (01) 587 22 62, *www.haydnkino. at*. All the latest English-language blockbusters.

Österreiches Filmmuseum, 1 Augustinerstrasse 1, **t** (01) 533 70 54, *www.filmmuseum.at*. Housed in the Albertina, this shows classic and cult screenings, and hosts retrospectives and film festivals. Films are always in the original language.

Votiv Kino, 9 Währinger Strasse 12, **t** (01) 317 35 71, *www.votivkino.at*. Excellent art house cinema showing films in their original language, and with a great Sunday morning film-plus-breakfast deal. They also do film screenings for kids and for babies.

Viennese Balls

The city hosts between two and three hundred balls a year, including the Vienna State Opera Ball and the Imperial Ball at the Hofburg. Most are held between December and February, although some, like the (very fashionable) Life Ball take place in March. The tourist office can provide a full list.

Nightlife in Vienna

Innere Stadt

American Bar, 1 Kärntnerstrasse 10, **t** 512 32 83. Adolf Loos designed this sleek modernist bar in 1908, and it still serves impeccable, if pricey, cocktails. *Open daily 12pm–4am.*

Flex, 1 Donaukanal/Augartenbrücke, **t** 533 75 25, *www.flex.at*. A popular club, with resident and guest DJs from around the world spinning the latest dance and electronic music. Good food and cocktails available at the adjoining Flex Café. *Open from 11pm, restaurant from 8pm.*

Krah Krah, 1 Rabensteig 8, **t** 533 81 93, *www.krah-krah.at*. Big, noisy Krah Krah remains enduringly popular, not least for its huge variety of beers (around 50). It also serves food. *Open Mon–Sat 11am–2am, Sun and hols 11am–1am.*

Oswald & Kalb, Bäckerstrasse 14, **t** 512 13 71. A sleek vaulted bar (and restaurant), where the wines are good and the clientele relaxed and well-heeled. *Open daily 6pm–2am.*

Vis à Vis, Wollzeile 5, **t** 512 93 50, *www.weibel.at*. This tiny bar is a great place to try a wide range of Austrian wines, perfectly accompanied by delicious little snacks. *Open daily 3pm–10.30pm.*

Zwölf-Apostelkeller, Sonnenfelsgasse 3, **t** 512 67 77. An old-fashioned brick cellar, with wooden tables, sturdy wines and traditional grub, this is a raucous but fun student hangout. *Open daily 11am–12am.*

Around the Ringstrasse

Aux Gazelles, 6 Rahlgasse 5, **t** 585 66 45. A sumptuous North African-themed restaurant-bar-club with hammam, where you can slurp some oysters at the oyster bar, and chill out in the beautiful cocktail bar and lounge, where DJs provide a soothing ethno-beat soundtrack. *Open Mon–Thurs 10am–2am, Fri–Sat 10am–4am, Sun 10am–9pm.*

Café Kunsthalle am Karlsplatz, Karlsplatz, **t** 587 00 73. A glassy pavilion on Karlsplatz with a huge terrace, this is one of Vienna's newest hot spots. Lounge on bean bags or sofas, and enojoy light meals during the day or cocktails with DJ sounds at night. *Open daily 10am–2am.*

Club–U, 1 Otto Wagner Pavilion, Karlsplatz, **t** 505 99 04. The location is the draw here – underneath one of Otto Wagner's twin frothy U-Bahn station pavilions (*see* p.74). It's a café by day (*9am–7pm*). *Open nightly from 10pm.*

Volksgarten, Volksgarten/Burgring, **t** 532 0907, *www.volksgarten-pavillon.at*. A restaurant by day and a club by night, this has a huge dance floor which opens up on summer nights. *Club open Wed–Sat from 11pm.*

Further Afield

Auslage, 6 Lerchenfeldergürtel 43, *www.auslage.co.at*. This minimalist bar and club is low-lit and loud, with resident and international DJs.

B72, 8 Hernalser Gürtel, Bogen 72, **t** 409 21 28, *www.b72.at*. Open nightly from 9pm. A great two-storey music bar in one of the vaulted arches under the U6 underground line, with excellent DJs and regular live music events.

Elektro Gönner, 6 Mariahilfer Strasse 101, **t** 208 66 79, *www.elektro-g.at*. A former electrician's shop has been strikingly modelled by architects to become one of Vienna's coolest hang-outs. As well as regular DJ sessions, there are film screenings and other events. (It's just off the courtyard at No.101.)

Mon Ami, 6 Theobaldgasse 9, *http://monami.at*. A very spacious, effortlessly cool café-bar serving light meals and drinks with a fashion store at the back.

Pratersauna, 2 Waldsteingartenstrasse 135, *www.pratersauna.tv*. A massive club complex with a summer pool in the Prater, this is the city's biggest venue.

Titanic Bar, 6 Theobaldgasse 11, **t** 587 47 58, *www.titanic.at*. Tucked behind the MuseumsQuartier complex, the Titanic Bar is a good spot for a cocktail, and you can head downstairs to the club afterwards. *Open Tues–Thurs 7pm–2am, Fri–Sat 7pm–4am.*

Day Trips from Vienna

It doesn't take long to escape the hubbub in Vienna: the glorious expanse of the Vienna Woods creeps up to the fringes of the city, sprinkled with wine villages and perfect for hiking and picnicking.

To the north, the Danube meanders through some of the most exquisite countryside in Austria, guarded by ancient castles and monasteries, and a paradise for gourmets and cyclists. The flat lands of Burgenland to the southwest offer more wine, a curious inland sea, and whitewashed Hungarian-style villages topped with untidy storks' nests. One of Europe's most panoramic railways clunks up to the extraordinary peaks of the Semmering range, where the Viennese come for summer hiking or winter sports.

Austria's efficient train system will whisk you in style to most destinations mentioned below, but a car is useful for exploring.

The Vienna Woods (Wienerwald)

Vienna is blessed with the leafy Wienerwald right on its doorstep, a gently undulating region of forests and hills which almost completely encircles the city and extends for more than 400 square miles. Much of it is protected forest, criss-crossed with excellent walking and cycling trails, but it's also peppered with elegant spa towns and unassuming wine villages full of excellent *Heurigen*.

Mödling

Mödling, 15km from Vienna, has a tiny but appealing old quarter, with 16th- and 17th-century houses clustered around cobbled squares, and a miniature Rathaus with a graceful loggia. Beethoven spent the summer of 1819 in Mödling, and rented rooms at the Hafernhaus, Hauptstrasse 79, which have been converted into a **museum**. He hoped to return the following summer, but was refused accommodation on account of his unpredictable and eccentric behaviour.

If sightseeing begins to pall, you can take a dip in the town's Jugendstil swimming pool, the **Stadtbad**, or head for the numerous **walking trails** which penetrate the forest from here. On the western fringe of the town, the **Seegrotte Hinterbrühl** is a former gypsum mine, which was flooded in 1912, and then drained and used by the Nazis to build jets during the Second World War. Tours (*in several languages*) culminate with a fun underground boat ride.

Beethoven Museum
t (02236) 26727; open Tues–Sun 9–12

Seegrotte Hinterbrühl
t (02235) 26364; www.seegrotte.at; open April–Oct daily 9–5; Nov–Mar Mon–Fri 9–12 and 1–3, Sat–Sun and hols 9–3.30; adm

Mayerling

West of Mödling, the unassuming hamlet of Mayerling is set in one of the most beautiful valleys in the Vienna Woods, with craggy

Getting to the Vienna Woods

There are frequent **trains** (every half-hour) to Mödling, Baden and Gumpoldskirchen from Vienna Südbahnhof. An infrequent bus service links Baden with Mayerling but, to explore the woods properly, it is best to have your own transport.

You can download **cycling** maps showing the enormous network of cycling trails from *www.mtbwiener wald.at* (German only), and the tourist office has maps and information on walking trails.

hills, swift-flowing rivers and dense forests. The village has become inextricably linked with the tragic suicide of Prince Rupert in 1889. The Imperial hunting lodge in which Rupert and his 17-year-old lover Maria Vetsera shot themselves was subsequently demolished by Emperor Franz Josef. A Carmelite **convent** was erected in its place, which now contains a few sticks of furniture and photographs of the tragic pair.

Maria Vetsera was buried at **Stift Heiligenkreuz**, a beautiful Cistercian abbey lost in a peaceful expanse of woods a few miles from Meyerling. The original abbey was built during the Middle Ages as a burial chapel for the Babenburg dukes, and, although it was substantially rebuilt after Turkish attacks in the 1690s, it still contains some lovely Romanesque and Gothic elements, particularly in the church, which was begun in 1135. The adjoining chapter house contains the oldest ducal tomb. Come for Mass if you can, movingly sung by the community of monks.

Baden

Southwest of Mayerling, the delightful spa town of Baden still oozes a slightly battered turn-of-the-20th-century charm. The Romans discovered the curative effects of its natural springs, and the town reached the height of its fame in the 19th century when celebrated artists, musicians and even the Imperial family would summer here and take the waters. The old centre is a higgledy-piggledy maze of 16th- and 17th-century mansions spiralling out from the Hauptplatz, which is dominated by a florid Baroque plague column. The **Kurpark**, a formal garden which merges into the surrounding forest, is a delightful place for a stroll or a picnic. You can still take the waters at one of the numerous **spas** (the

Mystery at Mayerling

No one knows why the prince and his lover chose to kill themselves in the early hours of 29 January 1889. Romantics insist it was for love, but Rupert was a notorious womanizer, and Maria Vetsera was merely the latest in a long line of pretty young mistresses. Some have suggested that he was frustrated with his lack of a real political role at court, and others that he had contracted a venereal disease which he believed to be fatal. Empress Zita was one of many who suspected he had been assassinated by political enemies. The real reason behind the suicide pact was buried with the prince, who was entombed with full Habsburg pomp and ceremony in the Kaisergruft (*see* p.55), despite his wish to be buried simply next to his mistress.

(i) **Baden** >>
Brusattiplatz 3, t (02252) 22600-600, www.baden. at; open summer Mon–Sat 9–5, Sun 10–12; winter Mon–Fri 9–5

(i) **Mödling** >
Pfarrgasse 2, t (02236) 400, www.moedling.at; open Mon–Fri 8–12, Sat 8–12 and 4–6

(i) **Gumpolds-kirchen** >>
Schrannenplatz 1, t (02252) 62101, www.gumpolds kirchen.at

(i) **Heiligenkreuz**
Heiligenkreuz 15, t (02258) 8720, www.heiligenkreuz.at; open Mon, Wed, Fri 8–12, Tues 8–12 and 4–6

Eating Out in the Vienna Woods

Mödling

Babenbergerhof, Babenbergergasse 6, t (02236) 22246, *www.baben bergerhof.com* (€€). Smart hotel-restaurant in the heart of Mödling.

Meyerling

Hanner, Hauptstrasse 54, t (02258) 23 78, *www.hanner.cc* (€€€). A spectacular restaurant in a luxury hotel (which also has an inexpensive restaurant).

Baden

Villa Nova, Helenenstrasse 19, t (02252) 209745 (€€). Thai, Mediterranean and Austrian dishes are on offer at this popular eaterie.

Gumpoldskirchen

Heuriger Bruckberger, Wienerstrasse, t (02252) 62230 (€). One of several traditional *Heurigen* clustered along Wienerstrasse and Neustiftsgasse.

tourist office provides a leaflet listing them all), or explore some of the numerous *Heurigen* in the area.

Gumpoldskirchen

With its redolent fairytale name, this is the most celebrated wine village in these parts. The town erupts twice a year with a fabulous **wine festival** (in June and August), and the countless excellent *Heurigen* produce the world-famous Gumpoldskirchner wines. Local tourist offices have an annual guide (*free*) listing all the best *Heurigen* throughout this region (*see also* 'Eating Out').

Up the Danube

The slow-moving river meanders gently through the verdant Danube Valley, past medieval villages, orchard-covered hills which blaze with blossom in spring, and snaking vines. The massive fortresses and monasteries which glower from the hills attest to the valley's strategic location at the crossroads of East and West, a reminder of hotly contested territorial battles that once ravaged the now-idyllic countryside.

The most beautiful section of the Danube Valley is the **Wachau**, the stretch of river which winds between Krem and Melks, a paradise for gourmets thanks to its abundance of excellent restaurants and vineyards, and for cyclists, who potter along the gentle riverside cycling paths. The area's stunning natural beauty and historical importance were recognized in 2000, when the Wachau was granted World Heritage Site status by UNESCO.

Tulln

Heading northwest from Vienna, the first major town is Tulln (about 30km from Vienna), which likes to call itself 'the Cradle of Austria'. The Romans established a garrison town here (a magnificent Roman watchtower survives), and it was effectively Austria's first capital under the Babenburgs. But Tulln was quickly

Getting to the Danube Valley

Tulln (25mins) and Krems (one hour) are served by suburban **trains** (S-Bahn) from Franz-Josefs Bahnhof. Trains for Melk (75 mins) depart from Vienna's Westbahnhof station, but there is also a single-line railway connecting Krems and Melk, which is slow but picturesque. There is also a tourist service, the Imperial Train, which leaves for Dürnstein on Thurs at 10.50am and returns at 5.50pm (costs €176); see www.imperialtrain.com for full details.

The Wachau is a popular destination for excursion companies, who run **bus or boat tours** of the region. There are countless **river cruises** along the Danube with stops at all the main towns and villages.

Egon-Schiele Museum
Donaulände 28, t (02272) 64570, http://egonschiele. museum.com; open Mar–Nov Tues–Sun 10–12 and 1–5; adm

eclipsed by Vienna, and is now a sleepy provincial town scattered with ancient churches including the magnificent **Minoritenkirche**. This has been lovingly restored, and the adjacent buildings contain a quirky museum with an eccentric collection of archaeological artefacts and historic fire engines. Nowadays, Tulln is best known as the birthplace of Egon Schiele, Austria's original *enfant terrible*, who was born above the train station (his father was station master) in 1890. The **Egon-Schiele Museum** dedicated to his life and work is located in the prison where he was briefly incarcerated in 1912 for corrupting minors with erotic drawings.

Krems an der Donau

Fifty kilometres west of Tulln, Krems an der Donau is a picture-postcard town at the start of the Wachau proper, enchantingly set in a sea of vines. Medieval Krems and Renaissance Stein, once separate settlements, have merged over the years, and the cobbled streets are lined with pretty ice-cream-coloured houses and a smattering of ancient mansions, many with elegant stone court-yards. Krems has been producing excellent wines for centuries and there are several wonderful *Heurigen* in the area: the tourist office, located in a former Capuchin monastery, has full details along with a wine museum. From the top of the town, you can see the romantic onion-domed spires of **Stift Göttweig**, an 11th-century abbey which was rebuilt in the 18th century after a devastating fire and has a flamboyant Baroque interior.

Stift Göttweig
t (02732) 85581, www.stiftgoettweig. or.at; open Mar–Nov daily 10–5; adm; visit by guided tour (German only)

Dürnstein and Beyond

About 8km upstream of Krems, medieval Dürnstein is piled winsomely on the river bank, dominated by the stony ruins of a battered castle. Richard the Lionheart was kept prisoner here by the Babenburg Duke Leopold V in the 12th century: according to legend, Lionheart was discovered by his faithful minstrel, Blondel, who searched the countryside looking for his master and finally found him by playing a song known only to the two of them beneath his window. Lionheart was eventually released after the payment of a huge ransom. The castle is now in ruins, although some efforts have been made to restore it recently, but it's worth the climb for the staggering views.

The river continues to wind sinuously past medieval villages like delightful **Weissenkirchen**, with its charming cobbled streets and terraced vineyards, and its larger neighbour **Spitz an der Donau**. Just beyond **Aggstein**, the fairytale castle of **Aggsbachdorf** is perched vertiginously on a rocky outcrop. Legend recounts that the castle's 13th-century owner, Georg Sheck von Wald, would force his enemies to leap to their deaths from the rock at the summit.

Melk

Stift Melk

t (02752) 5550; open Palm Sun–first Sun after All Souls daily 9–5; May–Sept 9–6; guided visits at 11am and 2pm in German only; adm to abbey, church free

The little Renaissance town of Melk huddles in the shadow of the extravagant **Stift Melk**, one of the most sumptuous Baroque monasteries in Austria and a huge tourist attraction. Once the site of a Babenburg fortress, the building was given to the Benedictines in 1089, and became a renowned centre of scholarship during the Middle Ages (described in Umberto Eco's *The Name of the Rose*, which is partly set here). The original monastery was destroyed by the Turks in 1683, but subsequently rebuilt and expanded in flamboyant Baroque style. It still houses a community of monks, who run one of Austria's most prestigious schools.

The highlights of the abbey museum are, frustratingly, only sporadically on view, but include the *Melker Kreuz*, a 14th-century gem-studded reliquary containing a fragment of the True Cross, an exquisite 11th-century portable altar, and a much venerated 13th-century reliquary containing the jawbone of St Kolomain (*see* below). The magnificent library is crammed with leather-covered tomes – there are more than 2,000 volumes from the 9th to the 15th centuries alone. A cloud of *putti* fly pudgily across the ceiling, in Paul Troger's lavish ceiling fresco allegorizing Faith.

The monastery was long a centre of pilgrimage thanks to its numerous relics, none more famous than the body of St Kolomain, an Irish saint with a gift for healing. His body (minus the jawbone, presumably) is hidden from view in the opulent church, topped with a vast dome, and oozing elaborately gilded stuccowork. There are plenty of other gruesome relics on view in the church's side chapels, with everything from glittering receptacles containing nails and hair to full skeletons leering from glass coffins.

(i) **Tulln >**

Minoritenplatz 2, t (02272) 67555, www.tulln.info

(i) **Krems >>**

Undstrasse 6, t (02732) 82676, www.krems.info

(i) **Melk >>**

Babenbergerstrasse, t (02752) 523 07410, www.nieder osterreich.at

Eating Out in the Danube Valley

Tulln

Der Floh, Tullnerstrasse 1, Langenbarn, near Tulln, **t** (02272) 62809, *www.derfloh.at* (€€€–€€). This welcoming, stylish, wood-panelled restaurant and guest house serves delicious gourmet Austrian cuisine from an award-winning young chef.

Krems

Hagmann, Landstrasse 8, **t** (02732) 83167 (€). There are countless fabulous *Heurigen* in the Krems area, or you could stop at this wonderful *Konditorei* for coffee and cakes.

Melk

Stadt Melk, Hauptplatz 1, **t** (02752) 525 47 (€€). Excellent Austrian fare and an extensive wine list.

Getting to the Southern Alps

The most spectacular way to get to Semmering is on the **train** from Vienna Südbahnhof (check train times in advance – there are only one or two direct trains a day, although changes are quick and easy). By **car**, it's an easy journey straight down the S6 motorway from Vienna.

The Southern Alps

Less than 130km from Vienna, the Alps make their last thrust before levelling out into the Hungarian steppes. The dramatic scenery and famously clean air drew wealthy 19th-century excursionists, and a spectacular railway was constructed through the Semmering Pass in 1854. This, along with a delightfully old-fashioned cog-wheel steam engine at Puchberg-am-Schneeberg, are still much-loved by the Viennese, who come to this region in droves to walk in summer, and ski in winter.

Semmering, an elegant mountain town sprinkled with Jugenstil villas, is the largest of the southern Alpine resorts. It sprawls across a hillside overlooking the Semmering Pass, and is liberally strewn with upmarket hotels (including the Imperial family's favourite, the Grand Hotel Panhans) and restaurants. In winter it's a popular skiing centre, with plenty of facilities (travel agents in Vienna sell special packages for a day or a weekend trip). The mountain railway, built in the mid-19th century, has been granted UNESCO World Heritage status, and is one of the most dramatic and beautiful train journeys in Europe, particularly the last section between Payerbach and Semmering. To the north of the resort, the **Höllental** (Valley of Hell) is a staggeringly beautiful, narrow gorge, carved out by the River Schwarza.

Schneeberg, at 2,076m, is the highest mountain range close to Vienna and another hugely popular destination for winter sports. In 1897, a cog-wheel steam engine was completed, which still makes a dramatic ascent up the mountain from **Puchberg-am-Schneeberg** to the small station at Hochschneeberg (with a hotel-restaurant). From here, you can linger over lunch or strike out into the surrounding peaks: the highest, Klosterwappen, is about an hour's hike.

ⓘ **Semmering** >
*Passhöhe 248,
t (02664) 20025,
www.semmering.at*

ⓘ **Puchberg**
*Sticklergasse 3,
t (02636) 2256,
www.tiscover.at/puch
berg-am-schneeberg*

Eating Out in the Southern Alps

Semmering
Restaurant Wintergarten, Hotel Panhans, Hochstrasse 32, **t** (02664) 8181 (€€€). Dine in style in the sumptuous restaurant of the beautiful Jugendstil Hotel Panhans.

Zum Stoasteirer, Zaubergasse 2, **t** (02664) 2498 (€€). This chalet-style restaurant offers excellent Austrian cuisine, which changes with the season, along with a good list of regional wines. There are welcoming staff and fabulous views.

Getting to the Neusiedler See

There are direct **trains** to Neusiedl am See from Vienna Südbahnhof at least every hour, with **bus** links to villages and towns around the lake including Rust and Mörbisch. There is one daily direct train to Eisenstadt from Vienna, but otherwise you will have to change at Neusiedl.

This area is perfect for exploring on two wheels and there are scores of **bicycle rental** outlets in every town and hamlet.

Around the Neusiedler See

The northern tip of Austria's easternmost province, **Burgenland**, is dominated by the vast, reed-fringed lake of the **Neusiedler See**. Thanks to its unusual microclimate, the lake attracts a wealth of bird and animal life and is now a national park. The baking heat of summer has made it a popular excursion for the beach-starved Viennese, who come to sunbathe and swim, while in winter it freezes to become an enormous ice-rink. Close by, Eisenstadt, the charming, tiny capital of Burgenland, retains vestiges of its Hungarian heritage (the region only became part of Austria after the First World War), and delightful Rust, the smallest town in the country, is famous for its wines.

Eisenstadt has long been linked with Haydn, who lived here for much of his life under the patronage of the powerful Hungarian Esterházy family. Their castle still dominates the town, an immense medieval fortress which has undergone numerous facelifts and is now primarily Baroque and neoclassical. The otherwise dull guided tours of the **castle** (still owned by the wealthy Esterházy family), include a visit to the lavishly frescoed Haydnsaal, where the composer once conducted his own works and where concerts still regularly take place. The highlight of the concert cycle is the Haydn Festival (*www.haydnfestival.at*), which takes place every September.

Close by, Eisenstadt's medieval Jewish quarter, the **Unterberg**, remains astonishingly intact, although its small community were sent to the death camps by the Nazis during the Second World War. The history of the Jews in Eisenstadt is recounted in the small **Jüdisches Museum** at Unterbergstrasse 6, which contains one of the only synagogues in the area to have survived the horrors of *Kristallnacht*.

Most of Eisenstadt's other attractions are linked to Haydn, and include his home, the Haydnhaus, on Josef-Haydn-Gasse (only for die-hard fans), and his mausoleum, in the frilly Baroque **Bergkirche**.

Close to the shores of the Neusiedler See, **Rust** is crammed with 16th- and 17th-century houses, many sporting an untidy fringe of storks' nests. Nesting storks bring luck, according to local superstition, but, if they fail to return, an unpleasant surprise is in

ⓘ **Rust >>**
Rathaus, Conrad-
platz 1, **t** *(02685) 502,*
www.rust.at

ⓘ **Eisenstadt >**
Schloss Esterházy,
t *(00800) 26837,*
www.eisenstadt.gv.at

ⓘ **Neusiedl**
am See >>
Obere Haupstrasse 24,
t *(02167) 8600,*
www.neusiedlersee.com

Eating Out in the Neusiedler See

Eisenstadt

Henrici, Schloss Esterházy,
t (02682) 62819 (€€–€). This is a fine restaurant in the castle itself, where you can linger over the papers in the café, or dine substantially on modern Austrian cooking.

Rust

Inamera, Oggauerstrasse 29,
t (02685) 6473, *www.inamera.at* (€€). A stylish whitewashed restaurant serving sophisticated local cuisine.

Neusiedl am See

Am Nyikospark, Landgasthaus,
t (02167) 40222 (€€). An elegant restaurant in the magnificent surroundings of the former Landgasthaus, with creative Austrian cuisine.

store. The reeds from the nearby lake are used in local crafts, including basketwork and thatching, but Rust is best known for its excellent wines (try to make it for Golden Wine week at the end of July).

To the north, brash and unappealing **Neusiedl am See** is the main transport hub of the region, with train and bus connections to Vienna, but it's not worth lingering here. South of Rust, the tiny village of **Mörbisch**, a straggle of brilliantly whitewashed houses with brightly painted doors, sits on the Hungarian border and feels distinctly un-Austrian. At the end of July, the village hosts an excellent operetta festival (more information at *www.seefestspiele-moerbisch.at*), with performances taking place on a floating stage. Close by is the formidable **Burg Forchenstein**, a virtually impregnable medieval fortress owned by Esterházy family, which now contains an enormous weaponry collection.

For swimming and other watersports, head for **Podersdorf am See**, on the eastern edge of the lake, which is the only village right on the water's edge (the other settlements are separated from the lake by reedy marshes).

Czech Republic: Practical A–Z

05

Climate and When to Go

Prague's climate is not extreme. The average temperature hovers at freezing point from December to February, climbing to shirt-sleeves weather in May. July and August are the hottest months, reaching the high 20s°C. The chill of autumn sets in in late September. The driest month is February and the wettest July, when warm showers drop lazily in the late evening.

Millions of tourists visit Prague each year, half of them in August, when the city resembles a theme park. Consider visiting in late June, early July or better still early September; Prague's buskers are still out in force, its gardens and islands are in late bloom, and the city heaves a sigh of relief at having survived the deluge.

Disabled Travellers

The Czech capital has made considerable provision for disabled travellers in recent years. Recorded announcements punctuate all train or tram journeys, and wheelchair-friendly buses are being introduced on several routes. The airport, main train stations and bus station are wheelchair-accessible, as are the following metro stations:

A line: Dejvická, Muzeum, Strašnická, Skalka, Depo Hostivar.

B line: Zličín, Stodůlky, Luka, Lužiny, Hůrka, Nové Butovice, Smíchovské nádraží, Vysočanská, Kolbenova, Hloubětín, Rajská zahrada, Černý most.

C line: All stations except I.P. Pavlova and Pražského povstání.

Further information can be found at branches of the Prague Information Service (*see* p.190), *www.prague-info.cz*.

Electricity

Czech electricity flows at 230v AC, and sockets take the two-pin plug that is standard across continental Europe. Many of the devices that you are most likely to be carrying, such as laptops and battery rechargers, have built-in AC/DC converters, and need only a physical adaptor to work off Czech mains. The same is true of British appliances in general. Other North American electrical goods will need a step-up voltage transformer; they are hard to find in Prague, so you should buy one before setting off on your travels.

Embassies and Consulates

In Prague

Canada: Muchova 6, **t** 272 101 800, *www.canada.cz*.

UK: Thunovská 14, **t** 257 402 111, *www.britain.cz*.

USA: Tržiště 15, **t** 257 022 000, *www.usembassy.cz*.

Czech Embassies Abroad

UK: 26 Kensington Palace Gardens, London W8 4QY, **t** (020) 7243 1115, *www.czechembassy.org.uk*.

USA: 3900 Spring of Freedom Street NW, Washington DC, **t** (202) 274 9100, *www.mzv.cz/washington*.

Health and Emergencies

Insurance

Several Prague clinics refuse to accept foreign health insurance policies, and before taking out travel insurance it is well worth checking that the provider can guarantee treatment at specific Prague clinics or hospitals. The following companies, one UK-based and the second North American, have well-established links with doctors and medical facilities in the city.

AXA PPP Healthcare, t +44 800 028 4188, *www.axappphealthcare.co.uk*.

IntegraGlobal, t 1-888 753 1377 (toll-free) or +49 6221 825 650, *www.integraglobal.com*.

Emergency Numbers

t 112 (pan-European emergency number, for all services)
t 150 (fire brigade)
t 156 (police)
t 155 (ambulance)

Money

An increasing number of establishments accept the euro, but the national currency is still the **Czech crown** (*koruna česká*), which comprises 100 heller (*haléř*). At the time of writing, the rate of exchange is 29kč to one pound sterling, 19kč to the US dollar, and 25kč to the euro. Prices fluctuate, but it's generally safe to assume costs are 10–20% lower than those of major cities at home.

Several smaller shops and restaurants do not accept credit or debit cards, but ATM machines are ubiquitous. Cash advances against cards and travellers' cheques can be obtained at 24-hour exchange offices across the city, or at one of the four main **Czech banks**: Česka spořitelna, Československá obchodní banka (ČSOB), Komerční banka and Živnostenská banka. Opening hours are Mon–Fri 9–5.

National Holidays

1 Jan New Year's Day
Easter Monday
1 May Labour Day
8 May Liberation Day
5 July Introduction of Christianity
6 July Death of Jan Hus
28 Sept Czech Statehood Day
28 Oct Foundation of the Republic
17 Nov Struggle for Freedom and Democracy Day
24 Dec Christmas Eve
25 Dec Christmas Day
26 Dec St Stephen's Day

There are a few other festivals worth noting. June 27 has been designated a day to remember people who were unjustly imprisoned and executed by the pre-1989 Communist regime: flickering candles are ubiquitous, and ceremonies are held at the memorial on the junction of Vitězná ul. and Újezd, over the bridge from the Slavia Café. Praguers traditionally light bonfires to ward off witches on **Walpurgisnacht**, the last night of April, and you should be able to find a blaze on Kampa Island. There are more fearful goings-on between **Hallowe'en** and **All Souls' Day** (2 Nov), when the city's Catholic cemeteries turn into galaxies of candles.

St Nicholas' Eve (5 Dec) is another eventful night: Praguers traditionally dress up as angels, devils, or a crozier-toting St Nick, and give children sweets and coal or drink themselves into a stupor, as the mood takes them.

Post

Correspondence can take anything from five days to two weeks to reach home. There is an **Express Service** that does not cost much and can halve that time. **Stamps** (*známky*) can be bought from tobacconists and card shops, as well as post office counters.

Price Categories

Hotels

A double room with bathroom in high season will cost:

Luxury	€€€€	over 5,000kč
Expensive	€€€	3,500–5,000kč
Moderate	€€	2,000–3,500kč
Inexpensive	€	under 2,000kč

Rates are 20–40% lower between November and March, except at Christmas and New Year. Several hotels also offer reductions during the dog days of July and early August.

Restaurants

A three-course dinner, including a couple of wines or beers, should cost the following:

Luxury	€€€€	over 1,500kč
Expensive	€€€	1,000–1,500kč
Moderate	€€	500–1,000kč
Inexpensive	€	under 500kč

Telephones

Most UK **mobiles** and tri-band American cellphones can be used throughout the Czech Republic, assuming that you've asked your company to activate roaming. Very few of Prague's public phones take cash, but phonecards are available from newsagents, post offices and hotels.

It can work out considerably cheaper to make calls with a Czech SIM card, though you will need an unlocked phone to use it. New cards can be bought in the Vodafone,

O2 or T-Mobile stores at Národní 28, 32 and 35 respectively.

All Czech numbers now have 9 digits and no area code. The **international country code** for the Czech Republic is **t** (00) 420.

Useful numbers: directory enquiries, **t** 120; international directory enquiries, **t** 0149; operator, **t** 0102; international operator, **t** 0131.

International dialling codes from Prague: to Canada, **t** 00 1; to Ireland, **t** 00 353; to the UK, **t** 00 44; to the USA, **t** 00 1.

Time

The Czech Republic is on Central European Time (CET) – one hour ahead of GMT – and operates in synchronization with British Summer Time (BST).

Tipping

Praguers will round up most bills by a few crowns, but there is no hard and fast tipping rule. Ten per cent has become the tourist norm. Tour guides in castles and at monuments outside Prague rely almost entirely on tips, so be sure to do the right thing.

Toilets

There are toilets in every metro station, and in strategic locations across town. If you're desperate, it is acceptable to rush into the nearest café or bar and ask for the *záchod*, a.k.a. WC (pronounced *ve tse*).

'Men' is *muži*; 'women' is *ženy*.

Tourist Information

The national tourist authority maintains a website at *www.czechtourism.com*, and has offices at the following addresses.

CzechTourism Great Britain, 13 Harley Street, London W1G 9QG, **t** (020) 7631 0427.

CzechTourism USA, 1109 Madison Avenue (at 83rd Street), New York, NY 10028, **t** (212) 288 0830, ext. 105, 101.

CzechTourism (Canada), 2 Bloor Street Wes, Suite 1500, Toronto, Ontario M4W 3E2, **t** (416) 363 9928.

The Foreign Ministry's website at *www.czech.cz* contains even more information, including news and current events, and includes links to several sites that may come in useful when planning your trip.

Czech Republic: Prague

Prague comprises some 242,002 inhabitants; 503 spires, towers and sundry aerial protrusions; 495 square kilometres; 10 districts; eight islands; seven hills (like most legendary cities); and an agglomeration of what were historically five separate towns.

Since 1989 it has barely stopped echoing to the rhythm of pile-drivers and, under the glare of oxyacetylene torches, the magical metropolis is being transformed into a city fit for the 21st century. It is still scarred by the barbed-wire wounds of the Cold War but, as it busks, dances, works and kisses its way back to the light, the old divisions are being healed on its streets.

GERMANY   POLAND

• Prague

CZECH REPUBLIC

AUSTRIA   SLOVAKIA

06

Don't miss

⭐ **Prague's jugular vein**
Charles Bridge, and the route along Karlova to Old Town Square **p.139**

⭐ **Baroque triumphant**
St Nicholas' Church **p.175**

⭐ **An Art Nouveau palace**
Municipal House **p.149**

⭐ **Castle in the air**
Prague Castle **p.158**

⭐ **A lost world**
The Jewish Quarter **p.152**

See map overleaf

Prague

250 metres
250 yards

N

PATOCKO

UL JELENÍ

UL MARIÁNSKÉ HRADBY

Royal Summer Palace

Royal Gardens

CHOTKOVA UL

NA OPYŠI

STARÉ ZÁM SCHODY

POD BRUSKOU

KLÁROV

Lion Court

Ball Game Hall

Orangerie

U PRAŠNÉHO MOSTU

Riding School

Basilica of St George

Malostranská Ⓜ

HRADČANY

PRAŠNÝ MOST

Prague Castle

Riding Hall

NOVÝ SVĚT

Archbishop's Palace

St Vitus Cathedral

VALDŠTEJNSKÁ

NA NÁSPU

Sternberg Palace

Old Royal Palace

Waldstein Palace

Waldstein Gardens

Capuchin Friary

KANOVNICKÁ

Martinic Palace

HRADČANSKÉ NÁM

VALDŠTEJNSKÉ NÁM

KEPLEROVA

ČERNÍNSKÁ

U KASÁREN

Tuscany Palace

Schwarzenberg Palace

NERVE ZÁMECKÉ SCHODY

SNĚMOVNÍ

TOMÁŠSKÁ

Vojan Park

Loreta

LORETÁNSKÉ NÁM

LORETÁNSKÁ

Thun-Hohenstein Palace

NAVE

THUNOVSKÁ

St Thomas'

DRAŽICKÉHO NÁM

KE HRADU

POHOŘICKÉ SCHODY

JANSKÁ

MALOSTRANSKÉ NÁM

St Joseph

DRAŽICKÉHO

Černín Palace

ÚVOZ

JÁNSKÁ

Morzin Palace

St Nicholas

MOSTECKÁ

NSENSKÁ

JÁNSKÝ VRŠEK

ŠPORKOVA

BŘETISLAVOVA

VLAŠSKÁ

TRŽ

ULICE

SASKÁ

LÁZEŇSKÁ

John Lennon Wall

Judith Tower

POHOŘELEC

St Roch and Galerie Miró

Lobkowicz Palace

Schönborn Palace

PROKOPSK

VELKOPŘEVORSKÉ

HROZNO

UL NA KAMPĚ

STRAHOVSKÉ NÁD.

VLADISLAVOVA CESTA

MALTÉZSKÉ NÁM

NÁM

Kampa Island

Strahov Monastery

MALÁ STRANA

HARANTOVA

NEBOVIDSKÁ

PELCLOVA

NOSTICOVA

U SOVOVÝCH MLÝNŮ

MALOSTRANSKÉ NÁBŘEŽÍ

Strahov Gardens

Petřín Gardens

Our Lady of Victory

HELLICHOVA

UL ÚJEZD KARMELITSKÁ

Hunger Wall

Model Eiffel Tower ★

VŠEHRDOVA UL

Strahovská

Maze

St Lawrence's

PETŘÍN HILL

Rose Garden

Funicular railway

LANOVÉ DRÁHY

BESEDNÍ

Dětský Ostrov

VANÍČKOVA UL

Štefánik Observatory

Nebozízek

RIČNÍ UL

VÍTĚZNÁ UL

OLYMPIJSKÁ UL

Hunger Wall Tower

PLASKÁ UL

Strahovský Stadión

CHALOUPECKÉHO UL

Observation Terrace

Hunger Wall

MĚLNICKÁ

PETŘÍNSKÁ UL

JEZDECKÁ UL

ROSIČKÝCH

ZBOROVSKÁ UL

JANÁČKOVO NÁBŘEŽÍ

ATLETICKÁ UL

ŠERMÍŘSKÁ UL

Kinský Gardens

NÁM KINSKÝCH

VODNÍ UL

MALÁTOVA UL

NÁBŘEŽÍ

KRAFTOVA UL

ELIŠKY PEŠKOVÉ

ZBOROVSKÁ

ZUBATÉHO

UL PAVLA ŠVANDY ZE SEMČIC

KOŘENSKÉHO UL

HOLEČKOVA UL

DRTINOVA UL

VIKTORA HUGA

ŠTEFÁNIKOVA UL

UL V BOTANICE

NÁBŘEŽNÍ UL

MOŠNO

ZÁPOVA UL

HOLEČKOVA UL

NA CÍCHUCE

GRAFICKÁ UL

ČÍCHUCE

KMOCHOVA

KOBROVA

STROUPEŽNICKÉHO UL

MATOUŠOVA UL

ERBENOVA UL

UL PALÍRKY

PLZEŇSKÁ UL

TOMÁŠ

NA

KARTOUZSKÁ

LIDICKÁ

Malá Strana cemetery

DUŠKOVA UL.

UL NA BĚLIDLE

Don't miss

🏛 Charles Bridge **p.139**

🏛 St Nicholas' Church **p.175**

🏛 Municipal House **p.149**

🏛 Prague Castle **p.158**

🏛 The Jewish Quarter **p.152**

Years of smears and smokescreens have added to the mystery that now surrounds Prague. It is the capital of Bohemia, which has been a byword for outlandishness for centuries. The kingdom began its ascent into the clouds in the mid-1400s: the pope spread the word that Bohemians made love on the streets, while in France a group of expelled gypsies waved their safe-conducts as they passed through, and the French duly noted that *un bohémien* was a gypsy – as he still is today. By the early 1600s, Shakespeare could get away with describing the landlocked and forested kingdom as 'a desert country near the sea' (*The Winter's Tale*).

In 1938, disingenuous ignorance was elevated to foreign policy by British prime minister Neville Chamberlain. Ten years later, Prague – farther west than Vienna, and considerably closer to Dublin than to Moscow – became lost in 'Eastern Europe'. The city of dreams began a 41-year nightmare; but, in the West, Bohemia did little more than hover somewhere between Bloomsbury and Hampstead.

And then, in 1989, a few million people pinched themselves, the tinpot emperors of Communism shivered, and the city returned to where it belongs: the heart of Europe.

Prague is now the capital of the Czech Republic – made up of Bohemia, Moravia and a slice of Silesia. It doesn't always feel dreamy – particularly as you chew through its accursed dumplings, wade through hordes of beer-hunting tourists or cross swords with a hobgoblin of the bureaucracy – but, if you pack your senses of humour, adventure and romance, a visit is an unforgettable jaunt into a city where history is in the making, and where a thousand years has already been made.

History

The First Přemysl

The story begins with the establishment of Bohemia's first ruling dynasty, the **Přemysls**, at the end of the 8th century. Myth and history are intertwined but, according to the former, the **Čech** tribe had established itself at Vyšehrad ('higher castle'), a rocky outcrop on the Vltava River that still bears the same name. Čech was a mass-murderer on the run, but it was his son, Krok or Crocus, who went down in legend as the putative founding father. Unable to produce a male heir, he was succeeded by his daughter **Libuše**.

When the men of the tribe insisted Libuše needed a husband, she went into a trance. Pointing towards distant hills, she told them to follow her horse, which would take them to a ploughman whose descendants would rule over them for ever. The horse trotted off, a sturdy farmer named Přemysl was brought back to wed Libuše, and

Getting to Prague

Many airlines fly direct to Prague from the UK, and from the USA and Canada (*see* **Planning Your Trip**, pp.21–2). You can also take the coach, or travel by train via the Channel Tunnel: *see* pp.22–4.

Getting from the Airport

Prague's international airport is Ruzyně, some 20km west of the city centre. **Taxis** to the centre cost 600–800kč and can be booked online before your departure: see, for example, *www.pragueairport.co.uk*. **Minibuses** leave for Náměstí Republiky, a central square, at half-hourly intervals until 9pm. That journey costs around 90kč per person, and they can also take you to a specific destination for approximately 300kč. The cheapest journeys into the city are on the municipal **bus** network. The 119 bus runs every 20mins or so between about 5am and 12.30am, to and from Dejvická metro station (line A). An express service operates along the same route between 5am and 9pm, and continues to Nádraži Holešovice, on metro line C.

a dynasty was born. The city of Prague owes its legendary origins to one of Libuše's prophecies too. According to Bohemia's venerable chronicler, Cosmas of Prague (*c*. 1045–1125), she was overcome by a vision involving 'a town, the glory of which will reach the stars'. Again the loyal subjects trooped off to a spot described by Libuše, where they found a man building a door-sill (in Czech, *práh* – hence the name Praha or Prague) for his cottage. This spot was said to be in Hradčany. Building started in earnest and the rest, as they say, is history.

Scanty archaeological evidence suggests, in fact, that the first people in the area were a Celtic tribe known as the **Boii**, who lived here long enough to leave the name Bohemia. The Čechs, a Slavonic tribe from Croatia, did establish a strong presence in the area in the 5th century, but there is no record of Crocus, and it is only in the later 9th century that the first historically attested Přemysl, **Bořivoj**, appears on the scene as ruler of Bohemia. The princedom was still an insignificant cog in the Greater Moravian Empire, which included most of the Slavs of central Europe, and was engaged in endless bloody tussles with the Holy Roman Empire to the west.

The **Great Schism** between the Roman and Byzantine churches had by now begun to open up, and German monks scurried across the Moravian Empire with their version of the Good Book. In about 863, the Empire's ruler, **Rostislav**, turned to the Eastern Church for help. Byzantine Emperor Michael sent along Brothers **Methodius and Cyril**, who arrived with a Bible and a liturgy written in a new Greek alphabet (Glagolitic, or Cyrillic script) that could deal with the grunts peculiar to the Slavs. Jealous Germans levelled charges of heresy, but the two men remained on good terms with Rome until their death. Bořivoj was dunked into the new religion by Methodius in about 874. Mass abandonment of storm and fertility gods followed.

Getting around Prague

The same type of **ticket** (*jízdenka*) is valid for the metro, tram and bus service. You can't buy them on board; get them in advance from the yellow machines at metro stations and tram stops, or at a tobacconist, café or news stand (look for the *tabák* and *trafika* signs). Journeys cost 18kč, unless you want to travel more than five subway stops, make a bus or tram journey longer than 20 minutes, or transfer between different modes of transportation, in which case you should buy a 26kč ticket. You can also buy 24hr passes for 100kč; 72hr passes for 330kč; and 7-day ones for 500kč. Your ticket or pass is not valid until it is time-stamped (look for the franking machines on trams and buses, and just before the escalators in subway halls) – and the system is enforced by inspectors with the power to issue instant fines of 700kč. Extensive information (in English) about the municipal transit system, including up-to-date tariffs and maps, is available at *www.dpp.cz/en*.

By Metro and Train

The **metro** is the easiest way to get around town. The chrome-plated Soviet-built network still runs with the efficiency of totalitarianism, and its trio of lines is simple enough to flummox only the drunk and the deranged. Trains run from 5am to midnight. The junctions are at Muzeum (lines A and C), Můstek (lines A and B) and Florenc (lines B and C).

Timetables and fares for intercity **train** journeys are available at *www.jizdnirady.idnes.cz* (then navigate to the site's English-language section).

By Tram and Bus

The cream-and-crimson **trams** shudder around Prague every 5–10 mins, 4.30am–midnight. Night trams (nos.51–58) prowl the major routes after midnight, and all pass through Lazarská Street in the New Town.

Buses feel less predictable than trams and subways, probably because they lack rails, but can come in useful. You can find information about city routes at *http://dpp.cz/en*; and about intercity journeys at *http://jizdnirady.atlas.cz/ConnForm.asp?tt=J&cl=E5*.

By Taxi and Funicular

Crazed and wily cabbies have long been a source of unhappiness for visitors, but they are considerably rarer today than they once were – and you're very unlikely to experience any problems at all if you use either **AAA Radio Taxi, t** 14014 (*www.radiotaxiaaa.cz*) or **Citytaxi, t** 257 257 257 (*www.citytaxi.cz*). Both companies have English-speaking controllers and accept online bookings; AAA will also return your text with a call (*see* website for details). Tip 10%. Main taxi ranks are in Wenceslas Square; on the corner of Národní and Spálená; in Malostranské náměstí; in Staroměstské náměstí; and in Náměstí Republiky.

Prague has a two-stop **funicular railway** on Petřín Hill. It runs between 9am and 11.20pm, connecting Újezd, the Nebozízek restaurant and the gardens at the top, and ordinary tickets and passes can be used.

Car and Bike Hire

All the big car hire companies have desks at the airport and pick-up locations elsewhere in Prague: for further details, go to *www.avis.cz*, *www.budget.cz* and *www.hertz.cz*. **Europcar** tends to be a little cheaper: its office in the Old Town is at Elišky Krásnohorské 9 (*open daily 8–8*): **t** 224 811 290 or 223 810 515, *www.europcar.cz*.

Pushbikes can be rented at City Bike: *www.prahaonline.cz/citybike* and Králodvorská 5, **t** 776 180 224. The less energetic might prefer rolling around town on a **Segway**: try *www.prague-segway-tours.com*.

Bohemia Takes Off

Although the Slavs had little sympathy for the Holy Roman Empire, its power could not be ignored. As the Přemysls struggled to control Bohemia, they began to turn away from the East. The influence of Germans in Bohemian affairs, which was to become a tragic motif over the next millennium, began to grow. In 885, **Pope Stephen V** declared the Slavonic liturgy to be heretical. The Přemysls took his word for it and began the switch away from Cyrillic, for which Western tourists can be eternally grateful.

Bohemia remained subservient to the Moravian Empire until the beginning of the 10th century, when rampant Magyars marauded across its southern and eastern borders. Little Bohemia was spared – and its history began to heat up.

In about 921, **Prince Wenceslas** (Václav) became Bohemia's ruler. A gentle Christian, he may have been a suitable subject for a 19th-century carol but he was not up to the rough-and-tumble of Dark Age intrigue. In 935, he was murdered on the way to Mass by his brother, **Boleslav the Cruel**. What Boleslav lacked in kindness, he made up for with political skill: he exterminated his rivals, extended his dominions, married his daughter into the Polish ruling family, and resisted political pressures from Rome.

In 973, under the rule of **Boleslav the Pious**, Bohemia's strength was acknowledged by the pope, who consented to the founding of a bishopric in Prague. Two more Boleslavs followed: **Boleslav the Third**, who reverted to type and murdered several unruly nobles at a banquet, and his brother, **Boleslav the Brave**.

Over the next two centuries, Bohemia was pulled ever deeper into the tangled politics of the Holy Roman Empire, and the popes and central European princes of late medieval Europe were regularly vying for influence over the region. A volatile social mix also began to brew at a lower level, with a decision by King Wenceslas I (reigned 1230–53) to invite German merchants into Bohemia's towns, where they were allowed to govern themselves and observe only their own laws.

Wenceslas' successor, Přemysl **Otakar II** (reigned 1253–78), gave even more ground to the Germans, literally, by allowing them to expel Jews from the left bank of the Vltava in 1257. Prague now developed into three autonomous units – the Old Town, the Castle District and Malá Strana – and a Jewish district established itself behind a walled quarter in the north of the Old Town.

Under Přemysl Otakar II, Bohemia's capital experienced the first of the many boomlets that have characterized its history. An expansion of trade and the discovery of silver deposits around Kutná Hora helped to fund major building works, and its Romanesque basilicas and houses gave way to the far more ambitious architectural style that would become known as Gothic. However, the king's own success sowed the seeds for ultimate failure. By the early 1270s, his realm stretched from the Baltic to the Adriatic – and Germany's princes finally looked up from their own internecine struggles to notice that they had a rival on their hands. Otakar made an all-or-nothing lunge for the imperial throne in 1273 – and missed. Rudolf of Habsburg allowed him to continue as king within Bohemia itself, but the empire that he had built lay in ruins.

Anarchy and Chivalry

In 1306, the Přemysl dynasty sputtered to a halt with the murder of the 17-year-old **Wenceslas III**. Anarchic Bohemia needed a steady hand on the tiller, but the victorious candidate left much to be desired. Fourteen-year-old **John of Luxembourg**, the son of the new German emperor, Henry VII, spent most of his reign on a warring spree across Europe. He cared little what Prague got up to as long as it kept the royal coffers full, so burghers and nobles made the most of the new opportunities: the Old Town got a town hall, a legal code and formal supremacy over every other town in the kingdom.

The Golden Age

John died a spectacular death in 1346 at the Battle of Crécy, where, old and blind, he led 500 horsemen to certain death under a hail of Welsh arrows. His son **Charles** was considerably more calculating. Appointed king of Bohemia and Holy Roman Emperor after his father's death, he proved expert at sidelining his enemies and achieving through diplomacy what John had singularly failed to win through war. He took advantage of France's battering at the hands of the English (the Hundred Years War had only just begun) to reduce it almost to vassal status. He spoke fluent Czech and encouraged the country's language and traditions. The emperor wrapped his reign in a series of legends, going back to Libuše and St Wenceslas. With the help of his friend and former tutor, Pope Clement VI, Prague had already been elevated to an archbishopric in 1344; Charles invited monastic orders from the far-flung reaches of the Eastern Church. While the Black Death devastated the rest of Europe in 1348, Bohemia lay protected by a screen of mountains and emerged as the Continent's most vital centre of Gothic art and architecture. As befitted a medieval town with pretensions of grandeur, it got a new bridge, cathedral and the first university in central Europe. For decades this was an academic vortex, sucking in scholars from as far away as Oxford. In the same year Charles founded the New Town, incorporating the straggling settlements outside the city walls into broad streets and marketplaces – the most successful and lasting piece of urban planning in Europe since the Romans.

Nationalism and Hussitism

The peace and prosperity enjoyed by Bohemia during Charles's reign were not to last. Tensions had long been building between German and Czech populations. The native nobility, although far from homogenous, resented the political influence of the Germans, while workers were jealous of their economic influence. At the same time, Charles's overtures towards foreign clerics inspired increasing hostility, as it became clear not only that medieval monks were as prone to screw around as anyone else, but also that those in Prague were being subsidized to do it. A sense was building that the Church needed reform – and a century before the birth of Martin Luther, Prague became an epicentre for the religious conflict that was to tear the Continent apart.

Charles died in 1378, and was succeeded by his eldest son, **Wenceslas IV**. Chroniclers had little time for the ruler, whose missteps supposedly began from the moment he urinated into his christening font. Although their accounts are as biased as that sounds, he undoubtedly lacked the mettle that his troubled times required, and lost his imperial title to his wily half-brother, **Sigismund**, in 1406. By then, a leader of far greater stature than both had emerged, however. In 1402 a young priest, **Jan Hus** (John Huss), influenced by the teachings of Oxfordshire parish priest John Wycliffe, was appointed rector of Charles University. Hus would never have regarded himself as anything but a Catholic, but his fiery sermons moved a long way from the party line. His assertion that clerical and papal decrees had to be tested against the Scripture amounted to a direct political attack on the power of the Church. The Hussites preached in the vernacular, and in about 1414 began the practice that came to characterize the movement: allowing the congregation the wine of the Eucharist as well as the bread. They became known as the **Utraquists** (from the Latin for 'in both kinds'). Hus was excommunicated in 1411 and burned at the stake on 6 July 1415. Wenceslas sympathized with the nationalists, but was under constant pressure from his brother to control the heretics. In 1419 things went from bad to worse when councillors at the New Town Hall were **defenestrated**, a novel form of political violence that was to become a regular feature of Bohemian history. The pressure finally became too much for Wenceslas, who bowed out of history by way of repeated apoplectic fits.

Sneaky **Sigismund** tried to take over, but encountered strong opposition from a coalition of Bohemian Utraquists, all anxious to prevent any restoration of Church privileges. Relations worsened in 1420, when Pope Martin V declared a crusade against Bohemia – the first of four that would be declared against the country over the next decade. As Prague's citizens absorbed the idea that they were at war with Christendom, a division opened up between moderates, who sought to compromise with the Church, and a radical faction who began to think in terms of total secession. It all came to a head in 1434, after Pope Eugenius IV agreed to the Compacts of Basle – allowing Bohemians to administer and receive communion in both kinds. The radicals thought that inadequate, so the moderates wiped them out at the **Battle of Lipany**.

Sigismund, finally recognized as king of Bohemia, died a few months later. His successor, **Albert of Habsburg**, followed suit in 1439, remaining alive just long enough to impregnate his wife, who produced **Ladislav the Posthumous**. He reigned briefly from 1453 to 1457, but the real ruler of Bohemia from 1440 to 1471 was an Utraquist nobleman, **George of Poděbrady** (Jiří z Poděbrad), who ruled as king from 1458. He hoped to establish a native dynasty, but was forced to sign a deal with the pro-Catholic Polish **Vladislav II of Jagellon**, in order to fight off the equally pro-Catholic **Matthias Corvinus** of Hungary.

Vladislav was elected king in 1471, and it was under his reign that the last flickers of popular Hussitism were extinguished. Anti-Catholic feelings still ran high among the population – a riot against Vladislav's officials in 1483 brought Prague's **second defenestration**, this time from the Old Town Hall – but the nobility increasingly looked after their own interests. Taking advantage of the king's absences (he preferred Buda Castle), nobles introduced serfdom in 1487, and began to brew beer (a long-standing privilege of the towns) on their feudal estates. Many kept to the Utraquist faith, but it came to signify little more than a tipple at communion. But even if the first flush of Czech nationalism was over, Bohemia was established as a centre of anti-Catholicism – and paid heavily over the next centuries.

The Habsburgs Arrive

When Vladislav's heir drowned in 1526, while fleeing a battlefield, another would-be dynasty bit the dust; and princelings from across the Continent headed for Prague to vie for the vacant throne. The electors' fateful choice was **Ferdinand I of Habsburg**.

The Bohemians initially had little cause for complaint. Ferdinand was tolerant enough in Christian terms, and busied himself doing battle against the Turks – then as close to capturing Vienna as they would ever be. But in 1533, he made peace with the infidel, and it became clear that his faith would have consequences closer to home. The universal claims of Catholicism were intrinsically linked to the political ambitions of the Habsburgs – and, since Protestantism was so closely associated with nationalist sentiment in Prague, a collision was all but guaranteed.

It came in 1547, when Ferdinand sweet-talked Prague's Protestants into financing an anti-Turkish army, which then marched west to attack Protestants in Saxony. Incensed nobles met in Prague to plot a response, but Ferdinand's troops massacred the Saxons in weeks, and headed straight back. The ringleaders were decapitated and Prague's privileges drastically curtailed.

Ferdinand ensured his eldest son, **Maximilian**, was crowned king and introduced the fiercely proselytizing Jesuit Order into

Prague in 1556 to counteract the spread of Lutheranism. In 1563, **Pope Pius IV** launched the militant programme of the **Counter-Reformation** at the Council of Trent.

Ferdinand died in 1564, to be succeeded as emperor by Maximilian (already king of Bohemia). In return for continued funding for his anti-Turkish forays, Maximilian granted Bohemia's Lutherans the right to organize independently of the old Utraquist church. The concessions enabled him to have his son elected king of Bohemia with little difficulty in 1576 and, when Maximilian died later that year, he was succeeded by **Emperor Rudolf II**.

Rudolfine Prague

Although relations between Catholic and Protestant were worsening across Europe by the late 1500s, there was still much to play for, and Czech burghers and nobles now offered to assume much of the imperial debt and build a new castle if Rudolf would relocate to Prague. With the Turks still within 100 miles of Vienna, it was a welcome offer – and in 1583, despite frantic lobbying by Viennese nobles, Prague became an imperial capital for the first time in two centuries.

Rudolf was the most singular monarch Prague had seen since Charles IV. The papacy had high hopes for the young emperor but Rudolf turned out to be a strange fish, imbued with a mystical spirituality that was far from the new orthodoxy the Church was trying to promote. Fanaticism was alien to him, but his education left him torn between hopes of a universal truth and the reality of a Christianity that was being reduced into two armed camps. The sensitive emperor was never able to resolve the dilemma, and teetered between profound pessimism and mild insanity for most of his reign. Legend and history remember Rudolfine Prague as a fantastic city of alchemy and astrology, suspended in time (*see* p.170), but its atmosphere was very much a product of the moment: the Counter-Reformation was gathering force in Austria and Styria; a part-time lunatic and full-time melancholic was on the throne; and mystics and zealots were massing in the city. Prague had become the embodiment of Europe's schizophrenia. It would have taken a genius to steer the empire through its crisis, and Rudolf, though certainly extraordinary, was not the man for the job. His younger brother **Matthias** had intrigued against him since his first major bout of insanity in 1600. By 1606, Matthias had launched an open mutiny and two years later Rudolf's reign as emperor came to an enforced end.

From Defenestration to Massacre

In 1617, **Emperor Matthias** proposed his fiercely anti-Protestant cousin **Ferdinand** as his successor to the crown of Bohemia. The

Bohemians finally took a stand against both men on 23 May 1618 when they hurled two of Ferdinand's hated councillors and a secretary out of a window. All three survived the 15-metre drop: the Catholic Church claimed a miracle; others claimed that their fall had been cushioned by a dung heap. Prague's **third defenestration** threw Europe into the Thirty Years War. By the time peace returned in 1648, the Continent would be in ruins – and Bohemia did not have to wait that long.

The city's nobles looked for a royal champion, and found **Frederick of the Palatinate**. They could not have made a worse choice. The allies he was expected to bring to the cause quickly flaked away, and it soon became clear that he had never fought in his life. The two sides finally met on 8 November 1620, just outside Prague at the **Battle of the White Mountain** (*Bílá hora*). The Protestant forces scattered into headlong retreat, bringing two centuries of anti-Catholicism to an ignominious end.

The Bohemian Counter-Reformation

The **Thirty Years War** ravaged Europe until 1648. It began as a struggle to assert Habsburg power, but by the 1630s the entire Continent was sorting out its differences by fire and sword. In Prague, where Protestantism and nationalism were inseparable, Ferdinand soon hitched the imperial cause firmly to that of the Church. He and his monkish allies extinguished the city's ancient powers: Protestantism was made a capital offence, and the independence of the Czech Estates was destroyed. When the dust settled, Bohemia was left with its population reduced by over a third.

The country plunged into a decline that lasted two centuries. **Frederick the Great** invaded Prague twice in the mid-18th century, but otherwise the city became a backwater, where you went when the bright lights of Vienna became too much. The Jesuits led the consolidation of the new faith with a Baroque building programme that transformed the face of the city, but were placed under a worldwide ban by a jealous pope in 1773. In 1781, the enlightened despot **Emperor Josef II** abolished most of the empire's other monasteries and convents. The corollary was the restoration of individual religious freedom for all save the weirdest sects, and Prague's Jewish population was finally allowed out of its ghetto.

The Nationalist Revival

During the early 19th century, Bohemia began to breathe again. People across Europe rediscovered or invented common cause in their ethnicity, and Czechs began for the first time in 200 years to imagine an end to German rule. The Czech language, which had all but died out, was resuscitated by a handful of writers and researchers – František Palacký and Josef Jungmann the most notable. In **1848** the citizens of Prague were up in arms, joined by the rest of the empire in a revolt against Metternich's iron rule from Vienna. The Habsburg empire was to prove incapable of accommodating the new power of nationalist sentiment. But as the empire sickened, the Czech nation quickened.

From Independence to Dependency

In the years before 1914, many Czechs and Slovaks felt with apprehension that their interests lay firmly in the enemy camp. Lingering pan-Slavism encouraged sympathy for even the corrupt Russia of Nicholas II, while democratic ideals and anti-German sentiment made others look towards France and Britain. When war broke out, two men – **Tomáš Garrigue Masaryk** and **Edvard Beneš** – began a four-year tour to persuade the world that the time was ripe for Czechoslovakia. In 1918, Masaryk signed a deal with Slovak émigrés in Pittsburgh, which persuaded President Woodrow Wilson to give 'Czecho-Slovakia' the green light.

Independence was declared on 28 October 1918 and, within two weeks, Masaryk had been elected president of the new Czechoslovakian Republic. With Beneš, now foreign minister, he staked out the borders of the new state. These encompassed the largely German-populated Sudetenland to the west, as well as areas claimed by the Hungarians and the Poles, but in the peace treaties the victors ratified the *fait accompli* with little discussion and no plebiscite.

Although the country's political structures rode the **Depression** with an astonishing stability, the ancient problem of the German minority was soon to explode with unparalleled ferocity. The Sudetenland separatist movement found a champion in Hitler, and Czechoslovakia became the eye of a building European storm. In the infamous 1938 **Munich Agreement**, Britain, France and Italy gave Hitler *carte blanche* to seize the Sudetenland. Within six months, the German army had invaded Czechoslovakia as Britain and France remained silent. Only after the invasion of Poland six months later did they declare war on Germany. The war left Prague's buildings almost unscathed, but its population was less fortunate. Thousands of intellectuals, politicians and Romanies were killed or imprisoned. Of the 90,000 Jews who remained in the Protectorate in 1939, only 10,000 survived.

When war broke out, Beneš, who had taken over as president in 1935, went to London to establish a government-in-exile. Within the Protectorate itself, armed underground movements began to operate, directed largely by the London government. On 5 May 1945, the capital's Resistance groups broadcast a call to arms and thousands rose up against the occupying Nazi forces in the city.

The **Prague Uprising** lasted only four days, but street fighting and last-minute executions left up to 5,000 Czechs dead. On 9 May 1945 the Soviet Red Army entered Prague to a rapturous reception. A provisional national assembly, with Beneš again as president, was set up in October. Mobs lynched collaborators, and three million Sudeten Germans were expelled, resulting in the deaths of thousands.

Communist Consolidation

The Czechoslovakian Communist Party led by **Klement Gottwald** swept the board in the 1946 elections, with 38 per cent of the votes. Beneš appointed Gottwald prime minister of a coalition government, but Uncle Joe Stalin had no intention of letting his protégé go to bed with a bourgeois. Gottwald's rabble-rousing skills and the weakness of Beneš led to the former's assumption of the presidency in February 1948. Within a month the popular foreign minister, **Jan Masaryk** – son of T. G. – who was less accommodating to the Communists, had died in a mysterious fall from his office window late at night. A **fourth defenestration** began 40 years of Communist rule; the Party was pleased to report 89 per cent support in new elections in May. Within a year the Terror had begun.

From Socialism to Normalization

During the mid-1960s, reformers at the lower levels of the Party began to work on revitalizing its links with the rest of society. In January 1968, Alexander Dubček was elected to the post of First Secretary. Dubček's politics had been formed in the crucible of the 1930s Soviet Union but, in the heady days of 1968, he finally began both to listen, and to learn. During the so-called **Prague Spring**, he proposed a radical reform of the country's political and economic institutions, partly out of his changing convictions but largely at the urging of more committed forces and individuals both within and outside the Party.

The Soviet Union, which had actually backed pliant Dubček for the leadership the year before, began to stir. General Secretary Brezhnev was soon considering how to help the Czechoslovak proletariat stave off 'a return to the bourgeois-capitalist system'. He took soundings of the other Warsaw Pact leaders and, on 21 August 1968, Czechoslovakia was invaded by five armies. The cultural and political renaissance of the mid-1960s was strangled in its cradle. The times were desperate. Fourteen philosophy students at the Charles University drew lots, and agreed to burn themselves alive one by one until press freedom was restored. 'Torch No.1' was **Jan Palach**. On 16 January 1969, the 20-year-old emptied a can of petrol over himself in Wenceslas Square, and flicked a lighter. Over the next three months, several others also killed themselves in protest.

In April 1969, Dubček was replaced by Gustáv Husák – Resistance hero, victim of the Terror and supporter of the Prague Spring. Brezhnev is said to have murmured, 'If we can't use the puppets, we'll tie the strings to the leaders.' Within a year, Husák began to dance. Some 500,000 people were deprived of Communist Party membership, in a process that was called 'normalization' (*normalisace*). When all was normal, the government declared that Czechoslovakia had achieved a state of *reálný socialismus* – an eerie phrase that is usually translated as 'real existing socialism'. A new generation grew up without even the memory of hope.

The Velvet Revolution

Even as late as mid-1989, with Hungary and Poland well on the path to reform, few observers saw Czechoslovakia as likely to follow in the near future. But, as the East German regime tottered, refugees began to flood into the West German embassy in Prague. The revolutions of 1989 had begun. On 10 November the West woke to the news that bulldozers were demolishing the Berlin Wall, and on 17 November Prague's students confronted a baton-wielding police force. The filmed scenes of police brutality against students armed with candles and flowers aroused the population from two decades of torpor. For the next six weeks, Prague was enfolded by its **Velvet Revolution**, an anarchic hubbub of strikes, pickets and celebrations, which culminated in the election of playwright and recently released political prisoner **Václav Havel** to the presidency on 29 December 1989.

Truth Will Out

The most dramatic of the messy truths to emerge since 1989 was the realization that Czechoslovakia itself was based on a fiction. The rhetoric of internationalism spouted by Communist leaders had both fuelled and concealed domestic rivalries and, within three years of the Velvet Revolution, Slovakian nationalism grew into a full-blown independence movement. On New Year's Eve 1992, each more or less amicably waved goodbye to the other, and the **Czech** and **Slovak Republics** were born.

The new nation's social conflicts do not have a solution as simple as a Velvet Divorce. The country's Romanies have suffered from official neglect and public ignorance for decades, and the replacement of totalitarianism by majority rule has in many cases done nothing but add a veneer of legitimacy to their stigmatization. The psychological legacy of Communism also fractures the country. As late as May 1988, the Party had more than 1.7 million members – that is, one in 10 of Czechoslovakia's total population –

and humdrum compromises with the regime were struck by millions more. As a result, measures taken since 1989 to break the institutionalized power of the Party have often had an irrational quality, scapegoating individuals for a system in which almost every adult was implicated to some extent. So far the Czech Republic has steered a precarious course between demands for revenge and the temptation of forgetfulness, but it is only when today's twenty-somethings reach middle age that it will be possible to say if normality has replaced the 'normalization' which plagued Czechoslovakia for 30 years.

The country has certainly made progress in throwing off its institutional past. A founder member of the Warsaw Pact, it joined NATO in 1999 and became a full member of the European Union in May 2004. But although a return to Communism is all but inconceivable, many obstacles and forks lie on the road ahead. Kickback scandals have been endemic since independence, bringing democratic reforms into disrepute and making early promises about the benefits of the free market ring hollow. The 2003 invasion of Iraq – opposed by most Czechs, but supported by the government of the day – also damaged the cause of those supporting continental integration, while winning the country no friends that it did not already have.

And while the Czech Republic has set its face firmly westwards, one of the most significant developments of them all has taken place in the other direction – where Russia, buoyed by surging energy prices, is re-emerging as a regional superpower. Prague's location at the crossroads of Europe, a slogan of hope after the Velvet Revolution, has always had its downside – in that crossroads are trampled – and though no one expects Russian tanks to be trundling back any time soon, the Czech Republic is again facing challenges from all points of the compass. But although uncertainties cloud the horizon, history makes at least one thing clear. Prague has seen it all before.

Art and Architecture

Romanesque

By the turn of the first millennium, Prague was already a thriving town of stone and mortar – as noted admiringly in the travelogue of a Jewish merchant named Ibrahim Ibn-Jacob, who passed through in 965. Its architecture drew on the forms and half-remembered engineering techniques of the Romans. The best surviving examples are **St George's Basilica** in the castle, and the **House of the Lords of Kunštát and Poděbrady** on Řetězová Street, in the Old Town.

Gothic

The cathedral builders of medieval France were the first Europeans to develop a distinctive architecture in a thousand years, and the new style – which would be christened 'Gothic' several centuries later – reached Prague in the mid-13th century. Characterized by soaring pinnacles and steeples, ornate sculpture and tracery-framed glass, it was soon making the rotundas and round arches of the past redundant. **St Agnes' Convent** and the **Old-New Synagogue** represent its earliest manifestations. By the early 1300s it was sweeping Prague – not least because the Vltava river had recently submerged the Old Town once too often, and the burghers had responded by burying it entirely, and rebuilding on top from scratch.

Under Emperor Charles IV (1346–78) Prague finally stormed the European stage. **Matthew of Arras** came from France to begin a new cathedral, but by the mid-14th century Germany led the field in church design. In 1353 Matthew's timely death brought 23-year-old **Peter Parléř** to Prague, where he built **St Vitus' Cathedral**, one of the grandest late Gothic churches of Europe. Artists began to produce unique Bohemian work, too. Paintings dating from the early 13th century show artists breaking free of rigid Byzantine rules. The Bohemian trend manifested itself in heavy modelling, which peaked in the work of **Master Theodoric**. His portraits of saints rank among the most distinctive work of the era in Europe.

The Renaissance

The 1526 coronation of Bohemia's first Habsburg king, Ferdinand I, brought Italian ideas and designers to Prague, but their impact on Gothic Prague was limited. Their finest product was Ferdinand's sublime **Royal Summer Palace**, but little else would survive the advent of Baroque art and architecture.

Mannerism

The highly stylized culture that emerged after the Renaissance got its name as a term of abuse – no uncommon phenomenon in art history – from critics who regarded its distorted perspectives and unnatural proportions as a deliberate affront to classical notions of beauty. It is nowadays seen as symptomatic of a far deeper malaise: at a time when the continent was being torn by religious turmoil, artists were concerned to find truths that transcended the mere world of appearances. One of the men who did most to promote the new trend was **Emperor Rudolf II** (1576–1611), who summoned artists to Prague from across Europe. One of the best known was **Giuseppe Arcimboldo** (1527–63), whose bizarre portraits, composed of objects such as fish or fruit, would be rediscovered with enthusiasm by the Surrealists four centuries later. A favourite theme was the apotheosis of Rudolf, who was repeatedly depicted as a Christian hero, or the defender of learning and wisdom against dark ignorance. Eroticism was another characteristic of the work produced in Prague during this time – not least because Rudolf himself would often instruct artists such as **Bartholomeus Spranger** (1546–1611) and **Hans von Aachen** (1552–1615) on the precise angle from which they should paint their nude models.

Rudolf's court was an ephemeral Camelot, and its culture evaporated with his downfall in 1611. His successor, Emperor Matthias, spirited parts of his collection to Vienna, and, as an atmosphere of quasi-Calvinism engulfed Prague, the visual arts went into crisis. The Protestant nobility sold off many remaining works in 1619, and most of what was left was looted by Swedish troops in 1648.

Baroque

The Baroque style arrived from Rome in the late 16th century, as the Council of Trent laid down its demand that art was to glorify the Church. Within a century it had utterly transformed the face of the city. The Baroque used movement, unnatural light and disproportion with a consistency that overwhelmed rather than intrigued. The new architecture elbowed its way into the **Waldstein Palace**, representing a transitional period. When the Thirty Years War ended in 1648, building began in earnest. Most of Prague's Baroque architects came via Vienna; the most prolific were **Francesco Caratti** and **Giovanni Alliprandi** (1665–1720).

By the early 18th century, Prague and Vienna had grasped the baton of Baroque. Two of the city's greatest architects were the Bavarian **Kristof Dienzenhofer** (1655–1722), and his son **Kilian Dienzenhofer** (1689–1751); their joint masterpiece, the Jesuit **Church of St Nicholas**, is one of 18th-century Europe's finest.

The Baroque reintegrated architecture and sculpture, after the Renaissance insistence that they were independent elements, establishing a tradition that influenced design into the 20th century. Baroque sculpture began with the relative restraint of **Jan Bendl** (1620–80) and **Matthias Jäckel** (1655–1738) and culminated in the epic works of **Matthias Braun** (1684–1738) and **Ferdinand Maximilian Brokof** (1688–1731).

Baroque painting in Bohemia is not up to sculpture. **Karel Škréta** (1610–74) followed Italian art of the *cinquecento*, and **Michael Willmann** (1630–1706) painted religious anguish and passion. The most accomplished works of Prague Baroque were experiments with light and colour by **Petr Brandl** (1668–1735) and the frescoes of **Franz Anton Maulpertsch** at the **Strahov Monastery**.

Neoclassicism

Under Emperor Josef II, the city's culture suffered a series of rapid blows. Fripperies had no place in the monarch's coolly rational world. What remained of Rudolf II's collection was auctioned off, and monks were turfed out of their monasteries, which were turned into barracks. A restrained classicism typifies the few grand buildings that were constructed in the city during the late 18th and early 19th centuries, but it had little impact on Baroque Prague.

Nation-building

In the mid-19th century, Prague's architecture was engulfed by the national revival movement, and a vogue for rehashing older architectural styles. The Renaissance was the favoured choice. Huge pediments triumphed, and stacks of disordered columns were considered noble. The result appears most clearly in the bombastic **National Museum**. The late 19th century also saw a wave of restoration of Bohemia's Gothic architecture. Artists also played a heroic role in the national revival, adorning buildings with mythological and allegorical works to express patriotic aspirations.

Art Nouveau

Prague's early 20th-century architecture was heavily influenced by a Continent-wide concern to shake off the previous decades' obsession with reviving historical styles. This manifested itself as a self-consciously new form of art – an Art Nouveau. Known in Bohemia as *secese* (a term derived from the 'secession' of various rebels from Vienna's official artists' association in 1897, *see* p.47), it was actually a confluence of two currents. The first, characterized by a fondness for natural motifs and whiplash curves, was epitomized by **Alfons Mucha**, who perfected his style in 1890s Paris and produced lush posters that still adorn many a student bedroom. The second, inspired by Charles Rennie Mackintosh's work in Glasgow, sought artistic novelty of a very different kind – through the type of rectilinear motifs and abstract patterns that would one day give rise to Constructivism and Functionalism. Its leading exponent in Prague was **Jan Kotěra** (1871–1923).

Two of the most original artists to emerge during the 1890s were, however, entirely unconcerned with such trends. The first was sculptor **František Bílek** (1872–1941), who linked ideas spanning music, literature and religion to produce a fascinating body of work. **František Kupka** (1871–1957) settled in Paris after 1896, where, after several years as a medium, he produced some of Europe's first deliberately abstract art.

Cubism

Prague's first modernist painting came out of **Osma** (The Eight), a group of artists founded in 1907. Its initial inspiration was the raw force of Munch but, as early as 1910, Czech artists such as **Emil Filla** (1882–1953), **Bohumil Kubišta** (1884–1918) and **Antonín Procházka** (1882–1945) had picked up on Parisian Cubism. For the next decade, Prague was the most important centre of the new art outside its birthplace. **Josef Čapek** (1897–1945) and **Jan Zrzavý** (1890–1977) also dabbled with Cubism, but were more interested in the primitivism that had inspired it.

Prague's painters largely followed the lead set by Picasso and Braque, but the sculptors and architects in the Cubist **Skupina** group produced maverick works. The leading sculptor was **Otto Gutfreund** (1889–1927), whose early work reflects the ideas of **Cubo-expressionism**. The most extraordinary Czech Cubism was in architecture. Three members of the Skupina, **Pavel Janák** (1882–1956), **Joseph Gočár** (1880–1945) and **Josef Chochol** (1880–1956) tried to restore depth and flexibility to buildings by using 3D geometrical forms on the façades.

Devětsil and Surrealism

The interwar years were among the most exciting in Prague's cultural life. The old world did not look good after the carnage of war, but Czechoslovakian independence had been won and, in the East, a rosy Bolshevik dawn was beginning. In 1920, a group of young artists led by **Karel Teige** (1900–51) founded **Devětsil** ('Nine Forces'). The political philosophy of the group was Soviet-style Marxism but, after a brief tinker with 'proletarian art', Devětsil spent the 1920s in a maze of artistic experimentation. In 1924 Teige hurled the group into the mêlée of the European avant-garde with a *First Manifesto of Poetism*. Like the Soviet Constructivists, he embraced the abstract beauty of the machine age, but also laid down his theory of 'Poetism', 'the art of pleasure', which was to condition the art produced.

Though Teige spent most of the early 1920s calling for 'the liquidation of art' (and the artist), early Poetism joyfully celebrated the imagination. The lyrical poets **Jaroslav Seifert** (1901–86) and **Vítězslav Nezval** (1900–58) worked on 'film poems'; the sculptor **Zdeněk Pěsánek** (1896–1965) created visual pianos and perhaps the world's first neon fountain; one of the group's most common form of art was the collage, or 'pictorial poem'. The group took the view that photography would replace the bourgeois art of painting, though its only full-time photographer was **Jaroslav Rössler** (*b*. 1902). Two other photographers emerged during the 1920s, **Jaromír Funke** (1896–1945) and **Josef Sudek** (1896–1976).

The group approved of cinema's popular non-élitism, and Devětsil also set up the **Liberated Theatre** in 1926. Devětsil had interests in common with French Surrealism, and the darker questions raised by Surrealism began to make inroads into the happy-go-lucky early Poetism of painters like **Toyen** (Marie Čermínová) (1902–80) and **Jindřich Štyrský** (1899–1942). Another Devětsil member, **Josef Šíma** (1891–1971), settled in Paris in 1921, and became a contact between the two movements. In 1932, one of the first international exhibitions of Surrealist art was held in Prague and in 1934 the **Prague Surrealist Group** was established.

Between the wars, internationalism and ideology led Prague's architects towards **Constructivism** and **Functionalism**. The first claimed that mass production and modern materials were beautiful; the second theoretically did not care, so long as a building served its purpose. By the 1930s the aesthetic differences, although still loudly argued over, were little more than nuances. Already primed by Art Nouveau, Prague hurled itself into a brave new world of glass and concrete. In 1924, Teige organized Czech participation in the first international **Bauhaus** exhibition and Adolf Loos built his **Villa Müller** on the outskirts of the capital. Standing outside any movement was radical Slovenian architect, **Jože Plečnik** (1872–1957), who modernized the castle and designed the Church of the Sacred Heart, a masterpiece of eclectic modernism that is well worth a visit if you ever find yourself in the vicinity of Jiřiho z Poděbrad metro station (line A).

From Nazism to Normalization

Culture, along with much else, was crushed by the Nazi invasion of March 1939, and Czechoslovakia's liberation in 1945 turned out to be short-lived. Within three years the Communist Party had manoeuvred itself into power, and individual creativity was being stifled in the name of **Socialist Realism**, a Soviet theory that valued art only insofar as it conveyed a political message simple enough for Bolshevik bureaucrats to approve.

After Stalin's death, cultural constraints were slowly eased. The **Surrealist movement** whooped into life again in the late 1950s. Important artists were **Mikuláš Medek** (1926–74), **Václav Tikal** and, most impressive of all, **Jiří Kolář**, who experimented with collage assemblages of image and word. In 1965, Prague's students elected Beat poet **Allen Ginsberg** as their king and carried him shoulder-high up Wenceslas Square. By 1968, the mildly insane **Milan Knížák** was slaughtering chickens to loud rock music.

The party ended on the night of 21 August 1968 as 200,000 Warsaw Pact troops turned the Prague Spring into winter. Potential centres of ideological resistance, such as theatre companies and

Czech Food and Drink

There are several types of eating and drinking establishments in Prague: beer joints (*pivnice*, *hostinec* or *hospoda*), wine bars (*vinárny*), cafés (*kavárny*) and restaurants (*restaurace*). The most distinctive delicacy of the Czech kitchen is the *knedlík*, or dumpling. Praguers treat it as the highest culinary expression of the country: if you say that you recently ate an unexciting one, you are almost certain to be told that you just have to know where to go. The main distinction is between floury *houskový knedlík* and *bramborový knedlík*, made of mushy potato. Both are usually served with a lump of meat in a thick gravy, and are staple fare in beer halls. *Špekové knedlíky* are marginally more interesting, mixed with bacon, while *kynuté knedlíky* are downright wild in comparison, centred on lumps of stewed fruit.

You're on tastier ground when it comes to cold meats. Prague ham (*šunka*) is of high quality, but it's generally agreed that the best salamis are the harder Hungarian varieties, particularly the flat *lovecký salám*, and *Uherský salám*. Sausages are much loved, and you can pick up a *párek* (two long porkers) in stands across the city. The frankfurter-like *Liberecký párek* and the paprika-flavoured *čabajka* are the best varieties. If you avoid pork, you can eat *hovězí párky* and *drubeží párky*, made of beef and chicken respectively.

Freshwater fish are a healthy alternative: carp and trout are bred in the lakes of southern Bohemia and, along with the pike and eel that are occasionally found with them, are widely available in Prague. Soups (*polévky*) are often delicious, and in cheaper beer halls and cafés they are often the most likely winners on the menu. *Dršťková* is one of the most popular soups and comprises floating pieces of a cow's stomach, while *zabijačková polévka* is a pungent concoction made largely of pigs' blood. The name, roughly translated, means 'slaughter soup'.

There are a few other snacks that you'll probably encounter. Stalls across the city sell *bramborák*, a garlicky potato pancake that is delicious if not too greasy. *Ďábelský toust* is a fiercely tasty mixture of meat (usually beef) on toast. *Smažený sýr* is fried cheese, which is more appetizing but no less unhealthy than it sounds.

Czech beer needs little introduction: Plzeň is the home of Pilsner Urquell, the first lager and the father of a thousand German imitators, while the brewing town of Budweis (České Budějovice) has become part of the American dream. US company Busch borrowed little more than the name, however, and the potent concoction produced in the Czech Republic puts the US slop to shame. (Perhaps realizing that, Busch has prevented its rival from marketing itself as Budweiser within the US for decades.) Both Czech beers are chock-full of alcohol and sugar, all created naturally during the brewing process, unlike that in additive-laden Western rivals. You may already like sweet beers, and if not you should acquire the taste: look out for beer halls and bottles marked Plzeňský prazdroj and Budvar. Prague also produces beers of its own – Staropramen, Braník and Smíchov – which are slightly more bitter. Czech wine might yet become a force to be reckoned with, but at present is best mulled; ask for *svařené víno*.

the Writers' Union, were dissolved, and artists who had supported the uprising were anathematized. Intellectuals and artists found work as taxi-drivers, or found fame abroad. The most courageous signed the **Charter 77** manifesto.

Resurrection

The changes unleashed in 1989 have seen stultification give way to hyperactivity. Within the space of a few short years, Czech artists have been unravelling their own mangled modernist traditions, while simultaneously learning the tricks and language perfected by a generation of Western postmodernists. The most provocative prankster to have emerged so far is **David Černý**, whose claims to fame include attaching large plastic infants to Prague's television tower (*Babies*) and floating a life-sized model of Saddam Hussein in a tank of formaldehyde (*Shark*).

Prague's architecture stands at an even more pivotal moment. The **Dancing House** (*see* p.184) designed by Frank Gehry and Croatian-born Vlado Milunič, proves that the city's traditions can accommodate inventiveness. The most striking impact of the free market has been to encourage renovations that were overdue decades ago. And yet, at the same time, garish malls and gloomy office developments stand as grim reminders that the hunger for money can still leech a city's soul.

Quite what comes next is anyone's guess, but those curious about Prague's cultural trajectory could do worse than head for the suburbs. Social energy has been flowing out of the centre for several years, and areas such as Karlín – the undisputed armpit of the capital for decades – are turning into magnets for the city's artists. As once derelict warehouses are colonized and disused factories become workspaces, a new culture is finally coalescing from a generation that was born after 1989.

But it's the ancient stone jigsaw at Prague's centre that will have drawn you to the capital, and whatever the artists may be scheming and the developers dreaming, it will endure. Even capitalism would have its work cut out to destroy that.

Around the City

Old Town (Staré Město)

The Old Town is the central European fantasy in microcosm: a topsy-turvy world of Baroque colour and Gothic gloom steeped in centuries of legend and history. It has witnessed catastrophes and revolutions that would have destroyed a lesser place – but, as you wander beneath its demented spires and towers, it can still seem as fantastic as a childhood dream.

Charles Bridge (Karlův most)

Charles Bridge

For centuries the Old Town's energy has squeezed over this bridge. Across its cobbles, invaders have advanced, armies have retreated, and a score of monarchs have headed towards their coronations – and, although the processions of yesteryear have given way to troupes of guided tourists, it remains Prague's jugular vein.

There was a wooden way across the river more than 1,000 years ago, if Cosmas the chronicler is to be believed: an incidental detail of his account of the murder of St Wenceslas is that the bridge was damaged in 932, requiring a spot of Divine Intervention to fly the pallbearers across. Nothing is left of that structure, but remnants of the Judith Bridge, built in 1158, survive in the piers of the present work. The Judith Bridge was destroyed by floods in 1342, but the civic pride of Charles IV, who ascended the throne four years later, ensured that Prague didn't remain bridgeless for long. Astrologers were asked to find a suitably auspicious celestial configuration, and in 1357 Charles's architect, 27-year-old Peter Parléř, got to work. Construction was completed in the early 1400s, and, for more than 400 years the bridge was Prague's only river crossing. It carried trams and buses during the early 1900s, and has survived innumerable deluges – most memorably on 14 August 2002, when the worst floods in Czech history came within two metres of overwhelming it entirely.

Old Town Bridge Tower (Staroměstská mostecká věž)

**Old Town
Bridge Tower**
*open daily
10–6, later in
summer; adm*

Designed by Peter Parléř and completed during the reign of Wenceslas IV, the titanic Old Town Bridge Tower is part of the city's fortification walls, and has had both symbolic and practical functions. After the execution of Bohemian nationalists in 1620, 10 heads hung putrefying from its first floor for a decade. In 1648 the final hours of the Thirty Years War raged around the tower, when Sweden's army went on a last-minute looting spree and the Old Town was saved by a motley alliance of bearded students and Prague Jews. A Europe-wide peace had been negotiated, but another truce was clearly necessary. It was signed on the middle of the bridge, in a wooden cabin partitioned to keep the factions from each other's throats. That battle destroyed most of the decoration on the western façade of the tower; the east still has its original 14th-century decoration, with sculptures of SS Adalbert and Procopius at the top, Wenceslas IV and Charles IV enthroned below, and St Vitus in the centre.

The view from the first floor is impressive: so much so that the Communist secret police used to sit here and point eavesdropping equipment and lenses at suspicious conversationalists on the bridge below.

Sculptures on the Bridge

The stark structure of the bridge is perfectly complemented by the 30 sculptures that now line it. The 14th century saw a simple wooden crucifix placed on the bridge; the Counter-Reformation knew a propaganda opportunity when it saw one and, during the late 1600s and early 1700s, an entire avenue of Baroque saints was added, inspired by Bernini's 1688 work on the Ponte Sant'Angelo in Rome. The hapless commuters of Prague were a captive audience to what would then have been an awesome array of gesticulating saints. Many of the works have now been replaced by copies to protect the originals from pollution, and there is some lifeless neo-Gothic statuary from the 19th century, but the overall effect of the sculpture is still superb.

The oldest work is the bronze *Crucifixion* (1657), third on your right going east to west, flanked by 19th-century works. The Hebrew inscription on the statue was the contribution of an outspoken Jew, who wandered past in 1695 muttering blasphemies. The fifth statue on your left shows **St Francis Xavier** being borne aloft by grateful bearers. It's a copy of a 1711 work by F. M. Brokof which was swept away by a flood in 1890. Ignatius used to stand on the opposite side of the bridge; after sinking in 1890, he was replaced by the youngest statue here, Karel Dvořák's 1938 sculpture of **SS Cyril and Methodius**.

About halfway across on northern side of the bridge, a small bronze **Lorraine Cross** is embedded in the wall. Rumour has it that the Dalai Lama recognized this point as the centre of the universe during his visit to Prague in 1990. It also marks the spot where **St John Nepomuk** was hurled into the river. Put your hand on it, make a wish and then go to his statue, the eighth on the right. John was a cleric who was put in a sack and dropped into the Vltava in 1383 by Wenceslas IV. He will get you across any bridge safely, despite his own misfortune, and he's the saint to turn to if you're ever wrongly accused.

Further along, **SS Vincent Ferrer and Procopius** deserve a mention: among the feats noted on their statue are the salvation of 100,000 souls, the conversion of 2,500 Jews, 70 exorcisms and 40 resurrections. A downcast devil, Turk and Jew support the saints. If you look across the bridge here, you'll see the statue of **Bruncvík**, a chivalrous character linked to the legend of Roland – a sanguinary epic of crusading Christianity.

Of the petrified melodramas that remain, take a look at Matthias Braun's **St Luitgard**. Generally agreed to be the best-crafted sculpture on the bridge, it shows Christ letting the blind saint nuzzle His wounds, a vision she enjoyed late one night. Two statues along is F. M. Brokof's pantomime-like tribute to the **Trinitarian Order**, established for the age-old purpose of ransoming Christian hostages from infidel clutches. The founders of the Order stand above a little grotto full of captives, guarded by a pot-bellied pasha and a mad dog.

Judith Tower
open daily 10–6, later in summer; adm

The western end of the bridge is punctuated by the **Malá Strana Bridge Tower**, which was built in the early 1400s, and the stumpy **Judith Tower**, which belonged to the 12th-century predecessor of the Charles Bridge. The inseparable duo, wearing tiled top hats and forming the parapet and arch into Malá Strana, frame St Nicholas's

Church and one of Prague's most tempting photo opportunities. As you walk through the gateway, cast your gaze up to the grooves on the southern wall; they're the scars of years of axe-sharpening, from the days when Malá Strana's executioner's rostrum used to stand here.

The Clementinum

Clementinum
Mariánské náměstí 5 or Seminářská 1, t 221 663 111; Baroque Library and Astronomical Tower open Mon–Fri 2–7, Sat–Sun 11–7

The Jesuits' former headquarters in the Old Town fills the entire block to the northeast of the Charles Bridge, at the Old Town end. During the uneasy peace that preceded the Thirty Years War (1618–48), it became the nerve centre of the Czech Counter-Reformation, relighting the Catholic flame in a city that had become 90 per cent Protestant. The Jesuit Order made up the Counter-Reformation's advance platoons. One of its most successful weapons was education. The Clementinum's success was such that, by the 17th century, non-Catholic families were queuing up to enrol their little ones. The college swallowed up its arch-rival, the Protestant Carolinum, in 1622, but in 1773 it was finally secularized. It now lives on as the **Czech State Library**.

The Jesuits took their architecture seriously. They moved into this site in 1556, but the present complex was built in protracted stages between 1653 and 1723, on the site of 30-odd houses, three churches, 10 courtyards and several gardens. Just two sections are open to the public – the Baroque Great Library and the Astronomical Tower, both handsomely restored in 2000. On display for visitors are some of the oldest illuminated manuscripts in the library's collection, a selection of Baroque astronomical instruments, and a pair of intriguing clocks made by Jan Klein, a maths teacher at the Clementinum. They illustrate just how much the quasi-rational Jesuits dithered over the position of the earth: on the left, it sits firmly at the centre of the universe, while on the right it circles the sun.

A step away is the **Great Library**, the grandest of all the Halls on the upper floor and the only one open to the public. It was designed by Kaňker in 1727, and its cherub-topped rococo bookshelves are overlooked by an enormous fresco in three parts. In the centre is a spectacular collection of Baroque globes. The **Astronomical Tower** at the very centre of the complex was the last part to be built (1721–3, remodelled in 1749). It was the college **Observatory** right up till 1928. Creak up the original wooden staircase to see the measuring device for establishing noon; light pierces through a tiny hole in the wall, and the narrow beam strikes a paved section in the wooden flooring. Kilian Dienzenhofer designed the **Chapel of Mirrors** in 1724, fusing glass and stucco decoration in a shimmering display.

The **Clam-Gallas Palace** (Clam-Gallasův palác) at Husova 20
contains the city archives and is only open to visitors for concerts.
Its colossal atlantes, built in 1713–19, were designed by one of the
masters of Austrian Baroque, J. B. Fischer von Erlach.

The ground floor of Franz Kafka's birthplace in U Radnice was
converted into the **Expozice Franze Kafky** in 1991. It contains a few
photos and a large selection of souvenir booklets.

Bethlehem Square (Betlémské náměstí)

True to Prague form, this tranquil square has had a tumultuous
history. It was here that Bohemia's religious reformers chose in 1391
to build a church where services could be held in the vernacular.
The idea was never a popular one in the Catholic Church. Papal
authorities granted permission for only a chapel – and began to
monitor events closely. Bohemians picked up the gauntlet, and
proceeded to construct the largest chapel in the country; with
panache, they centred it on the pulpit rather than the altar; and
with the Protestant preference for scripture over saints they
thumbed through the Bible for a name.

Countless heresies would be expounded from said pulpit at the
Bethlehem Chapel (Betlémská kaple), and the most threatening of
them all came from Jan Hus (*see* p.125). Hus's rejection of papal
authority prefigured that of Martin Luther by more than a century,
and when he began preaching in 1402 – before congregations of
up to 3,000 people – the city's clerics also pricked up their ears.
Prague's archbishop initially warned him to pipe down. When Hus
ignored the advice, he was excommunicated. An exasperated pope
finally decided to roast him in 1415. The building is a modern copy
of the original, which was all but demolished in 1786, and there's
now little to see inside other than daubed sermons preserved
on three walls.

Bethlehem Chapel
*generally open from
10–5 but times vary;
call* **t** *224 248 595 for
further information;
adm*

Old Town Square (Staroměstské náměstí)

The Old Town Square is the Brothers Grimm in stone: Gothic
towers, a sparkling white church and a pastel wave of pink and
blue Baroque rooftops. It is the strolling intersection of Staré
Město, and the perfect spot to soak up rays, history and a beer on a
summer's day. The best place for an overview is from the steps of
the **Monument to Jan Hus** (*see* box, overleaf). A bronze line in front
of the sculpture marks Prague's former meridian: a Marian column,
erected in 1649 to celebrate the Bohemian Counter-Reformation,
sent its midday shadow along here until it was toppled by a
patriotic mob in 1918. With independence, Prague gave up the
inconvenient tradition of calculating its own time.

The triangular junction known as the **Small Square** (Malé
náměstí), which leads into Staroměstské náměstí, threw up some

Jan Hus

Heretical Hus was burned alive in 1415. His death marked the beginning of decades of war in Bohemia. Two centuries later, his Protestant heirs were eradicated at the Battle of the White Mountain (see p.128) but, although the population reverted in droves, Hus never lost his position as the pre-eminent symbol of Czech nationalism. In 1900, as the Austro-Hungarian Empire doddered towards extinction, Prague's authorities commissioned a monument to their man, in preparation for the 500th anniversary of his martyrdom. The artist chosen was Ladislav Šaloun, whose lifelong attachment to Art Nouveau techniques (until 1946) placed him outside both the mainstream and the avant-garde of Czech sculpture. When this sculpture was unveiled in 1915, it was predictably showered with abuse. It shows Hus flowing from the bronze base, standing tall between two groups representing the crushed and the defiant. Some complained that Šaloun had created a sprawling mess, by letting his fascination with light effects run away with him; others found the very idea of allegory too disrespectful, although it's doubtful that they would have preferred Hus to be portrayed as the bald midget that he is thought to have been.

historical riddles in 1994, when workers stumbled on an 800-year-old cemetery. Archaeologists were drafted in to ponder the bones, and unearthed a village beneath the graveyard, only 15 years older. Nowadays, the square is dominated by the scenes of bucolic Bohemian happiness that cover the façade of the 19th-century **Rott Haus**, erstwhile home of art connoisseur, patriot and ironmonger Vincent Rott.

Old Town Hall (Staroměstská radnice)

Old Town Hall
Staroměstské náměstí 1; open Tues–Sun 9–6, Mon 11–6; adm; guided tours available

The Staré Město had fortifications built and a royal charter in the mid-13th century, and Wenceslas II grudgingly let Praguers have a clerk in 1296; but when they asked for a town hall to put the clerk in, he put his foot down. The townspeople had to wait until 1338, when they were able to take advantage of blind King John of Luxembourg. The burghers bought a house and turned it into the tower – the beginning of the Town Hall. As the receipts poured in, they were slowly able to add all the buildings to the left. It was a piecemeal process, involving the destruction of spinners' sheds and the roofing-over of the lane to the goose market, but the maroon and white 18th-century façades – encrusted with Gothic and Renaissance survivals from earlier days – now house a single interior, stretching from the tower to the end of the block.

The town hall's pride and joy is its **astronomical clock** (*orloj*); it chimes daily on the hour between 9am and 9pm. Prague woke up late to the idea of clocks – by the time this one was installed in 1410, every other major city in Europe had one – but they were still exotic devices, and the city's burghers were concerned that things should stay that way. Legend has it that when it was remodelled by a certain Master Hanuš in 1490, the Municipal Council took the precaution of blinding him to protect its copyright. A peeved Master Hanuš scaled the building, tossed a medieval spanner in the works, and promptly died. Prague's timepiece was out of joint for almost a century; but since 1572 it has ticked away without interruption, the occasional fire and artillery blitz notwithstanding.

Even into the 17th century, the connected notions of clocks, clockwork and perpetual motion were imbued with a mystery that is hard to imagine today. This one purports to tell the time, but that's only the beginning. Its astronomical symbols, pointers and interlocking circles also register the phases of the moon, the length of the day, the equinoxes, Babylonian time and the dates of innumerable mobile feasts. Every hour two cuckoo-clock windows open and statues of the 12 Apostles mince past while bony Death tinkles his bell. The great leveller is pooh-poohed by preening Vanity, and those bugbears of 15th-century Europe, the Turk and the Jew. The latter now lacks his beard and horns, and is politely referred to as Greed, having been sanitized following the Town Hall's bombardment in 1945. The post-Holocaust decision was understandable, but the paradoxical effect was to whitewash the bloody feature of central Europe's history that had just reached its culmination. A cock, and delighted children, screech when the ceremony is all over. The temporal theme is taken up by the painted calendar below the clock showing the monthly labours of rural folk.

The town hall's modern entrance is situated under the **Renaissance window** (1520). The Latin phrase means 'Prague, head of the kingdom', and was a motto extracted by the burghers from devil-may-care John of Luxembourg.

The small **Gothic chapel** on the first floor dates from 1381. A Nazi tank shelled it to smithereens at the height of the Prague Uprising, but it has been restored well. The chapel's main attraction is up on your right as you face the oriel: through a glass door, the figures of the 12 Apostles wait on the spokes of two wheels for their moment of glory. If your timing is right, you can be here to see the windows open and the figures twirl into life when the hour strikes.

From the chapel, begin the trek to the top of the **tower**, now made much easier by the construction of a glass lift – though the queues can be long enough for you to consider slogging up on foot. After gasping – and gasping – at the view, descend again for the guided tour of the **town hall's rooms**. The tour passes a **memorial cross** made from two charred wooden beams. At least 14 men died in the building during the Nazi assault; it was the headquarters of the committee that led the Prague Uprising. The Resistance fighters holed themselves up in the network of late 12th-century **cellars**. The clammy warren comprises a number of halls, a well, and a dungeon for those women who were thought to talk too much.

The rest of the tour takes you under painted Renaissance joists on the first floor; on the second are faded Gothic murals and a turn-of-the-20th-century drawing of Prague from Petřín Hill, minus the housing estates on today's horizon. The next two rooms contain four works by Václav Brožík (1851–1901), whose speciality was portraying turning-points of Bohemian history with a turgid solemnity. Until 1526, the country's king was chosen in the town hall, and *The Election of King George of Poděbrady* in the Assembly Room shows Hussite George being given the nod by the country's nobles in 1458. The equally monumental *Jan Hus's Trial at Constance* is one of several churned out by Brožík for the nationalist movement.

The **Old Council Chamber**, dating from about 1470, does most to conjure up the years when municipal powers were at their height. The haunting figure of Christ (*c.* 1410) implores them in Latin to 'Judge Justly, Sons of Man'. The councillors found themselves at the receiving end of some rough justice in 1483, when a Hussite mob threw the Catholic mayor and several cronies out of the window, in the second of Prague's four defenestrations (*see* p.126). Reformers then continued the 'good work' with a pogrom in the Jewish Quarter: eradicating Judaism was widely held to be a precondition of the Messiah's expected return in 1500. The scene of the defenestration is no longer known; the Renaissance window through which light now trickles into the chamber was installed 40 years later.

Other Buildings in the Square

The striking cream and brown façade of the **House at the Minute** (Dům U Minuty), adjacent to the Old Town Hall, fronts one of Franz Kafka's many childhood homes in Prague (1889–96). The only explanation that has been offered for its name is that 'minute' does not refer to time, but to the very small bric-a-brac that was once sold here. The *sgraffito* scenes that cover the building date from around 1610.

Goltz-Kinský Palace
t 224 810 758, www.ngprague.cz; open Tues–Sun 10–6; adm

The dainty **Goltz-Kinský Palace** (Palác Goltz-Kinských) dates from 1755–65, by which time Prague's Baroque frenzy had begun to exhaust itself. This is one of the best examples of rococo architecture in the city, with its frilly stucco garlands and pink and white façade. Kafka studied here from 1893 to 1901, and the family connection was resumed some years later when his father, no-nonsense Hermann, moved his haberdashery store into the ground floor. But its moment came in February 1948, when a vast crowd gathered in the square to hear Czechoslovakia's first Communist president, Klement Gottwald, roar from the balcony that the dictatorship of the proletariat had arrived. The gracious palace now hosts exhibitions of graphic art for the National Gallery.

Stone Bell House
t 224 827 526; open Tues–Sun 10–6; adm

The cream façade of the **Stone Bell House** (Dům u Kamenného zvonu), named after the stone bell set into the corner, belongs to the oldest intact Gothic house in Prague, built in the mid-13th century. Thorough remodellings after the late 1600s left it concealed until restorers in the 1960s realized what lay behind its unremarkable neo-Baroque façade. The onion-skins were peeled away, thousands of fragments pieced together or reconstructed and the house was opened to the public in 1986. It's now used for concerts and some of the city's best exhibitions of modern art. The Gothic tower, fronting a Renaissance courtyard, is the richest part of the building, but you'll find fragments of murals, pointed doorways and ribbed vaults throughout. The most complete decoration is in the chapel to your right as you walk towards the courtyard, once entirely covered with murals of the Passion (c. 1310).

Týn Church
open Tues–Sat 10–1 and 3–5, Sun 10.30–12

The 16th-century façade next door rises and falls in bulbous imitation of the building behind it – the 14th-century **Týn Church**. Its multi-pronged towers dominate the square, bristling like Gothic missile batteries, but the only access is through a tiny passage that burrows through house No.14. The building was founded in 1385, and was a hub of Hussitism until the Catholic victory at the Battle of the White Mountain in 1620 (*see* p.128). After a fire in 1679 the central vault was rebuilt, and its altars and decorations are as Baroque as you come to expect of Prague's churches, but those later additions barely register against the triple-naved church's cavernous Gothic structure.

At the end of the northern nave (to your right), past the tombstone of a dwarf, is a powerful Gothic *Calvary* from around 1410. If you cross to the other side of the church, you'll find the marble **tomb of Tycho Brahe** (1546–1601), imperial mathematician to Emperor Rudolf II for two eventful years until his death in 1601. Brahe was one of the most colourful men in a court that was hardly dull (*see* pp.127 and 140) and he continues to inspire fascination centuries after his death. A group of Czech scholars were once so curious about his metal nosepiece – worn to replace the original after he lost it in a duel – that they exhumed him in 1901 to analyse its composition (a gold, silver and copper alloy, for those who need to know). More recently, scientists saw fit to conduct a belated postmortem, which declared Brahe a victim of mercury poisoning. Given his alchemical interests, it sounds plausible enough, though the traditional tale is more in keeping with the irascible astronomer's life. It records that he died after a royal feast – because a combination of over-drinking and a polite reluctance to leave the table caused his bladder to implode.

Almost all the buildings lining the south side of the square bear a painted or carved house sign: the **Štorch House**, at No.16, has a swirling 19th-century depiction of a prissy St Wenceslas on

06 **Czech Republic: Prague** | Old Town (Staré Město)

horseback; and the older **House at the Stone Ram** is marked by a delicate carving of a miniature shepherdess and an enormous ram.

Estates Theatre (Stavovské divadlo)

Estates Theatre
Ovocný trh 1,
t 224 215 001; open for
performances only

The pediment and pillars of the theatre flow from the body of the building in concave curves, with all the elegance of neoclassical architecture at its best. It was a bastion of German opera for 150 years until 1945, and has been a minor place of pilgrimage among Mozart groupies ever since it staged a performance of Mozart's *The Marriage of Figaro* in 1786. Though it had been panned by the snooty Viennese, Prague's critics could not praise it too highly. Wolfgang came to town and was fêted by the city's bourgeoisie and nobility. The management knew a box-office success when it heard one and collared the composer. Commissioned to write another opera, he returned with the score of *Don Giovanni*, which he conducted here for the first time in October 1787, and the theatre's place in musical history was assured.

Also on this square is the **Carolinum** (Karolinum), the core of the Charles University, founded by Emperor Charles IV in 1348. It was central Europe's first university, as Prague's tourist brochures proudly recall, and the 35th on the Continent as a whole, as they generally forget.

Celetná

Celetná is one of the oldest streets in Prague. Behind the Baroque and rococo façades are remnants of earlier Gothic buildings and, below them, cellars that were once ground floors, buried along with the rest of the capital during the drastic flood-prevention programme of the late 13th century. Nowadays, it is a busy shopping street, packed with smart boutiques and Bohemian crystal outlets.

House of the
Black Madonna
Celetná 3; open
Tues–Sun 10–6; adm

Where Celetná meets Ovocný trh is the **House of the Black Madonna** (U Černé Matky Boží), a 20th-century Cubist curiosity housing temporary exhibitions and a permanent display of Czech Cubist art. (It's a small and unexciting collection; far more impressive are the grand keyhole staircase, and the attractive café on the first floor.) Designed by Josef Gočár, and built in 1911–12, the building is recognizable from the caged Virgin suspended above the portals, a 16th-century remnant of an earlier house on the site. Black Madonnas have long been a popular sideline of the Marian cult in Catholic Europe.

Just north of Celetná's Old Town Square end, enclosed between Štupartská and Týnská, is **Týn Court**. The courtyard originated in the 11th century as a kind of caravanserai for traders visiting Prague from lands further east, and had everything they could desire: a church, an inn and even a hospice in which moribund merchants could expire in comfort. Recent renovations have turned it into an enclave for commercialism of a more modern kind, and it now comprises a stack of restaurants, gift shops and cafés. Look out for the *sgraffito*-adorned arcade of the graceful **Granovsky House**, built by Týn's customs officer in 1560.

St James's Church (Kostel sv. Jakub)

St James's Church
Malá Štupartská,
t 224 828 816; open
daily 9.30–12 and 2–4

This church, founded in 1374, was redesigned during the Counter-Reformation – along with almost every other one in Prague – but it escaped the overkill that turned some others in grotesqueries, and it remains one of the most elegant in the city. It also has the city's finest acoustics, and the regular organ concerts that are held here make for spine-tingling listening.

Once past the rich stucco reliefs above the entrance – homages to the eventful lives of SS James, Francis of Assissi and Antony of Padua – you'll find yourself confronted by the second-longest nave in Prague. Its Gothic proportions keep the 21 Baroque altars firmly under control, even if the splendid **Tomb of Count Jan Václav Vratislav of Mitrovice**, at the far end of the northern aisle, tries its hardest to break free.

As you leave, you might look out for a less carefully crafted monument to human folly to the left of the main doors. It's a scraggly **human forearm** hanging from a chain – the remains of a miracle that reputedly took place in 1400, when a thief tried to pilfer jewels belonging to the Madonna who now sits at the high altar. She apparently grabbed the limb and held on so tightly that it had to be chopped off. A painting dimly depicts the glorious scene.

Municipal House (Obecní dům)

① Municipal House
Náměstí Republiky 5,
t 222 002 101,
www.obecni-dum.cz;
open daily 10–7; guided tours in English of the Smetana Hall and main rooms; adm

The Municipal House, with exhibition halls and auditorium, is an Art Nouveau masterpiece. The ornate façade, built between 1906 and 1911, is a successful contribution to the Czech national revival. Scores of Prague artists and architects contributed, notably Mucha, and the effect is a cacophonous *charivari* rather than a tight symphony in the new style. It is a forest of crystal and mirrors, whiplash curves, organic excrescences and sensual homages to Czechdom and civic virtue. It now hosts exhibitions of all things Art Nouveau, from poster art to photography.

A wander around the staircase between the ground-floor restaurant, the elegant *kavárna* (café) and the basement bars is free and gives a heady sense of the opulence of the age. But to see most of the interior, finally restored to its original lustre in 1997, you'll have to join a tour, starting with the massive cloakroom (*šatna*). Rising through two storeys at the core of the building is the **Smetana Hall**. Just off the Hall is the glittering **Confectioner's**

Room (*cukrárna*), complete with gilded display cases and an original samovar (1912), still gracefully dispensing coffee. The **Slovakian Lounge** (Slovácky salónek) has an Art Nouveau aquarium encrusted with brass snails, and the Turkish delights of the **Oriental Hall** are among the best-preserved in the building. The sumptuous Art Deco **Gregr Hall** is still used for chamber concerts and dances. In the circular **Mayoral Hall** (Sál primátorský) are violet windows, and paintings by Alfons Mucha.

Powder Gate (Prašná brána)

Powder Gate
*Na příkopě;
open daily 10–6, later in
summer; adm*

Originally one of the gates into the Staré Město, this Gothic hulk is now marooned in a 20th-century sea. Tethered by a small bridge to the neighbouring Municipal House and hemmed in by grim banks and a shiny shoe shop, it's a stately but forlorn reminder of a glory that never was. As long ago as the 11th century, traders with turbans, pelts, spices and slaves would roll into Prague from the East through a gateway here. Although this tower was begun in 1475 amid general festivities and merriment, it was rapidly abandoned by the mercurial Hussites. Later, it was given a temporary roof, a use (gunpowder storage) and an unimaginative name. It was bombarded by Frederick the Great, and emerged in an even sorrier state than before. It was finally put out of its misery by the zealous neo-Gothic touch of the Czech Josef Mocker; the ornate decoration of the façade, and much of the interior, is his work (1875–86).

The Eastern Old Town

The area south of the river and east of Kozí is one of the loveliest parts of Staré Město. The small houses and cobbled lanes, bathed in a sleepy hush, are a tantalizing glimpse of what a restored Josefov might have become. Off Dušní at Elišky Krásnohorské 10–14 stand some **Cubist Houses**, built by Otakar Novotný. With their jutting geometrical balconies, they were constructed between 1919 and 1921 when the old ghetto slums were still being cleared. They originally housed a teacher's collective, but are now private residences.

On the corner of Dušní and U milosrdných, the now deconsecrated church of **SS Simon and Jude** (Kostel sv. Šimona a Judy) has a net-vault that's an example of Prague's tenacious use of Gothic motifs into the early 17th century. Mozart and Haydn played on the organ in its heyday and nowadays it occasionally hosts chamber concerts featuring the Prague Symphony Orchestra. The Baroque façade, along with that of the one-time hospital next door, dates from the 1750s.

St Agnes' Convent (Klášter sv. Anežky)

St Agnes' Convent
*U milosrdných 17,
t 224 810 628, www.
ngprague.cz; open
Tues–Sun 10–6; adm*

St Agnes', the oldest remaining Gothic building in Prague, now houses the National Gallery's collection of **Bohemian and Central European Gothic Art**. The convent was founded by King Wenceslas in 1233, at the urging of his sister Agnes (Anežka) who had just signed up with the Order of the Poor Clares. Agnes was canonized as recently as 12 November 1989; the 750-year delay was because her body was never found. The long wait meant that, by the time she got the papal thumbs-up, the inevitable legend had arisen that her canonization would be accompanied by great marvels. The prophecy was duly fulfilled five days later, with the advent of the Velvet Revolution. Since 2000, the restored and expanded convent has housed the National Gallery's Gothic art collection. The earliest Gothic art in Bohemia dates from the beginning of the 14th century. The slender and elegant Madonnas in the **opening gallery**, their faces half turned away, show how Bohemian art was beginning to escape the rigid formality of its Byzantine progenitors, with ever more robust representations of the human form.

In the next room is the *Vyšší Brod (Hohenfurth) Altarpiece*. The most notable feature of the nine paintings is their use of contrasting colours to create an illusion of depth, a hundred years before the laws of perspective twinkled in the eyes of the clever Florentines. It is most remarkable in *The Descent of the Holy Ghost*: huddled Apostles swirl in a sea of reds and greens and indigos, yet the space around them appears almost three-dimensional.

The loud-mouthed creature with the droopy ears is called *Gargoyle-ibex*, though less goat-like a beast you never did see. Beyond its howling canine companion is the room containing the work of **Master Theodoric**, the first of Bohemia's painters to emerge from misty anonymity; as you gaze at the six paintings on display here, you'll understand the reasons for his fame. Bohemian artists' experiments with colour values and facial modelling reach their culmination in these panels, which have a vitality that survives six centuries. The panels are from the Chapel of the Holy Rood at Charles IV's castle at Karlštejn, where there are over 100 more (*see* p.204).

With Charles's death and the coronation of his wastrel son Wenceslas IV in 1378, Bohemian art became increasingly refined. Sophistication replaced spiritual mystery, and the paintings of women take on a doll-like charm. Look, for example, at the languid rosy-cheeked depictions of SS Catherine, Mary Magdalene and Margaret in the *Třebon (Wittingau) Altarpiece* of c. 1380. The line of Madonnas become romanticized images of motherhood: the *St Vitus' Madonna* shows the phenomenon in all its treacle; it's also apparent in the sculptures. The humanization trend takes a different form in most of the depictions of men of late Gothic art: the galleries are filled with hirsute and/or bald saints, while Christ suffers and is tortured with a greater intensity than ever before.

The work in the following galleries represents the final period of Bohemian Gothic art. By the time you get to the *Lamentation* of *c.* 1510–20, the regular cast of characters mourning the dead Christ show a restraint that's still utterly Gothic, but have begun to sprout the extra inches and shrunken pin-heads so characteristic of Mannerist art. The ground floor ends with the carvings of Monogrammist I. P., a shadowy character who lived in Prague from 1520 to 1550, and left behind a series of masterful woodcuts, showing the devotion to north European foliage characteristic of the Danube School.

Josefov

✪ Jewish Quarter

Josefov, standing on the land that once constituted the Jewish ghetto, has in recent years turned into the bourgeois district of boulevards and avenues that its Paris-inspired designers always wanted it to be. But, as you walk under the 19th-century façades, you can't help but hear whispers from the past. Its neo-Gothic strongholds and Art Nouveau citadels host airline offices and fashion stores today, but they tower over tiny synagogues and a melancholy cemetery, and fill land that was for hundreds of years at the very centre of the Jewish world. Elsewhere in Prague, history reeks from every stone, but in the Jewish Quarter it's the transformation that speaks.

Jewish Museum (Židovské muzeum)

Jewish Museum
t 221 711 511,
www.jewishmuseum.cz;
open Sun–Fri except
Jewish holidays,
April–Oct 9–6;
Nov–Mar 9–4.30; adm,
tickets sold at the
Pinkas Synagogue and
next to the Klausen
Synagogue; reserve in
advance in summer;
entry to the Old-New
Synagogue (see p.155) is
not included in the
museum adm charge;
the Jewish community's
website is at
www.kehilaprag.cz

The Jewish Museum comprises six major sites in the former Jewish Ghetto: the Maisel Synagogue, the Spanish Synagogue, the Pinkas Synagogue, the old Jewish Cemetery, the Klausen Synagogue, and the Ceremonial Hall.

Pinkas Synagogue (Pinkasova synagóga)

The Pinkas Synagogue stands over the 11th-century foundations of what may have been the first synagogue in Prague, at the southern edge of the cemetery. Rabbi Pinkas inaugurated its construction in 1479. After the Second World War it was chosen to house the Czech monument to the victims of the Holocaust: under the gilded ribs of the brick-red vault were listed the names of each of the 77,297 Czech Jews who died at Nazi hands. The synagogue was reopened in 1991, after being closed for over 20 years of so-called restoration, during which the Communist authorities allowed the memorial to crumble into indecipherability. They excused themselves by blaming rising damp. As you gaze at the

The Jewish Ghetto

No one knows when the first Jews came to Prague. Historical sources suggest that it was probably in the 10th century, and that Jews first lived in two separate communities on either side of the river. By the mid-13th century, however, an unhappy set of events had combined to create a single community here: Přemysl Otakar II wanted the left bank for his new town of Malá Strana; Staré Město was fortified; and, most crucially, in 1179 the Church had announced that Christians should avoid touching Jews, ideally by building a moat or a wall around them. Another set of walls was built within the Staré Město and, three centuries before the word was coined in Venice, Prague Jews began life in the ghetto.

The daily routine was much the same as that of Jews elsewhere in central Europe: pogroms, ritual murder allegations, and occasional banishments from the land. By day movement was free, but as the sun set, the portcullis was lowered. The gates would be locked throughout the Easter/Passover flashpoint. Jews didn't mind, as it kept out the crowds eager to avenge Jesus on Good Friday, but the authorities' concerns were no different from those of the mob. Medieval Christendom assumed that the Passover lamb was a cunning codeword for Christ and that, unless the gates were locked, Christian babies and virgins would end up on a Passover plate.

During the 16th century, the ghetto became a vortex of mysticism as interest in the kabbalah grew among both Jews and Christians throughout Europe. The mysterious cabalistic tradition – handed down orally from Adam – was reflected in the intellectual questing of Rudolf II's court; the exchange of cryptic data between rabbis and castle scholars was legendary. The period was to inspire a powerful image of the ghetto as a dank universe of miracles and poverty, its 7,000 inhabitants living cheek-by-jowl in a labyrinth of cramped lanes, subterranean passages and hypertrophied buildings. There's more than a little truth to the picture, but, although the ghetto was sealed, it wasn't all poor. The richest man in Rudolfine Prague was Jewish.

In 1784, under Emperor Josef II, the gates were thrown open. Josef, enlightened despot that he was, was being liberal only in an academic sense. The idea was to wipe the Jews out as an independent community: the use of Hebrew or Yiddish in business was prohibited, and separate schools were banned. That didn't stop him being honoured in 1850, when Jews were finally granted civil rights and the ghetto was formally incorporated into Prague under the name of Josefov. Integration proceeded apace: rich Jews moved out, and poor Christians moved in. By the end of the 19th century, the district was a set of 288 stinking slums, brothels and bars, a breeding ground for typhoid and tuberculosis. The authorities chose to destroy the buildings, along with an irreplaceable part of Europe's history. Broad streets, crowded with turn-of-the-century mansions, now stand over winding medieval alleys. Of the old ghetto, only six synagogues, the town hall and the cemetery were spared, and survive thanks to Hitler's macabre decision that they would house a postwar 'Exotic Museum of an Extinct Race'. Of the Jews themselves, some 80,000 of the 90,000 who remained in Bohemia and Moravia in March 1939 were killed.

In 1994 the State, which had taken over the Nazi collection after the war, finally relinquished control and the new Jewish Museum was opened by President Havel.

thousands of names, now repainted, only their tragedy can dwarf the scale of that insult.

Upstairs is a heart-rending exhibition of children's drawings from the camp at Terezín. Of the approximately 8,000 children who were transported east to the extermination camps, only 242 survived the war.

Old Jewish Cemetery (Starý židovský hřbitov)

Known in Hebrew as **Beth-Chajim**, or the House of Life, this Jewish graveyard is the second oldest in Europe and is an astonishing sight: the flash of a lost world that imprints itself on

Old Jewish Cemetery
entrance through Pinkas Synagogue

your memory. For more than three centuries until 1787 it was the only burial ground the Jews were permitted, its elder trees the only patch of green behind the ghetto walls. As space ran out, it was covered with earth, older gravestones were raised, and a new layer of burials was begun. Subsidence has turned the graveyard into a forest of some 12,000 madly teetering tombstones. Many are half-interred themselves; many have migrated far from the person they commemorate; and, as you walk through, there are thought to be some 20,000 people under your feet, buried in up to 12 subterranean storeys. Tens of thousands of people now visit annually, and for many reasons – including religious sensibilities and the fact that the cemetery was being padded down by a millimetre each year – walking routes have now been marked out.

The oldest known plot is that of poet **Avigdor Kara**, dating from 1439. In 1389, Kara lived through and lamented the most vicious pogrom in Prague's history, in which 3,000 were massacred: more than half the ghetto's inhabitants. His original gravestone, now in the Maisel Synagogue, has been replaced by a copy which you'll find on the path running along the eastern wall of the cemetery.

Along the western wall of the cemetery, near the Pinkas Synagogue, is the grave of **Rabbi David Oppenheim** (1664–1736), whose 5,000-volume library went on a tour across Europe, making it to Oxford's Bodleian in 1829 as the Oppenheimer Collection.

Just as you emerge from the Pinkas Synagogue courtyard into the cemetery, you can find the grand tomb of **Mordechai Maisel** (1528–1601), the mayor of the ghetto during the reign of Rudolf II. Maisel had to wear a yellow wheel and high hat like any Jew in Rudolfine Prague (badge and hat were an intermittent requirement throughout the ghetto's history) but he died one of the wealthiest men in Europe.

The best-known of all the cemetery's occupants, the subject of tales that are still told to awestruck New York children, is **Rabbi Loew ben Bezalel** (1512–1609). His tomb, covered in pebbles, is along the western wall, opposite the entrance gate. Loew, born in either Poznan or Worms, was one of the leading scholars of 16th-century Jewry. Most of his life was spent in Prague, and in 1597 he took over as chief rabbi of the ghetto; by the time of his death, he was already a legend (*see* box, p.156). His powers apparently extended even beyond the grave: he is surrounded by 30 faithful disciples, among whom is his grandson Samuel. Solemn Samuel set his heart on being buried next to his grandfather; Loew vowed that he wouldn't be disappointed. Bungling ghetto authorities filled the precious plot with another lucky corpse but, dead though he was, Loew had not forgotten. When Samuel expired, the rabbi and his sepulchre budged a couple of feet. Samuel's grave is the thin one on the left.

Ceremonial Hall (Obřadní síň)

Ceremonial Hall
*entrance at exit of
Old Jewish Cemetery,
on U starého hřbitova*

This crooked neo-Romanesque citadel, squatting on the edge of the cemetery, was built at the beginning of the 20th century. Its tenant was the Prague *Hevrah Kadisha*, or Burial Society – established in 1564, and responsible ever since for maintaining the graveyard was ensuring that its occupants were buried swiftly and in fit fashion. The building now contains a small collection of shrouds, some disconcerting corpse-cleansing implements, and a cycle of early 19th-century paintings that illustrate the society's deathbed-to-grave duties.

Klausen Synagogue (Klausová synagoga)

**Klausen
Synagogue**
*entrance by the
exit gates for the
Old Jewish Cemetery,
on U starého hřbitova*

The late 17th-century synagogue, remodelled in 1884, was built on the site of a mess of schools and prayer halls. Rabbi Loew taught in an older building. The synagogue now houses exhibits devoted to Jewish customs and traditions in daily life.

Maisel Synagogue (Maiselova synagoga)

The Maisel Synagogue was another of the mayor's gifts to the ghetto, but it was dully remodelled in neo-Gothic style at the end of the last century. The hall contains an exhibition devoted to the history of Jews in Bohemia from the 10th to the 18th century, including a spectacular silver collection.

Spanish Synagogue (Španělská synagoga)

The Spanish Synagogue, on the corner of Široká and Dušni, is the last of the synagogues to survive the great tidying-up of 1897–1917; three were destroyed, along with some 30 smaller prayer halls. Its arabesques and keyhole-shaped windows are the last reminder of the Sephardic Jews who settled in this part of the Staré Město after their mass expulsion from Spain in 1492. They themselves commandeered an ancient synagogue on the site, but this neo-Moorish structure dates from the end of the 19th century. It has been magnificently restored, and extravagant gilding now glistens throughout an interior that feels as much like a mosque as a synagogue. It contains an exhibition devoted to the modern history of Czech Jewry, and has a small display dedicated to Franz Kafka and the so-called Prague Circle: a clique of bickering, brilliant writers who made an important contribution to the last great flowering of German-Jewish culture in Europe.

Old-New Synagogue (Staronová synagoga)

**Old-New
Synagogue**
*corner of Pařížská/
Červená; opening times
are the same as those
of the Jewish museum
sites (see p.152), though
a separate ticket is
required; men must
cover their heads;
yarmulkes are provided*

One of the oldest functioning synagogues to survive in Europe, the Old-New Synagogue is still used today by Prague's Orthodox community. There are two explanations for the synagogue's name. The more prosaic offering is that it was coined when the building

The Legendary Rabbi Loew

Every community mythologizes its history, but with the legendary Rabbi Loew, Prague's Jews personified it. The legends begin on a touching note. When young Loew arrived in the capital, he was smitten by Pearl, daughter of one Reb Schmelke, who promptly went bankrupt. Loew was so in love that he agreed to wait until the dowry could be raised. Impetuous it may have been, but it was only 10 years before Reb Schmelke was back on his feet, thanks to a bag of gold that a contemptuous cavalier tossed at Pearl as he stole a loaf of bread. Loew, by now steeped in the Talmud, declared that that had been no ordinary horseman, but Elijah. The stage was set for an exceptional life.

Certain themes run through all the tales. The ghetto is under constant threat from Christians, the wickedest of whom is Brother Thaddeus, whose very mention brings a hiss to the throat. There is also the occasional good goy, most notably the weak but fundamentally sympathetic Emperor Rudolf. Pulling the strings together is mild-mannered Rabbi Loew, who checks Brother Thaddeus at every turn, dares to reveal to the emperor that his real mother was Jewish, and exchanges tips with other super-rabbis across Europe in his dreams. On the innumerable occasions that Rudolf begs him for help, the rabbi rescues him from jail, dethrones an impostor and overturns expulsion edicts. When a jealous flunky persuades the vacillating emperor to order Loew to hold a banquet, the scholar transports a shimmering palace from a distant land into his humble ghetto abode; and to the now jovial Rudolf II's uproarious laughter, the luckless lackey pockets a goblet and is rooted to his seat.

The legend now inextricably linked to Loew is that of the *golem*, or artificial man. The word, meaning 'unformed substance' (or 'unmarried woman') in Hebrew, is first found in Psalms 139:16. The idea that humanity could create life comes from the mystical cabalistic tradition that each mortal contains a spark of the divine. Jewish history is littered with pre-Loewian *golems*, but Rabbi Loew's has become the most famous, turned into a German silent film (1920), a French talkie (1937) and a tale to alarm good Jewish boys and girls. It all began while Loew communed with the cosmos one night. He was warned that danger loomed and told to make a *golem*, pronto. With his two youthful rabbi sidekicks, he hurried to the banks of the Vltava and built a man out of mud, walked around it several times and then placed the unknown name of God (the *shem*) in its mouth. 'Joseph Golem' was born. His adventures are laced with slapstick ghetto humour, but most are of a grimly heroic nature. Joseph once rescues a girl from being forcibly baptized and, when the community is on trial for ritual murder, he arrives with the exonerating evidence just as the verdict is about to be announced.

Joseph was eventually laid to rest in the roof of Prague's Old-New Synagogue. The annihilation of the capital's Jews gave rise to the last *golem* legend. It had been said that he would return if needed, but as the Nazi cattle trains filled and emptied, those Jews who remained declared that he had died for ever. It sounds likely, but Praguers still claim that on stormy nights, Joseph's footsteps can be heard on those streets of the ancient ghetto that survive.

was newly constructed on an older synagogue, but Jewish legend springs to the rescue with the claim that *alt-neu* ('old-new' in German) is actually a corruption of *al-tenai*, or 'with reservation' in Hebrew. Angels and/or outriders of the Diaspora are said to have built the synagogue from the rubble of the last Temple in Jerusalem, which they carried over in about AD 135. The name stands as a reminder that, when the Messiah finally arrives, Prague's Jews have to take it back.

Unless the legend is true, the synagogue appeared around 1270. The date was about 10 years before the level of the Staré Město began to be raised and, as you enter, you sink several feet to the level of (not quite) antediluvian Prague. The first chamber is the vestibule, and through the door on your left is the section where women are segregated during services. The gorgeous Gothic

tympanum over the portal, a stylized vine, is divided into sections that represent the 12 tribes of Israel and the three continents of the world then known to Europe. The splayed chinks of light, and the pillar supports, show how much the synagogue owed to Romanesque building techniques; but the vaulted naves, and the slenderness of the octagonal pillars themselves, represent the beginnings of Gothic architecture in Prague.

In the centre is the *almemar* (pulpit), surrounded by a 15th-century wrought-iron grille. Rabbi Loew apparently fought his final and most heroic battle here when, alerted by a dream, he hurried to the darkened synagogue and found an apparition waving swords, dripping with gore and ticking off a list of all Prague's Jews. Ninety-six-year-old Loew realized that this was Pogrom personified, and lunged for the beast. He ripped the scroll from Death's bloody grip, saved the ghetto from extinction, and missed only a scrap containing his name.

On the eastern wall is a screen covering the Torah (the scrolls containing the Pentateuch – the first five books of the Old Testament), in front of which are four messy cushions, where the rabbi used to circumcise wailing infants. The Hebrew psalms on the walls date from 1618. They were recovered in the 1960s, having been obliterated during so-called restoration in 1883. Among the other features that were simultaneously restored to oblivion were bloodstains belonging to people who had barricaded themselves in the synagogue during the 1389 pogrom. For 500 years the unwashed walls had been a memorial to those elegized by Avigdor Kara, 'destroyed in the House of God by the bloody sword of the enemy'.

When Rabbi Loew's *golem* (*see* box, left) eventually ran amok, as man-made creatures do, he went on a rampage through the synagogue. Loew was holding a service when he heard the news and, after consulting the scriptures to work out whether *golems* could be deactivated on the Sabbath, he stalked Joseph and eventually turned him back to clay. Suitably chastened by his dabblings with the laws of creation, he announced that he would never make another *golem*; lifeless Joseph was taken up to the steep brick roof, and has apparently been there ever since.

Jewish Town Hall (Židovská radnice)

The wooden clocktower of the Jewish Town Hall (*closed to visitors*) was donated to the ghetto by Mayor Maisel in 1586. Originally Renaissance in style, it was given a rococo revamp in 1765, when the tower and the clock below it were also added. The lower clock has Hebrew figures and, as the Jewish alphabet is read from right to left, its hands turn backwards. The town hall is still the administrative centre of Prague's Jewish community. For years it was a symbol of the moribund state of Jewish culture in the capital, but like so much else in the city it has fizzed back into unexpected life since 1989. There are still only about 1,500 registered Jews, but the number is growing and their average age has recently sunk – in the nick of time – from 80 to 57 years. The building contains a shop that sells kosher food, and a **restaurant** that is open for lunch every day except Sunday (meal vouchers can be purchased in the shop at Červená 1, opposite the Old-New Synagogue, **t** 224 800 806, *open Sun–Thurs 10–4, Fri 10–2*).

West of the Ghetto

Dominating **Náměstí Jana Palacha**, a square named after the student who burned himself to death in 1969 in protest at the Red Army invasion of Prague, is the **Rudolfinum**. The neo-Renaissance building's walnut-panelled and cut-glass rooms, ranging around a vast glass-roofed atrium, host temporary exhibitions (which usually showcase cutting-edge contemporary art), but the Rudolfinum is best known as the home of the Czech Philharmonic Orchestra. Its history is not purely cultural: the musicians perform under the globe-clustered chandeliers of the glorious **Dvořákovy sál** (Dvořák Hall), which used to host the legislative sessions of the Czechoslovak parliament until that was prorogued by the Nazis in 1938.

Rudolfinum
www.galerie rudolfinum.cz; open Tues–Sun 10–6, café open until 7.30; adm

Opposite the Rudolfinum is the **Museum of Decorative Arts**, founded in 1885, and inspired by the English Arts and Crafts Movement's dream of elevating public taste in the industrial age. Many of its holdings are in storage, or have been moved to the National Gallery of Modern Art, but the collection displayed is sumptuous: four rooms of household and palace furnishings from the Renaissance through to the mid-19th century. The work includes *escritoires* and cabinets inlaid with gemstones, time-pieces, Baroque bureaux and chests, porcelain (including works from Meissen, the first European factory to unlock the thousand-year-old Chinese mystery), Gobelin tapestries and furniture.

Museum of Decorative Arts
Uměleckoprůmyslové Muzeum; 17 Listopadu 2, t 251 093 111, www. upm.cz; open Tues 10–7, Wed–Sun 10–6; adm

Prague Castle (Pražská hrad)

From its beginnings as a pagan mound to the day when Václav Havel was sworn in as president, Prague Castle has been the backdrop for Prague's history. Its neoclassical veneer now stretches half a lazy mile over the capital, but it is the cathedral's onion domes and demented prongs, rising from its core, that hint at the true nature of what lies within. It is almost certainly the oldest continuously inhabited part of the city and, until the end of Bohemian independence in the 17th century, it was home to most

⭐ **Prague Castle**
tram 22 to Pohořelec and walk to Hradčanské náměsti; you can also take line A of the metro to Malostranská and climb the Old Castle Steps (Staré zámecké schodý), though you'll need to walk past the cathedral to get to the ticket office. **Castle grounds** *open daily April–Oct 5am–midnight; Nov–Mar 6am–11pm*

of the oddballs who ruled the country. It is still the seat of the president. Every building has its secrets, from the laboratory of Emperor Rudolf II's alchemists to the minuscule pastel cottages of the 400-year-old Golden Lane.

The **façade** of Prague Castle dates from 1753–75, when neoclassical façades were added with dull abandon, although, behind it all, huge chunks of the medieval castle survive.

First Courtyard (První nádvoří)

Enter the castle from Hradčanské náměstí through the main gateway under the Art Nouveau **Battling Giants**. Between the pine flagpoles of the First Courtyard is the **Matthias Gate** (1614), thought to have been designed by Vincenzo Scamozzi, a close follower of Andrea Palladio. The **Roman triumphal arch** is now unhappily immured in a building dividing the first two courtyards, but it originally stood proud and alone between two bridges crossing the outer moats of the castle.

Castle monuments open April–Oct daily 9–6; Nov–Mar daily 9–4; adm to the Old Royal Palace, Prague Castle Picture Gallery, St George's Basilica, National Gallery of Baroque Art, Golden Lane and Daliborka Tower (tickets available in third courtyard; St Vitus' Cathedral charges separately)

Changing of the guard hourly, with fanfare and main ceremony at noon

Prague Castle

The north wing is approached by way of the **Hall of Columns** (Sloupová síň), built between 1924 and 1926 and the work of Jože Plečnik (*see* p.137). Three rows of Ionic columns line the walls around the stone staircase, which marches up to double iron doors under a copper-panelled roof. Plečnik was appointed castle architect in 1920, with an unenviable brief: to modernize the castle in a way unimposing enough to suit the democratic ideals of the new Czechoslovakian state, dignified enough to honour that democracy's president, and tactful enough to complement the existing architectural scheme of the castle. In the context of the monumentalism that surrounded him, he carried off the balancing act with aplomb. The staircase leads up to the **Spanish Hall** (Španělský sál), which is used for concerts but otherwise accessible to the public only occasionally. On those occasions, queues of Praguers snake through, all curious to see the stucco-encrusted room that used to host the regular meetings of the Communist Party Central Committee. Opposite the Hall of Columns another glass doorway leads to the **presidential rooms**.

Second Courtyard (Druhé nádvoří)

The most notable feature of the Second Courtyard is the **Chapel of the Holy Cross**, which is now used for exhibitions. At the north end of the courtyard, beyond a Baroque fountain (1686) and a disused well, a gateway leads to the **Powder Bridge** where it crosses the Stag Moat. To the right of the gateway are the **Castle Stables**, once the home of 300 thoroughbred horses and now a sanitized exhibition space. To the left, another part of the former stables houses the Castle Picture Gallery.

Castle Picture Gallery (Obrazárna)

Castle Picture Gallery
t 224 375 531; open April–Oct daily 9–6, Nov–Mar daily 9–4; adm

The holdings of the gallery, including works of art kept in the castle since the reign of Emperor Rudolf II, are worth a brief visit to get a feel of the emperor's eclectic tastes and the decline of his Habsburg successors. No inventory survives, but as well as rhino horns, nails from the Ark and the like, Rudolf is thought to have installed some 3,000 pictures and 2,500 sculptures. The gallery was pillaged by occupying Protestant forces in the Thirty Years War: a mild pruning by the Saxons in 1631–2 was followed by a systematic ransack by the Swedes in 1648. What's left includes works by Massari, Guido Reni, Gentileschi, Tintoretto, Titian and Rubens.

Third Courtyard
Castle Information Centre, Third Courtyard, Prague Castle, t 224 373 368, www.hrad.cz; open April– Oct daily 9–6; Nov–Mar daily 9–4; tickets and audioguides, book tours, maps and leaflets

Third Courtyard (Třetí nádvoří)

An arched tunnel leads from the Second Courtyard into the Third Courtyard, bringing you up short before the looming St Vitus' Cathedral (Katedrála sv. Víta).

On the southern façade of the church is the **central tower**, which dominated the front of the cathedral until its modern completion.

The tower is almost 100 metres high, although a fair chunk of that (38 metres) is made up of the multi-storey Baroque dome. Four bells hang in the tower, of which the largest is **Sigismund**, an 18-ton monster on the first floor, dating from 1549. Bells caused no end of trouble in the 16th century. They couldn't be touched by anyone impure (a category that included all women), and pubescent boys dressed in white had to be engaged to transport them from foundry to belfry. The ornate golden grille in the arched window dates from Rudolf II's reign (hence the 'R' just above), as do the two clocks, the higher of which shows the hour, the lower the minute.

To the right of the tower is the **Golden Portal**, once the cathedral's main entrance. Above the gate is a **mosaic** of *The Last Judgement* dating from 1370–71, featuring Charles and his fourth wife, Elizabeth of Pomerania. Restoration funded by the Getty Foundation was carried out in 1998 and 2000, and the epic theme now shines out in glorious Technicolor.

Directly opposite the mosaic façade is the **Bull Staircase**, another ingenious Plečnik construction, which runs down to the **Garden on the Ramparts**. The garden contains pavilions and two obelisks that commemorate the miracle that followed Prague's third defenestration, in 1618 (*see* pp.128 and 164).

St Vitus' Cathedral (Katedrála sv. Víta)

St Vitus' Cathedral
open Nov–Feb Mon–Sat 9–4, Sun 12–4; Mar–Oct Mon–Sat 9–6, Sun 12–5 (until 6pm July–Sept); free entrance to the nave; adm to the crypt and chapels with a ticket you purchase in the church

This church, among the 14th-century's finest, began life as a mere rotunda in 929. Prince Wenceslas (a.k.a. Good King) had recently received Vitus's arm as a token of friendship from the Saxon King Henry I, and it was also hoped that a church in the saint's honour might assist conversion of the local pagans, who worshipped a four-headed rooster-venerating god of war and fertility by the name of Svantovit (St Vitus in Czech is svatý Vít).

Its present incarnation began to take shape in 1344. Charles IV was already eyeing the imperial throne (which he would occupy within two years) and needed a suitably glorious centrepiece for his capital. His first architect, who came from the papal court at Avignon, began an unexciting French design at the eastern end of the chancel – but, fortunately for the future of Gothic architecture in Bohemia, he died in 1352. A young Swabian named Peter Parléř took over, and his new plan for the nave inaugurated a half-century during which Prague became the most significant centre of Gothic architecture in Europe.

However, the entire western part of the church, including its grand façade, was only completed between 1871 and 1929, the neo-Gothic architects giving Prague's skyline a focus it had lacked for 500 years.

The Nave

Mammoth pillars line the noble arch of the nave. The stained glass is a modern addition dating from the 1930s. The original Gothic church is thought to have had only one coloured window, and its bold use of clear light was one way in which architect Parléř broke from the church's French origins. The windows have a garish splendour, but here it's hard not to wonder how different a completed 14th-century church might have been. The window in the third chapel was paid for by an insurance company, and celebrates prudent risk-assessment with the psalm, 'Those Who Sow in Tears Shall Reap in Joy'.

The original part of the building contains the **tower** of the old cathedral (*see* pp.160–61), which offers the highest vantage point in Prague; the view is as breathtaking as you would expect from a climb of 287 steps.

On the left of the building is the **choir** (1557–61), designed by Ferdinand I's court architect, Bonifaz Wohlmut, and surmounted by a tremendous organ dating from the later 18th century. Originally, it closed the western end of the church, but the whole shebang was moved in the 1920s.

St Wenceslas' Chapel, St Andrew's Chapel and the Crypt

To the right of the choir is Peter Parléř's shining goldmine of a chapel, built between 1362 and 1367. Gentle Wenceslas died at the hands of his brother Boleslav in 935, and has wielded more influence from his grave than he ever did during his life.

There are two doorways. The northern portal in the nave contains the ring to which the saint allegedly clung as he was hacked to death, although the church where the deed occurred, outside Prague, has always indignantly claimed to have the knocker concerned. The arch is flanked by sculptural warnings: on the left, a crumbling figure of Peter denying Christ, and, on the right, a vicious demon yanking Judas' tongue from his mouth; but the interior is an inviting mosaic of gilt plaster and semi-precious stones, unevenly framing and crowding over the painted Passion scenes below.

The chapel is a Gothic painting in three glittering dimensions, suffused with the shot of mysticism that ran through the otherwise eminent worldliness of Charles. The number of stones (about 1,370) corresponds to the date of its construction (and, if Prague's clerics were to be believed, the rough date of the Second Coming).

The emperor also gave the chapel tremendous secular significance by establishing a new coronation ceremony linked closely to the cult of Wenceslas. Much of it took place here, and the forged door in the southwest corner leads to a small room containing the old **crown jewels of Bohemia**. You'll have a job getting to see them, though: the door is secured by seven different locks. In any case, any pleb who puts them on signs his own death warrant. The legend was last fulfilled (or just possibly created) in 1942, when Reichsprotektor Reinhard Heydrich is said to have sneered with Teutonic arrogance when the grizzled guardian of the jewels warned him of the curse; shortly after trying on the crown, he was cut down by assassins.

St Vitus' in its heyday, like any cathedral worth its salt, served as a necropolis for the corpses of the high and mighty. In the central aisle is the white marble **Habsburg Mausoleum** (1566–89), containing the remains of the first two generations to rule Bohemia. More human remains can be found in the cathedral's **crypt**, a remnant of the 11th-century basilica. The journey through the church's innards ends at a spotlit sepulchre that contains various royal personages who were more or less reinterred at the time of the building's completion in 1928 and 1935. Emperor Charles IV lies here, next to a box containing all four of his wives. The room also contains most of Rudolf II, though his internal organs stayed at ground level and can be found in the Saxon chapel, just beyond the tomb of St John Nepomuk (*see* below).

Back in the Nave

From the crypt, you emerge back into the centre of the nave. The line of chapels on the right continues with the **Royal Oratory**. Opposite the **Waldstein Chapel**, with the Gothic tombstones of the cathedral's two architects, is a relief showing what looks a very orderly iconoclastic rampage through the cathedral, which occurred in 1619. You're now entering the oldest part of the church, but to go any further you have to get round the incandescent Baroque **Tomb of St John Nepomuk**. St John's not-so-humble abode was fashioned from 3,700 pounds of solid silver, after a design by Fischer von Erlach the Younger. Larger-than-life angels support the coffin, the swooning saint clutches a crucifix above the lid, and four heavenly bodies float over it all. As you pass the centre of the cathedral, pay your respects to the **altar to St Vitus** on your left. Vitus has not done well over the years, outshone first by Wenceslas and then by John Nepomuk; his tomb is an insignificant 19th-century affair.

On the right just past the choir is an amazing **wooden altar** (1896–9) by the Czech sculptor František Bílek. Its simplicity, and the pain that it exudes, owe much to the humanistic traditions of late Gothic art in Bohemia. Bílek's sculpture is a modern addition that works; the Art Nouveau **stained glass** by Alfons Mucha (a 1931 comic strip celebrating SS Cyril and Methodius) is one that doesn't.

Old Royal Palace (Starý královský palác)

Old Royal Palace
*open April–Oct daily
9–5; Nov–Mar daily
9–4; adm with
Castle ticket*

Since the castle was first fortified, the Old Royal Palace has been the site of the royal residence, and inside are three layers of palace, spanning the Romanesque and the Renaissance. The older halls are now below ground level – a feature you come to expect in Prague – as a result of the original unevenness of the Third Courtyard, which sloped steeply towards the east until paved during Rudolf II's reign.

The topmost palace, and the one you'll see first, is the **Vladislav Hall** (Vladislavský sál). It was built between 1486 and 1502 for Vladislav II of Jagellon, and represents the culmination of late Gothic architecture in Bohemia. In its magnificent vault, ribs shoot up like monstrous tendrils from its wall shafts, intertwining across five gently articulated bays and somehow meandering into star-like flower petals in the centre. The architect, Benedict Ried, used anything that seemed to fit the opulence required: the broad rectangular windows are pure Renaissance, sneaking into Bohemia years before the Italian influence began to be felt in western Europe; spiralling pillars and classical entablatures frame the doors of the hall. Horses fitted comfortably; mounted stewards and cupbearers lined the sides during banquets, and tournaments were a regular feature. Since 1918, the president of the Republic has been sworn in here.

To the right of the entrance is a door leading to the **Ludvík Wing**, and it was here that Prague's most significant **defenestration** took place on 23 May 1618. Count Thurn and a few other Bohemian Protestant noblemen confronted the two hated Catholic governors appointed by Ferdinand I and, after explaining their grievances, tossed both out of the window to the left; they survived after landing on a dung heap. The Church declared it a miracle, and two obelisks were set up in what is now the Garden on the Ramparts to commemorate the glorious event.

More steps descend to the predecessors of the Vladislav Hall. At the lowest level is the Romanesque gloom of the 12th-century **Soběslav Palace**.

Basilica of St George (Bazilika sv. Jiří)

**Basilica of
St George**
*open April–Oct daily
9–6; Nov–Mar daily
9–4; adm with Prague
Castle ticket*

The majestic chancel of St Vitus' looks across Jiřské náměstí (St George's Square) to the charming early Baroque façade of the Basilica of St George, with its asymmetrical towers (medieval rules said that a fat male tower had to protect a slim female tower from the midday sun). The perky orange-on-brown pilasters and dunce's cap of a dome cover an incongruously sombre Romanesque interior. The church was the second to be founded in the castle (921) and pre-dates St Vitus' Cathedral. Strictly speaking, its interior dates from 1142, when it was rebuilt after a fire, though zealous restoration at the end of the last century has turned it into a spanking-clean model of neatly hewn pillars and masonry.

Between the Baroque steps winding up to the chancel is the 12th-century crypt, containing the Romanesque **tympanum** that used to crown the southern portal of the church. At the top of the steps is the **chancel**, decorated with fading Romanesque frescoes of the Heavenly Jerusalem, and to the right is the **Chapel of St Ludmilla**. The saint was Prince Wenceslas' grandmother and spiritual adviser, strangled at prayer with her veil by his pagan mother Drahomirá, who hoped thereby to coax her son back into the barbarian fold. It was an optimistic scheme, and it soon collapsed: Wenceslas took Ludmilla's side and had her remains transferred here in 925, where they remain, grinning in a glass cabinet, to this day.

St George's Convent (Jiřský klášter)

St George's Convent
open daily 9–6; adm

This was the first convent in Bohemia, founded in 973, and it now houses the National Gallery's Collection of 19th-century Bohemian Art. The holdings are as soporific as they are patriotic, and well worth avoiding unless you harbour uncommon curiosity about the cultural roots of central European nationalism.

Golden Lane (Zlatá ulička)

Golden Lane
open April–Oct daily 9–6; Nov–Mar daily 9–4; adm with Prague Castle ticket

The huddled cottages along Golden Lane date from the later 16th century and look like a Matisse painting come alive: tiny blocks of colour stretching higgledy-piggledy down the street. There's barely enough room inside to fit a cat, let alone swing one. The cottages originally housed 24 of Rudolf II's marksmen, and nowadays constitute one of the most efficient ambushes in Prague, flushing visitors past a dozen twee tourist traps selling identical souvenirs. It wasn't always as busy. Franz Kafka lived at **No. 22** between December 1916 and March 1917, and found the house so congenial to writing that in just four months he produced most of the short stories that were published during his lifetime.

The street originated as part of Vladislav II's 15th-century fortification of the castle, and contains several reminders of its origins. At its eastern end (walk against the crowds) you'll find the **White Tower** (Bílá věž), which served as Prague's central prison for about 200 years after 1584 and contains a well-stocked torture chamber (*mučírna*). An upper corridor filled with suits of armour, lances, maces and muskets burrows through the parapets, and at the other end of the lane you'll find the **Dalibor Tower** (Daliborka).

Dalibor Tower
open April–Sept daily 9–5

It's named for a Robin Hood-like character of Bohemian legend, who supposedly re-emerges at midnight to play a spectral violin. Look out also for the oubliette, where troublesome detainees were once left to starve to death.

Royal Gardens (Královské zahrady)

Royal Gardens
*open April and Oct
daily 10–6; May and
Sept daily 10–7; June
and July daily 10–9;
Aug daily 10–8; adm*

The Royal Gardens stretch to the northeast of the castle; a gate links them with the **Chotkov Park** (Chotkovy sady) which in turn links up with **Letná Park** for a wonderful walk.

The Royal Gardens are best reached across the **Powder Bridge** (Prašný most), in the Second Courtyard. Ferdinand I built it and, in his weird Habsburg way, included a not-very-secret tunnel underneath, so that he could sneak off to his newly built Royal Summer Palace. His weirder grandson Rudolf II built a warren under the castle. The Communists were the weirdest of all: they constructed even more escape routes and hideaways, but suddenly got cold feet and filled the castle tunnels with concrete blocks in case anyone tried to invade through them.

Far below is the **Stag Moat** (Jelení příkop). It originated as a defensive ditch, but, with the invention of artillery, Vladislav II sensibly decided to rely instead on the powerful fortifications that you can see on the right. The Habsburgs filled the fissure with stags, who multiplied and gambolled here until 1743.

Over the bridge to the left is the **Riding School of Prague Castle** (Jízdárna Pražského hradu; *now home to temporary exhibitions of the National Gallery*). Animals were an important part of the life of a self-respecting 16th-century monarch, and just opposite the school, you'll see the **Lion Court** (Lví dvůr), which was once the Habsburg zoo.

Beyond the house is the *sgraffito*-covered **Ball Game Hall** (Míčovna), dating from 1567–9. The sculpture in front is *Allegory of Night* by Antonín Braun. Examine the monochrome façade closely. When restoring it after the war, the authorities, in a fit of Communist whimsy, added a few new details to the Renaissance decoration, such as the hammer and sickle discreetly tucked away next to the figure of Justice. The one-time **Orangerie** stretches along the slope below the garden.

Royal Summer Palace (Královský letohrádek)

Also known as the **Belvedere**, the palace (*no public access*) was constructed between 1538 and 1564 by Ferdinand I. It was built as a token of love for his wife – although he actually loved her rather too much: she died while giving birth to their 15th child, before the palace was completed. It's the purest example of Italian Renaissance architecture in Prague.

There are several pretty gardens on the hillside south of the palace, known collectively as the **Southern Gardens** (Jižní zahrady), with picturesque views of the red rooftops of Malá Strana. They can be reached via the Bull Staircase next to St Vitus' Cathedral.

Hradčany

This is the district that stretches west from the castle gates, and it has always been a world apart from the bustling city below. It was founded in 1320 as a set of hovels in which the royal serfs could sleep and breed, and, although it slipped out of the castellan's personal control in 1598, it never grew into a normal town. Locked into a slowly turning backwater, monks and nobles indulged their peccadilloes here for centuries; today, its cobbles and courtyards form a silent suburb of the castle which many visitors never see.

Hradčany Square (Hradčanské náměstí)

At the easternmost end of the square, furthest from the castle, is the early Baroque façade of the **Tuscany Palace** (Toskánsky palác; *closed to visitors*), a haughty structure that now forms part of the Czech Foreign Ministry. As you face it, the road to the right curves between a couple of notable houses. The **Martinic Palace** (Martinický palác), plastered with cream-on-brown scratchings, was built by a count of the same name in 1620, two years after his defenestrated descent into a dung heap plunged him into history's footnotes as one of the minor causes of the Thirty Years War (*see* p.128). Its *sgraffito* decoration, which draws on the Old Testament, includes a merry Renaissance retelling of the story of Joseph (of Technicolor dreamcoat fame): the wife of Potiphar is eagerly trying to lie with him, but he does his best to keep her at arm's length. On the opposite side of the street is a doorway that film buffs might recognise: it stood in for Mozart's house in Miloš Forman's *Amadeus*, which was filmed largely in Prague.

Schwarzenberg Palace (Svancenbersky palác)

Schwarzenberg Palace
Hradāanské nám. 2, t 223 081 713, www. ngprague.cz, open Tues–Sun 10–6; adm

This Renaissance beast, crawling with sgraffito triangles, dominates the southern side of the square. It contains the National Gallery's **Collection of Czech Renaissance, Mannerist and Baroque Art and Sculpture**. The holdings were built to complement the energetic architecture that marked the return of Catholicism to Prague after the Thirty Years War, and they look a little peculiar removed from their natural environments – something like fish twitching out of water – but they represent a peak in Prague's artistic history and certainly merit a visit.

The sensualism that permeated the court of Emperor Rudolf II is well represented by Adriaen de Vries's rippling *Hercules with the Apples of the Hesperides*, and the *Epitaph of the Goldsmith Müller* by Bartholomeus Spranger, an artist who found it hard to tame his taste for the erotic even when honouring the dead. There are also works by Maximilian Brokof and Matthias Braun, the two most accomplished sculptors of Baroque Prague. Best of all is Braun's *St Jude*, a heartstopping whirlwind of rags and varicose veins. Look out also for the excellent portraiture of Jan Kupecký (1667–1740): he lived off commissions and necessarily sought to please, but the demands of flattery struggle throughout with an urge towards honesty.

Sternberg Palace (Šternberský palác)

Sternberg Palace
Hradčanské náměstí 15, t *233 090 570, www.ngprague.cz; open Tues–Sun 10–6; adm*

Opposite the Schwarzenberg Palace stands the imposing rococo **residence of Prague's archbishop** (Arcibiskupský palác; *closed to visitors*), and concealed at the end of a winding lane next door is the entrance to the Sterrnberg Palace, which now houses the National Gallery's **Collection of Pre-Modern European Art**. It used to be the finest gallery in Prague, but it was decimated by a double-whammy in 2000: its superb modern collection was hived off to the Trade Fair Palace (*see* p.187), while many of its older works were returned to the monasteries and nobles from whom they had been confiscated. However, it still contains a few excellent pieces, and is worth a visit if you're in the mood for another gallery.

On the **first floor** you'll find **14th- and 15th-century Italian art**, **ancient and classical art** and **icons**, and **15th- and 16th-century Flemish art**. The triptychs and diptychs that make up the bulk of the work on this floor are no great shakes, but there are a few notable paintings in the Flemish section. One that you can't avoid is *St Luke Drawing the Virgin* (1513–16) by Mabuse (Jan Gossaert), which once adorned the altar of St Vitus' Cathedral. This floor also contains Pieter Brueghel the Elder's *Haymaking* (1565), a happy landscape of rural harmony which originally formed part of a cycle; only four other *Months* survive, in Vienna and New York. Finally, have a look at the exquisite *Bouquet* (1607–8), by Jan Brueghel, flower-painter *extraordinaire*.

The first rooms on the **second floor** contain work by **German artists of the 14th–16th centuries**, including a much-reduced selection of works by Lucas Cranach the Elder. The highlight is Albrecht Dürer's *Feast of the Rose Garlands* (1506), regarded as one of the most important paintings of the northern Renaissance. It represents Dürer's deliberate attempt to marry his country's late Gothic art with the technical tricks and new visions of the south, and this work – with its shimmering colour, noble proportions and beauty, and its use of perspective – was an attempt to beat the Venetians at their own game (Dürer painted it on a visit to the city). France and Spain are represented by a few minor works, least unremarkably Goya's *Portrait of Don Miguel de Lardizábal* (1815). The next wing continues with Prague's collection of **Italian Renaissance art**. The big names disappeared when the Swedes pilfered Rudolf II's massive collection in 1648. Of those that remain, look out for the two works by Agnolo Bronzino, *Cosimo de Medici* (1560) and *Eleanor of Toledo* (1540–43), both examples of the portraits produced by the artist for his Florentine patron.

Prague's **Mannerist** collection was unmatched in northern Europe until the Swedish heist. Although El Greco probably did not feature strongly, the gallery now holds one work by him, *Head of Christ* (1595–7), one of the most unforgettable in the gallery.

Baroque light effects fill the next few rooms. The works include Guido Reni's idealized *Salome with the Head of John the Baptist*; and Domenico Fetti's masterful *Christ on the Mount of Olives* (1615), convulsed by rippling movement and illumination. The gallery's Italian collection ends with Canaletto's *View of London from the Thames* (1746), painted from the balcony of Lambeth Palace.

The next wing of the gallery contains its collection of **Flemish and Dutch art from the 17th and 18th centuries**. The first room has two works by the Flemish Roelandt Savery: *Paradise* (1618) and *Landscape with Birds* (1622). Each is an excellent showcase for Savery's claim to art history fame as Europe's first painter of exotic animals. He developed his skills during the decade he spent at Emperor Rudolf II's court, and more particularly, during the time he spent in the imperial menagerie. The room also contains several works by Rubens, including the superb *Expulsion from Paradise* (1620), a preliminary sketch for one of 39 depictions commissioned by the Jesuits for their church in Antwerp. In the next room are landscapes by Salomon van Ruysdael, still lifes by Jan Jansz den Uyl, and a number of notable minor works.

The oval heart of the palace that you enter next contains the grandest Dutch and Flemish painting in the gallery. Rubens holds centre stage with his *Martyrdom of St Thomas* (1637–8), showing the dramatic skills of the artist at their larger-than-life best. Frans Hals, who like Rubens didn't waste a brushstroke, is represented by a masterful *Portrait of Jasper Schade van Westrum* (1645). The very different portraiture of Rembrandt, kneaded from the palette and laboriously formed on the canvas, is reflected in his *Scholar in his Study* (1634), an unknown character painted early in the artist's career, but showing the quizzical mystery of facial expression that was to obsess him in later life. The art of the Low Countries ends with some minor gems in the next room, including the eerie monochrome of *Ships in the Estuary* (1646) by Jan van Goyen, whose lifelong fascination with moody clouds placed him at the forefront of Dutch landscape painting of the 17th century. There are three notable still lifes: *Still Life with Lemon* by Willem Kalf, which depicts sparkling glasses and glistening fruit set off against a dark rug; Jan van de Velde's *Still Life with Smokers' Requisites* (1647), a strikingly simple example of Dutch still life; and Jan Davidsz de

Seers and Stargazers

The ear of Rudolfine Prague was attuned to speculations on all the highest planes, and soothsayers, croakers, necromancers and prophets of every description found the court of Emperor Rudolf II a congenial staging-post. In Rome, the shadow of the stake was a powerful disincentive to weirdness; in Prague, the character of an emperor whose horoscope had been cast by Nostradamus demanded it. His vast curiosity cabinet included mandrake root fetishes; he apparently carried moss from the bones of a hanged man in his back pocket; and wherever there was a mystery to be pondered, Prague thinkers could be guaranteed to deepen it.

Although the scope for quackery was immense, the astronomers of late 16th-century Prague were working at a pivotal moment in the history of science. For some 1,500 years the moon, planets, sun and stars had orbited the earth attached to Ptolemy's harmonious crystal spheres, but in 1543 the Pole Nicolaus Copernicus had revived the ancient heresy of heliocentricity. No one knew how to look at the universe any more. Successive imperial mathematicians at Rudolf II's court personified the critical juncture to which the heavens had come. The work of the first, the little-remembered Nicholas Ursus, was inextricably linked to that of the second, the Danish Tycho Brahe, who served at the court between 1599 and 1601. While still in Denmark, Brahe accused Ursus of plagiarism, setting off an arcane intra-Continental row that became vitriolic even for an age when scientists didn't mince their words. Brahe never quite matched his opponent's invective, but he was no more stable; and although his stellar observations did their bit for rationalism by putting the boot into Ptolemy's crystal spheres, in Prague he subjected poor Rudolf to endless astrological prophecies of doom. The emperor was told variously that he would die before 50, that he would be killed by a monk, and that he would follow his pet raven to Hell.

Heem's *Still Life with Fruit* (1652), which exemplifies the more opulent Flemish still-life tradition.

Nový Svět

The name Nový Svět means 'New World', and refers to both the street and the hamlet in general. The quarter grew up during the 1500s as ramshackle hovels for workers to trudge back to after a hard day's work at the castle. The last house at the eastern end of the street was the **home of Tycho Brahe** during his stay in Prague as imperial mathematician to Rudolf II (1599–1601; *see* box, above).

Around the corner on U Brusnice is the **Church of St John Nepomuk** (Kostel sv. Jana Nepomuckého), the first work that the younger Dienzenhofer built independently of his father in Prague. It dates from 1720–28, roughly the same time that he was finishing the elegant façade of the Loreta.

Loreta Square (Loretánské náměstí)

Loreta

Loreta
*t 220 516 740,
www.loreta.cz;
open Nov–Mar daily
9.30–12.15 and 1–4;
April–Oct daily 9–12.15
and 1–5; adm*

The original Loreto in Italy was one of the most visited shrines in Europe: it was the house where Archangel Gabriel told Mary the good news, rescued from pagan hands and flown over from Nazareth by a flock of angels in 1291. The cult was wildly popular, and hundreds of imitations appeared in the following centuries. After the Battle of the White Mountain, 50 were built in Bohemia as part of the re-Catholicizing miracle culture. The Prague franchise was the grandest. The shrine was begun in 1626, and three generations of architects perfected it.

The **façade** (1716–23) was the work of both Kristof Dienzenhofer and his son Kilian and it's a charmer: a boisterous mob of cherubs, green onion-domes and dinky towers cheerfully taunt the might of the Černín Palace opposite. Inside, the atmosphere is less sunny. The Loreta was established by Benigna Kateřina of Lobkowicz, one of the minor relatives of the Spanish Habsburgs. It was owned and run by an order founded by a Spanish warrior-saint, and it speaks the unearthly language of Spain's Counter-Reformation, the mixture of fanatical cruelty and sensual mysticism that spawned the Inquisition and the art of El Greco. Pleasure and pain are part and parcel of any shrine, but in Prague the new cult was being thrust on a people who had fought Catholicism for two centuries: it tapped into a morbid superstition and voyeurism that permeate it still.

The **cloisters**, built in 1661 to protect the hundreds of homeless pilgrims from heavenly deluges, are lined with rows of painted saints in pine cabinets. Halfway round the cloister, you're led into the **Santa Casa**, a replica of the Nazarene hovel itself, complete with rich Baroque stucco reliefs. You may feel that it is all slightly at odds with your understanding of the Gospels, but have faith: the exterior may be the work of mid-17th-century Italians, but inside is what it *really* looked like. The brick room is something of an anti-climax: a sombre box, with a cedar Virgin on the altar, surrounded by smiling silver cherubs who look as though they were put together with tin foil. Set into the bricks on the left are two beams from the original Loreto. The relief on the back shows the story of the angelic transportation.

Behind the Santa Casa is the **Church of the Nativity** (Kostel Narození Páně), which is well suited to the cruel and surreal spirit of the shrine. On the far right is a painting of the tortured martyr St Agatha – the patron saint of women with breast complaints – handing her own severed breasts like poached eggs on a dish to a welcoming angel. Even more macabre are the dummies in the glass cases on either side of the altar. The wax masks and dusty costumes shroud the skeletons of SS Felicissimus and Marcia, another Spanish addition to Loreta's box of tricks. The most preposterous Iberian addition to the shrine is in the chapel on the corner. The figure with the luxuriant beard, on the cross to your left, is not Christ (as you may realize from the sky-blue dress with silver brocade) but the Portuguese **St Wilgefortis**. She prayed on the eve of her wedding to be saved from her heathen suitor, and God in His mysterious way decided that the best remedy was facial hair, which she sprouted overnight. The prospective groom was suitably awed, and hastily withdrew from the wedding. Her father was less impressed; he crucified her.

Up the stairs just before the entrance is the **Loreta Treasury**, a glittering collection of baubles and reliquaries. The most impressive is a diamond monstrance, more than 6,200 of the stones splayed out like the quills of a horror-struck hedgehog. Designed by Fischer von Erlach in 1699, it formed part of the gift of Ludmilla Eva Franziska of Kolovrat, who left her entire estate to the Madonna of the Santa Casa.

Walking around the shrine, you may have heard the cacophonous chimes of Loreta's **carillon**, 27 mechanical bells that have been urgently trying to learn a recognizable tune every hour for three centuries. They were among the few to survive a central European bell holocaust in the First World War, when the Austro-Hungarians turned most of the metal they could find into cannons (Prague's 267 bells were rung for the last time on St Wenceslas' Eve in 1916). They're synchronized, for want of a better term, by grooved cylinders.

Černín Palace (Černínský palác)

The Černín Palace (*closed to visitors*) is the largest palace in Prague, and it is a monster. Its 30 Doric half-columns are still Renaissance in form; in its scale and deliberate repetition it belongs to the Baroque; and its pomp is redolent of nothing but power. Humprecht Černín was one of the wealthiest of the *arrivistes* who moved in after the Catholic victory at the Battle of the White Mountain in 1620. So concerned was he with micromanaging its construction that the palace remained incomplete at his death in 1682, and gloom has pervaded it ever since. The Nazis so appreciated it that they turned it into their wartime headquarters, and in 1948, it became the site of Prague's fourth (and so far, last) defenestration, when Foreign Minister Jan Masaryk was found dead here, beneath his office window. No one knows whether jumping or pushing was to blame – on the one hand, he was clinically depressed; on the other, he was hated by the Communists – but it remains a good subject to raise with a Czech whenever the conversation begins to flag.

Strahov Monastery (Strahovský klášter)

Strahov Monastery
Strahovská, t 220 516 671, www.strahov monastery.cz

Strahov Monastery gets its name from Strahov, derived from *stráž* ('guard'). It dates from the 14th century, when the western gateway of Charles IV's new fortifications around the left bank of Prague was built here. The Premonstratensian canons were an austere order – their insistence on celibacy did not make them popular among the licentious monks of the day – but they were also an honest and hardworking crew. On their hilltop retreat, they assembled a library that, despite sacks at the hands of Hussite swarms in 1420 and oafish Swedes in 1648, became the finest in Bohemia. The books came in useful in 1782, when Josef II announced the dissolution of almost all the monasteries and convents of the empire. While nuns and monks everywhere were being clapped in jail or told to find honest work, the wily abbot of Strahov, Václav Mayer, saved the day by turning it into a research institute for scholars. Strahov was one of very few monasteries to survive in Bohemia.

The Communists were tough cookies – in 1950 they mounted a night-time raid, sent the canons to gulags, and turned the cloisters into the national literary museum – but the Premonstratensians proved tougher still. Eight hardy survivors shuffled back after the 1989 revolution, and Strahov is once again a functioning monastery. The canons have been multiplying ever since, and though you're unlikely to glimpse so much as the flash of a white robe, there were 80 of them in place as of early 2007. Strahov has thereby resuscitated the tradition that it maintained for a millennium, in a country that has become, by several benchmarks, the least religious in all Europe. It's little short of a miracle.

Church of St Roch (Kostel sv. Rocha)

Church of St Roch
*Strahovské nádvoří 1,
t 233 354 066; open
daily 10–5; adm*

Just as you enter, you'll spot the crooked little church of St Roch, now the **Galerie Miró**, on your left. The church was built after Rudolf II promised the plague-resistant saint a church if he protected Prague from the approaching pestilence. It dates from 1603–12. St Roch did not share the luck of the monastery, and was closed down by Josef II in 1784. It now contains work by contemporary Czech artists and several paintings by Picasso, Miró and Braque.

Philosophical Hall (Filosofický sál)

**Phliosophical
Hall library**
*open daily 9–11.45
and 1–4.45; adm*

The Philosophical Hall library (*access with Strahov Monastery ticket*) was built in a frenzy between 1780 and 1782, after Abbot Mayer got wind of the new Emperor Josef's monastery-razing plans. After climbing the staircase, you'll find yourself in the **anteroom**. It contains a few illuminated manuscripts and monkish doodles, but it's hard to resist being dragged into the opulence of the hall beyond. Walnut bookcases, strung with overripe gilt rococo decoration, rise two levels. Any sensible library would stop at the gallery, but here the tomes march on, climbing 15 metres in all to the ceiling. There are more than 40,000 books, comprising works that Strahov had picked up from benefactors and monasteries less fortunate than itself, all lined up to prove to Josef that it was providing a useful social service.

The ceiling **fresco**, rising from the sombre stacks into a celestial blue, was the last work of the Viennese artist Franz Maulpertsch, and dates from 1794; it's called *The Struggle of Mankind to Know Real Wisdom*.

Strahov's Premonstratensians did not just bury their heads in books. They also stared at their collection of curiosities, displayed in the cabinets outside the hall: monstrous creatures of the deep, a sad crocodile and cases of shining beetles and butterflies. The musty, dusty leather-bound books that line the corridor lead up to a display case containing a replica of the oldest manuscript in the library: a 10th-century New Testament bound in fussy 17th-century encrustations.

Theological Hall (Teologický sál)

The Theological Hall library was built in 1671, during the restoration of the monastery after the Thirty Years War. It does not have the solemn majesty of the Philosophical Hall, but its stucco-laden barrel vault is even more sumptuous. Its ceiling frescoes extol the virtues of True Wisdom, painted by a member of the Order in 1723–7. The room also contains a reminder that the search for wisdom had its limits. Books banned by order of the pope once filled the cabinet above the far door, and a canon who wanted to flick through a dubious astronomical treatise or heretical tract would have to explain his reasons in detail to the abbot: a cumbersome process that ended during the *glasnost* of the 1780s, when the books joined their secular counterparts in the Philosophical Hall.

Strahov Art Gallery

Strahov Art Gallery

open daily 9–12 and 12.30–5; adm

Most of the works in the gallery, acquired over the centuries by the monastery, were confiscated by the Communists after 1950. Those that remain are unified by a humanistic and sometimes downright secular quality that is rare for monastic collections. The most notable early work is the *Strahov Madonna* (1340–50), whose matronly bulk and squirming infant clearly show Bohemian art's departure from the orthodoxies of Byzantium, while Lucas Cranach the Elder's *Judith* (c. 1530) turns the Old Testament head-hunter into a coquettish girl-about-town. There are several works from the Mannerist court of Rudolf II, including a portrait of the avuncular emperor by Hans von Aachen (1604–12) and an *Allegory of the Reign of Rudolf II* (1603) by Dirck de Quade van Ravesteyn. The latter is typical of many apotheoses that were produced to celebrate a pipe-dream vision of the emperor's crisis-ridden reign: Peace, Justice and Plenty fondle each other's breasts, while an iron-clad imperial bouncer keeps a curious Turk at bay. Most impressive of all the Rudolfine works is Bartholomeus Spranger's shimmering

Resurrection of Christ (*c.* 1576), in which the superhuman saviour shoots skyward from his tomb and the phrase 'faster than a speeding bullet' comes inexorably to mind.

Malá Strana

The name Malá Strana translates roughly as 'Lesser Quarter' or 'Little Side'. Sloping from the castle to the left bank of the Vltava, its swirling canopy of orange tiles and chalky-green domes covers one of the finest Baroque preserves in Europe. The quarter was founded way back in the 13th century, but a fortuitous fire and the Thirty Years War cleared out the rotundas and Gothic clutter in time for the carpetbaggers of the Counter-Reformation. Formerly a hive of opposition activists and artists, it has now become one of the most desirable residential districts in Prague.

Church of St Nicholas (Kostel sv. Mikuláš)

❷ Church of St Nicholas
www.psalterium.cz; open daily 9–4; adm (free to worship daily 8.30–9am)

The Baroque mass of St Nicholas' Church and adjoining one-time Jesuit College towers over **Malá Strana Square** (Malostranské náměstí). The church exudes the confidence and ideology of Prague Jesuitry at its height.

The **façade** was the work of Munich-born Kristof Dienzenhofer. It is a development of the undulating rhythm used by Borromini in 1667 for his church of San Carlo alle Quattro Fontane in Rome, but this one was not completed until around 1710. It is only when you enter the church that the mobility of Prague's late Baroque architecture finally overwhelms you. All of the city's churches built during this period sought to capture hearts and minds for the Church Militant, but none other has the potency of this Jesuit cocktail of illusion, threat and promise.

The nave's piers jut out at a diagonal, dragging your attention upwards, while the balconies sway forwards from pier to pier, over vast saints urging you onwards to the high altar. The vault adds to the intoxicating confusion, flowing almost imperceptibly from the pillars into three central bays, while the *trompe l'œil* extravaganza of the 1,500-square-metre **fresco** (1760) makes it almost impossible to say where construction ends and illusion begins. The fresco was the work of Johann Lukas Kracker, and opens the vault into the dark drama of the life of St Nicholas (better known to pagans as Father Christmas).

The east of the church, from the third vault on, is the work of Kristof's son, Kilian Ignaz Dienzenhofer, home-grown and educated by the Jesuits themselves in the Clementinum (*see* p.142). His contribution dovetails perfectly with that of his father. From the nave, the **choir** and **altar** seem almost irrelevant – but by the time you're standing under the diffuse light of the painted **dome**, it is the nave that has become an appendage. The size of the dome caused terror: no one would enter the church until a commission of experts certified in 1750 that it would not collapse. The painting, by Franz Xavier Palko, is the *Celebration of the Holiest Trinity* (1752–3).

God moves in mysterious ways while you keep your eyes heavenward, but there's little room for doubt when you notice the colossal statues (1755–7) stationed above and around you. The venerable *Doctors of the Church* standing at each corner of the stunted transepts have physiques more often associated with steroid abuse than religious devotion. Their brutality was no accident. SS Basil, John Chrysostom, Gregory of Nazianzus and Cyril of Alexandria are all associated with the early Christian struggle against heterodoxy in the East, and the Jesuits were drawing a parallel with their own cause in Bohemia. There are equally gargantuan statues of the Order's heroes, SS Ignatius and Francis Xavier, flanking the copper St Nicholas on the high altar.

Waldstein Palace and Around

Waldstein Gardens

entrance from Letenská St; open April–Oct daily 10–6; the palace itself now houses the Ministry of Culture and is closed to visitors

The **Waldstein Gardens** (Valdštejnská zahrada), a majestic maze of beech hedges, gravel paths and gurgling fountains that lazes under the silhouetted spires and halls of Prague Castle, are an idyllic summer retreat from the overheating city. They are a monument to General Albrecht Waldstein (1581–1634), perhaps the most epic megalomaniac that Prague has ever produced.

Waldstein's character oozes out of both his garden and his palace, built between 1623 and 1629. The magnificent terrace, or *sala terrena*, is approached through an avenue of sculpture by Adriaen de Vries (1545–1626). These green-streaked deities were among the last works to be produced by Netherlands-born de Vries, who died before completing his master's commission. The path of sculptures ends with a fountain of Venus, beyond which is Waldstein's terrace, designed by Milanese architect, Giovanni Pieroni, following the 16th-century rules of proportion to the letter. Waldstein clearly appreciated the triumphal possibilities of Baroque architecture, but his greatest tribute to his own genius lies under the stucco vault, in the **frescoes of the Trojan Wars** (1629–30) by Baccio Bianco.

In a small *salon* on the left as you face the *sala terrena*, the general would dine in the summer, under more heroic frescoes of the Argonauts' quest for the Golden Fleece. A **grotto** on the opposite side contains a door leading to what was once Waldstein's **observatory**. The general would stare at the grotto wall and listen to the warblings of his pride of peacocks when the pressures of devastating Europe became too much. Grottoes had become popular across the Continent during the later 1500s, and

Waldstein

Waldstein belongs to the dubious band of men whose influence on Europe is difficult to exaggerate. Friedrich Schiller turned his life into *Wallenstein*, a three-act tragedy, and the general himself was one of the first to recognize his own genius.

In 1618, while his countrymen were lobbing Emperor Ferdinand's men out of Prague's windows, Waldstein threw in his lot with the Imperial cause. The defenestrators were executed; Waldstein snapped up confiscated lands for a song, and was put in charge of the Imperial army, which he led through a decade of almost continuous victories over motley Protestant forces. But he was no employee. He provided the army to Ferdinand under a series of lucrative contracts and, with the help of an inflated currency scheme and manic organizational skills, Waldstein soon became the largest creditor of the Habsburg empire. Without the money to pay his general, Ferdinand had to reward him with other assets. Lands and honours poured through his hands, culminating with a princedom in 1627.

Ferdinand's Jesuit advisers already loathed Waldstein for his pragmatic attitude to a war that they saw as a crusade and, to many, the fact that he could now keep his hat on while chatting to the emperor was the last straw. The intrigues intensified until 1630, when Waldstein was relieved of his command. It was too late – his superbly run army had become indispensable. When Saxon Protestants retook Prague the following year, Ferdinand hastily recalled his champion, and appointed him *generalissimo* of the imperial forces. An almost omnipotent Waldstein finally decided to slip the leash. He began to negotiate with the enemies of the empire and, in January 1434, launched open mutiny against Ferdinand. Historians have spent three centuries discussing his reasons. Few doubt that he wanted to be king of Bohemia, but the riddle is whether he had been a Bohemian nationalist all along, whether he grew into one, or whether he was a power-mad traitor. The nuances did not really matter to Ferdinand, and the *dénouement* unfurled. As Waldstein crossed northern Bohemia in a crimson litter, looking for the allies who were suddenly and mysteriously fading away, Vienna's churches were put on alert and ordered to pray, for 'a matter of the first importance'. Four days later, placards appeared across the city blaring that the legendary Waldstein was to be taken dead or alive. The noble renegade's game was up, and he and the commanders who remained loyal to him were finally done to death by Scottish and Irish officers in the town of Cheb.

this pendulous foliage, growing tumour-like into a mass of hidden faces and shapes, reflects Waldstein's mystical pursuits. He had spent some years studying in Padua, a hotbed of the quasi-sciences of the day, and his astrological mania was public knowledge.

St Thomas' Church
www.augustiniani.cz

The grotto backs on to a former Augustinian monastery, and if you walk south along Letenská and turn right at Josefská you'll find the Baroque façade of **St Thomas' Church** (Kostel sv. Tomáše), looming over the tiny cul-de-sac. Once the church of a nearby Augustinian monastery, it nowadays serves as a centre for Prague's English-speaking Catholic community. Various evening classes and weekly Masses are held here, and anyone eager to confess their holiday sins will find a priest who more or less understands on the second Sunday of every month.

Vojan Park
U lužického semináře;
open April–Sept daily
8–7; Oct–Mar daily 8–5

If you take the other direction on leaving the Waldstein Gardens, you can find more greenery at the **Vojan Park** (Vojanovy sady). It's the oldest in Prague and – along with the Baroque **Vrtba Gardens** – among the most secluded.

Vrtba Gardens
Karmelitská 25; open
April–Oct daily 10–6,
www.vrtbovska.cz

Nerudova

This street is named after Jan Neruda (1834–91), a 19th-century Czech poet and journalist who lived here. His name was later filched by the Chilean writer, 1971 Nobel Laureate and inspiration for *Il Postino* Pablo Neruda, who apparently chose it at random, although he deposited flowers outside Jan's birthplace after finding out who he was. More a chasm than a street, its Baroque and Renaissance façades cling on to the incline. The street has more **painted house signs** than any other in Prague: multi-coloured beasts, birds and apparently random objects which sometimes date back 600 years. Walking up from Malostranské náměstí, at No.6 on the right is the narrow 18th-century façade of the **Red Eagle** (U červeného orla), one of the innumerable variations of the 26 avian species that adorned Prague's houses. There is another sign at the **Three Little Fiddles** (U tří housliček), a small restaurant at No.12. Three generations of violin-makers lived in the house, but legend insists that the sign has more to do with satanic fiddlers who gather here when the moon is full. Other signs to decipher as you walk up the street include a **Golden Goblet** at No.16 and a **Golden Key** at No.27, both from the 17th century, when castle goldsmiths used to heat and beat their metals along Nerudova.

The **Morzin Palace** (Morzinský palác; Nerudova 5), from 1713–14 and now the Romanian Embassy, shows the inventiveness of Giovanni Santini, one of Prague's late Baroque greats. Santini adapted three older houses into a palace, placed a balcony in the middle and curved both sides of the façade out towards it, making the asymmetry almost unnoticeable at first glance. The tension is thrown into even higher gear by the two atlantes, sombre Moors (the Morzin family emblem) who carry the balcony with ease and make a good job of supporting the rest of the façade.

Atlantes became fashionable during the 18th century, but if you look at the portal of the **Thun-Hohenstein Palace** (Thun-Hohenštejnský palác; Nerudova 20), now the Italian Embassy building, you'll see that they did not always work. It was built in 1721–6 for the Kolovrats, very soon after the Morzins had moved in at No.5. The newcomers liked the idea of the family emblem supporting the portal. Unfortunately, the Kolovrats' was an eagle, and Matthias Braun duly sculpted these two preposterous creatures.

Lobkowicz Palace (Lobkovický palác)

Running parallel to Nerudova are two quiet streets called Tržiště and Vlašská. Both are sufficiently off the tourist route to make for an attractive detour, and the second contains the **Lobkowicz Palace** – which now houses the German Embassy, and happens to be one of the finest Baroque palaces in the city. Its elliptical plan is best viewed from the **gardens**, accessible via a small path leading into woods at the rear of the palace, and while taking in the splendid architecture and landscaping you can also contemplate events of the more recent past. In September 1989, thousands of East Germans arrived in Prague, dumped their Trabants and clambered over these railings in the hope of being allowed to go west; they lived on the flower beds for a fortnight until permission was granted for them to emigrate. A whimsical tribute to the fleeing Ossies now stands in the garden, called *Quo Vadis*. It's a gold Trabant on four long legs. The gardens are closed, but you can glimpse the sculpture through the railings.

Ledeburg, Černín and Pálffy Gardens

Ledeburg, Černín and Pálffy Gardens
entrances at Valdštejnské náměstí 3, or through the Garden on the Ramparts; open 28 Mar–31 Oct daily 10–6; adm

The terraces that step up from Malá Strana, once vineyards, are the merged product of three gardens laid out during the 18th century. Handsomely restored (thanks in part to funding from Prince Charles), the walkways, balustraded staircases, and pavilions make for an excellently uncrowded route between ground level and castle, or a fine picnic destination in their own right.

Southern Malá Strana

Church of Our Lady of Victory (Kostel Panny Marie Vítězně)

Church of Our Lady of Victory
Karmelitská 9, t 257 533 646; open April–Oct daily 8.30–7

This sits on the site of Prague's first Baroque church (1611), given by Ferdinand II to the Order of Barefooted Carmelites. The structure is unimpressive, but the church has a famous exhibit: the **Bambino di Praga**, venerated throughout the Hispanic world. The Bambino's rise to stardom began when Polyxena of Lobkowicz, one of many Spanish brides taken by Czech Catholics during this period, gave the figure to the friars in 1628. Numerous miracles followed, and in 1741 enough money had been made to buy the doll its silver altar.

It has been given scores of costumes: after the Carmelites were expelled in 1784, an Order of English Virgins was allowed to continue dressing it, and even through the Communist era a prelate of St Vitus' Cathedral changed the Bambino regularly. The most mysterious (some say miraculous) tribute came in 1958 when an official delegation from Communist North Vietnam stepped off the plane with a set of silk clothes for the Bambino. To this day, no one knows why. Look out for outfit No.5, an apple-green number with gold embroidery, which was handed over personally by Queen Maria Theresa in 1754.

The John Lennon Wall

Opposite the very proper charm of the apricot-and-white French Embassy in the Buquoy Palace in Grand Prior's Square (Velko-převorské náměstí) is the polyglot scrawl of the John Lennon Wall, a colourful tribute to the Beatle-saint. The singer became a non-conformist symbol in Communist-ruled Europe after his murder in 1980, and this wall became the site of a surreal struggle between Prague's youth and the police. The wall is now encrusted with several years' worth of obscene *non sequiturs* and the scrawled greetings of hooligans from across the Continent. If you're around on the anniversary of Lennon's death on 8 December, come and join the dreamy types who spend much of the night imagining no possessions, greed or hunger. The dreamiest can add to the collection of 'love locks' attached to a nearby canal gate: the small padlocks are inscribed with lovers' names, and the key tossed into the water.

Kampa Island

Kampa Island (from the Latin *campus*, or field) is separated from the mainland by a sliver of the Vltava known as the Čertovka (Devil's Stream). You can reach it via a set of stairs alongside the Charles Bridge or from the John Lennon Wall (walk past the old mill-wheel, which the local Knights of Malta once used to make their bread). It's not the drowsy hideaway that it once was, but it can still offer a welcome gear shift on a hot Malá Strana day. Stroll along the embankment, laze on the grass, or investigate the modern art collection at the Museum Kampa (*www. museumkampa.cz*).

New Town (Nové Město)

The New Town is actually not very new, having got its name way back in 1348, when Emperor Charles IV established it to cater for the monks and merchants flooding into his new capital. Over the past century, Nové Město has become the commercial and administrative centre of the capital. Apart from Václavské náměstí (Wenceslas Square), these districts are overlooked by most visitors, but if you want to see what Praguers get up to while the tourists are not watching, take a walk.

Wenceslas Square (Václavské náměstí)

Wenceslas Square and the Charles Bridge were founded almost simultaneously in the mid-14th century by Emperor Charles IV. The square, in fact a half-mile boulevard, was the horse market that Charles needed for his new town; now it is the commercial centre of the city and significant for its recent history.

St Wenceslas

The equestrian figure silhouetted against the National Museum is one of the motifs of Bohemian nationalism. Although familiar to

English carol singers since the 1850s, Good King Wenceslas ruled as a prince rather than a king, until murdered by his notoriously cruel brother, Boleslav the Cruel, in 935. The saint's reputation arose from his Christianity, but over the years Wenceslas has metamorphosed from religious to national hero.

The symbolic importance of the statue came to obsess its designer, J. V. Myslbek, the grand old man of 19th-century Czech sculpture. He initially envisaged Wenceslas as a shaggy Slav but, as the reality of a nation state grew closer, he transformed the Dark Age prince into the serene and noble leader you see today. Ever since its unveiling in 1912, it has been a public rallying point. In 1918, Czechoslovakian independence was announced at Wenceslas' feet. After 1948, Communist May Day parades marched along the square, and following the Soviet-led invasion of August 1968 the monument became the focus of Prague's desperation. The happiest moment of the monument's recent history came in November 1989, when Wenceslas and his stallion Ardo made it on to millions of television sets across the world, at the head of the demonstrations that finally saw off the shoddy dictatorship.

National Museum (Národní muzeum)

National Museum
Václavské náměstí 68, t 224 497 111, www.nm.cz; open Mon–Tues and Thurs–Sun 10–6, Wed 9–6, every first Thurs of the month 2–6; closed first Tues of each month; adm

A museum of Bohemian history was a dream of early 19th-century patriots. They launched an appeal for objects, and, as the domestic appliances and folk art poured in, it became apparent that Bohemia's traditions would also need a suitably glorious home. In the 1870s Prague's council stepped in with this rent-free site. The grand neo-Renaissance building (1885–90) was meant to express the confidence of the Czech national revival movement; its effect was to shatter the balance of old Václavské náměstí, and encourage the almost complete renewal of the street's architecture. Paradoxically, the symmetry of the museum, its bulk set off by a central golden dome, now makes it an almost elegant point on the 21st-century exclamation mark that Václavské náměstí has become.

The museum is worth a visit for the open staircase that greets you beyond the entrance: three floors of veined marble pillars and banisters, globular lamps and swaying palm fronds. Wait for a very, very rainy day before exploring the rest of the building, which houses a stupefying collection of stuffed animals and anthropological knick-knacks.

Around the Square

Neon signs, techno music and waves of tourists have turned Václavské náměsti into an inner-city plaza similar to countless others throughout Europe, but it retains a few distinctive gems. One of the most appealing is the glorious Art Nouveau **Grand**

Hotel Evropa. Revolving doors spin you into a glittering room of mirrors, mahogany, crystal and carriage lamps – as sterile as a gilded lily these days, but considerably more attractive than any of the square's other tourist traps. Number 19, just across Jindřišská, was where in 1907 Franz Kafka began his career in insurance – dreaming, as he gazed from his office, of 'someday gazing upon sugarcane fields or Muslim cemeteries'. Wedged between two functionalist blocks on the opposite side is the **Hotel Adria** at No.26 – the last remnant of Baroque architecture on the square. Further north, at No.8, is the **Peterkův dům**: perhaps the most elegant, if understated, Art Nouveau façade in Prague. Designed by a 28-year-old Jan Kotěra and completed in 1900, it possesses the same geometric precision that would later inspire Czech constructivism – itself well represented by the **Bat'a** shop at No. 6.

The square ends with the so-called **Golden Cross**, a junction of shoppers, hookers and idle youth that marks the northern extent of Nové Město. It's a good place to shop till you drop, but if the free market's not your bag, you might alternatively visit the nearby **Museum of Communism** (Muzeum komunismu). Although it's above a McDonald's, you'll probably agree by the end of your visit that Prague has suffered even worse in its time than junk food.

Museum of Communism
Na příkopě 10, t 224 212 966, www. muzeumkomunismu.cz; open daily 9–9

Northwest Nové Město

Church of Our Lady of the Snows
open daily 6am–7.30pm

Off **Jungmannovo náměstí** is the **Church of Our Lady of the Snows** (Kostel Panny Marie Sněžné), one of the last remnants of Charles IV's New Town; he founded it in 1347, five years before the 1,000th anniversary of its Roman namesake, Santa Maria Maggiore. The interior is dominated by a splendid early Baroque altar.

Bristling with bizarre crenellations and turrets, the **Adria Palace** is a striking example of the 'rondo-Cubist' architecture that Pavel Janák tried to develop into a Czechoslovakian national style fit for the 20th century. Modern Prague would have been a curiosity of titanic proportions had he succeeded, but this urban citadel (1923–5) is one of only a few examples that got off the ground.

Národní třída (National Street) was built in the early 20th century when the New Town's defensive moat was filled in. At the end of it stands the **National Theatre** (Národní divadlo), erected at the height of the 19th-century Czech national revival. As the inscription at the entrance states, it was the 'nation's gift to itself', paid for entirely by a subscription to which almost every Czech contributed. It opened on 11 June 1881 with a performance of Smetana's opera *Libuše*: less than a fortnight later, it was a smoking shell after workmen accidentally set fire to the building. Once again, the Czech people dug deep and the National Theatre opened again just nine months later. Special trains were laid on to bring the Czechs to see their new theatre, decorated by the most famous artists of the day and bursting with statues and paintings trumpeting the glories of the Czech nation and its people. It remains a potent symbol of Czech nationalism.

Charles Square (Karlovo náměstí)

Now a park lined with 19th-century mansions, this was the original hub of the New Town. As well as serving as Prague's cattle market, it hosted an annual festival for the display of saintly relics, established after Charles IV persuaded the pope to let him put his large collection on regular show.

New Town Hall
open May–Sept Tues–Sun 10–6; adm

Today's **New Town Hall** (Novoměstská radnice) is descended from the 14th-century original. Only the tower (1425–6) looks its age, however, since the rest was completely rebuilt during the 19th and early 20th centuries. In 1419 its former windows were the venue for Prague's **first defenestration** (*see* p.125). Jan Želivský, a Hussite firebrand of a priest, led a rabble to the building to demand the release of some heretics, and the Catholic councillors lobbed stones at his monstrance – a misjudgement: the crowd stormed the building, hurled the councillors from the windows, and bludgeoned to death anyone who survived the fall.

Church of St Ignatius
Ječná 2; open daily 6–12 and 3.30–6.30

The **Church of St Ignatius** (Kostel sv. Ignác) once formed the Jesuit base in the New Town, along with the neighbouring college (now a hospital). The powerful arches of the chapels and broad nave are laden with half-immured cherubs and angels, and the gold and creamy pink interior has the usual ostentatiousness of Jesuit architecture. It was built in 1665–70.

Church of SS Cyril and Methodius
crypt open Tues–Sat 9–5 (last admission 4.30); adm

Just off Charles Square, a two-minute walk down Resslova St, the Orthodox **Church of SS Cyril and Methodius** (Kostel sv. Cyril a Metoděj) is recognizable by a pock-marked section of wall that commemorates one of the most dramatic events to occur in Prague during the Second World War. After the assassination of loathed Nazi Reichsprotektor Reinhard Heydrich, seven members of the group responsible holed themselves up here. They were betrayed and during the early hours of 18 June 1942 over 300 SS and Gestapo soldiers took up positions around the building. Through the night, wave upon wave of machine-gun fire slammed into the church, but only as dawn broke did the shooting from within stop. The Nazis entered to find that they had spent the night battling three men: four remained in the crypt. Gunfire resumed, and for another two hours the fighters held out in the catacombs against bullets, tear gas and hand grenades, until they finally took their lives after reaching the end of their ammunition. German troops had pushed a high-pressure hose through a vent, and with water flooding into the pitch-black crypt, and the Nazis on the point of blowing open a long-disused staircase, both men blasted themselves with their final bullets. The gashes of the shots still mark the walls. At the far end of the crypt is a metre-long hollow, smashed away with a pipe while the Nazis pumped gunfire and water through the ventilation hole overhead.

Although hundreds of troops had been stationed at sewage outlets along the Vltava to forestall any escape, the crypt is next to a Grand Central of Prague sewers. Had they hit the drain, the men would have been home and dry. They were 30 centimetres away from doing so.

A small exhibition includes photographs of the Nazi assault, taken by a Czech police officer with a camera in his lighter.

Along the Vltava

The point at which Resslova Street hits the river is dominated by one of Prague's more distinctive recent buildings, designed by Frank Gehry and Vlado Milunič. The **Dancing House** (Tančící dům) is said to have reminded its creators of the swirling skirt and trousered thigh of Ginger Rogers and Fred Astaire, though the structure's glassy curves also recall any number of Gehry's other works.

The top floor of the neighbouring house was once home to former president Václav Havel, who made a point of staying put after 1989; having made his egalitarian point, he subsequently relocated to discreetly luxurious lodgings behind the castle.

This stretch of embankment, all the way from the Charles Bridge down to Vyšehrad (*see* p.185), is also lined with dozens of splendid **Art Nouveau mansions**.

South of Charles Square

Effortlessly perched on a craggy curve, the **Church of St John Nepomuk on the Rock** (Kostel sv. Jana Nepomuckého na Skalce; Vyšehradská 49) is one of the most elegant of all Kilian Dienzenhofer's churches in Prague. A double staircase swoops serenely up the west front, and inside is a wooden version of the statue of St John of Nepomuk on the Charles Bridge. The twin towers of the narrow façade are echoed by the bizarre peaks of the **Slavonic Monastery** (Klášter na Slovanech) across the street. This Gothic monastery had its roof obliterated during an Allied bombing run in February 1945; the 1960s replacement, flowing into two spires, is one of the most distinctive pieces of postwar architecture in the capital.

Dvořák Museum
Ke Karlovu 20,
t 224 923 363; open
Tues–Sun 10–5; adm

Further east, the small **Dvořák Museum** (Muzeum Antonína Dvořáka) is housed in a gorgeous Baroque summerhouse designed by Kilian Dienzenhofer and set among sculptures by Antonín Braun. It contains photos, notebooks and other memorabilia.

Police Museum
open Tues–Sun 10–5; adm

A few hundred metres further down Ke Karlovu is the strange **Police Museum** (Muzeum policie), housed in a former convent. Once devoted to the activities of the National Security Corps, it has been cleaned up since the revolution and is now intended to laud the acceptable face of authoritarianism. Children will enjoy the outdoor playground with helicopter.

Church of Our Lady and Charlemagne
open Sun and hols 2–4.30

The crimson dome of the **Church of Our Lady and Charlemagne** (Kostel Panny Marie a Karla Velikého), also known as Na Karlově, glows at the end of the road. It was founded by Charles IV in 1358, for French Augustinians. Its unusual octagonal plan was loosely modelled on the Aachen burial church of Charlemagne. Its most awe-inspiring feature is the remodelled interior, shaped like a single star, 24 metres in diameter. Legend has it that the architect was a novice who built it with the devil's help; others claim that it was designed in about 1575 by Bonifaz Wohlmut, court architect to Ferdinand I. Either way, it is one of the grandest flourishes of (extremely) late Gothic architecture in Prague.

Outside the Centre

Vyšehrad

Vyšehrad
www.praha-vysehrad.cz; metro Vyšehrad; tram 3, 17 or 21

This ancient crag over the Vltava has spun a web of nationalistic lore. Praguers can still reel off the myths, but its romantic heyday was a century ago, when it was infested with poets and painters in search of patriotic inspiration. It is now a pleasant retreat on a lazy afternoon, with grassy parks covering the remnants of ancient walls.

According to the city's oldest legend, soothsaying Princess Libuše was standing here when she prophesied Prague. In the later 11th century, Vratislav II moved to the rock, prompted by dislike of his brother, who lived in the castle. The change of royal address lasted a century, but the only evidence is the heavily restored Romanesque **Rotunda of St Martin** (Rotunda sv. Martina). Near it are remnants of the fortification walls built by Charles IV in the mid-14th century.

Before leaving the area, be sure to see the **Cubist houses** designed by Josef Chochol between 1911 and 1913. There is a trio on the embankment below Vyšehrad, at Podolské nábř. 6–10, one at Libušina 3 and, most impressively, the prismatic apartment block jutting outwards and upwards from the corner of Přemyslova and Neklanova.

Smíchov

Smíchov
metro Anděl; tram 4, 6, 7, 9, 10, 12

This is one of Prague's most intriguing districts. Just half a mile along the river from Malá Strana, it was historically home to factories, a brewery and more Romanies than anywhere else in Prague – making for an urban flavour lacking elsewhere in the golden city. Gangs loafed, no-good kids yelled, and primmer Praguers tut-tutted at the disorderliness of it all. But change is very much afoot. Gentrification is sweeping the riverside roads, while the entire area east of Anděl metro station has been rebuilt as a grid of glassy multiplexes, showrooms and lounges. But if you walk a little further, beneath the new arterial overpass, you'll still find dodgy bars and grimy tenements on the streets around the district's spooky Baroque cemetery. Catch old Smíchov while you can.

The charming Villa Bertramka is one of the few houses of the suburban gentry to survive the dark advance of industry into Smíchov in the 19th century. It now houses the **Mozart Museum**; Mozart stayed here on three of his visits to Prague.

Mozart Museum
Mozartova 169,
t 257 318 461,
www.bertramka.cz;
open April–Oct daily
9.30–6; Nov–Mar daily
9.30–5; adm

Petřín Hill

Petřín Hill is the green and wooded hump on the left as you cross the Charles Bridge from Staré Město. The forest that used to stretch for miles to the south has disappeared, and vineyards no longer clamber up the hill, but its patchwork of gardens still makes for a perfect retreat. From the top, you can either stroll towards the Strahov monastery, or take the winding route down into Malá Strana. The latter offers one of the loveliest walks in Prague, along an asphalted path which turns into a forest track as it descends towards a sea of olive domes and orange tiles.

Petřín Hill
the funicular railway
can take you up and
down the hill between
9am and 11.20pm

Nebozízek, the first stop on the funicular, is marked by an eponymous terrace restaurant, on the site of a vintner's cottage. In the woods is a monument to the Romantic poet Karel Mácha, where generations of Praguers necked for the first time.

At the **summit** is a rose garden. Just to the north sits the **Štefaník Observatory**. In the opposite direction is the Baroque Church of St Lawrence and a **model of the Eiffel Tower**, built in 1891 (two years after the original) by the Club of Czech Tourists. The club was proud of its tower, but at 60 metres it falls well short of the Gallic symbol. The Tourists also contributed the nearby **Mirror Maze** (Bludiště), with a diorama depicting the Swedish attack on the Charles Bridge in 1648.

Štefaník Observatory
open daily except Fri,
with English shows and
audio translations,
t 220 999 001,
www.planetarium.cz

Model of the Eiffel Tower and Mirror Maze
open April–Oct daily
9.30–7; Nov–Mar Sat
and Sun only 10–5;
adm

The battlements of the **Hunger Wall** (Hladová zed') form a crenellated scar across Petřín as far as the Strahov Monastery. Charles IV constructed it in 1360 to enclose the inhabited left bank of Prague. The name recalls a legend that Charles did not really need a wall and built it to create jobs for peckish Praguers, although it seems neither more nor less functional than all the other walls, churches, castles and bridges that Charles erected during his hyperactive reign.

Letná Park

This expanse of greenery offers a stroll with views of the city. You can walk to the gates of the Royal Gardens in one direction and Stromovka Park in the other. Steps from the **Čechův most** (Czech Bridge) lead up to the graffiti-scrawled plinth of the former Stalin statue. (A giant metronome sits there now.) Uncle Joe was blown up in 1962, but his rocky remains are in chambers below. The nearby **Hanavský Pavilion** is an Art Nouveau exhibition piece that was moved here in 1898. To the north is the barren expanse of **Letná Plain**, devoid of interest save that it used to host Communist speech days (1 May) and, on 25 November 1989, it was the site of the demonstration that marked the death of the old regime, when a million people saw Václav Havel shake hands with Alexander Dubček. You could stop for coffee on the terrace of the **Letenský zámeček**, a 19th-century château with great views.

Trade Fair Palace (Veletržní palác)

The **National Gallery of Modern Art** is housed in the spectacular functionalist interior of the Trade Fair Palace, built between 1925 and 1928. In 2000 the collection was completely reorganized by its new director, Milan Knižák, a one-time member of the Fluxus movement.

Fourth Floor (1800–1900)

The 19th-century collection opens with the work of **J. V. Myslbek**, the country's most influential 19th-century sculptor. The following galleries are devoted to the National Revival movement of the 19th century. It produced some truly terrible art, but keep your eyes open for the out-of-place talents of **Josef Navratil** (1798–1865), represented by a number of accomplished still lifes and luminous lakeside scenes.

The next few galleries are piled high with the work of the 'National Theatre generation'. There are a couple of smouldering paintings by Sarah Bernhardt's favourite poster artist, **Alfons Mucha**, and a few feisty, bitter-sweet portraits by **Karen Spiller**, who created the mosaic above the entrance to the Municipal House. The prolific **Mikoláš Aleš** (1852–1913) defaced almost every public edifice of the era in Prague. Mainstream Czech **Art Nouveau** sculpture is represented by **Ladislav Šaloun** and a series of gentle copper and bronze reliefs by **Stanislav Sucharda**. The belated influence of Rodin, who exhibited in Prague in 1902, is reflected in the early works of **Josef Mařatka** and **Bohumil Kafka**, both of whom spent a couple of years working in the great man's studio.

Each floor has been allocated a series of galleries devoted to the **architecture** and **decorative arts** of each period. This one contains models and architectural plans of the National Theatre and several

Art Nouveau buildings, including the Municipal House and Hlavní nádraží train station.

Third Floor (Czech Art 1900–30 and 19th/20th-century French Art)

Prague's artists discovered Impressionism, postimpressionism and Cubism within a few years of each other in the first decade of the 20th century, and the collection shows the profound effect of this ferment. **František Kupka**'s mystical and ever more abstract art is well represented, and **Emil Filla**'s unique work is worthy of note, permeated with the moody tension of Expressionism but given form in a fluent style.

The most Czech work of this period is the **social realist** work of the 1920s and '30s, which was inspired by a genuine regard for the real lives of 'ordinary' people. **Otto Gutfreund** was one of the earliest practitioners, but his work went on to influence a whole generation of Czechoslovakian sculptors, including **Karel Pokorný**, **Jan Lauda**, **Karel Dvořák** and **Karel Kotrba**. Their works are complemented by the gentle naïve painting of **Jan Zrzavý**, and a collection of Czech **Surrealist** dreamscapes. **Toyen**, **Štyrský** and **Šíma** are the most eminent painters.

There is a distinctive collection of non-Czech art, including several works by **Rodin**, among which are the seminal *Age of Bronze* (1875) and *Balzac* (1898). When the latter was unveiled, critics called it 'a toad in a sack'. It has to be said that on the purely visual level the description is an accurate one, but the psychological mystery and Expressionistic power of the sculpture make it perhaps the most original ever produced by the artist.

The gallery's collection of early **Cubist** works is the best in central Europe. The director of the National Gallery in the 1920s, Vincenc Kramář, had lived in Paris during the early years of the century and unerringly appreciated the emerging style. Works by **Pablo Picasso** form the core of the collection. The plum is the artist's *Self Portrait* (1907), painted while he was still thinking his way out of the world of appearances. Other works include his *Woman* (1907) and *Nude Woman* (1908), and his first truly Cubist piece, *Woman in an Armchair* (1910). The style develops through *Mandolin and Glass of Pernod* (1911) and *Woman with a Guitar at the Piano* (1911), and explodes into obscurity with *Clarinet* (1911) and the murky mystery of *Toreador Playing the Guitar* (1911). The co-creator of Cubism, **Georges Braque**, is less well represented, but his *Violin and Glass* (1910–11) is an interesting still life.

As well as pieces of hazy Impressionism, there are a handful of works by the romantic heroes of **post-Impressionism**. **Gauguin**'s lifetime preoccupation with colour is reflected in his *Bonjour, Monsieur Gauguin* (1889), and his erstwhile friend **Van Gogh** is represented by the swirling undercurrents of *Green Rye* (1889). Considerably less anxious is **Le Douanier Rousseau**'s *Moi-même, Portrait paysage* (1890), the artist's only known self-portrait; look out too for the no less joyful *Circus* (1927) by Marc Chagall, and some sensuous nudes by Matisse.

Racked up in the **Decorative Arts and Architecture** galleries are dozens of stage sets for shows from the 1920s and '30s. There is also an assortment of wind-up gramophones, early telephones, vacuum-cleaners, irons and kettles, beautifully beaded flapper dresses and sketches for stage costumes.

Second Floor (1930–Present)

This floor opens with a bang: the gruesome **Surrealist** visions of **František Janonšek**, all swirling entrails and eyeballs. Behind them flicker **Zdeněk Pešánek**'s light-kinetic sculptures, created in 1936 and given a garish neon splash in the 1980s. There is Surrealism of a more contemplative bent too in **Josef Šima**'s dreamy landscapes. A small gallery is devoted to **Josef Sudek**'s early photography, exquisite experiments with light and shadow.

Cultural constraints eased in the years after Stalin's death, and by the mid-1960s, Czech artists were once again challenging the perceptions that two decades of propaganda had threatened to anaesthetize. There are powerful **Abstract Expressionist** paintings by **Mikuláš Medek**, and some quirky pieces by **Petr Štembera**, who 'grafted' a twig to his body and recorded the process. The director of the Trade Fair Palace, former Fluxus artist **Milan Knižák**, was an outspoken critic of the Communist regime; there is a photographic record of his *Demonstration of One* (1964), in which he asked spectators to crow as they passed.

The despair that followed the suppression of the Prague Spring in 1968 silenced many Czech artists, and the last two decades have lacked a consistent cultural voice. The most characteristic feature of works produced during the period is ironic humour, and, like their Western counterparts, they generally inspire smiles and shrugs of the shoulder in roughly equal measure. **Ivan Kafka**'s *Potent Impotency* comprises furiously ticking timepieces that busy themselves with everything but the time, while **Kurt Gebauer**'s *Swimmers* float with buoyant disengagement across the ceiling. The truly hip and cutting-edge can be found in this floor's 'laboratory of contemporary trends'. Installations have a mayfly longevity that's somehow appropriate; at the time of writing, you could find **Filip Turek**'s *From the History of Art*, which recreates famous works in supposedly witty ways. Botticelli's *Birth of Venus* is conjured up by three 1960s waterskiers in flowery bathing caps, for example.

First Floor (20th-century Foreign Art)

The first floor's collection of work from the first half of the 20th century work has a few gems: **Gustav Klimt**'s luscious *Virgin* (1913), which is displayed against the very different vision of feminine fecundity portrayed in **Egon Schiele**'s *Pregnant Woman and Death* (1911). Another tortured spirit, **Edvard Munch**, is represented by three paintings, including a lyrical and haunting *Dancing on the Shore* (*c.* 1900). Look out too for works by **Oskar Kokoschka**. He fled from Austria to Prague in 1934, and left for London four years after that; his *Red Egg* (1941) attacks fascism, with a stab at the appeasement policies that had betrayed Czechoslovakia at Munich in 1938.

Troja Château (Trojský zámek)

Troja Château
*U trojského zámku 1,
t 283 851 625, www.
citygalleryprague.cz;
metro Holešovice
nádraží, then bus 112;
open April–Oct Tues–
Thurs and Sat–Sun
10–6, Fri 1–6; adm*

The Baroque château houses a dull collection of 19th-century Czech art, but its fantastic, illusionistic interior decoration makes a trip out here worthwhile. Troja was built in the 1600s by an ambitious Czech nobleman so anxious to please Bohemia's masters that he covered his main hall with an apotheosis of the Habsburgs. Painted by the Flemish-born and Roman-trained Abraham Godyn between 1691 and 1697, it is the capital's richest *trompe l'œil*. Austrian triumphalism is the order of the day. The gaudy masterpiece heaps scorn on the Turks, who had been defeated at Vienna in 1683.

Tourist Information in Prague

ⓘ Prague >
*Prague Information
Service (PIS)
t 221 714 444,
www.pis.cz,
Railway Station and
Old Town Hall;
both open daily 9–7*

The **Prague Information Service** (PIS), www.pis.cz, has bilingual staff who can help you find accommodation, obtain tickets, and book excursions.

Prague Card

The Prague Card (*www.praguecity card.com*) allows free entrance to city museums and state-run galleries, with a supplement if you want to include free use of the public transport system. It is valid for two, three or four days, and an adult card costs from 790–1,200kč (not including tranport), or 990–1,600kč (with transport). There are reductions for students, children and seniors.

The Prague Card is available from most tourist agencies, including the PIS branches listed here and Čedok at Na příkopě 18, t 224 19 71 11.

Guided Tours

Walking tours are ubiquitous. Following a raised umbrella is often enough to get you on to one, but if you'd prefer to book ahead, try one of the following companies. All offer promenades on a few more or less predictable themes: Jewish Prague, revolutionary Prague, mysterious Prague, beery Prague, and so on.

Prague Walks, Jakubská 4, t 608 339 099, *www.praguewalks.com*.

City Walks, t 775 369 121, *www. praguer.com/citywalks*.

Prague Walking Tours, Vinohradská 28 t 222 516 064, *www.praguetravel.cz*.

Services in Prague

Internet Access

Most cafés now offer free WiFi access. Pay-per-minute connections can be found at:

Bohemia Bagel, Masná 2, Staré Město, *open daily 8am–9.30pm*.

Globe Bookstore and Coffeehouse, Pštrossova 6, Nové Město, *open Thurs–Sat 9.30–1am, Sun–Wed 9.30–midnight*.

On the Malá Strana side of the Charles Bridge, there's a no-frills collection of terminals through the passage at Mostecká 4, *open daily 9–10*.

Post Offices

The central post office is at Jindřišská 14, **t** 221 131 111, and its main hall is open Mon–Fri 7.30am–8pm. There are other branches at Kaprova 12 (Staré Město), Josefská (Malá Strana) and the Third Courtyard of Prague Castle.

Emergencies

There is an all-purpose crisis service for foreigners on **t** 112. Other emergency numbers are: **ambulance t** 155; **fire t** 150; **municipal police t** 156.

Hospitals and Clinics

Canadian Medical Care, Veleslavínská 1, **t** 235 360 133, *www.cmcpraha.cz*, *open Mon–Fri 8–6*. Somewhat pricy, but the most foreigner-friendly clinic in the capital. Doctors are permanently on call and will make home visits.

Nemocnice Na Homolce, Roentgenova 2, **t** 257 271 111, *www.homolka.cz*, *outpatient department open daily 7.30am–4pm*. The city's best-equipped hospital. It's accustomed to dealing with poorly foreigners, and should be the first port of call in serious cases. If you don't have a European Health Insurance Card (*see* p.20), upfront payment is required but the staff will liaise with your insurers to get you reimbursed.

Polyikinika na Národní, Národní 9, **t** 222 075 120, in emergencies out of hours call **t** 777 942 270, *www.poliklinika.narodni.cz*, *open Mon–Fri 8–6*. A private clinic in the centre of Prague. English staff and doctors are available and charges are relatively low.

Redeem prescriptions at any pharmacy (*lékárna*). The following are open 24 hours daily: Palackého 5 (Nové Město), **t** 224 946 982; Belgická 37

(Vinohrady), **t** 222 513 396; Štefánikova 6 (Smíchov), **t** 257 320 918.

Festivals and Events in Prague

The **Prague Spring Music Festival** in May and June is the highlight of the city's musical calendar. Details of its programme and tickets can be found at the Rudolfinum building (Nám. Jana Palacha, **t** 227 059 234) or via *www.festival.cz*. For more information on musical events in Prague, *see www.musica.cz*.

Shopping in Prague

In the city where a crate of olive oil could once attract a 20-strong queue you can now buy anything from a mango to a MiG-50 fighter jet. Malls have sprouted across the capital; the most disorientating one of them all is in Smíchov, replete with bowling alley and carousel. A more distinctly Czech form of consumerism survives in a set of shabby but elegant early 20th-century shopping arcades that radiate off the lower end of Václavské náměstí. Try the Lucerna complex or the Pasáž Rokoko. Prague's best department stores are Kotva in Náměstí Republiky (*open Mon–Fri 9–8, Sat 10–7, Sun 10–6*), and Tesco (a.k.a. My) on the junction of Národní and Spalená (*open Mon–Sat 8am–9pm, Sun 9–8; grocery open an hour earlier*). The swankiest street for designer goods is Pařížská: bargains are thin on the ground, though if you're the kind of person with sudden needs for a Hugo Boss suit or a Louis Vuitton valise, you probably don't care.

Bookshops (English-language)

Big Ben, Malá Štupartská 5, **t** 224 826 565, *www.bigbenbookshop.com*. Small but well-stocked, with a decent selection of international magazines and periodicals. *Open Mon–Sat 10–8, Sun 11–6*.

The Globe Bookstore and Coffeehouse, Pštrossova 6, **t** 224 934 203, *www.globebookstore.cz*. An expat fixture. Internet access, an eclectic selection of new and used books, and grizzled travellers exchanging yarns and numbers. *Open Thurs–Sat 9.30–1am, Sun–Wed 9.30–midnight.*

Clothes and Accessories

Art Deco Galerie, Michalská 21, **t** 224 223 076, *www.artdecogalerie-mili.info.* Pre-war glassware, ornaments and clothing, and some '60s items. *Open Mon–Fri 2–7.*

Vintage, Michalská 18, **t** 777 273 238. A selection of Prague cast-offs, from chiffon skirts and spangled bras to dirndls. *Open Mon–Fri 10–8, Sat 11–6, Sun 12–5.*

Crystal

Celetná Crystal, Celetná 15, **t** 222 324 022, *www.czechcrystal.com*. Three floors' worth of glassy objects, from dainty brooches to ornate chandeliers. *Open daily 10–7.*

Moser, Na příkopě 12 (first floor), **t** 224 211 293 (*see* corporate website at *www.moser.cz*). This Karlovy Vary-based company has been manu-facturing its uniquely lead-free crystalware since 1857, and claims several popes and kings among its satisfied customers. That may or may not impress, but the selection in this store certainly dazzles. *Open daily 10–7.*

Where to Stay in Prague

Current rates are generally posted on hotels' websites, and several places can be bargained down by email, especially during low season. The listings below represent some of the best hotels, but independent-minded travellers might prefer to rent a self-contained **apartment**. An online search will quickly produce several options: try *www.happyhouserentals. com*, *www.prague-city-apartments.cz*, *www.prague-hotel.co.uk*, or *www. apartments-in-prague.org*.

For an explanation of the price categories, *see* p.115.

Staré Město

Four Seasons, Veleslavínova 2a, **t** 221 427 000, *www.fourseasons.com/ prague* (€€€€). Impeccable service, larger than usual rooms, and

⭐ Hotel Josef >>

magnificent views over the Vltava river – at a price.

The Iron Gate, Michalská 19, **t** 225 777 777, *www.irongate.cz* (€€€€). A punctiliously restored townhouse, with wings dating back to Gothic times and original features peppering the building. So posh that the kitchenettes are hidden in antique wardrobes.

Buddha-Bar Hotel, Jakubská 8, **t** 221 776 300, *www.buddha-bar-hotel.cz* (€€€). Buddha Bars have grown distinctly tired since they began rolling out of Paris in the early 2000s, but this place has been getting rave reviews. It's certainly quiet and well-located, and if your idea of Zen-like calm involves sumptuous luxury, it may appeal.

Hotel Josef, Rybná 20, **t** 221 700 111, *www.hoteljosef.com* (€€€). A minimalist maze of frosted glass, curved chrome and white walls, with more mod cons than you can shake a stick at. To really unclutter your mind, splash out on one of the terraced rooms on the 7th and 8th floors.

Hotel U Prince, Staroměstské nám. 29, **t** 224 213 807, *www.hoteluprince.cz* (€€€). An ancient town house opposite the Astronomical Clock. Slick service, two vaulted restaurants, a magical roof terrace, and rooms stuffed with antiques.

Hotel U Červené židle, Liliová 4, **t** 296 180 018, *www.redchairhotel.com* (€€). A friendly family-run boarding house in a quiet street, halfway between the Charles Bridge and the foot of Wenceslas Square.

Old Town Square Hotel, Staroměstské nám. 20, **t** 221 421 111, *www.otsh.com* (€€). On the one hand, this place has no lift and it can be noisy. On the other, many of its rooms look out on to one of the most picturesque locations in central Europe. (There's a cheaper alternative a couple of doors away: *see www.grandhotelpraha.cz*.)

Penzion U medvídků (The Little Bear), Na perštýně 7, **t** 224 21 19 16, *www. umedvidku.cz* (€€). Simply decorated rooms, some with Gothic rafters and painted ceilings, in a former brewery. The adjoining beer hall has been getting Praguers drunk for generations.

⭐ **U černe hvězdy**

U černé hvězdy (The Black Star), Seminářská 6, t 222 220 033, *www.blackstarhotel.com* (€€). Six simply but tastefully furnished suites, four with kitchenettes, on a curving lane just metres from the Charles Bridge. Good value. There are two neighbouring hotels – details viewable on *www.uzlatestudny.cz* and *www. clementin.cz* – with prettier façades, but less attractive rooms.

U Krále Jiřího (King George's), Liliová 10, t 221 466 100, *www.kinggeorge.cz* (€€). Cosy, stylish, Baroque *pension* in the middle of the Old Town and a stroll away from the Charles Bridge. Good value, but you'll generally need to book quite some time ahead of your travel date.

U Staré paní (The Old Lady), Michalská 9, t 224 228 090, *www.ustarepani.cz* (€€). Centrally located accommodation in a gas-lit street, with a jazz bar in the basement.

U Tří Bubnů (The Three Drums), U radnice 8/10, t 224 214 855, *www.utribubnu.cz* (€€). Spacious rooms with character, and the cheapest hotel you'll find on the Old Town Square.

Dlouhá Pension and Hostel, Dlouhá 33, t 224 826 662, *www.travellers.cz* (€). A long-established and central hostel, offering accommodation ranging from snore-filled dorms to triple rooms with showers. There are five other locations, all bookable online.

⭐ **Aria Hotel »**

Hotel Haštal, Haštalská 16, t 222 314 335, *www.hotelhastalprague.com* (€). Reasonably priced rooms in a calm quarter of the Old Town.

Hostel Týn, Týnská 19, t 224 828 519, *www.hostel-tyn.web2001.cz* (€). Very basic rooms, but they're clean, cheap and just off the Old Town Square.

⭐ **U Zlaté studně »**

Penzion Attractive, Smetanovo nábřeží 14, t 222 220 523, *www.attractivepenzion.cz* (€). Spacious rooms and attic apartments on the Vltava embankment, several of them with riverside views. So long as you don't mind the aromas that waft from the café below, this place offers self-catering at a decent price.

Prague Castle/Hradčany

Romantik Hotel U raka (The Crayfish), Černínská 10, t 220 511 100, *www.romantikhotel-uraka.cz/english* (€€€). A family-run collection of six double rooms in a restored 18th-century timber barn. It's set in one of the prettiest, drowsiest corners of Prague, far from the madding crowds, and the owners can sort you out with taxis, dinner reservations and even bookings at a beautician. All rooms are non-smoking.

U Krále Karla (King Charles's), Úvoz 4, t 257 533 594, *www.romantichotels.cz* (€€€). A Baroque house, cluttered with fireplaces, painted ceilings, and stained glass, at the tranquil top end of steep Nerudova street.

Golden Tree Guest House, Nový Svět 13, t 233 354 082, *www.goldentree.cz* (€). Cheap bed-and-breakfast accommodation and self-contained flats, in picturesque locations on the castle side of the Charles Bridge.

Hotel Loreta, Loretánské nám. 8, t 233 310 510, contactable via *www.hotelloreta.cz* (€). A kind of Baroque chalet, offering quiet and clean rooms in a quiet square to the west of Prague Castle.

Malá Strana

Aria Hotel, Tržiště 9, t 225 334 111, *www.aria.cz* (€€€€). A musically themed boutique hotel, with extensive business facilities, a wonderful roof terrace and unfailingly courteous staff.

The Augustine, Letenská 12, t 266 112 233, *www.theaugustine.com* (€€€€). Amazing luxury at eye-watering prices. Good for anyone with an expense account to burn.

U Zlaté Studně (The Golden Well), U zlaté studně 4, t 257 011 213, *www.goldenwell.cz* (€€€€). A gate at the end of a cobbled cul-de-sac takes you into this four-storey Baroque hideaway, nestling under the castle gardens. The terrace restaurant has a good reputation and a breathtaking view over the orange tiles and green domes of Malá Strana.

The Golden Wheel, Nerudova 28, t 257 535 490, *www.thegoldenwheel.com* (€€€€–€€€). A stylishly converted

14th-century building, with impeccable service, 17 unique rooms and plush lifts to whizz you between them. A tiny garden looks up to the castle.

Residenze Lundborg, U lužického semináře 3, t 257 011 911, *www. lundborg.cz* (€€€). An ancient townhouse next to the Charles Bridge, built on flagstones from its 12th-century predecessor. It's a beautiful place to start and end your day in Prague.

Residenze Nosticova, Nosticova 1, t 257 312 513, *www.nosticova.com* (€€€). Set on a quiet corner of Kampa Island, with rooms that look ready to stage a historical drama and bonuses including a small pool, a beauty spa and sushi bar. The attached **Alchymist** restaurant radiates neo-Baroque bling, from its gold flock wallpaper to the zebra-striped chairs, but serves food that is reputed to be excellent.

The Charles, Josefská 1, t 257 532 913, *www.thecharleshotelprague.com* (€€). Friendly, well-appointed, and just a hop, skip and jump away from the Charles Bridge. The exterior is Baroque; the inside is a sumptuous mess of velvet curtains, engraved furniture, painted ceiling beams, and rug-laden wood and terracotta floors. The rates are particularly good value if you book online sufficiently far in advance.

Dům U velké boty (The Big Shoe), Vlašská 30, t 257 533 234, *www. bigboot.cz* (€€). Charming lodgings in an ivy-festooned 17th-century townhouse that's dreamy even by Malá Stana standards. Most rooms have twin beds; note that some are cheaper than others, but lack an ensuite bathroom.

Little Town Budget Hotel, Malostranské nám. 11, t 242 406 964, *www.littletownhotel.cz* (€€). The best-value bed and breakfast in central Malá Strana.

U páva (The Peacock), U lužického semináře 32, t 257 533 360, *www. romantichotels.cz* (€€). Charming and well located, in one of the quiet corners of Malá Strana. A small premium gets you a castle view over the gorgeous Vojan Gardens.

⭐ **Penzion U šuterů** >>

U Tří Pštrosů (The Three Ostriches), Dražického nám. 12, t 257 532 410, *www.utripstrosu.cz* (€€). A 16th-century townhouse that's all but built in to the Charles Bridge. After years of overpriced snootiness, it has pulled its rates down and now constitutes quite a bargain, though its central location might not suit light sleepers.

Hostel Sokol, Nosticova 2, t 257 007 397, *www.hostelsokol.cz* (€). A bargain for the budgetarily challenged. The rooms are clean, it's on the edge of a park next to the river, and you're a short stroll from the Charles Bridge.

Nové Město

Carlo IV, Senovážné nám. 13, t 224 593 111, *www.boscolohotels.com* (€€€€). Elegantly built out of a former bank, with a shimmering cigar bar and restaurant in the former vault and a luminous 17-metre pool in the basement. Several rooms are disappointingly cramped, but the facilities are top-notch.

Hotel Esplanade, Washingtonova 19, t 224 501 111, *www.esplanade.cz* (€€€). A hotel dating from 1927, left to crumble under the Communists, but now sumptuously restored. Comfortable, if a little chintzy, and relatively good value if you book online in advance.

Grand Hotel Evropa, Václavské nám. 25, t 224 215 387, *www.evropahotel.cz* (€€). Prague Art Nouveau at its most impressive, with a melancholy café on the ground floor and dusty chaises longues, lanterns and palm fronds scattered around the skylit corridors above. The rooms themselves are drab, and many lack private bathrooms at worst, but they remain the cheapest on Wenceslas Square.

City Penzion, Záhřebská 16/Belgická 10, t 222 522 422, *www.hotelcitybell.cz* (€). A basic but friendly *pension*, in a quiet, cobbled avenue that's a stroll away from Wenceslas Square and even less distance from several pleasant cafés.

Penzion U šuterů, Palackého 4, t 224 948 235, *www.usuteru.cz* (€). An elegant *pension*, with vaulted and beamed whitewashed rooms, in the centre of the New Town. It comes with a cosy restaurant next door.

Eating Out in Prague

Thousands of tourists feast daily on rubbery meats and desiccated vegetables on Prague's main streets, but short detours can produce meals that are far cheaper and tastier. Note that all the following restaurants still allow smoking, unless stated otherwise, and kitchens generally shut down an hour before the advertised closing time. For an explanation of the price categories, *see* p.115.

Staré Město

Bellevue, Smetanovo nábřeží 18, **t** 222 221 443, *www.bellevuerestaurant.cz* (€€€€). Elegant furnishings, attentive service, excellent food and extraordinary prices in a riverside restaurant with views over to the castle. There's live jazz at a champagne brunch on Sundays. *Open 12–3 and 5.30–11.*

V Zátiší, Liliová 1, **t** 222 221 155, *www. vzatisi.cz* (€€€€). One of the first restaurants to bring modern cuisine to Prague, serving some of the capital's best cooked dishes. *Open daily 12–3 and 6–11.*

Chez Marcel, Haštalská 12, **t** 222 315 676 (€€€). French-owned bistro, serving steaks, mussels, frites, soups and so on in a cobbled church square. Perfect for idling away an evening over a bottle of wine or two. *Open daily 11.30am–1am.*

Klub Architektů, Betlémské nám. 5a, **t** 224 401 214 (€€). Candlelit wooden tables in a atmospheric warren of Gothic chambers. The Czech-based menu is almost endless, and though the preparations are hit-and-miss, portions are hefty. *Open daily 11.30am–midnight.*

Kolkovna, V kolkovně 8, **t** 224 819 701, *www.kolkovna.cz* (€€). An updated incarnation of the Czech *pivnice*, serving several vegetarian dishes alongside meaty meals that offer more choice than usual. *Open daily 11am–midnight.*

Kozička (The Little Goat), Kozi 1, **t** 224 818 308, *www.kozicka.cz* (€€). Hot and cold meals, with a handful of vegetarian options, in a lively cellar bar. The kitchen usually closes around

⭐ **Kolkovna** >

1am. *Open Mon–Fri noon–4am, Sat 6pm–4am, Sun 7pm–3am.*

Lehká hlava (Clear Head), Boršov 2, **t** 222 220 665, *www.lehkahlava.cz* (€€). A hole-in-the-wall in a cul-de-sac, serving spicy vegetarian and vegan dishes. Non-smoking, with children's portions available. This place is popular, so reservations are advisable. *Open Mon–Fri 11.30–11.30, Sat–Sun 12–11.30.*

Maitrea, Týnská ulička 6, **t** 221 711 631, *www.restaurace-maitrea.cz/en* (€€). Vegetarian food with an Asian theme. Non-smoking, child-friendly, and comfortable, with extra seating downstairs. *Open Mon–Fri 11.30–11.30, Sat–Sun 12–11.30.*

Orange Moon, Rámová 5, **t** 222 325 119, *www.orangemoon.cz* (€€). Spicy south and southeast Asian dishes, including several vegetarian options. An excellent spot to warm up in midwinter, or anytime else for that matter. *Open daily 11.30–11.30.*

U červeného kola (The Red Wheel), Anežská 2, **t** 224 811 118, *www. ucervenehokola.wz.cz* (€€). Czech steak and duck, in a sublime corner of town close to the St Agnes' Convent. *Open daily 11–3pm, 5pm–11pm.*

Bohemia Bagel, Masná 2, **t** 224 812 560, *www.bohemiabagel.cz* (€). Fresh bagels, squeezed juices, and tasty salads. *Open daily 8am–9.30pm.* There's another branch just over the Charles Bridge at Lázenska 19 (*open 7.30am–7pm*).

Pizzeria Rugantino, Dušní 4, **t** 222 318 172, *www.rugantino.cz* (€). Italian-owned, serving the best pizza in town. *Open Mon–Sat 11–11, Sun 12–11.*

U Kata (The Executioner), U radnice 6, **t** 224 236 363 (€). An old-time boozer just behind the Old Town Square, named in honour of Prague's headsman, who used to have special dispensation to eat in the restaurant next door. The food is basic, but helps soak up the beer. *Open Mon–Sat noon–12.30am, Sun 12–11.*

U Vejvodů, Jilská 4, **t** 222 251 282 (€). An over-renovated but enduringly popular 14th-century beer hall, with stodgy Czech delicacies and lashings of Pilsner to wash them down.

Open Mon–Thurs 10–3, Fri–Sat 10–4, Sun 11–2.

Josefov

Pravda, Pařížská 17, **t** 222 326 203 (€€€). Situated next to the Old-New Synagogue, this is the elegant sister of trendy **Barock** on the other side of the road. The international menu is exhausting (everything from asparagus to zucchini, most of it seared or drizzled), but anyone eating to impress will find something to his or her taste. *Open noon–1am.*

(★) Hergetova Cihelná >>

Café Colonial, Široká 6, **t** 224 818 322 (€€). The best place for a swift lunch in the Josefov if you're after non-kosher food. None is done very well, but on a busy afternoon you'll probably be pleased that it is done at all. *Open daily 10am–midnight.*

King Solomon, Široká 8, **t** 224 818 752, *www.kosher.cz* (€€). An amiable kosher restaurant. Try to get a seat in the bright conservatory at the back. *Open Sun–Thurs 12–11pm, shabbat meals on Fri and Sat with reservations.*

Shalom Restaurant, Maiselova 18, **t** 224 800 806, 224 810 929 (€). Kosher lunches in the Jewish Town Hall. Vouchers for meals have to be bought in advance from the shop opposite the Old-New Synagogue (*open Sun–Thurs 10–4pm, Fri 10–2pm*). *Open Mon–Sat 11.30–2pm.*

(★) U Modré Kachničky >>

Prague Castle and Hradčany

Bellavista, Strahovské nádvoří 1, **t** 220 517 274, *www.bella-vista.cz* (€€€). Italian cuisine served up in a vaulted cellar behind the monastery; in summer, eat out on the terrace for a heart-melting view of the city below. *Open daily 11–noon.* There's a cheaper restaurant and microbrewery opposite the entrance to the library (Klášterní pivovar, *open daily 10–10*).

Peklo (Hell), Strahovské nádvoří 1, **t** 220 516 652, *www.peklo.com* (€€). Fairylights line a stone staircase into 12th-century beer cellars owned by the Strahov Monastery. *Open daily noon–11pm.*

Malý Buddha, Úvoz 46, **t** 220 513 894, *www.malybuddha.cz* (€). Cheap Czech Chinese. You can also join the owners for meditation on Mondays between 7 and 8pm. *Open Tues–Sun 12–10.30.*

Malá Strana

Kampa Park, Na Kampě 8b, **t** 257 532 685, *www.kampapark.com* (€€€€–€€€). From the moment you step along the oil lamp catwalk to enter this place, you're dining in style. The menu drizzles with tasty French/Italian offerings, while the location next to the Charles Bridge is what you came to Prague for. The city's most glamorous restaurant, even if it does insist on proving it with photos of celebrity diners. *Open 11.30am–1am.*

Hergetova Cihelná, Cihelná 2b, **t** 296 826 103, *www.cihelna.com* (€€€). One of the best restaurants on this stretch of the Malá Strana embankment, with great views, a stylish interior, and meals that are both light and fresh. Several vegetarian options. *Open daily 11.30am–1am.*

Pálffy Palác, Valdštejnská 14, **t** 257 530 522, *www.palffy.cz* (€€€). This ornate restaurant, set in one wing of a Baroque palace, was once among the most romantic in Prague, but the interior has become rather too crowded to be fun. The food and service remain excellent though, and if you manage to reserve a spot on the summer terrace, beneath the fragrant castle gardens, chances are you won't forget a meal here for a very long time. *Open daily 11am–11pm.*

U Modré Kachničky (The Blue Duckling), Nebovidská 6, **t** 257 320 308, *www.umodrekachnicky.cz* (€€€). The first post-revolutionary restaurant to take Czech food seriously. Game is a speciality. Intimate, eccentrically cluttered, and a quiet walk away from Charles Bridge. *Open daily 12–4 and 6.30–11.30.*

Artisan, Rošických 4, **t** 257 218 277, *www.artisanrestaurant.cz* (€€). Global cuisine, using fresh and seasonal ingredients, in an quiet street on the lower slopes of Petřín Hill. Intimate surroundings, friendly service and decent value. *Open daily 11–11.*

Gitanes, Tržiště 7, **t** 257 530 163, *www.gitanes.cz* (€€). A Balkan-Italian menu, eclectic but often delicious, with outdoor seating in the summer. *Open daily 12–11.*

Malostranská Beseda, Malostranské nám. 21 **t** 257 409 112, *www. malostranska-beseda.cz/en* (€€). The ground-floor restaurant in the square forms part of a four-floor entertainment complex, with a beer hall beneath and music venue and bar upstairs. *Open daily 11am–11pm.*

Noi, Újezd 19, **t** 257 311 411, *www.noirestaurant.cz.* (€€). When you've had one dumpling too many, head over here for sizeable and tasty Thai dishes in stylish surroundings. Baby- and child-friendly. *Open daily 11pm–1am.*

St Nicholas, Tržiště 10, **t** 222 530 204 (€€). A cosy tunnel of a restaurant/bar, with friendly staff and a pizza oven in operation until 1am. *Open daily 12–2am.*

Vinárna Čertovka, U Lužického semináře 24, **t** 257 534 524, *www.certovka.info/eng* (€€). A secluded riverside terrace at the foot of the narrowest staircase in town. Nondescript meals, but a great location. *Open daily 11.30am––12 midnight.*

U Hrocha (The Hippo), Thunovská 10, **t** 222 516 978 (€). Hidden at the foot of the New Castle Steps, this pub has somehow survived the gentrification that has swept away so many others in Malá Strana. Food on offer includes sausages, dumplings and *pivní* – a rank cheese that you're supposed to squash into a beery paste. The raucous regulars guard many secrets, but confident drinking and kneading can at least earn their respect. *Open daily 12–11.30.*

Nové Město

La Perle de Prague Dancing House (Tančící dům), Rašinovo nabřeží 80, **t** 221 984 160, *www.laperle.cz* (€€€). *Haute cuisine* from the 7th-floor heights of Gehry's 'Fred and Ginger' building (*see* p.184), with a view as spectacular as you might expect. *Open daily 12–2 and 7–10.30pm.*

Dynamo, Pštrossova 29, **t** 224 932 020 (€€). A canteen-like restaurant, with a good range of fresh, well-made Czech and Mediterranean dishes. *Open daily 11.30–12.* It's often packed, in which case take a look at the nearby **Universal** at V Jirchařích 6

(**t** 224 934 416; *open daily 11am–1am*) and **Velryba** (The Whale) at Opatovická 24 (**t** 224 912 484; *open daily 11–12*).

U šuterů, Palackého 4, **t** 224 948 235 (€€). A cosy eatery, serving Czech standards like duck, dumplings and sauerkraut. It's become a little pricy for its long-standing regulars, but remains good value by Western standards. *Open Mon–Sat 11–11, Sun 12–10pm.*

Cafés in Prague

Staré Město

Bakeshop Praha, Kozí 1, **t** 602 101 443. Excellent bakery and café, offering pastries aplenty, copies of the *International Herald Tribune* and the *Guardian*, and window seats from which to watch busier folk hurry by. *Open daily 7–7.*

Café Montmartre, Řetězova 7, **t** 222 221 244. This was a watering hole for Prague's pre-war intellectuals and dandies, but the decadence has been slow to return since its post-revolutionary reopening. A pleasant place to contemplate one's novel, all the same. *Open Mon–Fri 8am–11pm, Sat–Sun 12 noon–11pm.* There are a couple of nearby alternatives: the **Café Ebel** next door at number 9 (*open Mon–Fri 8am–8pm, Sat–Sun 8.30am–8pm*) and the **Literární kavárna** on the other side of the street at number 10 (*open Mon–Fri noon–11pm, Sat–Sun 5–11pm*).

Grand Café Orient, Ovocný trh 19, Staré Město, **t** 224 224 240, *www. grandcafeorient.cz.* An elegantly geometric corner café, serving particularly good breakfasts, on the first floor of the Cubist house in Celetná street. *Open Mon–Fri 9am–10pm, Sat–Sun 10am–10pm.*

Erra, Konviktská 11, **t** 222 220 568. A semi-subterranean and slightly gay café, especially good for breakfasts. *Open daily 10am–midnight.*

Gourmand Au Gourmand, Dlouhá 10, Staré Město, **t** 222 329 060. A tiled and mirrored delicatessen, serving good coffee, quiches, pastries and snacks just steps away from the offensive eateries of the Old Town Square.

⭐ Grand Café Orient >>

Open daily Mon–Fri 8am–8pm, Sat–Sun 8.30am–8pm.

Obecní dům Kavárna, Náměstí Republiky 5, Staré Město, **t** 220 002 763. The most glamorous Art Nouveau café in town. *Open daily 7.30am–11pm.*

U Zlatého Kohouta (The Golden Cock), Michalská 3, **t** 224 213 435. Tea, tea, and more tea – nigh on 200 varieties, in three cosy rooms and a pretty little courtyard. As and when you thirst for something stronger, there's a clutch of long-established wine bars nearby. *Open Mon–Fri 10–9.30, Sat–Sun 2–9.30.*

Nové Město

Café-Café, Rytířská 10, **t** 224 210 597, *www.cafe-cafe.cz*. A stylish coffee and cocktail bar: breakfasts, salads and small meals served by some of the most attractive waiting staff in town. *Open daily 10–11pm.*

Café Imperial, Na poříčí 15, **t** 246 011 440, *www.cafeimperial.cz*. A splendid coffeehouse, forested by ceramic pillars, encrusted by wall-reliefs and oozing pretensions of faded glory. A good place to mourn Mitteleuropa, eat schnitzels and so on. *Open daily 9am–1am.*

⭐ **U Zavěšeného Kafe >>**

Café Meduza, Belgická 15, **t** 222 515 107, *www.meduza.cz*. A charming mahogany hideaway on a quiet avenue at the edge of the New Town. *Open Mon–Fri 10am–1am, Sat–Sun 12–midnight*. There's another café serving Mexican food four doors away at no.11 (**Žlutá pumpa**, *open Mon–Fri noon– 12.30am, Sat–Sun 4pm– 12.30am*) and another on the corner of Záhřebská (**Hlučná samota**, *www.hlucna-samota.cz, open Mon–Fri 11–11, Sat–Sun 12–11*).

Café Louvre, Národní 20, **t** 224 930 949, *www.cafelouvre.cz*. A bright and airy café, originally opened in 1902, well-suited to newspaper perusal, conspiratorial meetings, pool-playing (five tables), and time-wasting in general. *Open daily 8am–11.30pm.*

Evropa, Václavské nám. 25, **t** 224 215 387. An Art Nouveau gem, not quite as glamorous as the Obecní dům (*above*) but worth visiting if you are on Wenceslas Square anyway. Breakfast is served in the gallery from 7–10am.

Open daily 10–midnight (restaurant until 11.30pm).

Friends Coffee House, Palackého 7, **t** 272 049 665, *www.milujikavu.cz/en*. The unremarkable entrance opens into a non-smoking, kiddie-friendly and thoroughly relaxing café. Bagels, sandwiches, fresh juices and decent coffee. *Open Mon–Fri 8am–10pm, Sat–Sun 12–9pm.*

Kavárna Slavia, Smetanovo nábřeží 2, **t** 221 771 651. A legendary haunt frequented by dissidents, secret policeman and pretty much everyone else in Prague for most of the 20th century. Come join the gossiping students and good-for-nothing grandmothers who lounge their lives away here. *Open Mon–Fri 8am– midnight, Sat–Sun 9am–noon.*

Zahradka U Kristiána. Smetanovo nábřeží 6. A rickety cafe that floats on the river. Nothing to eat except bread, cheese and ham, but live music and a view of bridge and castle mean that there are far worse places to mull over your next move. *Open April–Oct daily noon–10pm.*

Prague Castle/Hradčany

U Zavěšenyho Kafe (The Hanging Coffee), Úvoz 6, **t** 257 532 868. Excellent home cooking in a charming neighbourhood café on the steep hill leading from Nerudova to Strahov. *Open daily 11am–midnight.*

Malá Strana

U Malého Glena (Little Glen's), Karmelitská 23, **t** 257 531 717, *www.malyglen.cz*. A cosy American-owned café serving a mishmash of Czech, Tex-Mex, soup andsandwiches. It turns into a small and lively jazz club during the evening. *Open Sun–Thurs 10am–2am, Fri–Sat 10am–3am.*

Smíchov

Savoy, Vítězná 1 (Smíchov), **t** 257 311 562. A glamorous Art Deco counter-point to the **Slavia**, on the far side of Legion Bridge (Most Legii). Worth a drink, though better and cheaper French cuisine can be had elsewhere. *Open Mon–Fri 8am–10.30p,, Sat–Sun 9am–10.30pm.*

Entertainment and Nightlife in Prague

The *Prague Post* publishes a supplement called 'Night and Day' with up-to-date listings, and free guides are nestled amid the debris in most tourist-friendly establishments. You'll avoid commission by dealing directly with the venue concerned, but the following agencies can obtain tickets for a fee (check websites for retail outlets and opening times): **Bohemia Tickets International**, *www.bohemiaticket.cz*; **Ticketpro**, *www.ticketpro.cz*; **Ticketstream**, *www.ticketstream.cz*.

Opera and Classical Music

Prague's operatic community split into two companies in 1992. The **National Opera** is based in the National Theatre at Národní 2 (**t** 224 901 448, *www.narodni-divadlo.cz*), and the **State Opera** is at Wilsonova 4 (**t** 224 227 266, *www.state-opera.com*); both addresses are in Nové Město. The **Estates Theatre** (Stavovské divadlo) remains part of the former but devotes its energies to Mozart; it's at Ovocní trh. 1 in the Old Town (**t** 224 215 001, *www.estatestheatre.cz*). The **Prague Symphony Orchestra** operates out of the Art Nouveau Obecní dům at Náměstí Republiky 5 (**t** 222 002 100, *www.obecnidum.cz*), and the **Czech Philharmonic** is based at the Rudolfinum on Alšovo nábřeží 12 and has its own websites at *www.ceskafilharmonie.cz*. *See also* festivals, p.191.

Theatre

The two largest are the **National Theatre** (Národni 2, Nové Město, **t** 224 901 448, *www.narodni-divadlo.cz*) and the neighbouring **Laterna Magika Theatre** (Národní 4, **t** 224 931 482, *www.laterna.cz*), squatting under what looks like a very big piece of bubble wrap. The latter company sparked off an entire genre on the basis of one gimmick – the fact that actors in black clothes can invisibly move things against a dark backdrop – and you'll find 'black light theatre' advertised on fliers across the capital.

Prague's smaller theatres have been undergoing a renaissance in recent years, and two dynamic ones are the **Divadlo na zábradlí** (Anenské nám. 5, Staré Město, **t** 222 868 868, *www.nazabradli.cz*) and the **Švandovo divadlo** (Štefánikova 57, Smíchov, **t** 234 651 111, *www.svandovodivadlo.cz*). The city's most innovative productions are often found on the three hydraulically controlled stages of the **Divadlo Archa** (Na poříčí 26, Nové Město, **t** 221 716 333, *www.archatheatre.cz*). With a strong bias towards music and dance, the theatre is relatively accessible to non-Czech speakers – well worth investigating if experimental drama is your bag.

Dance

The **Czech National Ballet** (*www.balet.cz*) generally performs either at its home at the National Theatre or at the Estates Theatre. Visiting companies sometimes stage shows at the State Opera. *See also* 'Festivals', p.191.

Bars

Blue Light, Josefská 1, Malá Strana, **t** 257 533 126. Small, dark and highly cosy, with a soundtrack of R&B and a friendly, eclectic crowd. *Open daily 6pm–3am.*

Bombay Cocktail Bar, Dlouhá 13, Staré Město, **t** 222 324 040. A lively place to drink and dance. *Open Sun–Wed 7pm–4am, Thurs 7pm–5am, Fri–Sat 7pm–6am.*

Chapeau Rouge, Jakubská 2, Staré Město, **t** 222 316 328. An alcoholic maelstrom that sucks in and spits out about half of Prague's party people on any given evening. A good place to begin the night if you have no idea where you want to end it. *Open daily 4pm–5am; till 4am in winter.*

Club Zero, Dušní 8, Staré Město, **t** 737 282 354. An eclectic crowd of drinkers and dancers in a small cocktail lounge-cum-dance floor not far from the Old Town Square. *Open Wed–Sat 8–4am.*

Duende, Karoliny Světlé 30, Staré Město, **t** 775 186 077, *www.duende.cz*. A block away from the Old Town end of the Charles Bridge, but so mellow you'd hardly guess. Friendly staff, convivial co-drinkers, and occasional live acts. *Open Mon–Fri 1pm–midnight, Sat 3pm–midnight, Sun 5pm–midnight.*

Hergetova Cihelná, Cihelná 2b, Malá Strana, **t** 296 826 103, *www.cihelna.cz*. Capacious cocktail lounge with sofas and pool table, above the elegant riverside restaurant of the same name. *Open daily 11.30am–1am.*

Klub solidní nejistota, Pštrossova 21, Nové Město, **t** 224 910 593, *www.solidninejistota.cz*. A place to eye-up and be eyed, with a circular bar and a small, packed dance floor. *Open daily 6pm–6am.*

Klub Újezd, Újezd 18, Malá Strana, **t** 257 316 537, *www.klubujezd.cz*. This was the first club to operate after the Velvet Revolution, and remains popular among grungy nostalgists of a certain age. *Open daily 8pm–4am (ground-floor bar open from 2pm).*

Kozička, Kozí 1, Staré Město, **t** 224 818 308, *www.kozicka.cz*. Buzzing cellar bar, packed with trendy regulars. *Open Mon–Fri noon–4am, Sat 6pm–4am, Sun 7pm–3am.*

Le Clan, Balbínova 23, Vinohrady, *www.leclan.cz*. A semi-private drinking club that doesn't get going until around 2am, and disgorges its last guests some time after sunrise. It serves as a terminus for some of Prague's most restless clubbers, but there can be few dive bars more civilized. *Open Tues–Sat until very late.*

M1, Masná 1, Staré Město, **t** 227 195 235, *www.m1lounge.com*. A sleek lounge close to the Old Town Square, playing at least as much R&B as anyone could reasonably hope for. Unpleasantness from the officious bouncers is minimised by reserving a booth online in advance. *Open Sun–Thurs 7pm–3am, Fri–Sat 7pm–5am.*

Nebe, Křemencova 10, Nové Město, **t** 777 662 081, *www.nebepraha.cz*. A friendly and semi-slick subterranean bar cum dance floor. *Open daily Mon–Sat 6pm–5am.*

Tretters, V kolkovně 3, Staré Město, **t** 224 811 165, *www.tretters.cz*. Swanky and cocktail-heavy, crowded with Czech and foreign thirty-somethings in the money, on the pull, or both. *Open Mon–Sat 7pm–3am, Sun 7–2am.*

U Černého Vola (The Black Ox), Loretánské nám. 1, Hradčany, **t** 220 513 481. A popular pub, with delicious dark Kozel on tap, located just beyond the castle. Subject to alcoholic intake, it's a good place from which to launch a walk into the Petřín woods or a descent towards Malá Strana. *Open daily 10am–10pm.*

U Fleků, Křemencova 9–11, Nové Město, **t** 224 934 019, *www.ufleku.cz*. Prague's best-known beer hall, with all that that entails: bassoonists, heaps of dumplings, and droves of crooning, *stein*-clashing Germans. If 14° beer and five and a half centuries of brewing tradition tempt you nevertheless, come and claim one of the 500 seats. *Open daily 10am–11pm.*

U Zlatého Tygra (The Golden Tiger), Husova 17, Staré Město, **t** 222 221 111. A dank Pilsner pub. Grizzled Prague regulars used to colonize every inch of this place, but, for better or worse, they're increasingly ceding ground to curious foreigners. *Open daily 3pm–11pm.*

Zanzibar, Lázeňská 6, Malá Strana, **t** 602 780 076. A lively cocktail bar near the Charles Bridge. *Open daily 5pm–3am.*

Clubs

Akropolis, Kubelíkova 27, Žižkov, **t** 296 330 911, *www.palacakropolis.cz*. This place is a taxi ride from the centre, but its enduring popularity should earn it a place in any comprehensive club-crawl. Two decrepit bars, a restaurant, and live acts from across the world. *Open daily 7pm–5am (coffee bar 10am–midnight; restaurant Sun–Thur 11am–12.30am, Fri–Sat 11am–1.30am).*

Cross Club, Plynární 23, **t** 736 535 053, *www.crossclub.cz*. A kind of steampunk inferno in the wilds of Holešovice. Not for the faint of heart, but an excellent destination for desperadoes in the mood for a mission. *Open Mon–Sat 9–6am.*

Duplex, Václavské nám. 21, Nové Město, **t** 224 232 319, *www.duplex.cz*. Anyone determined to sample one of Wenceslas Square's many techno clubs may as well do it here. Two layers of dance floor, five bars, go-go dancers and a vertiginous view, all contained within an immense glass cube six storeys above street level. *Open Wed–Sat 10pm–5am.*

Jazz Dock, Janáčkovo nábřeží 2, t 774 058 838, www.jazzdock.cz/en. A long bar, decent food and a flexible space in a modern riverside building make this one of Prague's most comfortable venues for local and visiting jazz acts. *Open Mon–Sat from late afternoon until 4am, Sun until 2am.*

Karlovy Lázné (Charles Baths), Karlův most, Staré Město, t 2 22 220 502, www.karlovylazne.cz. Four dance floors in the Old Town's erstwhile public baths, close to the Charles Bridge. Its neon sign serves as a beacon to countless stag parties and tour groups; if you fancy meeting leery compatriots in a disused swimming pool, this may be the club for you. *Open daily 9pm–5am.*

Radost FX, Bělehradská 120 (just south of Wenceslas Square), Vinohrady, t 224 254 776, www.radostfx.cz. The fulcrum of Prague fabulousness in the early 1990s, and still popular among the city's club kids. Pocket dance floor; excellent vegetarian food in the café upstairs (until 1am). *Open 10pm–5am.*

Reduta, Národní 20, Nové Město, t 224 933 487, www.redutajazzclub.cz. The city's oldest jazz club, established in 1958. It's always been a hotbed of mild nonconformism, and when Bill Clinton hit Prague on his 1994 Europe tour it was here that he blew his sax. *Open daily 9.30pm–midnight.*

Roxy, Dlouhá 33, Staré Město, t 224 826 296, www.roxy.cz. A former cinema stripped down to its concrete essentials, fond of hosting foreign DJs and acts. *Open sporadically 8pm–5am.*

SaSaZu, Bubenské nábřeží 13, Holešovice, t 733 640 771/3, www.sasazu.cz. A hangar-sized dance floor in a converted abbatoir, alongside an Asian fusion restaurant and more beautiful people than you could shake a stick at. *Open daily 12 noon–3am.*

Day Trips from Prague

Karlovy Vary

Carlsbad, as the Germans called it, was long one of central Europe's most elegant watering holes. Goethe and Schiller drank deep of its draughts; its casino and promenades were the playground of Russian aristocrats and European monarchs; and every Romantic composer worth his salt took the cure. The frolics ended in the 20th century. As part of the Sudetenland it was stolen by the Nazis in 1938, and after the war the toffs were dispossessed by the Communists. A dreary parade of postwar potentates, from Haile Selassie to Kurt Waldheim, came to dip their toes in the waters. But although the beau monde has been replaced by German tourists, lovers of bygone charm will find few better spots in Bohemia. Le Corbusier called Karlovy Vary a 'cream cake' – no compliment from a modernist – but less doctrinaire types will revel in the confectionery.

Built along the bubbling Teplá river, the town climbs wooded hillsides in pastel blocks. The town's famous springs are forced up from subterranean hot rocks two kilometres down, and reach the surface at temperatures of 30 to 72°C, but until Emperor Charles IV stumbled upon it in 1358 little Wary was just a village of clean and healthy folk. It received its royal charter in 1370, and now 12 of the

Getting to Karlovy Vary

Karlovy Vary is 132km west of Prague. By **car** join the E48 on Milady Horákové running north by Letná Park. **Coaches** leave Florenc bus station more or less hourly and take 1½–2 hours; a one-way ticket costs around 200kč. There is a **train** each morning from Hlavní station. It leaves at 07.31, takes 3½hrs, and costs about 300kč. There are two **funiculars** in the town.

60 springs have established medicinal benefits. Beware the hypochondriacal regulations that apply along the promenades – no dogs, smoking or loud noises – and in the colonnades, where 'long objects' are forbidden too. Up the Teplá from the landmark **Thermal Hotel**, **Dvořák Park** (Dvořákovy sady) has a lily pond and the wrought-iron colonnades that survived a Habsburg cannon-metal hunt during the 1914–18 war. Further upriver is the neoclassical splendour of the **Mill Colonnade** (Mlýnská kolonáda), where five springs hiss and gurgle to the surface. It is the favourite ambulatory of the town's hydrophiles, who drink waters through the spouts of teapot-like *pohárky*.

In the centre of town is the wooden **Market Colonnade**. Here you will find the **Vřídlo** ('Spring'), the fountain responsible for Karlovy Vary's rise to glory, housed in a glass Communist-era temple. When Charles IV chanced upon a spring while deer-hunting he was advised by his physician that it was suitable only for bathing; but in 1522, its oral advantages were publicized by early spa maniac Václav Payer, who recommended a daily dosage of 60 cups and 12-hour baths.

The street that runs up the hill from the plague column takes you past the circular colonnade of the **Castle Spring**, under a tower built by Charles, to **Stag Leap** (Jelení skok), the tall rock where Charles' quarry was sighted – leading him to the spring.

Salvation of the soul always took second place to sins of the flesh in Karlovy Vary. The town was blessed with just one Counter-Reformation masterpiece, the oval **Church of St Mary Magdalene** (Kostel sv. Marie Magdalena), built by Kilian Dienzenhofer in 1732–6, on the hill across the river. An enjoyable approach is by **funicular** (*lanovka*), walking down again past bulbous spires. In the same square is the **Vítězslav Nezval Theatre** (Divadlo V. Nezvala), financed by toilet admission fees. Its stage curtain was painted by three Viennese painters in 1885, one of whom was a young Gustav Klimt. The embankment beyond the theatre is called **Old Meadow** (Stará louka), and is lined with the oldest houses in town. On the right at the end is another **funicular**. It takes you to a view so good that it is disillusioning, revealing the spa a tiny oasis amidst the greyness of a 20th-century town.

The 500-bed **Grand Hotel Pupp**, the core of which is 300 years old, marks the end of the town. The twilight splendour of the

(i) **Karlovy Vary** >
*Infocentrum,
Lázenská 1, t 355 321 171,
www.karlovyvary.cz*

Spa Treatments in Karlovy Vary

The town's clinics handle conditions from indigestion to quadriplegia. Treatments can be booked at Čedok offices abroad. In the town, **Infocentrum** (next to the Vřídlo; *see* left) can tell you if Karlovy Vary can treat your ailment. It can also book hotels and guides.

Of the municipal baths, Baths III and V, luxurious Bath I and the new Bath VI are open to foreigners. They offer watery services from massage to low-voltage electric shock. If you just want a dip, there's an outdoor pool on the hill behind the Thermal Hotel, filled with water from a cool spring. Sparkling clean and with a breathtaking view over the town, there are few more satisfying swims in Bohemia (*open Mon–Sat 8–8, Sun 9–8*).

The town also has a few dietary specialities. Look out for *oplatky*, sweet wafers designed to mitigate the foul taste of the waters, and the ubiquitous Becherovka, a herbal tipple

developed by town chemist Dr Becher in the 19th century. Porcelain from its factories and Moser snifters are the town's most popular souvenirs – the latter balloon-sized glasses that have the sole purpose of making superior cognac taste even more superior.

Eating Out in Karlovy Vary

Cafe Elefant, Stará Louka 30, t 353 222 544 (€€). A local favourite since the early 1800s. Luscious cappuccinos, cakes, fruit salads and sundaes, complemented by excellent people-watching opportunities.

Embassy, Nova Louka 21, t 353 221 161 (€€€). To dine in the style that Karlovy Vary deserves, make a reservation at the dark and discreet Embassy, and gorge yourself on smoked eels and asparagus tips. The cure wouldn't be worth it without the indulgence.

Promenáda, Tržiště 31, t 353 22 56 48 (€€). Huge, Baroque *vinotheque* for fine dining or sampling the regional wines.

neo-Renaissance **Bath 1** (Lázně 1), opposite the hotel, offers the chance to munch water biscuits in Emperor Franz Josef's imperial bathtub, before heading upstairs for the roulette tables. A few hundred metres down **Goetheova stezka** is a bust of Goethe, who paid Carlsbad thirteen visits.

Karlštejn

Karlštejn
*t 311 681 617, www.
hradkarlstejn.cz;
opening times vary
widely over the year
and the castle is always
closed on Mondays;
check websites for
details; amission is by
guided tour only, and
visits to the Holy Cross
chapel should be
booked in advance
online*

Bohemia is full of Gothic castles. Karlštejn is one of the closest to Prague; its slate roofs and towers perched on their limestone peak are almost too perfect to believe. Karlštejn was begun in 1348 by Charles IV, and by 1367 it had been turned into a vast symbol of the strange universe that the emperor inhabited. Its three components were designed to mark a mystical ascent from the mundane level of temporal power (the emperor's quarters), up 260m to the pinnacle of the castle, the Chapel of the Holy Rood. In the late 19th century it was restored according to the neo-Gothic theories of Josef Mocker. Much of its interior suffered, but it is still well worth a visit.

The tour of the lowest level takes you into a richly panelled **Audience Hall**, past an altarpiece by Tomaso da Modena (1325–79),

Getting to Karlštejn

Karlštejn is 28km southwest of Prague. To get there by **car** follow signs on Strakonická (south), the western embankment of the Vltava. There are regular **trains** from Hlavní nádraží; the journey takes 40mins and costs about 50kč.

The castle is a 2km walk from the railway station. Hiking routes through the hills and forests are marked on tree trunks and cairns. If you don't fancy the walk from the station, there are hundreds of Prague-based tour operators who'll deposit you at the door in a coach.

The road up the hill to Karlštejn is lined with cafés eager to sap the pockets of day-trippers. Eat in Prague before leaving, take pot luck wherever there's a table, or picnic in the woods.

and into the **Luxembourg Hall**. A minuscule model shows how the original room looked.

Spiritual concerns begin to take over in the **Church of the Virgin**, where Charles is still honoured with a requiem on 29 November. Its lively *Relic Scenes* (*c*.1357) are among the earliest European portraits. They show the emperor receiving oddments of the Passion from Charles V of France (left), and placing them in his Reliquary Cross. *Scenes of the Apocalypse* cover the other walls; you can just make out hallucinations suffered by John on Patmos, including a city collapsing into topsy-turvy destruction, and the fiery seven-headed and ten-horned Beast itself.

Next to the church is **St Catherine's Chapel**, consecrated to one of Charles' patron saints, adopted by the emperor after she saved his life on an Italian battlefield. The oratory is studded with chalcedonies, amethysts and jaspers set in gilt stucco. Paintings of the seven Bohemian patron saints line the side of the chapel. On the altar is a votive scene of the emperor kneeling under the Virgin.

In the third and last stage of Karlštejn the fervent chiliasm of the emperor and his age reaches a climax in the **Chapel of the Holy Rood** (Cross). Accessible only via a corkscrew staircase and fortified with walls that are up to 5.5 metres thick, the chapel was designed by Charles to house his crown jewels and Reliquary Cross. It also represented the promised Heavenly City, where he could contemplate the bliss of salvation after the tribulation of revelation in the church below. Under its gilt vaults, studded with hundreds of glass stars, a moon and a sun, he would pray in the light of 1,300 candles. The emperor's painter, Master Theodoric, painted over 120 saints, prophets and angels to guard Charles and his jewels – Gothic gems.

Kutná Hora

Kutná Hora means 'mining mountain'. The town grew out of nothing in the late 13th century, when silver and copper were discovered in the hill. The Přemysl kings muscled in on the operation, and the city boomed as it began to yield up thousands

Getting to Kutná Hora

The scenic route by **car** is the 333 (from Vinohradská); the fast route the D11 motorway to Poděbrady, then the 38 via Kolín.

There are regular **buses** from Florenc station. It takes 1hr 20mins, 60kč one way.

Regular **trains** from Hlavní nádraží take less than an hour and cost about 100kč.

You can walk everywhere, and the town is well signposted.

of tons of precious ores annually. It was granted a royal charter (1308), grew into one of the largest towns in Europe, and became the second home of King Wenceslas IV in 1400 – and then, in the mid-16th century, its silvery life-blood was finally exhausted. But its crumbling Baroque and rococo townhouses are peppered with some of the finest Gothic architecture in Bohemia.

The highlights of the town are packed south of the main square, including the 82-metre tower of the **Church of St James** (Kostel sv. Jakub), which rises incongruously from a curving lane of pastel cottages. The citizens started to build it in 1330, but, splendid as it is, it was just a trial run for their later effort.

Church of St Barbara

open April and Oct Tues–Sun 9–11.30 and 1–4; May–Sept 9–5.30; Nov–Mar Tues–Sun 9–11.30 and 2–3.30; adm

The **Church of St Barbara** (Kostel sv. Barbora) was built between 1388 and 1558 and ranks among the most splendid Gothic churches in Europe. Its three steeples and web of gargoyle-bedecked flying buttresses can be seen from across the town. The church is even more fantastic when you consider that it was miners who financed it, in honour of their patron saint (shared by anyone who faces sudden death). Bohemia's finest architects worked on the church for over 150 years. Peter Parléř began the eight eastern chapels. The most striking feature of the church, the wondrous flowers and stars of the nave's vaulting, was the work of Benedict Ried. The Jesuits moved in their Baroque baggage – the chapels at the west end have altars dedicated to SS Ignatius and Francis Xavier – but the original Gothic decoration is superb. Three of the chapels are covered with late 15th-century frescoes: *The Crucifixion*; *The Queen of Sheba*; a colossal *St Christopher Fording a Fishy Stream* (he is another protector against sudden death); and *Miners at Work*. Local traditions have influenced the art of the period with striking effect in the church's architectural grandeur. At the southwest end an entire wall is covered with images of coiners and angels, neither group more glorified than the other.

Italian Court

Havlíčkovo náměstí 552, t 327 512 873; open Mar and Oct Tues–Sun 10–5; April–Sept Tues–Sun 9–6; Nov–Mar Tues–Sun 10–4; adm by guided tour only

As you walk through the streets of the town, look out for the late 15th-century **stone fountain** in Rejskovo náměstí, the **plague column** of 1715 at the junction of Husova and Šultysova, and the Gothic façade of the **Stone House** (Kammený dům) on Radnická.

The **Italian Court** (Vlašský dvůr) was set up as a mint in 1300 by Wenceslas II after Florentine financial experts suggested he make money by producing coins. The *groschen* became the euro of its time, used by merchants across Europe. You can see it in the

(i) **Kutná Hora >**
Infocentrum,
Palackého nám. 377,
t 327 515 556,
www.kutnahora.cz

Eating Out in Kutná Hora

U havířů, Šultysova 164 (near the plague column), **t** 327 513 997 (€). Pub serving beer and tasty daily specials. *Closed Mon.*

Dačický pivnice, Rakova 8, **t** 327 512 248, *www.dacicky.cz* (€). Big wooden beer hall serving beer and Czech pub grub. Breezy summerhouse.

Hrádek Mining Museum
Barborská 28, t 327 512 159; open April and Oct Tues–Sun 9–12 and 1–5; May–Sept Tues–Sun 9–12 and 1–6; adm by guided tour only

museum, alongside the *taler*, precursor of the dollar. Wenceslas IV moved his royal residence here in 1400, with a **Session Chamber**, used when troublesome nobles wanted a word. Diets (parliaments) assembled here into the 16th century. The same king built the chapel, smothered by garish neo-Gothic painting from 1904.

The **Hrádek Mining Museum** is built over a mine shaft, and is the perfect spot to contemplate the drowning, burning and asphyxiation that were the causes of premature death in medieval Kutná Hora.

Beyond the museum on Barborská is the former **Jesuit College**, built in the mid-17th century and the largest outside Prague; to your left is an avenue of the Baroque sculpture so loved by the Society of Jesus.

Hungary: Practical A–Z

07

Addresses

Addresses in Budapest follow the same formula, which can be confusing at first. First comes the district, designated by a number in Roman numerals; then the street name, followed by the number of the building; then the floor and apartment numbers, separated by a slash. For example, VIII. Lónyay u. 11, III/312, means: apartment 312, 3rd floor, 11 Lónyay Street, 8th district.

Climate and When to Go

In summer Budapest can be uncomfortably hot. Many establishments close in July and August. Winter can be bitterly cold, the average temperature around the freezing mark, troughing in January. So the best time to visit is late April–June or September and October.

Crime and the Police

Police: t 107 or **t** 112
Tourist police (Budapest): V. Vigadó u. 6, **t** 438 8080
Ambulance: t 104
Fire: t 105

Most of the crime in Budapest is organized crime. It is generally safe to walk at night, but use common sense in outlying districts, especially District VIII. Look out for pickpockets in the tourist areas, especially around crowds and on public transport.

Beware tricksters. Never change money on the streets. A common ploy is for a girl to pick up a foreign male and take him to buy her drinks. The bill is extortionate, and the man pressurized to pay. The same tactic is used in red-light venues.

If anyone claiming to be the police asks to see money or a credit card, it is a scam. Demand to be taken to the police station and watch them run. Watch out too for fake transport police, who try to extort 'fines' (which they immediately pocket) if you can't produce a ticket on the tram or metro, or if you have failed to validate it correctly. The police – whether the city police or the transport police – are not allowed to accept cash as payment for fines. Call the police or contact the **Complaints Office**, Budapest Municipal Police HQ BRFK: XIII, Teve u. 6.

Disabled Travellers

Budapest is not geared up for disabled travellers. Wheelchair access is limited. Most sights and museums are housed in 19th-century buildings with copious steps, and most major roads can only be crossed by subway.

Apart from some stops on the M1 metro line and the Airport Minibus, transport is also poorly adapted for wheelchair-users, although things are slowly improving: some low-level buses and trams have been introduced on city routes, but there is still a long way to go.

For more information, contact the **Hungarian Disabled Association (MEOSZ),** San Marco utca 76, **t** 388 2387/88. MEOSZ can also arrange the city's newly introduced public minibuses, which operate a door-to-door system for travellers with disabilities.

Electricity

The Hungarian electricity supply is 220V and the plugs are of the standard continental type with two round pins. Bring an adaptor.

Embassies and Consulates

In Budapest

Australia: XII. Királyhágó tér 8–9, **t** 457 9777, *www.hungary.embassy.gov.au. Open Mon–Fri 8.30–4.30.*

Canada: XII. Ganz út 12–14, **t** 392 3360. *Open Mon–Thurs 8.30–4.30, Fri 8–1.30.*

Ireland: V. Szabadság tér 7–9, **t** 302 9600. *www.embassyofireland.hu. Open Mon–Fri 9.30–12.30 and 2.30–4.*

New Zealand: VI. Nagymező utca, **t** 302 2484. *Open Mon–Fri 11–4.*

UK: V. Harmincad utca 6, **t** 266 2888, *www.britishembassy.hu. Open Mon–Fri 9–5 (consular and visa services 9.30–12.30).*

USA: V. Szabadság tér 12, **t** 475 4400, *http://hungary.usembassy.gov. Open Mon–Fri 8–5.*

Hungarian Embassies and Consulates Abroad

UK, 35 Eaton Pl, London SW1X 8BY, **t** (020) 7201 3440, *www.mfa.gov.hu/kulkepviselet/uk/hu.*

USA, 3910 Shoemaker St NW, Washington DC 20008, **t** (202) 362 6730, *www. huembwas.org.*

Canada: 299 Waverley Street, Ottawa, Ontario K2P 0V9, **t** (613) 230 2717, *www.mfa.gov.hu/kulkepviselet/CA/en.*

Ireland, 2 Fitzwilliam Place, Dublin 2, **t** (01) 661 2902, *www.mfa.gov.hu/kulkepviselet/IE/en.*

Health

No vaccinations are required to enter Hungary. Medicines can be obtained with prescriptions written abroad, and most common over-the-counter drugs are available.

See **Budapest**, p.293, for English-speaking doctors, dentists and pharmacies.

Money

The Hungarian currency is the **forint** (Ft in this book, sometimes HUF elsewhere). Coins come in 1, 2, 5, 10, 20, 50 and 100Ft; notes in 200, 500, 1,000, 2,000, 5,000, 10,000 and 20,000Ft. The rate of exchange at the time of writing was approximately £1 = 305Ft, €1 = 267Ft, $1 = 185Ft. Hungary joined the EU in 2004 but it has not yet achieved the fiscal requirements for entry into the Eurozone.

The best way to travel is using a bank card and **ATMs**, which are very numerous. Major **credit cards** are also accepted just about everywhere. Rates for exchanging cash vary wildly, the worst in hotels and tourist spots, the best rates from banks and certain exchange offices. In the latter, always double-check the rate and commission that apply to you.

Travellers' cheques are almost impossible to change, and the commission/rates are unfavourable. The AEB Bank is best (there's one at Astoria). The Magyar Külkereskedelmi Bank, V. Szent István tér 11, transfers money from abroad.

There's a **24-hour exchange service** at V. Apáczai Csere János u. 1. Leftover forints can be exchanged up to 20,000Ft, more with an exchange receipt. Avoid changing money at the airport if possible, which charges higher commissions and offers lower rates.

National Holidays

1 Jan New Year's Day
15 Mar Revolution Day
Mar/April Easter Monday
Mar/April Whitsun
1 May Labour Day
20 Aug St Stephen's Day
23 Oct Remembrance Day
24–5 Dec Christmas (*Karácsony*)

On these dates, public buildings will all be closed. *See* p.294 for an explanation of what goes on during these and other festivals.

Price Categories

Hotel Price Categories

Prices for hotels are almost always quoted in euros (€), even when payment is expected in forints. The approximate price you should expect to pay, for a double room with bath in high season, is as follows:

Luxury	€€€€	over €180
Expensive	€€€	€140–180
Moderate	€€	€80–140
Inexpensive	€	under €80

Restaurant Price Categories

The approximate price for a three-course meal with wine is as follows:

Luxury	€€€€	over €50
Expensive	€€€	€35–50
Moderate	€€	€20–35
Inexpensive	€	under €20

Telephones

The **international code** for Hungary is **t** (00) 36. The **code for Budapest** is **t** 01, which is not necessary to dial if you're there. To dial Budapest from abroad, dial **t** 00 36 1 (i.e. drop the 0 from the code).

The code for **long-distance calls within Hungary** is **t** 06. You also have to dial **t** 06 before calling mobile phones.

For **international calls** from Hungary, dial **t** 00, wait for the dialling tone, then dial the country code, area code and number (1 for the USA and Canada, 44 for the UK, 353 for Ireland, 61 for Australia, and 64 for New Zealand).

Useful numbers:

Operator: t 191
Domestic directory enquiries: t 198
International enquiries: t 104, or **t** 311 1666

Sending a **telegram** in Hungary: **t** 192

Public phones are common. A few still take 20, 50 or 100Ft coins, but almost all now take cards, available from post offices, hotels, supermarkets and newsagents, costing 800Ft or 1,800Ft. International calls are very expensive, but much cheaper if you use an international card (from tourist offices or news stands).

Time

Summer time, from early March to late October, is GMT + 2hrs, Eastern Standard Time + 7hrs, Pacific Standard Time + 10hrs. In winter clocks go back an hour to GMT + 1hr.

Note that Hungarians represent times in a way which can be confusing to Westerners: ½8 means 7.30.

Tipping

Service in restaurants is usually 10%, but check the bill to see whether it has been included or not (many establishments popular with tourists include the service charge on the bill). Tell the waiter how much change you expect. If you say 'thank you' (*köszönöm*) when handing back the bill and payment, it means you expect them to keep all the change.

Give a small tip to cloakroom attendants, taxi drivers or changing room attendants at the baths. Most people leave 10% where appropriate, or 50Ft.

Toilets

Public toilets (*WC* or *toalett*; *nöi* or *nök* is women and *férfi* or *férfiak* is men) usually charge a small fee and have a concierge.

Tourist Information

Tourist information abroad is available from embassies (*see* above). The following websites are also useful:

www.budapestinfo.hu: Budapest's official home page.

www.budapest.hu: A site maintained by the mayor's office.

www.budapestweek.hu: Listings.

www.chew.hu: A food blog, with good restaurant reviews.

www.funzine.hu: Online version of a free English-language listings magazine.

www.pestiside.hu: Witty and incisive insights into local politics, culture, food and society. Linked to the excellent *www.caboodle.hu* website, with useful listings in English.

Hungary: Budapest

Wherever you are in Budapest, a point comes in the late afternoon when a magical quality of refracted light calls you to the Danube. The other cities that straddle this most celebrated of Europe's waterways have largely resisted her charms, but here she is queen, and the atmosphere she commands is one of romance.

Destroyed and rebuilt many times, Budapest seems to have learned something from other famous riverside cities. It has its bridges and promenades for pedestrians, Paris-like; a castle and a cathedral on the hill, Prague-like; and a London-inspired Parliament building adorning one bank. The key sights here are the two panoramas, so perfect on the Buda side that the whole stretch has been assigned UNESCO World Heritage status.

08

Don't miss

⭐ **Exquisite painted details**
Matthias Church **p.241**

⭐ **The handsome link between Buda and Pest**
The Chain Bridge **p.249**

⭐ **Outdoor bathing and Art Nouveau**
Széchenyi Baths **p.282**

⭐ **St Stephen's Sword and Mantle**
National Museum **p.271**

⭐ **Budapest's grandest avenue**
Andrássy Út **p.273**

See map overleaf

500 metres
500 yards

N

MOSZKVA TÉR

Moszkva tér

II

ATTILA ÚT

Museum of
Military History

KAPISZTRÁN
TÉR

Telephone Museum

National Archives

BÉCSI
KAPU TÉR

Commerce & Catering Museum

Jewish Prayer
House

Várhegy
(Castle Hill)

HESS A.
TÉR

SZENTH
TÉR

Music History
Museum

Matthias Church

Fisherman's
Bastion

VÍZIVÁROS

DONÁTI UTCA

GYORSKOCSI UTCA

Tomb of
Gül Baba

MARGIT

Lukács
Baths

TÖRÖK UTCA

FRANKEL LEÓ ÚT

CORVIN
TÉR

Calvinist
Church

St
Anne

Batthyány
tér vá.

FŐ UTCA

Király
Baths

Capuchin
Church

SZILÁGYI
D TÉR

BATTHYÁNY
TÉR

Church of the
St Elizabeth Nuns

BEM   RAKPART

BEM
JÓZSEF
TÉR

Margaret
Island
(Margit-sziget)

AKADÉMIA UTCA

ZOLTÁN UTCA

Kossuth
Lajos tér

Parliament

SZÉCHENYI RAKPART

BALASSI BÁLINT UTCA

KOSSUTH
LAJOS TÉR

FALK
MIKSA

MARKÓ

VERTANÚK
TERE

Ethnographical
Museum

LIPÓTVÁROS

NÁDOR UTCA

Soviet Army
Memorial

HONVÉD UTCA

POZSONYI ÚT

SZABADSÁG TÉR

Post Office
Savings Bank

ALKOTMÁNY UTCA

SZEMERE UTCA

NAGY IGNÁC UTCA

Vígszínház
Theatre

TÁTRA UTCA

St Stephen's
Basilica

Batthyány
Monument

VADÁSZ   UTCA

BIHARI   UTCA

MARKÓ
J. UTCA

KATONA J. UTCA

Arany j. u.

Nyugati Pu.

XIII

HEGEDŰS

GYULA

Opera House

NAGYMEZŐ   UTCA

LOVAG UTCA

PODMANICZKY UTCA

Nyugati Pu.

VÁCI ÚT

Opera

Thália
Theatre

MOZSÁR UTCA

TERÉZ KÖRÚT

Lehel tér

Ernst Museum

JÓKAI
TÉR

SZONDI

Terézváros
Parish Church

Oktogon

VI

VÁCI ÚT

LISZT FERENC
TÉR

OKTOGON

House of
Terror

CSENGERY UTCA

VÖRÖSMARTY

UTCA

PODMANICZKY UTCA

Pekáry
House

Liszt Academy

TERÉZVÁROS

LEHEL UTCA

ERZSÉBET KÖRÚT

CSENGERY UTCA

Vörösmarty utca

RÓZSA UTCA

Liszt Museum

Puppet Theatre

ERZSÉBETVÁROS

KIRÁLY UTCA

ANDRÁSSY ÚT

SZÍV UTCA

SZINYEI MERSE

SZONDI UTCA

Kodály Memorial
Museum

KODÁLY
KÖRÖND

BAJZA UTCA

MUNKÁCSY MIHÁLY UTCA

DÓZSA GYÖRGY ÚT

To Hősök tere
(Heroes' Square and City Park
(550 metres)

Budapest is of course two cities, which grew as separate entities until their union less than 130 years ago, and which have maintained their own distinct characters. Buda is hilly and green, lorded over by the elevated Castle Hill area, whose cobbled traffic-free streets and grand old buildings huddle around the vast Baroque Royal Palace and the picturesque Matthias Church, just about maintaining the atmosphere of a medieval village despite the tour buses. Just two centuries ago, most of its inhabitants still spoke German and kept themselves apart from the expanding metropolis across the water. That flat expanse on the east bank is Pest, a vibrant, thoroughly modern city in all respects but for the complete lack of skyscrapers. There is so much to see here, so spread out, that the onslaught of tourism is easily absorbed.

Almost the entire town was built at the end of the 19th century in an unparalleled period of expansion. After centuries of having to defend itself from invaders and neighbouring empires, Hungary became part of the Austro-Hungarian Dual Monarchy, and set about transforming its newly united capital into a city that would compete with and even surpass Vienna in its grandeur. This rapid development was catalysed by the 1896 Hungarian Millennium, the 1,000th anniversary of the arrival in the Carpathian Basin of the city's Magyar founding fathers. In the four years leading up to this date, at least 3,700 buildings were completed. At 80 square miles Budapest had become the biggest city on the Continent, with the mainland's first metro system, electric street-cars running since 1880, three bridges spanning the Danube and a fourth well under way and, also nearing completion, two of Pest's most important constructions: its cathedral, St Stephen's Basilica, and its Parliament. No wonder Mark Twain had this reaction in 1899: 'Budapest was a surprise for me, really. Civilised, cosmopolitan, spacious. Young and ambitious. Can this Chicago-paced development go on forever, one wonders.' It did so long enough to benefit fully from the exciting Art Nouveau era, of which it ranks alongside Barcelona as the world's premier exponent. The progress was halted, however: by two world wars, then 40 years of Communism.

Budapest is not what the visitor expects. The predominant characteristic of Hungarian architecture is an almost obsessive love of the eclectic, a mix-and-match combination of Gothic, Baroque, Renaissance, Romanesque and Art Nouveau. Lawns, parks, gardens and great playgrounds abound, making this as child-friendly as cities get. Giant plane trees line the roads. The city's inhabitants are as varied as its buildings: from the start, Hungary has been a melting pot of Slavs, Serbs, Croats, Romanies, Germans, Austrians, Italians, Turks and, of course, Magyars. The visitor expecting the cliché-ridden Russian-style temperament will be surprised

Getting to Budapest

See **Planning Your Trip**, pp.21–22, for flights to Budapest. You can also travel by train or coach, *see* pp.22–4.

Getting to and from the Airport

Budapest's Ferihegy Airport is 20km (15 miles) southeast of the city. Airport information at *www.bud.hu*, or **t** (01) 296 7000; the website has live arrival/departure information. Most of the main airlines, including Málev, Austrian Airlines and British Airways, use Terminal 2A or 2B; budget airlines use Terminal 1. The terminals are linked by bus services.

An airport shuttle **minibus service**, bookable at the booths in the arrival halls or online at *www.airportshuttle.hu*, will take you anywhere in Budapest (2,990Ft single, 4,900Ft return). To arrange pick-up for the return, call **t** (01) 296 8555, or email *booking@airportshuttle.hu*.

Trains from Nyugati pu train station depart regularly from 8am–10pm for Terminal 1, where you can connect with bus 200E. See timetables at *www.mav-start.hu*.

Public bus nos. 200E and 93 run from outside the terminals (buy a ticket from the machine, and validate it on the bus) to the M3 metro station in Kőbanya-Kispest. The total journey to the centre is about an hour. The last bus leaves the airport at 11.45pm. The last **metro** leaves at 11.10pm.

Zóna Taxi, **t** (01) 365 5555, *www.zonataxi.eu*, and Fő taxi **t** 222 2222, or *www.fotaxi.eu*, provide **taxi** services to from the airport. The fare should be around 3,600–6,000Ft .

at how Mediterranean the Hungarians seem. People here are passionate and fun-loving, needing little excuse to get dressed up.

In fact, on a superficial level, it already feels as if 40 years of enforced Communism, with the implied atmosphere of bleak, apathetic fatalism and crippling inefficiency, never happened. The service in shops and restaurants is not always great, but it has improved even in the last five years. People still have not learned to clear a fast lane on metro escalators, but maybe this is a symbol for what the Communism-imposed deceleration of Budapest has preserved. Whereas the modern age of advancing technology, multinational corporations and information superhighways has led to cities looking increasingly similar, in Budapest the effect has been dampened. As the generation educated in post-Communist years assumes greater control, however, things are changing fast – for the better and worse. Budapest's tacky and commercial districts are losing their character, but other areas are just finding theirs, with more colours on their palette to choose from.

History

Migration, Migration, Migration

The history of Budapest cannot, technically, be spoken of until the year 1873, when the two municipalities of Buda on the right bank and Pest on the left bank were united. But the human history of the region is older even than St Stephen and his sometimes problematic crown.

The earliest settlements in the area we now know as Budapest can be traced back to the 2nd millennium BC. Subsequent waves of

Getting around Budapest

The Budapest transport company **BKV**, *www.bkv.hu*, runs a fast, efficient and relatively cheap network consisting of three metro lines (a fourth is under construction, due to open in 2012, and a fifth is slated for 2015), buses, trams, trolley-buses and local trains (HÉV). All run between about 4.30am and 11.30pm. A few night buses ply the busier routes. The website has route planners, maps, ticket prices, traffic news and other info. The Budapest Card (*see* p.292) includes unlimited use of public transport.

Tickets and Passes

The same tickets are used for all modes of transport, one ticket good for one ride on one vehicle only: if you change metro lines, you need to have another validated ticket (or else buy a special transfer ticket, *see* below). Tickets can be bought at any metro station, from some news stands, and from vending machines at busier bus/tram stops, which only accept change and often don't work. Single tickets are more expensive when purchased from machines at stops or on trams (400Ft instead of 320Ft). To minimize frustrating moments when a ticket just isn't available, buy a **book of tickets** or a **pass**. Don't be tempted to travel without one: plain-clothes inspectors will fine you 2,000Ft. Tickets must be validated (punched) for each journey. In the metro, this is fairly obvious, but on some buses and trams you might have to watch someone else first. Tickets cost 320Ft, 2,800Ft for 10; a 24-hour pass is 2,400Ft, a 72-hour pass 3,850Ft, a 7-day pass 4,600Ft, a 14-day pass 6,500Ft, a 30-day pass 9,800Ft (requires an ID card: bring a photo). Children up to 6 travel free.

By Metro

Trains are identified by destination rather than direction or name, Paris-style. There are currently three lines: yellow (M1), red (M2) and blue (M3), all connecting at Deák tér, with a fourth line, the M4, slated to open in 2012. A Metro Short Section ticket for 3 stops on one line costs 260Ft. *See* p.335 for a metro map.

By Tram

At rush hour, though packed, these are a godsend. The most useful routes are 4 and 6, which follow the Nagykörút (*see* p.233) all round Pest, terminating at Moszkva tér in Buda. Line 2, hugging the Danube on the Pest side, has great views; line 19 follows the Buda embankment from Batthyány tér to beyond the Gellért hotel.

By Bus

Most buses are very modern, with displays showing the next stop. When you want to get off, press the button on the rail next to the doors. Especially out of the centre, the distance between stops can be very considerable. Buses with a red square around their number are express and make fewer stops. Those with red numbers follow different routes. A useful route is the 86, following the Buda embankment from Óbuda past the Gellért hotel. The No. 906 **night bus** follows the 4/6 tram route round the Nagykörút; No.909 runs the length of Andrassy Út. Timetables and routes can be found online. They run every 15mins or so, and begin as normal transport ends.

migrations left their mark, with the **Scythians** arriving from modern-day Russia in the 6th century BC and the **Celts** from what is now France around the 4th century BC. In the 2nd century AD, the **Romans** built a city called **Aquincum** on the western bank of the Danube, designating it the capital of their easternmost province of Lower Pannonia. Aquincum's population had grown to more than 40,000 by the 3rd century but, as the empire declined, the Romans could not hold off attacks from successive waves of eastern nomadic peoples. When the **Huns**, led by their king, Attila, attacked in the 5th century, the Romans abandoned the site. The excavated ruins, now a low-key tourist attraction with its small museum in Óbuda, make a pleasant outing, easily reached by public transport (*see* p.309). The fortifications the Romans built on the eastern side of the river to protect them from the barbarians became the beginnings of the town of Pest.

By Local Train

There are four suburban train (HÉV) lines; you are most likely to use the one from Batthyány tér (M2) to Óbuda and Szentendre. A normal ticket is valid as far as Óbuda, since it is officially within city limits.

By Boat

Ferries (t 369 1359, *www.bkv.hu*) run every couple of hours from May to early September between Boráros tér, at the Pest end of Petőfi Bridge, and Római part, just north of Aquincum. The last ferry stops at the Pest end of Margaret Bridge.

By Taxi

Taxis that hang around outside major hotels, tourist spots, stations and the airport often overcharge; phoning a cab is always a safer bet. Ask roughly how much the journey will cost before getting in, and check the meter is working. Taxis are prohibited from charging more than the following rates anywhere in Budapest, and should issue a receipt on request. **6am–10pm**: 300Ft basic fee, 240Ft/km, and 60Ft/min waiting fee; **10pm–6am**: 420Ft basic, 340Ft/km and 85Ft/min waiting. The following have good reputations, and the dispatchers speak English:

Budataxi, t (01) 233 3333.
Fő Taxi, t (01) 222 2222.
City Taxi, t (01) 211 1111.

Car Hire

Driving in the city itself is a bad idea. If you do drive, be aware that the use of dimmed headlights is obligatory even during daylight out of city limits. The speed limit is 80km/h unless stated. In city limits it is 50km/h.

All the major companies are at the airport.
Avis, V. Szervita tér 8, **t** (01) 318 4240, airport **t** (01) 296 6421, *www.avis.hu*.
Budget, I. Krisztina krt 41–3, **t** (01) 214 0420, airport **t** (01) 296 8197, *www.budget.hu*.
Hertz, V. Apáczai Csere János utca 4 (Hotel Marriott), **t** (01) 266 4361, airport **t** (01) 296 0988, *www.hertz.hu*.
Europcar, V. Deák tér 3. **t** (01) 328 6464, airport **t** (01) 296 8105, *www.europcar.hu*.

Bike Hire

Riding a bike around town is no more recommended than driving. However, it can be a very good idea in the Buda Hills, or on Margaret Island.
Nella Bikes, V. Kálmán Imre utca 23, **t** (01) 331 3184, *www.nella.hu*.
Yellow Zebra, V. Sütő utca 2, and VI. Lázár utca 16, **t** (01) 269 3843, *www.yellowzebrabikes.com*.
Bringó Hintó, XIII. Hajós Alfréd sétány 1, Margaret Island, **t** (01) 329 2073, *www.bringohinto.hu*. Pedal cabs.
Velo-Touring, Előpatak utca 1, **t** (01) 319 0571, *www.velo-touring.hu*.

After Attila's death in 453, the **Avars** took over and ruled for several centuries. Finally the conquering **Magyars** or Hungarians got to Hungary in 896, led by their chieftain Árpád. The nomadic Magyars were similar in habits to other central Asian tribes, except for their everlastingly unassimilable language, which was of Finno-Ugric origin. The Europeans confused them with the dreaded Huns, which may account for the eventual name of Hungarians. In their last attempt at European conquest, the Magyars were defeated at Augsburg in 955, after which they retreated to the Carpathian Basin to consolidate and establish a kingdom. A descendant of Árpád, King Géza, was the first to be baptised by missionaries from Charlemagne; they also baptised his son Vajk. This son was to be renamed István or **Stephen**.

Stephen was a strong king, who helped organize a feudal state out of the formerly tribal territories. After his death in 1038, the country continued to develop, despite squabbling among former chieftains and 'pagan' revolts, and despite pressure from the Byzantine and Holy Roman empires. Then in 1241 the **Mongols** arrived, sacking the city and burning Pest to the ground. But the Mongols quickly retreated with the death of their leader, and the Hungarian king **Béla IV** ordered castles – including one at Buda – built to fortify the country.

Matthias and the Hungarian Renaissance

When the House of Árpád died out with the death of King Andrew III in 1301, the throne was taken over by the Neapolitan Angevin kings, who established the royal seat at Buda, encouraged trade and built a university. In 1456, under the leadership of **János Hunyadi**, the Turks – the next set of invaders – were temporarily staved off at Belgrade. This breathing space before the eventual arrival of the Turks (the newly established Habsburgs, too, were eyeing Hungary) was to provide the country with a fertile era during which Buda became one of the most cultivated courts in Europe. Mátyás, Hunyadi's son, reigned from 1458 to 1490, romanizing his name to **Matthias Corvinus** (his emblem was the crow). He was by all accounts a gifted ruler and a cultural visionary, bringing Italian artists and literary figures to the court and amassing a huge and valuable library, the Bibliotheca Corviniana; Matthias' reign became known as the **Hungarian Renaissance**. After his marriage to an Italian, Beatrice of Aragon, Matthias' table evidently became as sophisticated as his library.

First Turks, then Habsburgs

In 1526 the Hungarians were defeated by the Turks at Mohács, and in 1541 Buda Castle fell. For nearly 150 years Hungary became part of the **Ottoman Empire**, with a slice of the country to the west ruled by the Habsburgs, and Transylvania as a separate principality. Buda and Pest were depopulated, and churches were converted to mosques. Little other building occurred except for defensive fortifications. In 1686 a pan-European Christian army led by the **Habsburgs** and partly financed by the pope mounted a six-week siege to recapture Buda and release the Hungarians from their bondage. At the end, Buda and its castle were in ruins, as was Pest, a result both of the siege and of the post-victory depredations of the 'liberators'.

The Turks left behind little in the way of cultural artefacts except for several fine baths, still functioning, and the tomb of Gül Baba. They had made no effort to convert the Hungarians, and in fact a strong wave of Protestantism had converted many from the

Roman Church to a Calvinist faith. But the Turks' real legacies were twofold: the habit of drinking coffee, a custom that became crucial to the social, literary and political life of Budapest; and the use of that quintessentially Hungarian seasoning, paprika.

The Habsburgs Are Coming – and Staying

After the defeat of the Turks, Hungary was ruled from Vienna, in a connection that ended only with defeat at the end of the First World War in 1918. The new rulers brought in settlers from Austria and Germany to replace the depleted population, and instituted strong Counter-Reformation measures against the growing power of Hungarian Protestantism. A failed **War of Independence**, led by **Ferenc Rákoczi** between 1703 and 1711, which united nobles and peasantry, is still seen as one of the great moments in Hungarian history. When it was over, the Austrians destroyed fortifications and castles throughout the entire country to make sure no such rebellion would happen again. Reforms that defined the rights of the peasants and initiated public education were introduced under Maria Theresia and Josef II, but they made small inroads on the essentially Imperial-colonial relationship between ruler and ruled.

Although Latin was the official **language** of government, German and French were the main languages of the privileged; Hungarian was spoken by peasants and now also by an enlightened intelligentsia looking towards revolutionary nationalist ideas. In 1795, seven of these revolutionaries, the 'Hungarian Jacobins', were executed. As in other countries struggling towards nationhood, language became a powerful issue at the end of the 18th century, along with the attempt to define a specifically Hungarian artistic and architectural style. It was important and threatening enough that Ferenc Kazinczy, a leader in the reform of the language, was thrown in jail. Anyone who has tried to learn Hungarian as a second language will understand how special this linguistic experience is; some might argue that this linguistic uniqueness makes it possible for the best Hungarian minds to 'think outside the box'. A surprising number of Hungarians have won Nobel Prizes in the sciences, including the quantum mechanics physicist Paul Dirac and the father of vitamin C, Albert Szent-Györgyi. Think, too, of Rubik's Cube, an invention almost as baffling as Hungarian grammar.

Independence Gets on the Agenda

The so-called **Reform Period** of the second quarter of the 19th century is notable for the presence of a star, the liberal politician **Count István Széchenyi** (1791–1860). A sophisticated, multi-talented figure, he was an anglophile who admired England's modern inventions, from steam shipping to flush toilets. He founded the Hungarian Academy of Sciences, introduced horse racing, and had the Chain Bridge built. But liberal reforms within the framework of Habsburg rule were not enough for revolutionaries such as **Lajos Kossuth**, who called for immediate and total separation from Austria. With the help of the nationalist poet Sándor Petőfi, Kossuth called for the abolition of the feudal system along with a new constitution that would grant Hungary far greater autonomy. The **Revolution of 1848–9** began, in what was to become a typical Hungarian fashion, with a meeting in a literary and political café, the Café Pilvax in Pest. Frightened by the show of support for Kossuth, the Austrians acceded to the initial demands, which included making Hungarian the official language, and instituting a ministry headed by, among others, Széchenyi. But Kossuth, now finance minister, upped his demands for even greater separation from Austria. The rebellious Hungarians were easily defeated in 1849 when the new emperor, Franz Josef, called for help from the Tsar of Russia. In the wake of the uprising, the government outlawed public gatherings, theatre performances, displays of the national colours and Kossuth-style beards. Kossuth himself went into exile. Széchenyi suffered a nervous breakdown, and eventually committed suicide.

But Hungarian independence was permanently on the agenda, and the idea soon fell on more fertile ground. When the Austrians were defeated in 1866 during the Austro-Prussian War, the weakened empire looked for an agreement with the Hungarians. The **1867 Compromise** created the **Dual Monarchy**, with separate governments and parliaments. Under the new arrangement, the Habsburg emperor was King of Hungary, and the two countries shared finance ministries; but the Hungarian government, with a prime minister, cabinet and parliament, took control of its own domestic affairs. The arrangement did not satisfy the most radical reformers, nor did it please members of various ethnic minorities living in Hungary. Still, it marked the beginning of an unprecedented period of peace and prosperity. That period ended with another nationalist eruption and the outbreak of the First World War.

Building a Modern City

One outward sign of the newfound solidity was a population explosion. The 1870s also saw the creation of a public works council, based on the London model. Then, when the two main cities were combined into **unified Budapest** in 1873, an immense architectural plan was implemented, featuring the creation of that still magnificent boulevard, Andrássy út, as well as the rebuilding of Pest's inner city. By 1900, shortly after the millennium celebrations, Budapest had a population of 773,000 and enjoyed modern utilities and transport. Commerce and industry blossomed during this period of relative stability, Hungary's **Golden Age**, and Budapest became the centre of a rich intellectual and social life, with poets and literary figures haunting the coffee houses.

The architecture of today's Budapest reflects the prosperity and style of the turn of the 20th century. The buildings that largely characterize the city's current skyline were built during this period: the faux-Baroque palace, the faux-Gothic Matthias Church, the fantastic Fishermen's Bastion, the Parisian-style Opera House and the London-style Parliament.

The First and Second World Wars

In June 1914, Hungary entered the First World War along with the rest of Austria-Hungary as an ally of the Germans. Luckily for the Hungarians, the war was not fought on their soil, but they suffered heavy losses on the Russian and Italian fronts. The war and the defeat that followed underscored the social weaknesses that lay just beneath the heady pre-war prosperity. Ethnic divisions and economic inequality led to political instability. For a brief moment, an independent republic was established under the leadership of **Count Mihály Károlyi**, and universal suffrage and freedom of the press were proclaimed in 1918. Then in March 1919 a short-lived (4½-month) Communist regime was installed under **Béla Kún**, who dealt brutally with all opposition. On 16 November 1919, **Admiral Miklós Horthy** rode into Budapest on a white horse at the head of a Hungarian army, beginning a right-wing regime that lasted until the regent, as he was called, was kidnapped by the Germans in 1944. Under Horthy's 'White Terror', the Communist Party was banned and a *numerus clausus* restricting the enrolment of Jews in universities was instituted.

Hungary's most devastating wounds from the First World War, politically and psychologically, came from the amputation of its territory by the **Treaty of Trianon**. Romania gained Transylvania and a number of primarily Hungarian towns; and, using the Danube as a convenient border, southern Slovakia got an area packed with Hungarians. But, during the Horthy regime, prosperity, albeit an uneasy one, settled back on Hungary. Despite the backbeat of hunger and social unrest, tourism rose as celebrities and ordinary people from all over Europe and America came to enjoy Budapest's hospitality, its spas, music and good food. The period came to be designated as the **Silver Age**.

Perhaps the most dangerous result of dismantling Hungary's former territories after the First World War was to send the country into the arms of Nazi Germany at the start of the Second. Hungary was a reluctant and recalcitrant ally of the Germans, although it became a source of natural resources, food and forced labour for the Axis powers. When huge numbers of Hungarians were lost on the Eastern Front in 1943 the government withdrew its troops and began secret negotiations with the Allies. In addition, the Horthy regime, despite its history of home-grown anti-Semitism, refused to go along with the murderous German demands for the ghettoization and deportation of Jews. Until now, Budapest had been spared air raids, but, as the Russians moved in from the east, the British and Americans began bombing the country.

In March 1944, the Germans occupied their ally, Hungary, and the round-up of anti-Nazi citizens began. Jews were forced into ghettoes and deported to the death camps. A few thousand of Budapest's Jews survived because of the heroic efforts of Swedish diplomat Raoul Wallenberg.

When the Germans kidnapped Horthy in October, Hungary's murderous **Arrow Cross** Fascist party took over. The Nazis occupied Buda Castle, preparing for a siege during the winter. They held out for several months, but the city was finally 'liberated' in February by Soviet forces fighting street by street. The Germans surrendered in April 1945. Seventy-four per cent of the buildings in the city had been damaged and more than a third destroyed. Along with Berlin and Warsaw, Budapest was one of the three European capital cities to suffer the greatest damage in the war.

Communism, Real and Goulash

The Hungarians welcomed their Soviet liberators uneasily; the advance guard of Russian troops were known to be a particularly brutal lot. A kind of local government was established, with elections that gave the Communists only 17 per cent of the vote. A new currency, the forint, was created, helping to stave off disastrous inflation, and a land reform act distributed agricultural land to peasant families. But by 1948 a Soviet-style government was put in place, a Stalinist, one-party system, with typically inefficient five-year plans that succeeded in destroying the Hungarian economy, collectivizing farms and emphasizing heavy industry at the expense of agriculture and commerce. A Communist secret police force, the AVO, took over the building on Andrássy út formerly occupied by the fascist Arrow Cross party. In 1949, the Moscow-appointed hard-liner **Mátyás Rákosi** became prime minister. In 1951, as part of the effort to extinguish the bourgeoisie, more than 13,000 citizens were deported into the countryside for hard manual labour. Hungary became a failed Soviet-style economy, driven by a deadly combination of shortage and waste. On the death of Stalin in 1953, Rákosi was replaced by a less extreme Communist, **Imre Nagy**. His more relaxed form of government, the so-called **New Course**, permitted economic and social reforms. But the struggle between hard-liners and moderates tipped again towards Moscow, and Rákosi was returned to power in 1955.

The 1956 Revolution

In late October 1956, in the midst of a particularly warm and pleasant autumn, the world watched with horror as Russian tanks rolled into Budapest to crush what Hungarians and others had believed would be a well-supported revolt against Communist rule. The USA and other Western powers, who the revolutionaries had understood were prepared to back their cause with force of arms, were unfortunately distracted by the simultaneous events of the Suez Crisis and did nothing. The revolution was a failure; exhausted and disillusioned, 200,000 Hungarians left the country to start new lives elsewhere. But in the long run the 1956 revolution meant that Hungarians began once more to see themselves as agents, rather than simply as observers or victims of their own history. Totalitarianism in Hungary was broken; **János Kádár**, Hungary's new leader, was a relatively moderate figure in the Communist spectrum. His oft-quoted formulation, 'Those who are not against us are with us', suggests an edge of renascent humour, along with the possibility of a new political and cultural freedom. During the 1960s Budapest began once again to rebuild, and a reinvigorated, sophisticated culture was on the rise.

The End of Communism

Budapest, which had come to be known as 'the jolliest barracks' in the Eastern bloc, in a country that practised 'goulash Communism', began to live up to its reputation. During the late 1970s, major construction of hotels began, to accommodate foreigners coming to conferences and sporting events. Enormous, faceless housing blocks had been built during the 1950s and '60s but, as prosperity grew, so did the attempt to protect the historic face of the city. In 1983, the City Embellishment Association of Budapest was founded to encourage preservation and restoration.

In June 1989, Imre Nagy was reburied in an emotional ceremony. That summer and autumn, all over the Eastern bloc, walls and barbed wire came down. The Hungarians allowed thousands of East Germans to go west through its territory. In Budapest, streets and squares shed their Communist designations and recovered their old names. With enormous enthusiasm, Hungarians generated over 100 political parties, of which about six survived. That authentic emblem of capitalism, a tiny stock exchange, reopened. After a series of elections and run-offs, the **Hungarian Democratic Forum party (MDF)** eventually took power, with a conservative coalition led by Prime Minister **József Antall**. His government was replaced in the 1994 election by the **Socialist Party (MSZP)** and their coalition partners, the **Free Democrats (SZDSZ)**, with **Gyula Horn** as prime minister. The 1998 elections returned another conservative coalition, **FIDESZ**, with **Viktor Orbán** as prime minister and **Árpád Gönz** as president. The concerns of this government included efforts to preserve the environment, reflected in a struggle over a Danube dam on the Hungarian-Slovak border, and an increasingly comfortable relationship with Western Europe and its capitalist-democratic ideology. In the end, the swing to the right proved too much for the ever-divided Hungarian psyche, especially when Orbán started promoting a return to pre-war Christian and Nationalist values. In 2002, FIDESZ unexpectedly lost the election – albeit narrowly – to the Socialists under **Péter Medgyessy**, a finance minister with the old régime. He was replaced in 2004 by **Ferenc Gyurcsány**, who hit international headlines in 2006 after apparently confessing to lying in order to win the election. Despite calls for his resignation, he managed to cling on to his position until 2009, when he finally resigned in the face of Hungary's increasing economic problems. A successor acceptable to all the main political parties was chosen, businessman **Gordon Bajnai**, who reluctantly took the helm for a limited term in order to preside over the introduction of an austerity package designed to halt the impact of the global financial crisis. Bajnai stood down at the 2010 elections, which were won with a two-thirds majority by the conservative FIDESZ party under **Victor Orbán**. Orbán commenced his second term as prime minister with a mandate for change after what was widely perceived as eight years of corruption and mismanagement by the outgoing Socialists. But popular support evaporated rapidly when the government aggressively assumed control of formerly independent entities, most controversially introducing a media law that gave the goverment unprecedented powers and which was widely regarded – both within Hungary and beyond its borders – as an attack on the freedom of the press. Demonstrations held in spring 2011 in support of a free press were widely reported to be the biggest in the city since the dismantling of Communism. FIDESZ candidate **Pál Schmitt**, a former Olympic fencing champion, was elected as president in mid-2010, publicly, if controversially, declaring his intention to further the political policies of the incumbent government. Budapest's spiralling debt and poorly managed investment in infrastructure ended liberal-progressive **Gábor Demszky**'s 20-year-long stint as mayor, when **István Tarlós** (FIDESZ) took over the job and promised to rein in spending.

Having joined NATO in 1999, Hungarians voted overwhelmingly in a referendum to join the **EU**, and did so on 1 May 2004. They are committed to joining the euro, but the country doesn't currently fulfil the fiscal requirements for entering the Eurozone and a date has yet to be set.

Art and Architecture

The city's greatest period of prosperity came after unification in the 1870s, and the magnificent boulevards of Pest are the manifestation of a dramatic era when Budapest and Chicago were the fastest-growing cities on earth. The building of Pest coincided with Hungary's greatest artistic flowering; its streets are crowded with exquisite architectural decoration and powerful buildings. The wealthy, however, often moved out to the leafy hills of Buda, so the city's finest architecture is widely spread; to see it all is a mammoth undertaking. Whether you have a weekend, a week or a year, the key to the city's architecture is to stroll and look around. Look at the details, the doorways and their wonderful ironwork, wander into the courtyards, sit in the cafés and observe one of Europe's most coherent capitals.

Roman to Ottoman

The history of Hungarian architecture is of dramatic leaps forward and devastating setbacks, a stop-start affair which makes it hard to trace any single line of development. The earliest surviving works were left by the **Romans**: a few morsels, including the military amphitheatre (1st century AD), are in Aquincum, in modern Óbuda. The art and architecture of Hungary's early years (c. 1000–1200) was **Romanesque**; there is little of it in Budapest. The work of art embodying the early Hungarian nation is the **crown of St Stephen**; its blend of Byzantine and Romanesque reflects Hungary's position between East and West. Mongol invasions from 1241 destroyed much and, once the barbarians retreated, the focus of Hungarian building efforts was fortification.

The ruke of King Matthias Corvinus (1458–90), who brought the Renaissance to Hungary, was the pivotal period between the **Gothic** and the **Renaissance**; the buildings from his reign blend Gothic and Classical motifs. A few fragments from this period survive throughout the Castle district, a window here, a door there. The brilliant polychromatic **Matthias Church** is a true mish-mash, this incarnation dating from the 13th century. It has been remodelled almost every century since. The **Royal Palace** also dates from the 14th century, but only a few Gothic foundations survive. Some of the finest Hungarian art of the period can be seen inside.

The Turkish invasions of the 16th century swept away Hungary's burgeoning Renaissance and artistically the country stagnated for 150 years. The Turks left few monuments, but they are worth seeing. The **Király Baths** in Buda date from the 1560s and survive in almost unaltered form. The dome in the **tomb of Gül Baba** is original; the rest has been rebuilt several times.

Baroque

Turkish occupation was followed by Habsburg domination from the end of the 17th century. For the next 150 years **Baroque**, which crept in during the last years of Turkish occupation, defined the city. Baroque was the architectural language of the Counter-Reformation, its curvaceous forms a riposte to the puritanism of Calvinist and Protestant architecture and, although it appeared in secular buildings, its greatest expression was in **ecclesiastical architecture**. Although the great Baroque monuments are churches, most 18th-century buildings were affected by the style. The Castle district presents endless examples of Baroque embellishment. During this period, a lot of foreign artists, mostly Italian, Austrian and German, were at work in Budapest; there was a snob value in employing them, although many were second-rate. Ironically, with so many foreign artists in Hungary, many Hungarian artists were forced abroad.

Neoclassicism and Romanticism

The Baroque remained a powerful force in Hungarian art and architecture through the 19th century, when it was dominant in the historicist rebuilding of Pest. But gradually, under the influence of changes in Germany, Britain and France, the **neoclassical** emerged as the style that would most stamp its mark on the city during the first half of the 19th century. The key building of this era was the **National Museum** (1837–44), the last major neoclassical museum in Europe. Neoclassicism, the style based on the Greek model, seemed everything Baroque was not: cool, urbane and intellectual. Associated with the French Revolution and the American republic, it represented democracy, rationalism and science. With Hungary under the yoke of Habsburg oppression, it was inevitable that Mihály Pollack's museum of national history, culture and aspirations, the distillation of the nation's image of itself, should be executed in a grand neoclassicism. In art, neoclassicism was represented by sculptor **István Ferenczy**.

Historically and artistically the turning point of Hungarian art and architecture was the failure of the 1848 Revolution. On one hand the defeat led to a self-pity which penetrated the arts to their core. On the other, Hungary's economic success and growth after the Revolution led to the Dual Monarchy. **Romanticism**'s inherent sense of longing and loss struck a deep chord with Hungarian artists. In France, Germany and Britain, Romantic artists celebrated lost worlds of chivalry, the passion of revolution or an emotional desire for ancient pastoral landscapes; Hungarian artists celebrated death and heroic failure. If you walk through a Hungarian art gallery you will be astounded at the misery, poverty and intense mourning on display. Hungarian art of this period was Europe's most miserable art by far: see the work of **Viktor Madarász, Mihály Munkácsy, Gyula Benczúr** and **Bertalan Székely**. The stronghold of Romanticism and historical genre painting was only challenged at the end of the 19th century, when Hungarian artists brought their Impressionist influences home from Paris.

Eclecticism: Building the Capital

Industrialization, the population boom and the uniting of the city necessitated a huge building programme. Town planning, based around two new concentric ring roads, was based on the Viennese model. The infrastructure and council of public works were based on London. The aesthetic came from the broad, tree-lined boulevards and grand buildings of Paris. The first step was the building of the earliest permanent bridge between Buda and Pest, the **Chain Bridge** (1839–49). It was followed by the layout of key parts of Pest as aristocratic Buda waned and Pest became the engine of Hungarian recovery. The style of the new city was **Eclecticism**, a pompous but urbane blend of neo-Renaissance, neo-Baroque and Parisian grandeur. Eclecticism allowed unprecedented freedom of expression with a pick 'n' mix range of architectural elements. **Imre Steindl**'s fairytale **Parliament** (1884–1902) is an ambitious example of extremist Eclecticism, blending Gothic verticality, a Florentine dome, Baroque planning and Ruskinian dreaming spires with great success.

National Expression, National Romanticism and Folk Art

After the failed 1848 Revolution there was a great desire to rebuild a Hungarian architecture independent of foreign sources, leading to a surge of interest in Hungarian folk art and the origins of the Magyars. Ethnographers traced the nation's roots to Central Asia and India by similarities between Hungarian folk art's motifs and those of other nations. These researches were often spurious but they prompted some remarkable architectural approaches.

The architect who succeeded (briefly) in reviving the ideal of a truly Hungarian architecture was **Ödön Lechner**, and his master-piece is the **Museum of Applied Arts** on Üllői út. Lechner's building was created to house the best international applied arts as a resource for Hungarian designers. His fascination with Eastern forms explains the domes and ogee arches, the dragons' heads and Middle Eastern courtyards which so influenced this building. The decorative elements are almost all executed in brightly coloured Zsolnay tiles. **Vilmos Zsolnay** was a ceramicist of world renown who had travelled with Lechner to study design in London. His ceramic factory was pivotal in the spectacular success of Hungarian decorative art. The company's products, in particular its glazed tiles, grace the roofs of a number of buildings that define Budapest's skyline, including the Matthias Church and the **Post Office Savings Bank** (1899–1901), Lechner's other great masterpiece. Lechner was a contemporary of Gaudí, with whom comparisons are instructive.

Influenced by William Morris and the British Arts and Crafts movement, and Finnish National Romanticism, and inspired by Lechner's attempts, the next generation set about creating a new *œuvre*. Its rural roots gave this style more success in the country than the city, but Budapest has some examples, the most concentrated area being the **Wekerle Estate** around Kós Károly tér (well off the tourist map), a version of the Arts and Crafts garden suburb. The bastion-like gates around the main square are particularly impressive. Nos.2–3 were designed by **Károly Kós**, the influential leader of this group. Kós continues to exert great influence on Hungarian architects, and modern architects working in an organic vein are inspired by his use of folk art and architecture. Hungary's most internationally renowned architect, **Imre Makovecz**, who was taught by Kós, owes a deep debt to his mentor's vision.

Art at the End of the 19th Century

If Hungarian art had been morose in the mid-19th century, it underwent a stunning *volte-face* towards the end of the century. **Pál Szinyei Merse**, who spent much of his career in Munich, was a contemporary of the French Impressionists and his work paralleled theirs. Sunny, colourful and *en plein air*, Szinyei Merse brought sunshine to the gloom of Hungarian art. He was followed by **József Rippl-Rónai**, who lived in France and represented the post-Impressionist phase of Hungarian art; his works echoed the bold outlines and powerful forms of Toulouse-Lautrec, with graphically simplified figures, but he blended these with the expressive colour of Van Gogh and Gauguin. Rippl-Rónai also designed fine tapestries and ceramics and painted frescoes, and was instrumental in fusing arts and architecture, an ideal of Hungarian Art Nouveau. The artist who stands out from this period as unique and unclassifiable is Tivadar Csontváry Kosztka. Known as **Csontváry**, he was a true eccentric who began painting at 30. His deeply odd paintings blend biblical symbolism, Expressionist emotion and complex symbolism and iconography rooted in Hungarian history.

Art Nouveau and Secession

The *fin de siècle* in Budapest was dominated by the **1896 millennium** of Magyar settlement. A huge programme of

Hungarian Food

The image conjured up by the words 'Hungarian food' is of stodgy dumplings, thick stews, lots of meat and lard, and paprika in everything. For the most part this is still true, but, as Hungary embraces the possibilities of a more global perspective, more and more Budapest chefs are breaking away from the undeniably tasty but heavy traditional meat-based fodder, stretching their range of ingredients and techniques, taking chances, and embracing a lighter, pan-European fusion cuisine.

Often this is coupled with a rediscovery of pre-Communist Hungarian cooking. From the Mongols, the Magyars learnt the secrets of stewing meats in their own juices, the basis of *tokány* stews. The great Renaissance king Matthias is said to have imported the likes of dill, capers, figs, turkey and garlic from Italy. From Austria came *schnitzel*, meats fried in breadcrumbs (*rántott*), and the cooking of vegetables in a roux of lard and flour and/or sour cream (*fő zelék*). In the 19th century, the Francophile tastes of aristocrats encouraged chefs to lighten the traditional fare, substituting butter for lard, and introducing such subtleties as herbs and truffles. The most famous Hungarian flavour, **paprika**, came with the Turks, and is usually surprisingly subtle: sweet and fragrant. Along with onions, fat and smoked bacon, paprika forms the basis of the classic stews called *pörkölt*, which usually include cubed meat. *Paprikás* is the same thing with sour cream. These are what we know as goulash, while *gulyás* is actually a thick meat soup cooked slowly with onions, vegetables, paprika and potatoes or small noodles. In their milder, unground form, paprika peppers are the basis, with tomato, of the classic summer dish *lecsó*, a kind of ratatouille often served with meat. In winter an old favourite is stuffed cabbage, *töltött káposzta*, made of sauerkraut, minced pork and smoked sausage dumplings.

As well as these dishes, a typical menu will offer a range of **meats**, often including pheasant, wild boar, hare, venison, goose, goose liver and duck, cooked in a variety of ways, usually with sauces containing fruit, wine or cheese. They are generally delicious. **Fish** from Hungary's many rivers and lakes is also abundant: the delicious pike-perch and trout, abundant carp and rather bony catfish. Particularly worth trying is the hot and sour fish soup called *halászlé*. **Vegetarians** have always been ill-served here: theirs is a credo alien to the Magyars, for whom healthy eating for centuries meant shovelling down enough fat to make it through the next winter. Breaded and fried mushrooms (*gombafejek rántva*) and cheese (*rántott sajt*) feature heavily. Salad (*saláta*) has no fixed meaning and could amount to a pile of pickled cabbage, gherkin or pepper. Among **desserts**, look out for the strudels (*rétes*), apple, cherry or curd-cheese. Curd-cheese balls (*túrógombóc*) are also recommended, as are the pancakes stuffed with walnuts and topped with chocolate sauce named after the famous chef (*Gundel palacsinta*). It's fun to stretch the culinary experience to a second venue and have coffee and a delicious cake or pastry in a *cukrászda*.

rebuilding celebrated both this and the phenomenal progress that Hungary had made in the years since 1867. The legacy of the celebrations is staggering. The **metro**, the first in continental Europe, still runs to Hősök tere, focus of the celebrations. Beyond is the **Városliget park**, built for the Millennium, within which is **Vajdahunyad**, an impressive theme-park re-creation of a 15th-century Transylvanian castle.

In the first few years of the 20th century, artists and architects reacted against the established appearance of the city in Hungary's **Art Nouveau**, known as **Szecesszió** after the breakaway from the academic system of Vienna. By Western European standards, Budapest arrived at Art Nouveau late. The highlights occurred in 1905–15, by which time this approach was distinctly *art vieux* in France, Belgium and elsewhere. Nevertheless the Secessionist architecture and decoration in Budapest is

Wine, Beer and Spirits

Hungary's 20 **wine**-producing areas have a tradition as long and accomplished as those of France, Italy or Spain, broken by 40 years of Communism, from which the industry is still recovering. Grape varieties include cabernet sauvignon, merlot and pinot noir for reds, chardonnay, sauvignon and riesling for whites, and local central Eastern European varieties. There are also some rosés and natural sweet whites. The Hungarian wine with the greatest reputation is of the latter kind: Tokaji Aszú, which Louis XIV called 'the wine of Kings, the King of wines'. It is made using grapes desiccated by long hours of sunshine and *Botrytis cinerea*, or 'noble rot'. The number of hods of these raisin-like grapes added to each batch of base-wine made from non-botrytized grapes is expressed by a number from three to seven *puttonyos*, the higher the number the greater the quality, the finest known as Tokaji Eszencia. The mixture of grapes is then refermented, without all of the sugar turning to alcohol.

Of the reds, the most famous, not necessarily the best, is known internationally as 'Bull's Blood' and locally as (Egri) Bikavér, Eger being the best-known but not the only region to produce it. Indeed, some of the finest hail from the Szekszárd area, which generally makes some of the best red wine to be found. The other key region for reds is Villány, whose wines are the most full-bodied, with high tannin and alcohol content. Eger reds tend to be more delicate and complex. For whites the North Balaton area is recommended. The small Somló region produces very acidic whites, said to be utterly unmistakable. Otherwise, chardonnays are generally a good bet, as is the Tokaji Furmint or Hárslevelű. Note that Hungarian sparkling wine can be every bit as good as champagne and considerably cheaper.

Hungary is not historically a **beer**-drinking nation and, while the younger generation are moving in this direction, Hungarian brewers are yet to catch up. Dreher, the most common brew, is acceptable ice-cold on a sweltering day. Borsodi is only slightly better. The best bet is to look for Czech beers such as Budweiser Budvar (not to be confused with the inferior American product) and Pilsner Urquell, or Belgian brews like Leffe and Belle Vue. Normally two sizes are offered: a *korsó* is almost a pint, a *pohár* almost a half. Some places sell glasses by the decilitre (*deci*).

The most famous national **spirit** is *pálinka*, a strong fruit brandy or eau-de-vie. The best is apricot (*barack*), but also worth trying are plum (*szilva*), pear (*körte*) and cherry (*cseresznye*). A national institution is Unicum, a dark brown liqueur containing 23 different herbs, with a horribly bitter taste and a kick like a mule.

fantastically varied, of very high quality and worth examining in detail. Among the larger works of Art Nouveau, the **Ferenc Liszt Music Academy** (1904–7) is the supreme *Gesamtkunstwerk*. Another towering work of this era is the **Gresham Palace**, designed by **Zsigmond Quittner** and **László and József Vágó** in 1905–7, a similarly mountainous structure adorned with jewel-like inlays of gold and swirling Art Nouveau tendrils.

At this time Budapest was the fastest-growing city in Europe. Pest's phenomenal growth was fuelled by rapid economic and industrial expansion: it was the engine of the Austro-Hungarian Empire, a city of factories, banks and pan-European trade. This industry also gave rise to a new field in Hungarian arts: **graphic design**. The **poster** became the driving medium in the popularization of Art Nouveau, and graphic design as well as illustration became an important part of the new art. Posters for Tungsram light bulbs, Unicum liquor and Törley champagne are among the most distinctive, each developing a specific brand image and style.

Modernism

The First World War, the loss of two-thirds of Hungary's territory and its reactionary post-war regime crippled its art and architecture while Modernism was fermenting throughout Europe. **György Lukács**, the cultural commissioner under Kún in 1919, encouraged radical art and design, but the government was not able to put its ideas into practice, and artists who had been associated with it had to flee the country after it failed. Other radical architects left the capital for more promising environments and Hungary lost a generation of brilliant young artists. The **Bauhaus**, the German home of radical Modernism, was full of Hungarians. **Marcel Breuer**, best known for his invention of tubular furniture, designed the UNESCO building in Paris (1953–8). **Vilmos Huszár** was a key figure of the De Stijl movement in Holland. **Ernő Goldfinger** was pivotal in the development of Modern architecture in England. **André Kertész**, perhaps the finest Modern photographer, worked in Paris. **Sándor Bortnyik**, **Andor Weininger** and **Lajos Kassák** all proselytized for European Modernist and Constructivist art in Hungary but were also at the apex of the development of these art forms.

Café Society

Coffee was introduced here by the Turks a century before it was heard of in Paris or Vienna. The burgeoning coffee culture reached its apotheosis at the turn of the 20th century, when there were between 400 and 600 cafés in Budapest. At a time when most people lived in cramped, dark surroundings with few amenities, coffeeshops were a convivial place to relax and socialize. These were forums for views to be aired and disseminated. The 1848 Revolution even began in the Café Pilvax, Petőfi's regular haunt, where he spent so much of his time that he advised his friend János Arany to address any letters there. Cafés would list on the wall like a menu those publications to which they subscribed, and provide paper and ink for the journalists and writers, who spent much of their time gaining inspiration from the free flow of ideas and opinions. Naturally, they were favoured by the whole intellectual and artistic community. Different groups or professions, artists, writers or businessmen, would have their own coffee shop. Thus the Japán on Andrássy út was the regular den of artists and architects such as Ödön Lechner, József Rippl-Rónai and Csontváry, whereas the New York was dominated by writers, clustered around dramatist Ferenc Molnár. It says something for the standing of coffee shops that the New York, which opened in 1894, was designed by the architect in charge of the Royal Palace, Alajos Hauszmann.

The New York, now under renovation, is the only survivor of those glory days. Cafés were such renowned bastions of free thought that the Communists closed them down. With those years gone and the the promise of consumerism in the air, even optimists harboured no real hopes that the halcyon coffee house days would return, but somehow, gloriously, it is happening. All over the city, new establishments have opened with a genuine sense of style. The Central Kávéház on Ferenciek tere is a perfect example, and the coffee itself (espresso rather than filter) is probably better than ever.

Along with this rebirth, the kind of trendy cafés found in Paris, London or Amsterdam, modern alternatives to pubs and bars, are also represented in abundance, serving alcohol as much as caffeine. Finally, Budapest is famous for its *pâtisseries*, known here as *cukrászda*, selling a variety of creamy *gâteaux*, tortes, tarts, pastries and pies, freshly made on the premises.

A few artists scraped a living in Hungary during these lean years. By the early 1930s, architects like **Kozma** were beginning to get work once more as the country slowly liberalized and began to prosper. A few Modernist villas appeared in the Buda hills as business began to boom and entrepreneurs and industrialists looked for the latest fashions. By the mid-1930s, the political climate was more receptive, and **Functionalist** buildings were beginning to appear in the city centre.

Towards the end of the decade a more streamlined version of Modernism blended the aerodynamic curves of classic ocean liners and cars with the clean, simple lines of Functionalism. This resulted in a number of wonderful apartment blocks, the best of them the building at **Margit körút 15**, a sleek, travertine-clad apartment block with lifts encased in glass cylinders. Good modern buildings went up in the early years of the Second World War and resumed quickly in the socialist regime of the immediate postwar years. The finest example of architecture from this early, idealistic period of socialism is the **Erzsébet tér bus station** (István Nyíri, 1949). By the early 1950s, however, Stalinism had established a grip and Modernism was out.

Socialist Realism to Post-Modernism

Stalin decreed that modern art was decadent, the preserve of an urban bourgeois élite, and that it could only have value if it realistically represented the life and work of the people. This art came to be known as Socialist Realism, or **Soc-Real**. The architecture of the period was derivative, a classicism that appeared bolder and stronger than it was. This heroic period of Socialist Realism lasted only a few years, and the late 1950s and early 1960s were dominated by the rebuilding of the city after the brutal suppression of the 1956 revolution. By the time Hungarian art and architecture recovered from that shock, it had fallen into line with Western trends. Architecture from the late 1950s to the 1980s has little to recommend it. The lasting architectural legacy of the Kádár era is the dreadful concrete tower blocks that surround the city.

Art of this era was dominated by a few figures, whose state-sponsored status has inevitably tainted them. **Margit Kovács** was probably the best known; her naïve, folk-influenced ceramics remain popular. **Imre Varga** was one of the regime's most favoured sculptors. The best-known Hungarian artist of the era was **Victor Vasarely**, creator of Op Art, who studied under Constructivist Sándor Bortnyik in the 1920s but left Hungary to live in France.

By the early 1980s Hungary's more liberal politics and tolerant regime allowed artists a degree of expression unthinkable in neighbouring countries. Conceptual and absurdist art were a vehicle for criticism of the regime. Hungarian **Pop Art** too took on radical overtones, aiming criticism at Soviet political imagery and Western consumer culture. From 1989 the **political poster** became a powerful and evocative tool, the voice of democracy against the still Communist-controlled mass media. One of the artists most vocal against the inhumanity of Communism was **Imre Makovecz**, renowned for his organic approach to building, his revival of forms drawn from folk art and architecture, and his unparalleled use of sculptural timber forms.

Castle Hill
the Siklό (funicular), its cars resembling old-fashioned black and yellow trams, glides up to Castle Hill from the Buda side of the Chain Bridge in about a minute (7.30am–10pm daily; closed every other Mon, 840Ft single, or 1,450Ft return); to walk, follow the slope (negotiable by wheel-chair to the top) to the left as you face the Siklό, then take the stairs to your right; or take the M2 metro to Moszkva tér, then pick up the Várbusz from beneath the turret of the castle-like building; however you get up to Castle Hill, it feels like a journey back in time

Around the City

Castle Hill (Várhegy)

Perhaps the best place to start a tour of Buda is at the other end of the **Chain Bridge** on Roosevelt tér. Your first view of Castle Hill will then be in the context of the landscape that it crowns. A mere 60 metres above the level of the Danube, it's not high enough to be aloof, but demands your attention: the Royal Palace, Matthias Church, the whole centuries-old centre, hanging above the city like a mirage of the past.

First to see the strategic potential of this location was the Hungarian king, Béla IV, who, following the Mongol invasion of 1247, had a fortress built here, recognizing it as a more defensible location than Esztergom. A civilian population grew up around it and, when the 'New Palace' was built during the 1387–1437 reign of Sigismund of Luxembourg, it became the new royal seat in an extended period of peace that culminated in Matthias Corvinus'

Orientation

Finding your way around Budapest is easy. Buda is the hilly part to the west of the Danube, Pest the flat. busy area to its east. The river runs near enough north–south, so that when you are in Pest west means towards the Danube, east away from it.

Two circular roads service Pest. The inner semi-circle or **Kiskörút** (Little Boulevard) traces the boundaries of the Inner City, called Belváros. It runs from Szabadság (Liberty) Bridge in the south to Széchenyi Lánchíd Bridge at Roosevelt tér, changing names as it goes: Vámház krt., Múzeum krt., Károly krt., and József Attila utca Roughly where the last two sections meet, Bajcsy-Zsilinszky út strikes north, marking the eastern boundary of Lipótváros (Leopold Town, the City). Together, Belváros and Lipótváros, stretching from Liberty Bridge to Margaret Bridge, constitute district V, and contain the lion's share of Pest's sights. The outer ring-road, or **Nagykörút** (Great Boulevard), running from Petőfi Bridge to Margaret Bridge as Ferenc, József, Erzsébet, Teréz and Szent István krts., possesses its own more gritty appeal and many extraordinary buildings that are being renovated one by one.

Budapest's numbered **districts** fan out from the inner ring, divided by the spokes of major roads. Of these, the most important is Andrássy út, which runs northeast to Heroes' Square and City Park. The Nagykörút continues on the Buda side, almost making a perfect ring, with Moszkva tér as its main transport hub on the west bank.

rule (1458–90), a Golden Age when Buda played its part in the European Renaissance.

All that died with the king. A period of decline set in, and this weakness was seized upon in 1541 by the Ottoman Turks, who plundered what they could from the town and left the rest to fall apart around them, a job of destruction finished off in 1686 by the Habsburg-led Christian armies that drove them out. This self-proclaimed royal family built their own palace (though they ruled from Vienna) and restored the town, only to raze it again during the 1848–9 War of Independence. Again the castle was rebuilt and again destroyed, this time in 1945, when German troops, besieged by the conquering Red Army, held out for a month, during which Castle Hill was reduced to rubble. It was the city's 31st siege. Phoenix-like, it rose again.

This persistence is important to remember when roaming these streets, which still follow the course dictated by the shape of the castle walls. As the rubble was cleared away after the last destruction, many remains dating back to the Middle Ages were found which would otherwise have been forever hidden. In the rebuilding that followed, these were left visible, and complemented by architectural styles that evoke every period of Buda's eventful history. It would be both easy and unjust to dismiss the whole area as a historical theme park. Instead we should see the preservation of its past as a gesture of pride on the part of a people who have always been a buffer zone between East and West, and have always bounced back.

The Turul Statue

If you ascend by the steps, a great bronze eagle suddenly looms over you, clutching a sword and squawking, wings spread, poised for flight. This is the **turul-bird**, which can also be seen guarding the Liberty Bridge (Szabadság híd) and Parliament's main gates. It occupies a curious place in Hungarian myth, beginning its job as national protector by raping the grandmother of Magyar chieftain, Árpád. As the hero led his people to conquer the Carpathian Basin, it flew overhead, bearing the sword of Attila the Hun. Descent from an eagle, symbol of the Creator, implied that holy blood coursed through Magyar veins. It's ironic that this particular turul, created in 1905 by Gyula Donáth, was placed here by Habsburg Emperor Franz Josef to present himself as a second Árpád, founder of a thousand-year Dual Monarchy.

In the palace gardens beside the bird is the **statue of Eugene of Savoy**, considered the finest work of József Róna, a self-made man from a poor background. It pays tribute to the man who liberated Hungary by driving out the Turks, though rumour has it that the Austrian Eugene couldn't stand Hungarians.

The Royal Palace (Budavári Palota)

Plain as it may be, few would be unimpressed by the sheer scale and symmetry of the Royal Palace. Occupying much of the southern portion of Castle Hill and dominating the Buda skyline, its lineage reflects the changing fortunes of the town.

Nothing remains of the castle and fortifications of King Béla IV, and nobody is even sure where it stood. The Angevin kings, living in less drastic days, built more impressive quarters, bettered in turn by Sigismund of Luxembourg, who commissioned a large Gothic palace, protected by a new set of external walls. Matthias Corvinus went one better, ordering a whole new set of buildings and renovating the old ones to suit the latest Renaissance tastes. As the palace reinvented itself as a melting pot for the new ideas on art, politics and culture, artists and scholars from all over Europe were commissioned to supply paintings, sculptures, fountains and lavish banqueting halls; and stayed on, no doubt to enjoy the famous hospitality, state-of-the-art hot and cold running water, wine, women and song.

Alas, the Turks were waiting in the wings to trash the place, using the Royal Palace to stable their horses and store their gunpowder. Defeating them entailed reducing Matthias' pleasure-dome to such tatters that the Habsburgs just had to build a new one. It started small under Charles III (early 18th century), grew to 203 rooms under Maria Theresia, and just kept growing through the 19th century, despite the lack of royalty. The Viennese court left it to be enjoyed by their viceroy, which added to the rancour of the Hungarian public and no doubt fuelled their restless desire for independence. After the great Compromise was made in 1867, large-scale extensions were carried out under Miklós Ybl, then Alajos Hauszmann. This neo-Baroque monolith was completed in 1905, and never did house an actual monarch.

After the First World War put an end to the Dual Monarchy (though not to the palace, which came off uncharacteristically unscathed), the locals again had to put up with an impostor walking the corridors, this time in the shape of the Allies' viceroy Admiral Horthy. In 1945, of course, the walls came tumbling down again, more completely than ever. The medieval remains uncovered were incorporated into the new structure, which, alas, was based not on the Matthias model but on the vast Habsburg edifice completed by Hauszmann, though with a simpler roof and the addition of a neoclassical dome, which is probably its finest feature.

The interiors were not designed with royalty in mind but for the benefit of cultural institutions; and today the palace is occupied by the National Gallery (wings A, B, C and D), the Budapest History Museum (E), and the National Széchenyi Library (F).

Hungarian National Gallery (Magyar Nemzeti Galéria)

Hungarian National Gallery
www.mng.hu, t 375 5562 or t 020 4397 331; open Tues–Sun 10–6, last adm at 5pm, dome open until 5pm; closed Mon; adm (separate adm for dome and crypt, crypt visits by prior appt only, call t 020 4397 325; 600Ft)

Unlike many National Galleries, this one really is national. Everything is Hungarian, ranging from the Middle Ages to the present. It is a large collection but not intimidating: a couple of hours should be enough. Paintings are labelled in English, but there is no further elaboration and no guidebooks or tapes. It hardly seems to matter, since these are all artists the layman is unlikely to have heard of, with names that are impossible to get a hold on, who often allude to historical events only a Hungarian would know. What does matter is that there is much of quality that will help you understand a little better the national soul of the country.

Ground Floor: First port of call is the Lapidarium, which displays stone objects reclaimed from the past after the 1945 destruction. Note the black marble statue of King Béla III's head, thought to date from around 1200, and the two red marble bas-reliefs of King Matthias and his wife Beatrice. Most people agree that one of the highlights of this museum is the collection of 15th- and 16th-century Gothic altarpieces and panel paintings, found on both the ground and the first floor. Many seem weird and wonderful to the modern eye, but that is part of the fun. Note the *Madonna* from Bártfy, rare among Gothic art in that it is complete, and the *Death of the Virgin from Kassa*. These, like most of this collection, are from Slovakia, once part of Upper Hungary; those in the Magyar heartland were mostly destroyed by the Turks.

First Floor: Of the late Gothic altarpieces, look out especially for *The Annunciation* by Master G. H. and *The Visitation* by Master M. S. In the Baroque rooms, most notable is the 1712 *Portrait of Ferenc Rákóczi* by Ádám Mányoki, which might prepare you to go back through the middle section and face the vast canvases of battle scenes that you hurried past. The most unavoidable, right at the top of the stairs, is Peter Krafft's *Zrínyi's Sortie*, dominating a small gallery found off the stairs between the ground and first floors, which captures that suicidal moment when the army defending Szigetvár took on the Turks outnumbered 50 to one. These skilful, but to many unappealing, works form part of a wave of nationalism which shows itself in every aspect of the 19th century, when Hungary was sick of being ruled by the Habsburgs or anyone else. Here the response was a return to the glories, even glorious defeats, of the past. András Török mentions the word *honfibú*, which he translates as 'patriotic sorrow': 'There is the grief of generations behind this word. The grief common to all for their ill-fated country.' The nationalist fervour is only too evident in Bertalan Székely's historical works such as *The Return of Buda in 1686*, but the grief is there also, maybe more profoundly, in his portraits.

It is easy to see the influences from the rest of Europe, particularly France, but for the most part these styles are given a distinctly Hungarian turn, and the artists are at their best when they rise above outside influences and bare their souls, as in László Mednyánsky's dark, brooding Expressionist oils. A room in wing B is devoted to the works of Mihály Munkácsy and László Paál. The former, who worked largely in Munich and Paris, was one of the few to gain recognition in the rest of Europe. He is well known for paintings with a social conscience such as *The Condemned Cell* and *Tramps at Night*, but also produced landscapes such as the Turneresque *Dusty Road*. Paál mainly painted landscapes of a Realist nature. Also in wing B, look out for works by the 'father of Hungarian Impressionism', Pál Szinyei Merse, such as *Picnic in May*, and several Impressionist style works by Károly Ferenczy. The varied collection of Károly Lotz – whose frescoes adorn the ceilings of almost every major building in town – includes the beautiful, life-size *Woman Bathing*.

Second and Third Floors: These floors contain the 20th-century and contemporary art collections, plus two major temporary exhibitions. Much of the permanent work is by The Eight, a group from the influential artists' colonies such as Nagybanya, who established Hungary's first avant-garde school. The most notable examples of their work are Róbert Berény's *Woman Playing the Cello*, and Ödön Márffy's *The Old Toll-house at Vác* and *The Oarsmen*. One of the most immediately likeable artists is Károly Ferenczy. His work seems characterized by a certain serenity, such as in his *Self-portrait: The Painter*, or the informal peasant setting of his *Sermon on the Mount*. Note also the extremely idiosyncratic style of Tihanyi Lajos' portraits.

In the works of the 20th century, general trends are ever more apparent, though the critics are not always sure what to call them. József Rippl-Rónai has been called Art Nouveau and Impressionist; see his works such as *Woman with a Birdcage* and decide for yourself. Somewhere between Art Nouveau and Symbolism are János Vaszary (*The Golden Age*) and Simon Hollósy (*Dancing Girls at the Outskirts of the Forest*). One artist everyone agrees on, even Picasso, is Tivador Csontváry Kosztka. It seems that this enigmatic, possibly mad visionary discovered that he could draw when he sketched, on the back of a prescription form, a dozing ox tied to a cart outside a chemist's shop. He is considered self-taught, though he studied in Rome, Paris and Munich. When Picasso first saw his work he apparently asked to be left alone with the paintings for an hour with the doors locked, and said, 'And I thought I was the only great painter of our century.' Csontváry is represented by a handful of paintings including *Pilgrimage to the Cedars of Lebanon* and

Ruins of the Greek Theatre at Taormina. Most of his works, apparently saved after his death just as his family were about to sell them off as tarpaulin, are in Pécs, about 125 miles south of Budapest.

Amongst all this, everyone will surely find much that appeals. In spite of, maybe because of, its difficult history, Hungary has quietly amassed a wealth of artistic achievement of which any country would be proud. And this without even mentioning the sculpture. Here you will have to follow the dictates of your own tastes, for if anything this is an even more subjective art form than painting.

The museum has recently opened tours of its glassy **dome** – from here, the views over the entire city are heart-stoppingly lovely. At the end, if you still haven't had enough, for a fee you can be taken on a tour of the **Palatine crypt** below, which was built in 1715. Ask at the reception desk for details.

Outside the museum, on the square behind the main entrance, is the **Matthias Fountain**. It is based on the legend of Szép Ilonka (Helen the Fair), a peasant girl who fell in love with the king when he was out hunting, accompanied by his head huntsman and Italian chronicler. Upon discovering his identity and understanding the hopelessness of her love, she died of a broken heart. To the left is the chronicler, while to the right is poor Ilonka, cosseting the animal her beloved is intent on killing.

To the right, two lions guard the gate which leads into the courtyard named after them, within which are entrances to the National Library and the Budapest History Museum.

Budapest History Museum (Budapesti Történeti Múzeum)

Budapest History Museum

www.btm.hu; open Mar–Oct Tues–Sun 10–6; Nov–Feb Tues–Sun 10–4; closed Mon; adm, audioguide in English available

This is definitely worth a visit, since it helps to bring Budapest's tumultuous history to life. It's also well presented, with a reasonable amount of information in English. It is probably best to start on the top floor, where the history lesson begins with artefacts and accounts of those original Magyars descended from the turul-bird. There is little left to show of the intermediate period of the city's past, when the Mongols and Turks seemed bent on all-out destruction, but this deficiency is made good by the splendid, well-designed permanent collection 'Budapest in Modern Times', from the overthrow of the Turks in 1686 to the present.

Downstairs in the basement are exhibited the remains of the **medieval palace** that in its heyday was praised as one of the grandest in all Christendom. Alas, the rooms that it was possible to restore were only of minor importance. The best are the vaulted royal chapel and a Gothic hall which is home to the collection of Gothic statues unearthed in 1974. Ironically, these only survived the Ottoman ravages because in the 15th century no space could be found for them, so they were dumped out in a yard that was later filled in. In summer, a door leads from here to the bastions and courtyards on the palace's southern side.

National Széchenyi Library (Országos Széchenyi Könyvtár)

National Széchenyi Library
www.oszk.hu, **t** *224 3700; open Sept–July Tues–Sat 10–9; closed Aug, Sun and Mon; adm; bring passport or other ID for entry*

This library was founded in 1802 thanks to Count Ferenc Széchenyi, father of the famous reformer and national hero. He scoured the country for books, which he bought out of his own pocket and donated to the nation, a collection of some 17,000 books and manuscripts. Today the library contains five million books, including everything that has ever been published in or about Hungary or written by a Hungarian. There are also newspapers, journals, small prints, and collections of maps, music and theatre history. Chief among its treasures are the earliest surviving records of the Hungarian language, from around the 13th century, and the Corviniani, a collection of ancient books and manuscripts, some beautifully illustrated, which originally belonged to King Matthias. There are usually some items being exhibited.

North to Matthias Church

Castle Hill's biggest asset is its atmosphere. Here the past presents itself through the accumulation of details, so, as you wander these ancient streets, observe how each house distinguishes itself through countless tiny variables, hinting at its own secret story. Look at the huge doors; the windows with their bars and boxes; the roofs dotted with spikes, vents, chimneys or tiny windows; the wrought-iron grilles, torch-carriers, sign-holders; the pastel shades, murals, niches, sculptures, plaques. Take in the street-lamps, the cobbled streets, the tiny alleyways and the listed-building (*műemlék*) signs giving details you won't understand.

As you walk away from the Royal Palace past the Sikló, another giant of a building looms, looking as if it must contain something terribly important. This is the **Sándor Palace**, now the official residence of the president. Its only claim to fame occurred on 2 April 1941 when the prime minister, Count Pál Teleki, shot himself as a gesture of disgust when Hungary joined Germany in its invasion of Yugoslavia only months after signing with them a treaty of eternal friendship. Next door is the grand **National Dance Theatre** (*see* p.306). Originally built for the Carmelite order in 1736, it housed the first ever play in Hungarian, performed by the first professional acting troupe in 1790.

Golden Eagle Pharmacy Museum
18 Tárnok utca; open Tues–Sun 10.30–5.30; closed Mon; adm

On the other side of **Dísz tér** (Parade Square) the road splits. Tárnok utca, now sadly all dug up, leads to Matthias Church via the small **Golden Eagle Pharmacy Museum**. This 15th-century house was the second home of Buda's oldest pharmacy, established after the defeat of the Turks and here since the mid-18th century. A

08

Hungary: Budapest | Castle Hill

reconstruction of an alchemist's laboratory features various dried creatures along with the alembics. Original texts include an early 17th-century Paracelsus, a 13th-century Roger Bacon and a 16th-century Geber. Look out for the 17th-century Italian map showing Buda's fortifications at the time of the Turkish occupation, with Pest nothing but a tiny village. There's no labelling in English but the enthusiastic lady will gladly guide and explain.

Úri utca (Lord Street), on the left, runs to the northern end of Castle Hill and is probably its finest street. The stand-out house is No.31, its almost entirely Gothic façade thought to look as it did in the late 15th century, though the core dates back to the 14th century. In 1862 it was redesigned in a Romantic style but, after these decorations were destroyed in 1945, great efforts were taken to restore the medieval façade. No.49, the former Poor Clares' cloister, houses the delightfully quirky **Telephone Museum**, containing everything from ancient Bakelite contraptions and a still-functioning old switchboard to state-of-the-art technology.

Telephone Museum
www.postamuzeum.hu; t 201 8188; open Tues–Sun 10–4; closed Mon; adm

Buda Castle Labyrinth
Úri utca 9, t 212 0207, www.labirintus.com; open daily 24 hours; adm

Buda Castle Labyrinth (Budavári Labirintus)

Castle Hill is topped by an 11m-thick layer of limestone, within which thermal springs have hollowed out a series of natural cavities. The first Magyar inhabitants of the hill developed and connected them. Through centuries of invasions, the cave network repeatedly proved its worth, growing in length and sophistication all the while. Sometimes it was the invaders themselves, such as the Turks, who saw their military potential. In peaceful times, the caves were partitioned and used as cellars. In the Second World War they were used as air-raid shelters for up to 10,000 people and contained a hospital. During the Cold War they held a secret military installation. Nowadays you can visit a small section of the 10km labyrinth of passages. Attractions include copies of the most famous European cave paintings such as Lascaux, reconstructions of historical scenes, images of labyrinths from different ages and cultures, and the chance to test your courage and sense of direction by walking around alone. After 6pm they offer a range of tours, including one by oil lamp.

Szentháromság Tér

Dominated by the Matthias Church and Fishermen's Bastion, the broad, cobble-stoned Szentháromság tér is the focal point of Castle Hill, thronged by tourists, tricksters, leaflet-distributors and buskers. All the more reason to arrive early or late. At night the church is more beautiful, and the whole area timelessly romantic.

The large bronze equestrian **statue** between church and bastion represents King Stephen, justly, as a grim and powerful figure. At the end of the 10th century he unified the Magyar tribes into one nation, of which he was the first king. Born Vajk, he became Stephen (or István) when he converted to Christianity and forced his nation to do the same, a move that facilitated their integration into Europe. He is depicted here wearing the famous crown sent for his coronation by Pope Sylvester II. The relief at the back shows Frigyes Shulek (*see* below), who designed the neo-Romanesque plinth, kneeling modestly before the king, offering him a model of the Matthias Church. Nearby, a spiral staircase leads down into the **Szent Mihály Kápolna**, an atmospheric, cavernous brick and stone chapel full of modern artworks. The square is named for its central **Holy Trinity Column**, erected in thanksgiving for the end of the plague in 1713, and in the hope of fending off another.

On the square's southwest corner is the former **Buda Town Hall**, bearing a statue of Pallas Athene, protector of cities. Turn west for the famous **Ruszwurm Cukrászda** (*see* p.303), whose lavish antique interior makes it as much a part of the historical tour as a great place for coffee and cake. Opposite is the statue of András Hadik, better known as the **Hussar Statue**. These infantrymen, first organized by King Matthias in 1480, wore no armour because their weapon was speed. Armed with sabres, pikes and pointed daggers, they specialized in fast, unexpected attacks, with such success that soon every army in Europe had a similar regiment. As well as capturing the poise of effortless understanding between horse and rider, this statue has another interesting feature: its gleaming, smooth testicles. Touching them is said to bring luck in exams.

Matthias Church (Mátyás Templom)

Matthias Church
currently undergoing extensive renovation, so check opening hours; Mon–Fri 9–5, Sat 9–1, Sun 1–5; mass 7am, 8.30am and 6pm, also Sun and hols 10am (Latin mass) and noon; more info, including a list of concerts, at www.matyas templom.hu

The Matthias Church is undoubtedly one of Budapest's finest buildings, though its effect is diminished by the surrounding fence (despite appearances, it's still open to visitors; just follow the signs). Its chequered past began way back in the early 13th century, following the Mongol invasion. It originally resembled the northern French Gothic, before Sigismund of Luxembourg remodelled it into a hall-church in high Gothic style. Matthias made his own improvements and was married here twice. Under the Turks, the furnishings were destroyed, the walls whitewashed and the church restyled as a mosque. Back in Christian hands after the siege, it was given to the Franciscans, then the Jesuits, who decorated it in a Baroque style. Poor as its condition was by 1867, it was still considered worthy to host the coronation of Franz Josef as King of Hungary, for which Liszt's *Coronation Mass* was specially composed.

Like so much of Castle Hill, this building is neither old nor new, but rather a composite of many past ages. When much-needed reconstruction was undertaken between 1873 and 1896, architect Frigyes Schulek was so keen to preserve its multi-layered past that he noted all the original features revealed as the walls were pulled down, and built them into his new structure, including much of the wall decoration. He also added a lot of his own. Thus, he kept the original tower intact up to the third floor, after which he followed his own vision.

It takes a while to realize why the church makes such an impact. Partly it is the proliferation of detail and the colourful tiling of the roof, but mainly it is the sheer height of the tower. At 80 metres, it could lose a whole section without appearing squat. Before going inside, have a closer look at the front left **Béla Tower**, named after the church's original founder, which has retained many Gothic features; and the stained-glass rose window, which is unfortunately hidden inside by a pipe organ. Above all, have a good look above the door at the **Mary Portal**, Schulek's reconstruction of one of the greatest pieces of Gothic stone carving in Hungary, depicting the *Assumption of the Virgin Mary*.

Inside, every inch of wall space has been painted, not like the Sistine Chapel – there are few biblical scenes or figures – but with repetitive patterns of a floral or geometrical nature, sometimes resembling Polynesian, Aboriginal or Native American art, and adding up almost to an Art Nouveau effect. They were designed by Bertalan Székely. The overall effect is one of infinite warmth, in marked contrast to the starkness of so many churches. Here the worshipper – for this is still above all a place of worship – is not overawed and intimidated, but cheered and welcomed. The God who resides in this house feels much more approachable than most. But he still has a penchant for gold. Much of that present is on the altar, whose design was based on Gothic triptychs, and which repeats the Trinity figures from the column outside.

The three arched stained-glass windows on the south wall were designed by Schulek, Székely and Károly Lotz. The participation of these latter two artists helps to explain the overall quality of the art present. Above the Mary Portal are five circular paintings by Lotz showing the birth and childhood of Christ. To its right is the original coat of arms of King Matthias. Nearby, inside the **Loreto Chapel** below the south tower, is a Baroque *Madonna* in Italian style from the 17th century. Legend has it that the original was set into a wall during the Turkish occupation. When the walls were crumbling during the siege of 1686, she reappeared, scaring the Turks out of their wits and assuring them of their imminent defeat.

On the north side in the **Trinity Chapel** lies the tomb of King Béla III and his wife Anne de Châtillon. Their double sarcophagus lies below a richly carved stone canopy. In the crypt is a red marble sarcophagus housing bones from the royal tombs in Székesfehérvár. A stone staircase leads up to the small museum in the upper gallery, which contains a collection of ecclesiastical treasures and relics. The museum includes **St Stephen's Chapel**, with a bust of the king, and various scenes from his life, and culminates in the **Royal Oratory**, which exhibits a replica of the Hungarian crown (the 'Saint Crown of Hungary' which is thought to have divine powers), and the coronation thrones of Emperors Franz Josef and Karl IV.

Try to attend a concert in the church; the acoustics are excellent.

Fishermen's Bastion (Halászbástya) and Hilton Hotel

In the Middle Ages there was a fish market near to this spot, and the Guild of Fishermen were responsible for defending this part of the **wall**. Nowadays, this rampart fulfils a strictly aesthetic function. It was designed by Schulek to complement the Matthias Church. In both, the mood is one of romantic chivalry, playfulness and an almost childlike sense of wonder. With its zigzagging white ramparts, curving stairways and ice-cream-cone turrets (seven, symbolizing the Magyar tribes who founded the nation), it looks as if it has leapt from the pages of a fairytale book. It also offers some of the best views of Pest available.

Opposite is the ugly **Hilton Hotel** which, despite the funky reflections of church, statue and bastion thrown off by its dated copper-glass façade, looks all wrong here. It does have some redeeming features, though. Follow the bastion to its northern end and go through the (normally open) gate that leads behind the hotel, and you will find yourself in the remains of a medieval church from 1254. This Dominican courtyard, uncovered during excavations in 1902, was incorporated by architect Béla Pinter into the hotel's design, and now provides a stage for concerts and operettas during the summer season. The hotel's **Faust Wine Cellar** is a reconstruction from remains of the original monastery wine cellar. Round on Hess András tér, the hotel's frontal façade has been built to integrate remains of a late Baroque Jesuit college. To the left of the entrance is **St Nicholas' Tower**, containing a copy of the 1486 *Matthias Relief* from Germany, generally considered to be the only genuine likeness of the great man. The overall achievement is admirable, and from the Pest embankment the hotel's bulk looming behind the church is discreet enough to take little away from the scene.

North of Matthias Church

Music History Museum
www.zti.hu, t 214 6770; open Mar–Dec Tues–Sun 10–6; closed Mon and Jan–Feb; adm

Three streets run north from Szentháromság tér, roughly parallel to and east of Úri utca. Furthest east is Táncsics Mihály utca, which contains the **Music History Museum** at No.7, in the grand Erdödy Palace where Beethoven stayed in 1800. In this fascinating selection of 17th–19th-century instruments, the classical exhibits

08 Hungary: Budapest | Castle Hill

include finely ornamented lyres and a unique tongue-shaped violin, while the folk section has a gardon (a primitive cello), bagpipes, zithers and cowhorns. The emphasis is on the instruments as works of art. As well as temporary exhibits, there is a collection of Bartók's scores and scribblings. Down the street at No.26 is the **Medieval Jewish Prayer House**. The foundations of a large synagogue dating back to the 15th century were discovered here. The interest of the museum lies not so much in the small exhibition of tombstones and liturgical objects, but in the space itself, used as a house of prayer during the Turkish occupation.

Medieval Jewish Prayer House
www.btm.hu, t 225 7816; *open May–Oct Tues–Sun 10–5*

The **Museum of Hungarian Commerce and Catering** is much more interesting than you'd expect. The commerce section includes early 19th-century advertisements, antique shopfronts, a provincial grocery store, Hungary's first electric billboard (advertising beer) and, the *pièce de résistance*, an HMV dog that taps its paws against the window to catch the attention of passers-by. It regularly hosts special events, including concerts and popular film screenings.

Museum of Hungarian Commerce and Catering
V. Svent István tér 15, t 375 6249, *www.mkvm.hu; open Wed–Mon 10–7; closed Tues; adm*

Hess András tér was named after the man who established the nation's first printing press. His workshop is believed to have occupied the site of the Fortuna Restaurant. At No.6 is the **House of Hungarian Wines** (Magyar Borok Háza), whose extensive cellar holds some 550 different wines from Hungary's 20-odd growing regions, making it one of the biggest wine collections in Europe. For a few forints you can help yourself to a selection of 60 or 70 of these, taking as much time as you like, and learn everything about Hungarian wine. Farther west, Országház utca (Parliament Street) gained its name from a period in the 1790s when the Parliament (Diet) met in the large building at No.28, originally a convent of Poor Clares.

House of Hungarian Wines
www.winehouse.hu; open June–Sept Mon–Fri 1–9, Sat and Sun 11–9; Oct–May daily 11–7

At the northern end of Castle Hill, all streets converge on two conjoined squares. To the east is Bécsi Kapu tér, named after the **Vienna Gate**, built to celebrate the 250th anniversary of the recapture of Buda. Climb on top of the gate for a better view of the Lutheran Church, built at the end of the 19th century, with its unusual spire. Through the gate and to the right is **Europa Grove**, so named because in 1972 city mayors from all over Europe planted 16 types of tree in honour of the centenary of the unification of Buda, Óbuda and Pest. Lovas utca, curving left under the castle walls, has a collection of Budapest street-lamps dating from 1844 to 1944.

Military History Museum
open Oct–Mar Tues–Sun 10–4; April–Sept Tues–Sun 10–6; closed Mon; adm

Back on the square, the hulking neo-Romanesque **National Archives** building is saved from total po-facedness by the multicoloured roof. Next door is the **Military History Museum** in a former barracks. Permanent displays include 'The History of Hand Weapons from the Stone Axe to the Pistol', exhibits on the 1848

Revolution, and an evocative look at the 'Thirteen Days' of street-fighting during the 1956 Uprising (*newsreel footage at 11am and 2pm*). Outside is a **statue of Friar John Capistranus**, after whom this bigger square, Kapisztrán tér, is named. This zealous Italian Franciscan urged the Crusaders on to victory in the siege of Belgrade in 1456. Here he stands over a dead Turk, exhorting the soldiers to produce more. Over the road is the **Mary Magdalene Tower**, modelled on the original Baroque spire, after the war destroyed the rest of the church. In the Middle Ages, Hungarians worshipped here, while the Germans got Matthias Church. The remains of the foundations stand between this strangely solitary tower (housing a private art gallery) and the even more eerie sight of a single tall window. Adding to the oddness is the tower's peal of ornamental bells, apparently capable of rattling through a melody compiled by a jazz pianist.

A chestnut-tree-lined street, Tóth Árpád sétány, hugs the western ramparts of the hill, offering views of the Buda Hills, Gellért and Tabán. The entrance to the Military History Museum is on this street, announced by a collection of historical cannons. Round the corner is the **Abdurrahman Memorial**, a tomb with an inscription in Hungarian and Turkish that reads: 'It was near this site that the last governor [pasha] of the 143-year-long Turkish rule in Buda fell in battle at the age of 70. A valiant foe, may he rest in peace.'

Gellért Hill and Tabán

These two areas line the Buda embankment from the Liberty Bridge (Szabadság híd) in the south to the Chain Bridge (Széchenyi Lánchíd) in the north.

Gellért Hill (Gellért-Hegy)

As well as providing a backdrop to the Buda skyline, the 460ft dolomite cliff of Gellért Hill offers the best views of Pest and Castle Hill. For centuries its lower slopes were used for cultivating grapevines. The name Gellért derives from an 11th-century Benedictine abbot from Venice, Ghirardus (Gellért in Hungarian, Gerard in English), whom King Stephen asked to help convert the Magyars to Christianity, as well as tutoring his son, Imre.

The Gellért Hotel and Baths

Budapest's most famous hotel sits like a country mansion at the end of the elegant Liberty Bridge, which looks as though, like a driveway, it were constructed for this purpose alone. (In fact it was built for the Millennium celebrations in 1896, when it was opened by Franz Josef, whose name it originally bore.) It is a spectacular, unabashedly Art Nouveau building, with cylindrical towers and turrets and many fine details, such as the lyre and bird motifs on the elaborate balustrades of the balconies. Purpose-built as a spa hotel in an attempt to promote Budapest as a spa town, it occupies a spot whose hot springs have been revered for their healing properties for at least seven centuries. An old legend has it that spring comes to Gellért Hill three weeks earlier than the rest of Budapest thanks to the dynamic power of the thermal waters. In the Middle Ages a hospital stood on the site, and the Turks, who know about such things, constructed their own baths. Sadly, the year after its completion the hotel was taken over by Béla Kún's Communist régime, then by the Romanian army, and finally by Admiral Horthy following his entry on a white horse and declaration of intent to cleanse the 'sinful city'. Despite this interlude, the Gellért lived up to the hopes invested in it, becoming in the 1920s a social high spot for Budapest's upper classes and later enjoying an international reputation that attracted the royal, powerful, rich and famous from all over Europe. After the party-pooper of 1939, it was goodbye to all that: only the outer walls survived the war.

Though not original, the interior is as magnificent as the outside, and should not be missed. Step into the busy entrance hall to admire the mosaics and statues. On the right, at the top of a flight of stairs, is a radiant stained-glass window, which recounts the story of the magic stag, an old Hungarian legend famously rendered in the poetry of János Arany.

Gellért Baths
www.gellertbath.com, t 466 6166; tram 47 or 49 from the Kiskörút; open daily 6am–8pm; adm

The entrance to the **baths** is on the hotel's right flank as you face it. They offer sheer opulence, decorated throughout in ornate Art Nouveau style replete with statues, columns, mosaics, glazed tiles, ornate ceilings, lion-headed spouts and myriad other details only the wealthy could once afford. Ignore those around you and imagine that you are royalty. Rarely does life offer the opportunity to partake of so much grandeur for so little money. The baths are mixed-sex, with segregated hot-tubs and steam-rooms. They offer all the variety of pools, plus an outdoor swimming pool and sunbathing terrace.

The Cave Church (Sziklatemplom)

Opposite the entrance to the baths, a path leads a short way uphill (to the right) to the Cave Church (*wheelchair-accessible*). Established in 1926 and based by designer Kálman Lux on the shrine at Lourdes, the church was intended for the Pauline order of monks. This is the only order indigenous to Hungary, traditionally confessors to the king, founded in 1256 by Eusebius of Esztergom and dissolved in 1773 by Josef II. It was built and they came – 15 of them, back from a 150-year exile in Poland. Unfortunately, in the 1950s the Communists jailed the monks for 'treasonable acts' and sealed the entrance of the church. It was reopened in 1989.

It may be in a cave, but everywhere the coldness of ceiling and walls is enlivened by potted plants, stained glass and art. At the very back a giant bronze Polish eagle contains a copy of the *Black Madonna* of Czestochowa. In the chapel, look for Béli Ferenc's wooden sculptures, and check out some of the whimsical art in the area behind the altar. All of this is rather let down by the gaudy plastic Christ above the altar. But then this is not a tourist attraction: it is a working church, and a busy one at that. A large congregation attends the hour-long masses at 11am, 5pm and 8pm, during which times tourists are asked to remain outside and silent.

The Citadella and Liberty Statue

On the summit of Gellért Hill squats the low, bulky **Citadella**, not an attraction as much as a pinnacle from which to see everything else. The site was chosen by the Habsburgs with this in mind. After quashing the 1848–9 Revolution, they constructed this grim edifice, a stronghold from which to survey and control, and which was impossible to ignore. After the Compromise of 1867, citizens breached its hated walls and called for its destruction. For all that, only in 1897 did the Austrian soldiers leave. Since then it has housed a prison camp, an SS regiment, the homeless, an anti-aircraft battery and, nowadays, a restaurant, café, hotel, nightclub and a small museum about the Celtic Eravisci, the first inhabitants of this hill, 2,000 years ago.

Mainly, though, people come for the views, among them that of the adjacent **Liberty Statue**, which is far too tall to take in from below. Designed by Hungarian sculptor Zsigmond Kisfaludi Stróbl, Lady Liberty stands 46ft high (100ft if you include her colossal pedestal), and can be seen clearly from anywhere in Pest. The story goes that this statue was originally commissioned by Regent Miklós Horthy to commemorate his son István, killed in a plane crash on the Russian front. But after the German units were finally prised out of Castle Hill, a Russian marshal supposedly saw this figure in a sculptor's workshop and had the propeller she was intended to hold swapped for a palm leaf, thus creating a monument to the Soviet soldiers who died in the 'liberation'. Funnily enough, this really is just a story: it was a Communist monument from the start. When the Communists retreated, many locals wanted the statue destroyed or removed. In the end it was simply recycled: the figure of a Russian soldier (now in the Statue Park, *see* p.291) and a plaque listing Russian war casualties were removed. For all that, something about the pedestal marks this out as a Soviet creation.

Gellért Monument

A quarter of the way up Gellért Hill, facing Elisabeth Bridge, stands this statue of the eponymous saint (bear left on your way down from the Citadella). The pagans he was converting put up with Gellért's evangelizing while King Stephen was alive, but legend tells that in 1046, eight years after the ruler's death, a rebellion erupted against Christianity during which the saint was put into a barrel and pushed off this hill into the Danube. The barrel could have been nail-studded or merely a wheelbarrow, depending which version you choose to believe.

Now that Christianity again has the upper hand, Gellért has been restored to his full dignity. Built in 1904, this near-40ft statue shows him holding his cross aloft in perpetual reproach to the sinners across the water in Pest, while at his feet kneels one of the newly converted Magyar heathens.

An alternative way down the hill involves following the paved road past the viewing spot until you hit a junction, then bearing right and getting lost amidst the maze of lanes and narrow streets. This would appeal to lovers of grand houses and mansions, with which this green area is overflowing. Most of them are embassies. If you keep going down you will, of course, eventually get back to the river and the jumble of roads that carve up the area of Tabán.

Tabán

This area gets its name from the tanning workshops clustered here during the Turkish occupation. The Turks took advantage of the thermal waters, building two magnificent baths, the only part to survive the siege of 1686. When the Turks retreated from Hungary, they still occupied the Balkans, and many Serbs fleeing from them settled here. Around 1700, 95 per cent of the area's inhabitants were Serbian (Rácok in Hungarian). As Greeks and Romanies followed suit, a dense, cosmopolitan and essentially impoverished population gave the quarter a run-down, bohemian flavour, famous for its bars, brothels and gambling dens, ancient rambling streets, whitewashed houses with red tile roofs, wine gardens and orchards. Unfortunately, this nostalgic simplicity also entailed open sewers, and in 1908 the City Council declared the whole area a health hazard and razed it. Thankfully the baths survived, as did the splendid Tabán Parish Church on Attila út. The arterial roads that now choke it were constructed during the Communist years and mean that the area is only worth visiting for one of its notable sights.

Rácz Baths
l. Hadnagy utca 8–10,
www.raczhotel.com,
t 266 0606; adm

The **Rácz Baths**, at the foot of Gellért Hill where it meets Tabán, are named after the Hungarian word for Serb. The 19th-century exterior has been remodelled into a plush luxury hotel (*see p.296*) which opened in 2011, but still retains the original Turkish octagonal pool and dome, although a fancy new VIP zone has been added. The waters are good for chronic arthritis and muscle and nerve pain. The **Rudas Baths**, built in the 16th century on a site occupied by baths since the 14th century, are the most atmospheric of the Turkish baths. The original octagonal pool and cupola combined with the dim, rather dank interior, saturated with steam and echoing sounds, make for a timeless experience. Light slants in at different angles through small octagonal windows in the dome. As well as six pools of differing temperatures, including the hottest in town at 46°C, there are three saunas and two steam rooms. A fountain allows you to drink the warm, sulphurous water, said to be good for gastric complaints. Occasionally, the Rudas plays host to a uniquely Budapestian phenomenon known as *Vizimozi*, basically a rave in the main swimming pool accompanied by silent movies shown on a big screen, or ethno-trance music in the Turkish baths. It also offers bars, a gallery, and a dance floor in the hallway. The baths have recently been substantially renovated: some of the new amenities are welcome, but much of the battered, time-worn charm has been lost.

Rudas Baths
I. Döbrentei tér 9,
t 356 1322,
www.rudasbaths.com;
open Mon–Fri
6am–6pm, Sat and Sun
6am–1pm; Mon, Wed
and Fri are men-only;
Tues is women-only
weekends are for men
and women; adm

The **Semmelweis Museum of Medical History** (Semmelweis Orvostörténeti Múzeum), near the Rudas Baths, exhibits items relating to medicine, including a medieval chastity belt and some 18th-century beeswax anatomical models. It's based in the house where Dr Ignác Semmelweis (1818–65) was born.

Semmelweis Museum of Medical History
I. Apród utca 1–3,
t 375 3533; open mid-
Mar–Oct Tues–Sun
10.30–6; Nov–mid-Mar
Tues–Sun 10.30–4;
closed Mon; adm

The striking white **Elisabeth Bridge** (Erzsébet híd) which leads from the jumble of roads across to Pest was named after Franz Josef's wife. Nicknamed Sisi, she was a beautiful and tragic figure, unsuited to the straitjacket of royalty (*see* p.62). Much loved by the Hungarians, whose language she spoke, she was greatly mourned following her assassination in 1898. This was the only bridge destroyed in the war not rebuilt according to its original form, although it does imitate the old chain bridge's much loved arch. Constructed in 1964, the bridge has almost become a symbol for the city.

Chain Bridge (Széchenyi Lánchíd)

⭐ Chain Bridge

Before the 1840s, Buda and Pest were by necessity separate towns because they were divided by the Danube. It was impossible to build a bridge of wood and stone over a river this wide. A pontoon bridge operated between autumn and spring, there were occasional ferries, and in winter the water froze so that sometimes even carts could cross, but still people got stuck on the wrong side for weeks when a sudden thaw set in. Like many examples of 19th-century progress, the first permanent bridge across the Danube was István Széchenyi's initiative. In 1820 he had to wait a week for a ferry across to attend his father's funeral, and decided it wasn't good enough. He sent to Britain for an English engineer, William Tierney Clark (who designed London's Hammersmith Bridge), and a Scottish masterbuilder, Adam Clark (no relation), and even had the iron shipped over. In 1849, before it was completed, the Austrians tried to blow it up, but Adam Clark thwarted their plans by flooding the anchorage chambers and destroying the pumps that could have been used to drain them. The colonel who tried to use explosives despite this was blown to pieces. But the Uprising failed, and the bridge was completed under Austrian command. As a further irony, the first person to cross the bridge at its opening was the cruel and much hated General Julius Haynau, at whose behest the equally despised Citadella would be constructed.

A story has it that Adam Clark was so proud of his masterpiece that he swore he would drown himself if the slightest fault was found with it. Eventually it was noted (erroneously) that the splendid lions at either end had no tongues, and Clark allegedly duly topped himself. Again, just a story. Actually, Clark liked the city so much that he married a local girl and stayed to construct the **tunnel** that runs under Castle Hill as a direct continuation of the bridge, whose style it complements. Flanked by two pairs of Doric columns, it was clearly built with an eye to the aesthetic. The joke amongst Budapesters at the time was that it would be a good place to put the new bridge when it rained. Today the Chain Bridge is a symbol of the city, for its beauty as much as its technological prowess. When, 95 years after its construction, the Germans blew up all the Danube's bridges, this was the first to be reconstructed, to the same design.

The **Sikló** running up to Castle Hill (*see* p.233) starts its journey in Clark Ádám tér. At its foot, a small garden contains a curious concrete doughnut. This is the **Kilometer Zero stone**. Sculptor Miklós Borsos intended it to express not just zero but the beginning of everything, the origins of all life. It signifies that this is the centre of Budapest: all distances in the country are measured from here; and justly so, for this is where the three component towns of Pest, Buda and Óbuda were given their first permanent physical link, paving the way for their official union in 1872.

Víziváros

The thin stretch of land north of the Chain Bridge and west of the river has been called Víziváros or 'Water Town' since the Middle Ages. While the royal court and its associated gentry enjoyed the views from the hill, people down here were mainly fishermen, craftsmen and traders. The Turks depopulated the area, turned its churches into mosques and left behind the Király baths. The 18th century witnessed a boom time when some of Buda's more socially elevated citizens built many of the grand houses that can be seen here today, but extensive construction a century later put an end to the small-town atmosphere and the advent of the car killed it off.

Today Víziváros has the feel of a neighbourhood that has known better times and will know them again. In contrast to Castle Hill, many grand old buildings have been let go, the churches are closed, the principal square feels seedy, and the main road heaves with traffic. Yet on a Sunday morning, when the churches are open and the roads less busy, it is still possible to catch a whiff of the history that permeates these buildings. It is not dead, only sleeping.

Fő Utca

Literally meaning 'Main Street', this thoroughfare leading northwards from Clark Ádám tér dates back to the times of the Romans. Looking up at the façades, it is clear that this has the potential to be a beautiful, refined district when future waves of yuppies restore the faded buildings. Check out the three-sided Romantic building at No.2, or the 1811 remodelling of a medieval house at No.20, with its unusual turreted cylindrical window and reliefs. Past the ugly Postmodernist pile of the French Institute with its Constructivist sign, already looking dated in a way these older buildings never will, past the **Capuchin Church**, whose fine statue of St Elizabeth has unfortunately been painted brown, pretty **Corvin tér** stands newly renovated. Across the road are four striking houses, recently renovated and painted in pastel shades to form the western face of the art'otel (*see* p.296), demonstrating what could be done with the whole street. A statue of St John of Nepomuk stands in the niche on No.3's Baroque façade, whilst the neoclassical No.5 carries four reliefs, the three above the windows depicting King Matthias as farmer, scholar and commander, the one above the door showing the interior of an alchemist's shop.

Fő utca continues in its unrenovated form practically to Margaret Bridge and contains at least two churches that shouldn't be missed. If the traffic gets too much, try the quieter Iskola utca, parallel on the left.

The Calvinist Church (Református Templom)

On Szilágyi tér off Fő utca, this neo-Gothic church (finished in 1896) was planned by Sámuel Pecz according to a design traditionally used for medieval Catholic churches. It is one of the most distinctive points of the Buda landscape and an extremely complex, impressive construction. Castle-like and angular, squat and solid rather than elegant, and buttressed on all sides, it still manages to achieve a certain sublime beauty, maybe thanks to the three shades of brick used and the glazed, polychromatic roof-tiles, maybe due to its very complexity. Note the unusual shape of the central 10-sided tower, its roof splaying at the last moment to connect with the walls, or the way the spire is set off to one side. Whatever the appeal, viewed from Pest it stands out as one of a trio with the Matthias Church and Fishermen's Bastion. The inside is similarly unornamented but aesthetic, its most showy feature the intricate upper half of the pulpit. Unfortunately, it's usually closed.

The **statue** on a fountain in this square is of the church's architect Pecz dressed as a medieval master builder, a guise the sculptor claimed to have seen him wearing at a fancy-dress ball. The square itself is remembered for one of the more grim events of 1945. This stretch of water is one of the areas where Jews and anti-Fascists were brought to be shot. Even after the departure of the SS, the Fascist Arrow Cross rounded up and massacred hundreds of Jews here and dumped their bodies in the river. A plaque commemorates the spot.

Church of St Anne (Szent Anna Templom)

Church of St Anne
open only for services, Mon–Fri 6.45–9 and 4–7, Sun and hols 9–1; for details of concerts, ask at the tourist office or in the Angelika café (see p.302)

Located on faded Batthyány tér off Fő utca, this twin-towered parish church is one of Budapest's most beautiful Baroque buildings. Commissioned by the Jesuits, work began in 1740 but was interrupted by financial constraints, an earthquake in 1763, and the abolition of the Jesuit order in 1773. It was not consecrated until 1805. It was badly damaged in the Second World War, and almost pulled down during the construction of the metro due to fears that its foundations would be undermined. On the **façade**, note, from bottom to top, the allegorical figures of Faith, Hope and Charity above the entrance, the central niche with a statue of St Anne and the child Mary, the Buda coat of arms in the tympanum, and above it the eye-in-the-triangle symbol representing the Trinity, flanked by two kneeling angels. Farther up loom the distinctive twin towers, crowned by magnificent Baroque spires with funky green square domes.

Much of the **interior** dates from the 18th century. The spectacular **high altar**, representing in typically Baroque fashion the child Mary being presented by her mother Anne at the Temple of Jerusalem, was completed in 1773, the finest work of Károly Bebó, who also created the gilded Baroque pulpit swarming with cherubs. The painted **ceiling** in the cupola of the chancel is a 1771 depiction of the *Holy Trinity* by Gergely Vogl, while the side altars by Antal Eberhardt date from 1768. Note also the delicately carved baptismal font and the figurative scenes carved into the wooden panels of the choir pews. Yet, for all the gold and excess of decoration, the green wallpaper, carved wooden Stations of the

Cross, vases of flowers and oval portraits create a homely, small-town atmosphere, such that, as in the Matthias Church, the God who resides within these walls comes across as welcoming rather than intimidating. The church regularly hosts organ concerts (ask at the tourist office for details), and the former presbytery contains the delightful Angelika café (*see* p.302).

Batthyány Tér and on down Fő Utca

Batthyány tér epitomizes the current nature of Víziváros, surrounded as it is by grand edifices gone shabby. Note, for instance, the old market building that resembles the best kind of railway station but now houses a supermarket. Worth seeing, though, are the bas-reliefs on the façade of the 18th-century **Hikisch house** at No.3. Reminiscent of sketches from an alchemical treatise, they are depictions of the four seasons. The rococo-style house next door is the former **White Cross Inn** where Casanova is reputed to have stayed. The square is good for views of Parliament.

Carrying on down Fő utca, you will pass the **Church of the St Elizabeth Nuns**, looking like a big cake. Inside, the Baroque decoration is absurdly rich, with gold-draped figures everywhere: fixed to the walls, loafing around the edge of the pulpit or flanking the paintings, admiring them or pointing to encourage us. The altarpiece of St Francis receiving the stigmata is worth seeing, as is the fresco of St Florian saving Christians from a fire in 1810. All the more pity that it too is locked outside service times.

Király Baths
II. Fő utca 84, t 201 4392; open Tues, Thurs and Sat 9–8 for men; Mon, Wed, Fri 7–6 for women; adm

Farther on are the Turkish **Király Baths**. One of Budapest's most striking and atmospheric baths, featuring a 16th-century Ottoman pool and several smaller pools beneath the original cupola, it was completed by the third Turkish pasha in 1570 just inside the Víziváros castle gates, so that the garrison could bathe even during a siege. The classical section was added in the early 18th century. All the normal baths are here. The surviving Turkish section faces Ganz utca; the neoclassical wing facing Fő utca dates from 1826.

Bem József tér is named after the Polish general whose statue it contains. He fought in the Polish uprising of 1830–1, the Vienna revolt of 1848 and the War of Independence in 1848–9. Demonstrations often begin here, as did the march on Parliament at the beginning of the 1956 Uprising.

Lukács Baths
II. Frankel Leó utca 25–9, t 326 1695; open Mon–Fri 6am–7pm, Sat–Sun 6am–5pm; adm

The road changes name but continues, leading (maybe farther than you would want to go) to the peaceful neoclassical complex of the **Lukács Baths**. These mixed-sex baths are set in attractive grounds containing two outdoor swimming pools and the normal thermal pools. The waters are said to be good for orthopaedic diseases.

Tomb of Gül Baba
II. Mecset utca 14;
open April–Sept
Tues–Sun 10–6;
Oct 10–4

A short detour off Frankel Leó utca takes you to the **Tomb of Gül Baba**. The name of this Turkish Dervish, a member of the Sufi Bektaşi order, means 'Father of the Roses'. Legend has it that he introduced the rose to Hungary and gave Rózsadomb, this area, its name: Hill of Roses. Hungarians revere him for this even though he participated in the hated Turkish capture of Buda (after which he died at the thanksgiving service). His life has inspired works by the Danish writer Hans Christian Andersen and the Hungarian composer J. Huszka. The site has been restored by the Turkish government and surrounded by a colonnaded parapet. The octagonal tomb is a 1962 reconstruction of the one built in the 1540s by the third pasha of Buda, but the dome that covers it is original. The interior is decorated with Arabic calligraphy citing the Koran, pictures and Turkish carpets.

The City (Lipótváros/Leopold Town)

Covering the northern section of inner Pest, this is the financial, banking and business heart of the capital, containing its Parliament and cathedral. Planned in the early 19th century and named Lipótváros after Habsburg Leopold II, it is buzzing on weekdays with people in suits talking on mobile phones, and a ghost town at weekends and in the evenings. Since what is of most interest here is the buildings (of which there are too many striking examples to take in), these quiet times are probably the best ones for a visit. There is a lot to see here, and the selection below is only the cream. But, as is so often the case, it is a good idea just to stroll around, get slightly lost, and see what you see.

Roosevelt Tér

Situated at the Pest end of the Chain Bridge, Roosevelt tér is a big grassy expanse, choked by relentless traffic. Its main draw is the **Gresham Palace**, an Art Nouveau gem designed by Zsigmond Quittner and brothers József and László Vágó in 1906, with details crafted by many of the leading artists of the day. Built for an insurance company, it became an apartment block with exclusive boutiques in the arcade, a famous café, and a cabaret. Badly damaged by the retreating German army in 1944, it was used by Allied military for a while, became a library, then Communist state offices, before slipping into complete neglect. Fortunately, the Four Seasons hotel group has recently completed the painstaking reconstruction that has restored its former glory, sticking as close as possible to the original design. The fresh white façade is very subtle, dotted with fragments of glistening gold mosaic designed by Miksa Róth. The relief of a male head in a ruff at the top portrays Sir Thomas Gresham, who first commissioned the building. Guests pass through exact copies of the original delicate wrought-iron peacock gates into an interior that is far more overtly Art Nouveau. The floor is a swirling mosaic; the lobby, inner courtyards and sweeping staircases overflow with showy details in stained glass, wrought iron, and Zsolnay ceramics. Arched glass ceilings focus on the restored original glass cupola.

At the north end of the square is the neo-Renaissance **Hungarian Academy of Sciences**. The six statues on the main façade represent the Academy's original six departments: law, sciences, mathematics, philosophy, linguistics and history. On the same level are statues of six scientists: from the river, Newton, Lomonosov, Galileo, Miklós Révai (a Hungarian linguist), Descartes and Leibnitz. The building was finished by German Friedrich August Stüler in 1865.

The statue in the middle of the square is Count István Széchenyi, surrounded by Minerva (trade), Neptune (navigation), Vulcan (industry) and Ceres (agriculture). Farther south is a **statue of Ferenc Deák**, a moderate, liberal politician known as 'the nation's sage'. It is appropriate that his statue should be close to that of Széchenyi, whose belief in the gentle path of reform he shared throughout the turbulent 1840s. Ever opposed to war, he was largely responsible for the 1867 Compromise with Austria that led to the Dual Monarchy. Here he is shown with figures representing Justice, Patriotism, Popular Education, National Progress and Compromise. In 1858 he wrote, 'Primarily the task is to keep alive in the nation a sense and enthusiasm for constitutional liberty, because in a more favourable moment the Hungarian constitution can be restored by the stroke of a pen, and within 24 hours we can again be a free constitutional state.'

The large bronze relief on the Akadémia utca side of the Academy depicts the moment of its formation. On 3 November 1825, Count István Széchenyi (dressed here in a Hussar officer's uniform) announced to the Diet (Parliament) that he would donate a year's income towards the establishment of a learned society for the development of Hungarian arts, science, language and literature. When asked what he would live on, he answered, 'My friends will support me.' It was the first major act of a life of extraordinary philanthropy.

Between Roosevelt tér and Parliament, **Akadémia utca** is recommended for its buildings, though Nádor utca has the appealing **Central European University**, whose best feature is its interior. Nip inside for a look: just say you're going to the fine academic bookshop if anyone asks. The university was established by George Soros, a billionaire economist born in Budapest in 1930 at the tail end of a period which saw an unfeasible number of geniuses educated in the city.

St Stephen's Basilica (Bazilika)

**St Stephen's
Basilica**
*V. Szent István tér,
t 317 2859; **basilica** open
Mon–Fri 9–5, Sat 9–1,
Sun 1–4; **treasury** open
daily 10–5; adm;
dome open April–May
daily 10–4.30; June–Aug
9.30–6; Sept–Oct
10–5.30; adm; **guided
visits** in English are
held Mon–Fri at 11am,
2pm, 3.30pm and on
Sat at 11am; adm*

Sitting on Szent István tér with its back to the main road, and surrounded by buildings almost as high as itself, Budapest's cathedral tends to creep up on you. It's hard to get a good look at it except from the front, which is easily the most attractive part anyway. The back is too overcrowded with competing architectural features for its own good, and has provoked accusations of ugliness. The detractors are silenced now, however. Freshly cleaned and free of scaffolding, the basilica looks fantastic.

History has also hitherto been unkind to the building. Over 50 years and three architects were required to complete it, to the point that it became a standing joke: 'I'll pay up when the Basilica is finished.' After decades of talk and three years of a failed Revolution, work finally began in 1851 under József Hild, whose neoclassical design followed a Greek-cross floor plan. When Hild died in 1868, Miklós Ybl took the helm and was shocked to find cracks in the walls. He had the site fenced off, just in time: eight days later during a storm the dome tumbled down, breaking more than 300 local windows. Ybl began afresh with new plans, including the neo-Renaissance dome that is the church's finest feature today. After he died, the church was finished by József Kauser and consecrated in 1905. During his opening speech, the story goes, Franz Josef was seen to throw nervous glances at the dome. Though it is not shaped like a basilica, it received the title Basilica Minor in 1938, on the 900th anniversary of the death of St Stephen, to whom it was dedicated.

The city around the Basilica changed long before it was finished. Originally it had backed on to low buildings and narrow streets, but by the time Ybl took over the major thoroughfare now called Bajcsy-Zsilinszky had been built, necessitating a second façade. He cleverly provided this by adding the Ionic colonnade surmounted by statues of the 12 apostles. The dome is 96 metres high (315ft), the same as the Parliament's dome, this number alluding to the date of the legendary arrival of the Magyar tribes: AD 896. Its four niches carry statues of the four Evangelists. The tympanum between these contains figures of Mary surrounded by Hungarian saints. The main door features carvings of the 12 apostles. Above it is a bust of King (St) Stephen, and higher still a mosaic of the Resurrection.

The interior, which can hold 8,500 people, is spacious, impressive but not oppressive. The marble walls and pillars carry mosaics, paintings and sculptures of a very high standard, mostly produced by Hungary's finest 19th-century artists. The mosaics were designed in Hungary (the dome is by Károly Lotz) and made in Venice. Highlights of the statues are the mournful St Rita, and the subtle Joseph, which has Jesus looking like a normal little boy yet with something intangible extra. Of the paintings, Gyula Stettka's *Golgotha* on the left middle deftly portrays Christ's passion as realistic yet larger than life. Opposite, also excellent, is Gyula Benczur's treatment of a famous scene from Hungarian legend. King Stephen, left heirless after his son Imre's premature death, is portrayed shrewdly offering his crown, and therefore his country's future, not to the pope or the Holy Roman Emperor but to the Virgin. Since then she has been considered the Patroness of Hungary. Stephen is featured on the main altar, wearing a halo and a sword, a combination that raised no eyebrows in the past. (Note, for instance, the statue of St Ladislaus, the hilt and blade of his sword held up as a cross, a tell-tale crescent symbol protruding from beneath his foot.) The reliefs behind Stephen depict scenes from his life.

Strangely, it was in death that the great king provided the church with its most famous attraction. His mummified **Holy Right Hand** (and forearm), Hungary's most important relic, is daily taken from its chapel and displayed in front of the painting of Stephen offering his crown. It lives in a highly ornate golden model of the Matthias Church, which a 100Ft coin will illuminate (it is tucked away in a small chapel behind the main altar). When Stephen was canonized, his tomb was opened, and the corpse's right hand was found to be missing. It was found in the manor of the keeper of the royal tombs. An abbey was designed to contain the hand, but not for long: it made a mini-world tour before it wound up in its new gilded home. The custom has been revived of parading it through the streets every 20 August in a procession celebrating the anniversary of the king's 1083 canonization.

A tiny room contains the few items of the **Treasury**. The best items are monstrances, gifts from abroad. More worthwhile is the **panorama** from the top: this vantage point offers excellent views, including the best view of the roof of the former Post Office Savings Bank (*see* p.259). You can get a lift part of the way, but 146 more steps remain. You don't get to see the inside of the church, but the space between the inner and outer domes is a curious spectacle.

Before leaving Szent Istvan tér, check out the wonderful green-tiled Art Nouveau façade of the building at No.13.

Szabadság Tér (Liberty Square)

Flanked by stretches of glorious green that are home to a wide range of tree species, with a great playground at its southern end, Budapest's largest, most important square would almost resemble a park, were it not for the intrusive fencing and frequently high police presence. Scattered throughout this almost innocuous space are objects of great national and political import, and around its edges stand some huge, imposing buildings, most of them banks. The biggest is now the home of Magyar TV, though its original function as a stock exchange suits it better. Built in 1905, incorporating touches of Greek and Assyrian temple architecture, it occupies the whole of the square's western side and would be terribly intimidating were it not for the cheap and nasty MTV Televízió sign above the door. It was on these steps that tens of thousands of people assembled on 15 March 1989, when the air was thick with long-awaited political change, to hear actor György Cserhalmi announce the 15 points of the new opposition parties. It was also the scene of fierce clashes between police and protestors in October 2006, the 50th anniversary of the 1956 Uprising.

In the park in front is the **Memorial to the Martyrs of the New Building**, a modest monument to a tragic piece of history. The New Building (Újépület) stood here, an enormous Habsburg barracks in which countless Hungarians were imprisoned and executed. Among them were the country's should-be leaders, including, killed on 6 October 1849, its first independent prime minister, Count Lajos Batthyány. Loathed even more than the Citadella, the New Building's destruction in 1897 gave the square its name of Liberty. Across from here is a rather dull statue of Harry Hill Bandholtz. He was a US general present when Romanian troops tried to make off with the treasures of the National Museum, which he saved by blocking the doors with censorship seals.

The façades of the four similar grand buildings on the square's northern end curve gently in a semi-circle that faces the fenced-in **Soviet Army Memorial**, a large white obelisk topped with a gold star, its base covered in reliefs that depict Red Army soldiers 'liberating' Budapest in 1945. From 1928 till then, a flag stood on this spot, permanently at half-mast, over a mound of soil from territories lost in the 1910 Treaty of Trianon, which gave away two-thirds of Hungary's lands and a third of its population. It was accompanied by a quotation from British press baron Lord Rothermere, who campaigned against the unfair treaty, gaining such gratitude that he was even offered the Hungarian Crown. The Soviets removed the flag, and four statues called North, East, South and West, which also symbolized the lost territories. Why this ugly Soviet memorial has been allowed to remain in this symbolically charged location when all the others have been removed is puzzling, but may explain those fences.

Ironically, it stands close to the former HQ of the Fascist Arrow Cross and right in front of the **US Embassy**. This 1901 building, decorated in a Viennese Art Nouveau style, is where Cardinal Mindszenty, Hungary's Catholic Primate, was sheltered for 15 years following the 1956 Uprising. The situation, exacerbated by

Mindszenty's uncompromising attitude and the coverage it received around the world, became embarrassing for the USA and the Vatican, which eventually persuaded him to leave for Austria in 1971. Most of this eastern side is taken up by **Hungarian National Bank** buildings, of which the one on the southeast corner is the most impressive. Built in 1905, it shows an eclectic combination of historical styles. Two large bronze statues in front of the tympanum symbolize agriculture and industry, while a series of limestone reliefs at the first-floor level depict mainly crafts and trades – the means by which the majority made money. This potentially corny idea works thanks to the sympathetic treatment of the subjects, each imbued with an air of nobility. Note also the carved faces representing the many nations of the world. A pretty kiosk-style café in the centre of the park provides relief from the pompous buildings and statues.

Post Office Savings Bank

On Hold utca, behind the National Bank and now belonging to it, sits one of Budapest's architectural highlights, the former Post Office Savings Bank. Ödön Lechner combined Art Nouveau with Hungarian folk art to forge a new nationalist architecture. 'Hungarian style has no past,' he said, 'but it does have a future.'

The **façade** is all curves and gentle colours, simple motifs so delicate and playful that it's hard to do them justice. A wealth of small, lovingly conceived details adds up to a whole much greater than the sum of its parts. If you have children with you, this is one building they will also like. Look for the ceramic bees climbing up the gable walls towards the hives on the roofs – the accepted interpretation is that these symbolize savers accumulating their wealth, but anyone familiar with the works of Gaudí, with whom Lechner has much in common, may remember the great Spaniard's interest in the architectural prowess of bees, whose constructions and techniques he was keen to study.

These hives and the yellow majolica curlicues are the only hints from below of the extraordinary roof that is the building's finest feature. Here, multi-coloured hexagonal tiles from the Zsolnay factory are ornamented with flowers, dragon tails, angel wings and Turkish turbans, a world of fairytale folk imagery. When asked who would enjoy such details, Lechner answered, 'The birds.' The best view of the roof is from the top of the Basilica (see p.257) with binoculars. Even the façade is difficult to see owing to a lack of vantage points and the many plane trees.

Over the road is one of Budapest's still-functioning **produce markets** (Vásárcsarnok), startlingly clean and orderly inside. On the way to the Parliament, where Hold utca meets Báthory utca, an **Eternal Flame** inside a giant lantern commemorates the execution of Count Lajos Batthyány on this spot (then inside the New Building) on 6 October 1849. He was a conservative patriot, not a revolutionary, who had attempted to find a compromise with Austria and later headed a failed peace delegation. From here it's not far to **No.3 Honvéd utca**, which has one of the nicest, most original façades you'll see: very Art Nouveau, very playful and another one for the kids. Note the balconies, each utterly distinctive, and the use of glazed ceramics. There are roses, sunflowers, fruit, and more comparisons to be made with Gaudí.

Imre Nagy Monument

In Vértanuk tere (Martyrs' Square) is the monument to Imre Nagy. After Stalin's death in 1953, the strong-arm dictator Rákosi fell from grace with Moscow, partly because of his personality cult, which surpassed locally even that of Stalin. When Imre Nagy replaced him as prime minister, a period known as 'the thaw' began. Investment policies were implemented, encouraging a healthier economic structure; forced collectivization was abandoned and peasants were allowed to leave their co-operatives; the ideological atmosphere was relaxed, and silenced writers and poets were allowed to re-enter the literary scene. The reign of terror had come to an end. When Nagy's protector in Moscow was dismissed, however, he too was removed from power (after just two years), and his changes criticised and reversed. Though a Communist, he had become much loved, so that, during the 1956 Uprising, the people called for him to speak. Eventually persuaded to address the crowds, he simply urged them to go home. Nevertheless, he accepted the position of prime minister for the 11 or so days when the Uprising seemed to have been successful, and attempted to appease both the revolutionaries and the Soviets.

In the end, the broader political picture sealed the country's fate, the Russians deciding they could not allow Hungary independent rule, and the Western powers agreeing not to interfere. So the Russian tanks appeared, and Nagy sought amnesty in the Yugoslavian embassy. After accepting an armistice, he was imprisoned for two years in Romania, then secretly tried in the spring of 1958 and executed on 16 June. During the trial he could have saved his own life by co-operating, but refused to revise his opinions. Though he never stopped being a Communist, Nagy really believed in the people, their freedom and independence, and he was not prepared to compromise those beliefs in the name of Moscow's policies. This spiritual defection is symbolized by his statue's position on a bridge, his back to the Soviet Army Memorial, looking towards Parliament. Nagy himself is not romanticized, but treated as an imperfect, very human individual, who lived a difficult destiny.

Kossuth Lajos Tér

This is another square that really wants to be a park. Either side of the gargantuan Parliament building are grassy tree-filled areas that could be joined were it not for a car park the size of a football pitch. On the square's southwest corner is a statue of **Attila József**, the popular working-class poet. Despite left-wing tendencies, he was too interested in life's bigger questions and the tragically fragile beauty of the human condition ever to conform to any ideology, and was not as popular with politicians as with ordinary people. Sculpted with tremendous empathy, the statue captures all this. The face is forlorn and troubled, too sensitive, too intelligent. Just as much is said about his state of mind in the way he's holding his hat, the coat thrown in a heap beside him. He is one of the greats, and he bears his nation's woes to a degree his fellows will never understand. He committed suicide in 1937, aged 32.

Right in front of Parliament is a far less enjoyable **statue of Ferenc Rákóczi II**, a prince of Transylvania who led the 1703–11 struggle for independence against the Habsburgs. Latin inscriptions on the plinth read 'For Country and Liberty' and 'The wounds of the noble Hungarian nation burst open'. The sentiment is echoed on the other side of the car park by an odd Modernist block carrying an **Eternal Flame** in memory of those who died here during the Uprising of 1956, particularly on 25 October, when Soviet snipers started taking pot-shots at the peaceful demonstrators below, who were socializing with Soviet tank crews at the time. The shots came from the roof of the Ministry of Agriculture, the nicely proportioned neoclassical building behind Rákóczi fronted by a massive Corinthian colonnade. Outside stand unmarked statues of noble peasant types. The Reaper Lad seems to be eyeing Parliament with numbed bewilderment, while the Female Agronomist looks stubbornly away.

The neo-Renaissance **palace** next door was built to house the Supreme Court and Public Prosecutor's Office, hence the fresco on the ceiling of the vast and ornately decorated main hall, which depicts Justitia, Goddess of Justice, surrounded by allegorical representations of Justice and Peace on the right, Sin and Revenge on the left. By Károly Lotz, it outshines his fresco in the Parliament.

Ethnographical Museum
open May–Oct daily 10–6; Nov–April daily 10–5; adm

The palace is now the **Ethnographical Museum**, worth visiting as much for the building as for its contents. On the first floor, starting on the left, 13 rooms contain the permanent exhibition 'Folk Culture of the Hungarians'. By the 18th century the population of ethnic groups equalled that of Hungarians, so there is a wealth of diversity to be covered. Enlarged old black and white photos are often more interesting than the exhibits themselves and give a flavour of how life really was. The temporary exhibitions held here are also invariably excellent.

In the park outside the museum is a **statue of Lajos Kossuth**, the most powerful figure from the struggles of the 1840s. A brilliant writer and speaker, he revolutionized the Hungarian media with his newspaper *Pesti Hírlap*, which he used, along with inflammatory speeches in Parliament, to rouse the people to demand separation from Austria. He was a contrast to the likes of Széchenyi and Batthyány, whose moderate stance he opposed. Széchenyi understood that Kossuth's insistence on revolution threatened to enrage the Austrians and destroy all the progress made by the more subtle path of reform, and history proved him right. When the inevitable war with Austria began, Batthyány stepped down, and Kossuth took up the prime minister's reins. He travelled the country rousing the people to arms, which is the subject of this statue, the six figures around him supposedly typical citizens. Unfortunately, the ensemble looks rather silly, like seven ham actors striking poses. Maybe the original statue was better: it depicted the gloom after the war with Austria was lost. The Soviets had it replaced with the present offering presumably because it was too downbeat, or maybe because Kossuth was surrounded by his aristocratic ministers such as Batthyány, Széchenyi and Eszterházy.

Just northwest of here is another little square, which contains a **statue of Mihály Károlyi**, a.k.a. the 'Red Baron'. He wasn't a fighter pilot but a wealthy landowner who became a radical liberal politician and in 1919 Hungary's first president. This was a very difficult time, at the end of the First World War when the Allied powers were preparing to confiscate two-thirds of Hungary's territory, and the people were swinging ever further to the left. Eventually forced to resign in favour of Béla Kún's Communist party, he went through two separate periods of exile. In this statue by Imre Varga he looks old and sad but stubbornly dignified, standing under two halves of an arch that do not meet.

Parliament (Országház)

Parliament
t 441 4415; tours in English leave at 10, 12, and 2 on days when Parliament is not in session; tickets (2,070Ft, children 1,035Ft, free to EU citizens so bring your passport) can be bought in advance by telephone

Occupying 880ft of the Danube embankment, there is no ignoring Budapest's most famous building. Based on – and reminiscent of – the House of Commons in London, it's a magnificently bold feat of virtuosity, so extravagant and pompous that the temptation is to belittle it. The 20th-century poet Gyula Illyés called it 'no more than a Turkish bath crossed with a Gothic chapel', drawing attention, even in this put-down, to the eclecticism so integral to Hungarian architecture. The ground plan is Baroque, but the façade is a fusion of neo-Gothic and neo-Renaissance. Designer Imre Steindl wanted 'to combine this splendid medieval style with national and personal features'. Tharaud spoke in 1899 of 'those Hungarian architects, with their bizarre passion for medievalism, without reason'. But there was a reason, which can be understood by comparing this structure with the frigid Baroque Royal Palace on the other side of the water: the Gothic harks back to better days, when Hungary was free to choose its own buildings. Whatever your reactions to the result, awe will be among them. As Patrick Leigh Fermor put it in 1934, 'Architectural dash could scarcely go further.' Upon completion, it was the largest parliament building in the world. The plan is one of perfect symmetry centred on the magnificent dome. The two wings are mirror images down to even the smallest details, one originally holding the House of Commons and the other the House of Lords.

It was in 1843 that the Hungarian Diet (Parliament) decided to build a permanent 'House of the Motherland'. For centuries before, they had met wherever they could. A competition was held which Steindl won. The second- and third-place designs were also used, the former now housing the Ethnological Museum, the latter the Ministry of Agriculture. Work began in 1885 and involved an average of a thousand people every day for 17 years, by which time it was six years too late for the millenary celebrations it was meant to crown, and Steindl was a sick old man giving directions from a chair. He died five weeks before it was completed.

Inside there are 20km of stairways and 691 rooms. Much of the trimming is painted with 22- or 23-carat gold, 60kg of it. On the guided tour you will only see a fraction of what is there. Just inside the main entrance on Kossuth Lajos tér is a model of Parliament made from 30,000 matchsticks. The 96 steps of the ceremonial staircase, with ceiling frescoes by Károly Lotz, lead to the 16-sided hall below the 96m-high dome. As in St Stephen's Basilica, these numbers allude to AD 896, when the Magyars arrived in the Carpathian Basin. The dome is the building's finest feature both outside and in, where it is decorated with intricate gilding leading the eye to an exquisite chandelier. Round the giant pillars that support the dome are statues of some of Hungary's rulers. All are staring straight ahead except Árpád, who is looking to his right, as if saying, 'What are those Habsburgs doing here?' Below the dome is the latest resting place of Hungary's crown jewels.

In the old Upper House, the colour scheme is blue, representing the blood of the lords. Outside the Lords' Chamber, used for conferences since their discontinuation, you'll see the brass ashtrays, numbered so that each member could retrieve his own cigar on returning from hearing the speaker who had lured him away from it. The length of cigar turned to ashes was an indication of the speaker's quality. These days, only the offices of the president, prime minister and speaker are here. All other MPs work in the White House, an ugly modern building farther north, which for 32 years was the power base of Communist dictator János Kádár.

North to the Nagykörút

The northern chunk of Lipótváros is a paradise for lovers of big buildings. Many of the modern ones are just as impressive as the old stalwarts which they are clearly designed to complement. For a first-class selection of both, try this suggested circuit, remembering that not all of the best buildings are on the route, though they are visible from it. From Kossuth Lajos tér walk down Alkotmány utca, turn left on to Bihari János utca, then left on to Markó utca which crosses Nagy Ignac utca. This last and Bihari János retain their quality up to the Nagykörút.

If you feel like going this far, turn right for the beautiful **Nyugati Station** building. Constructed by the famous Eiffel company in Paris, it was the largest station in Europe until 1880. Known as the Western Railway Station, this was the site of the first such building in Hungary, from where the first train ran in 1846. Behind it on Váci út (not to be confused with the famous Váci utca in Belváros) is the postmodern **West End City Centre** shopping mall, packed with designer boutiques, cafés and bars.

To the west the Nagykörút heads past the delightful **Vígszínház** (Comedy Theatre) to **Margaret Bridge** – with its own fantastic views, especially at night – and Margaret Island (*see* below). A path beside the Danube leads back south to the Chain Bridge.

Margaret Island (Margit-sziget)

Margaret Island
tram 4 and 6, or bus 26 from Nyugati station

Margaret Bridge (Margit híd) is the northernmost bridge you are likely to encounter. It is easily recognizable by the 'elbow' in its middle, a 150° angle which allows it to continue the line of the outer ring road (Nagykörút) of which it is a part. At this elbow, a third section leads to Margaret Island. Essentially one big park, Margit-sziget is greatly appreciated by Budapesters, offering as it does a slice of tranquillity minutes from the city centre.

Named the 'Isle of Rabbits' in the Middle Ages, the island was used by the Árpáds as a royal game reserve. From the 12th century onwards various monastic orders replaced the hunters: Premonstratensions, Franciscans and the Order of St John. Béla IV had a convent built for the Dominican nuns, of which his daughter Margaret was the best-known inmate. Tradition has it that, during the Mongol invasion of 1242–4, Béla vowed that if Hungary survived he would have her brought up as a nun. In 1252, aged nine, she was confined to the convent, where she died 19 years later after many holy acts, which won her canonization (in 1943) and a place of honour in the Hungarian pantheon. In a change of pace, the Turks destroyed most of the island's holy buildings and used it for a harem. Open to the public since 1869, the park's popularity with lovers generated the saying, 'Love begins and ends on Margaret Island.'

The island is primarily attractive as a park, especially for children. There are plenty of open areas for games and sports, playgrounds, and much natural beauty. At either end, rental facilities are available, including roller-skates, bikes, two-seater pedal-cars and electric cars. Choice – and prices – are greater at the northern end. Along the road that runs down the western side are the **Alfréd Hajós Swimming Pools**, designed by and named for the gold-medal-winner of the 100-metre and 1,200-metre swimming races at the first modern Olympics in 1896. More fun, and extremely popular in summer, is the **Palatinus Strand bathing complex**, 300 metres farther on. There are several open-air thermal pools, a water chute, wave machine, segregated terraces for nude sunbathing (a gay favourite), and a 100-metre pool, one of the longest in Europe.

Palatinus Strand bathing complex *t 340 4505, www.budapest gyogyfurdoi.hu; open June–Aug Mon–Thurs 9–7, Fri–Sun 9–8; last week of Aug 10–7; closed Sept–May; adm*

East of here is the oval-shaped **rose garden**; southwest the scant remains of a 13th–14th-century **Franciscan church**. East of the rose garden is a small **wildlife reserve** with goats, donkeys, peacocks and cranes. North is the park's most prominent feature, the 57-metre **water tower**. A pioneering structure when built in 1911, it now houses exhibitions in the summer, and is next to an **open-air theatre** that hosts operas, rock operas and plays.

To the southeast stand the ruins of the **Dominican church and convent**, a series of low walls (currently being renovated). A marble shrine within marks Margaret's original burial place. Farther north stands the 1931 reconstruction of a 12th-century **Premonstratension chapel** in the Romanesque style. The bell hanging in the tower was made by master craftsman Hans Strous, was lost for centuries, then found in the roots of a tree torn out during a storm in 1914.

Two giant hotels stand sentinel over the northern end of the island. The **Danubius Grand** is one of Budapest's classic hotels, built as a sanatorium in 1873 by Miklós Ybl. The baths to which it was attached are contained within the ugly concrete 1970s-style hotel (now also part of the Danubius chain) next door. To the west is a **rock garden** whose warm-water ponds contain tropical fish, bullrushes, sculptures and lilies of varied colour. A network of small canals and bridges links the ponds and paths. What with the artificial waterfall and a small gazebo, this is one of the most attractive areas in the park.

Public toilets can be found between here and the hotels, or at the water tower.

Belváros: The Inner City

The Kiskörút (Little Boulevard) runs along the line of medieval Pest's walls, containing the city centre known as Belváros. Not much remains to identify this as the site of historic Pest: the town was razed when the Turks were driven out in 1686. What can be seen today is mainly a result of the massive expansion at the end of the 19th century. There are a few sights, but the thing to do here is stroll – along the Dunakorzó, whose whole waterfront stretch has been declared a UNESCO World Heritage site, or around the lively hubs of Vörösmarty tér and Váci utca.

Deák Tér

Sitting on the Kiskörút at the junction of Pest's four inner districts and three metro lines, Deák tér is undeniably the city's main hub, a busy and until quite recently rather sleazy spot. Its landmark is the squat, spireless **Lutheran Church** with its gently curving green roof. The inside is simple, and can only be seen during services or via the **museum** next door, whose exhibits include a facsimile of Martin Luther's will and a copy of the first book printed in Hungary, a 1541 *New Testament*. The more attractive **Lutheran School**, a couple of buildings west, is a candidate for the best school of all time. As well as György Lukács, the Marxist philosopher who survived his country's changing politics relatively unscathed, and Sándor Petőfi, who didn't, three Nobel Prize-winners were educated here, plus pioneer scientists John von Neumann and Edward Teller. The best thing on this square is the neo-Gothic **VW building** at No.3, its corner topped by a turret. Across the main road, the giant mustard-yellow **Anker Palace** continues to crumble.

In the metro is the tiny **Underground Railway Museum**. The line (now M1) underneath Andrássy út, inaugurated in 1896, was mainland Europe's first metro, and the world's second after London's Metropolitan line. The exhibits are two refurbished carriages on a stretch of track.

The wide open space north, where Deák and Erzsébet squares collide, was proposed by Budapest's former mayor as the site for a new National Theatre, until political wranglings from the FIDESZ government moved the theatre to a far less appropriate spot way south by Lágymányosi Bridge. Now one of central Budapest's greenest and most attractive spaces has emerged. A vast expanse of shallow water, with a glass case full of growing crystal floating around on top, is surrounded by park-benches and modern sculptures, with a broad stairway leading down to a club/music venue. **Erzsébet tér** to the west is a giant square of tree-lined paths converging on the **Danubius Fountain**. The male figure on top

Lutheran church museum
open Tues–Sun 10–6; closed Mon; adm

Underground Railway Museum
open Tues–Sun 10–6; closed Mon; adm a transport ticket

symbolizes the Danube, while the women on the lower basin represent tributaries, the Tisza, Dráva and Száva. The original, whose basin was carved from a single 100-tonne rock, was destroyed in the war.

Vörösmarty Tér

Free from traffic and lined by the terraces of cafés, dotted with graceful iron lamp-posts and dominated by half a dozen giant trees, Vörösmarty tér has long been a focus of social activity – or inactivity, for it has always been a nice place to just hang out and watch. Locals lost this relaxing corner of the city to building works while the square was gutted as the new metro was tunnelled, but it's hoped that things will go back to normal by 2012/13.

At the centre is a **statue of Mihály Vörösmarty**, romantic reform writer and giant of 19th-century Hungarian poetry. On the front of the monument are the famous opening words of his *Szózat* (Appeal), which became a second national anthem: 'To thy Fatherland be unshakeably true, oh Magyar!' The black spot above this is supposedly the coin donated by a beggar towards the monument's cost. Festivals sometimes take over for a day, or a week, and street musicians and artists perform in the summer.

Alive and atmospheric, the square never feels busy, tacky or sleazy. This is partly due to the hallowed institution on the north side, the **Pâtisserie Gerbeaud**. This 1861 building has been a café-confectioner's since 1870. Emil Gerbeaud bought it in 1884 and turned it into a landmark, famous as a meeting-spot as well as for its cakes. The three vast rooms that face the square resemble an English palace, exquisitely decorated with turn-of-the-20th-century furniture. The marvellous building with turret-like corners on the square's south side is the **Bank Palace**, housing the Budapest Stock Exchange, which reopened in 1990, 42 years after the Communists closed it down. Ignác Alpár, who designed the Magyar TV and National Bank buildings in Szabadság tér, considered it his major work.

To the north is **József Nádor tér**, flanked by fantastic buildings: the Romantic **Postabank** building on the south side, its façade alive with detail; **Credit Lyonnais** on the corner, lovingly restored; the **Ministry of Finance** on the west side, another Alpár construction, its top ledge boasting a statue of Mercury holding a model of the building on which he stands; the **OTP** (also Postabank) **building** on the east with an arcade running through the middle. Overlooking the square from József Attila utca is the **Merkantil Bank** building with an Art Nouveau façade. The statue in the square's centre is of the archduke whose name it carries. Habsburg Palatine from 1796 to 1847, he was a friend to Hungary. In 1808 he helped establish the Embellishment Commission for the restoration and development of Pest (an ongoing process). The Commission's leading supporter was architect János Hild, whose son József built the neoclassical **Gross House**, No.1 on this square, next to the Ministry of Finance.

Vigadó Tér to Petőfí Tér

West from Vörösmarty tér is a small square named after the Romantic **Vigadó Concert Hall**, whose name approximates to 'making merry'. It was so badly damaged in the Second World War that reconstruction wasn't completed until 1980. The symmetrical façade, cleaned and renovated in 2006, is richly embellished, with a ledge running like a frieze along its top, bearing the heads of Hungarian rulers and celebrities, and the old coat of arms at its centre. The columns carry reliefs of dancers, and statues of musicians line the first-floor ledge in front of the five arched windows. The foyer, while grand enough, is a mere prelude to the Great Hall's dazzlingly rich colour scheme: unfortunately, restoration works to the interior, due for completion several years ago, have stalled, and no one knows when it will finally emerge from behind the hoardings and scaffolding. On the square's railings, look out for a bronze statue, the *Little Princess* (1990). Prince Charles has a copy and invited the sculptor, László Marton, to exhibit his work in London.

The **Dunakorzó** has wonderful views of the Buda panorama, especially at night when lights dance on the water and the air is suffused with romance. In the 1900s this area was surrounded by fancy hotels, and the promenade was *the* place to stroll, to see and be seen. They are trying to recapture that atmosphere, and the tramlines keep the traffic at a distance.

Petőfi tér contains a giant Celtic tombstone, and the statue of Sandor Petőfi. More maybe than any other national hero, he stirs patriotism in the Magyar soul, thus his statue – despite making him look slightly silly – is a popular site for political demonstrations. Behind him is the Baroque **Greek Orthodox church**.

Greek Orthodox church
closed except for services

Inner City Parish Church (Belvárosi Plébániatemplom)

Inner City Parish Church
open daily 6.30am–9pm; Mass Mon–Sat 6.30am and 6pm, Sun 9, 10 (Latin), 12 and 6

Petőfi tér runs into Március 15 tér and Pest's oldest building, the Inner City Parish Church. From the outside it's nothing special. The plaster is crumbling in places and the paint peeling, the niches are empty and the Holy Trinity above the door look sadly decrepit. Even Christ's cross is rusting. Yet this is Budapest's only building east of the Danube to reflect anything like the history encountered on the other side. Sources disagree over how old it is. Some say that a church was founded here as a burial site for the martyred St Gellért in 1046. Others speak of a triple-aisled Romanesque church built at the end of the 12th century. Certainly the first occupant of this site was the 3rd-century Roman fortress

Contra Aquincum, whose remains can be seen in the square beside the church. The original was razed during the Mongol invasions, though a single Romanesque arch survives in the southern tower. The 14th-century Gothic replacement provided the basis of what you see today. The Turks converted it into a mosque and then returned it so that for a while it was the only Christian church in Pest. When they were kicked out it was damaged, then in 1723 it burned down. Reconstruction in a Baroque style saw the addition of today's twin towers and façade, resulting in a hybrid curious even by Budapest's eclectic standards: the back is Gothic, the front Baroque. After all that, the church was inevitably war-torn and then almost pulled down when the Elisabeth Bridge was built.

Inside, the historical mish-mash, as well as the grandeur, is much more apparent. The **nave** features a barrel-vaulted Baroque ceiling and is simple, with little use of gold and few paintings or figures. The **chancel** is much more ornate, its complex vaulted ceiling-arches edged with geometric shapes. On the right side are five **chapels**. The first three are Baroque; the fourth contains a beautiful Renaissance tabernacle of red marble and white limestone, its pedestal holding the crest of the Pest city council who commissioned it in 1507; the fifth is Gothic. The original **high altar** was destroyed during the war; this one dates from 1948 and is the work of sculptor Károly Antal and painter Pál C. Molnár. Behind the altar are Gothic **sedilia** and to the right is a souvenir from the church's time as a mosque, a **prayer-niche** (*mihrab*). You can only get a close look at these after Latin Mass on a Sunday. The fine wooden **pulpit** is neo-Gothic, from 1808. On the chancel's left side is a reconstructed Gothic tabernacle. The chapel before the chancel contains the remains of the church's frescoes. The last chapel holds the extravagant neoclassical tomb of a newspaper editor, constructed in 1835 by István Ferenczy.

Váci Utca

Váci utca runs the length of this district and was once Pest's main road. For the last 150 years it has held Budapest's premier boutiques, where rich ladies would seek the latest fashions, stroll among the gentry and enjoy the sophisticated café terraces. Over 30 years ago the northern half of the street, still considered by natives to be 'the' Váci utca, was pedestrianized, leading to a return of the boom times. It has become increasingly Westernized, tacky even, so you won't be very surprised by anything you see (unless you look up above the shop fronts). You will end up here anyway. It is gloriously traffic-free and humming with action, a place to watch the locals (who are probably there to watch the tourists). Its lively atmosphere is particularly worth seeking out at night. The southern half of Váci utca, only pedestrianized in 1997, is calmer and feels less like a tourist trap.

Szervita Tér

Walking north on Váci utca, before you get to Vörösmarty tér, a little square overflowing with terrace tables opens up on the right. This is **Kristóf tér**, and at its centre is a statue of a *Fisher-Girl* which originally belonged at a fish-market nearby on the embankment, and apparently caused a stir due to the girl's skimpy attire: strange, given the number of naked classical statues everywhere. It leads into **Szervita tér**, centred on a copy of a 1729 **Immaculata column** with figures of Joseph, Anne and Joaquim at the base. The square is named after the run-down 1732 Baroque **Servite Church**, whose most interesting feature is the large bas-relief to the right of the entrance, with Christ cradling a dying hero. This 1930 monument is dedicated to the VIIth Wilhelm Hussar Regiment, who gave their lives in the First World War. Inside, the church is excessively lavish, with winged or haloed figures everywhere, lots of gold, and a pastel pink and blue ceiling covered with frescoes.

The real reason for visiting this square may elude you until you look up to the west. The building known as the **Turkish Bank House** (which it used to contain) looks at ground level like any other shop. Follow it up and things get more interesting. The whole façade is covered with vast arched windows. At the top in the playfully curved gable is Miksa Róth's masterpiece, an Art Nouveau mosaic entitled *Glory to Hungary*. Angels, shepherds, and heroes such as István Széchenyi, Lajos Kossuth and Ferenc Rákóczi, pay homage to a bethroned *Patrona Hungariae* (Our Lady, Patron of Hungary).

Two doors to the left, **Rózsavölgyi House** is interesting for its distinctions between retail, office and residential levels, a typical trait of the father of Hungarian Modernism, Béla Lajta, one of Ödön Lechner's students. The upper storeys' ceramic decoration reveals his earlier links with the Romantic school, while the whole anticipates the avant-garde.

Ferenciek Tere

This is the main route for east–west traffic and very busy, which may blind you to its charms. As ever, the key is to look up. Stand where the bridge stretches away before you and you will notice that two near-identical buildings, the **Klotild Palaces**, flank the road like mirror images, creating a gateway for the bridge. This 'gateway' is different but equally impressive coming the other way. Beneath the bridge in the subway is a collection of enlarged black and white photos taken by György Klösz which show details of this area before and after the building of the bridge. Opposite are modern photos of the same region.

On the north-facing wall of the **Franciscan church** that gives Ferenciek tere its name is a large memorial relief recalling the catastrophic flood of 1838 when the whole Inner City was under water and over 400 people died. It depicts Count Miklós Wesselényi, who rescued many in his boat.

Over the main road, the corner building smothered with gold-leaf mosaics, ironwork, busts and reliefs is the Párizsi Udvar or **Paris Arcade**. Note the naked figures striking poses either side of the clock (stopped at 12), and the fancy carving around the roof-line and towers. Above the third storey, naked figures appear from the waist up, as if plunging out of the wall. Such details met with disapproval when the building was erected as the Inner City Savings Bank. More in keeping was the theme of bees and the guardian archangel Gabriel on the relief below the gable. Have a closer look at the mosaic inside this porch. Theatrical masks, swirling patterns and gorgons' heads are all the more striking for the colours: gold and an amazing range of blues, greens and reds. Inside it is gloomy and contains nothing worthwhile except for a bookshop, but the décor is astounding, full of sculpted wood, wrought iron, Art Nouveau mosaics and stained glass, of which the apotheosis is Miksa Róth's neglected glass dome.

Southern Belváros

In the calm of these narrow back streets you can catch a whiff of the past and the true spirit of the present. There is little sightseeing to be done. At Károlyi Mihály utca 16 is the neoclassical **Károlyi Palace**, mostly built 1832–41. It contains the **Petőfi Museum of Hungarian Literature**, which has little to interest foreigners beyond the chance of seeing the building's interior. Right behind it, off Magyar utca, are the **Károlyi Gardens**, a secret oasis popular with playing children and smooching couples. **Kálvin tér** to the southwest contains the **Calvinist church**, worth a quick look. Plain but elegant on the outside, the interior possesses its own grandeur. Decoration is almost non-existent, as befits the denomination, but the ceiling is enlivened with brass reliefs of floral motifs, particularly effective on the dome. The combination of the church's many curved planes particularly pleases the eye, drawing it back to the centre, in this case the altar, without so much as a cross. **Raday utca** shoots south from here, Budapest's most exciting nightlife street, pedestrianized and lined with trendy bars and restaurants.

Petőfi Museum of Hungarian Literature
t 317 3611, www. pim.hu; open Tues–Sat 10–6; adm for temporary exhibitions only

⭐ **National Museum**
Múzeum krt. 14–16, t 338 2122, www.mnm.hu; open Tues–Sun 10–6; adm for temporary exhibitions only

National Museum (Nemzeti Múzeum)

This grand neoclassical edifice is just off Kálvin tér. The huge central portico consists of eight Corinthian columns supporting a large tympanum filled with statues, chief among them Pannonia, the name of the ancient Roman province that occupied western Hungary. Opened in 1848, when it was far from the centre of town, it soon played host to one of Hungarian legend's most important scenes. A huge crowd gathered on 15 March 1848 to listen to the leaders of the young revolutionaries, and heard the popular poet Sándor Petőfi recite his now famous *National Song*, marking in a sense the beginning of the revolution. 'Choose! Now is the time! Shall we be slaves or shall we be free?' he cried, and the people chose.

As with the National Library, the National Museum was the inspiration of the great Count Ferenc Széchenyi, father of István. The count's extensive collection of manuscripts, prints, coins, coats of arms and maps was the basis of the museum's collection. Today the exhibits tell the story of Hungary's history in two halves: from the foundation of the state to its reconquest from the Turks, and from the end of the Turkish wars to the 1990s. Its two great treasures are **St Stephen's Sword** and the **Coronation Mantle**, both on the first floor. In the basement is a **Lapidarium** with a collection of Roman remains, mainly tombstones.

The permanent exhibitions are upstairs. On the ceilings and walls above the grand staircase are a series of frescoes completed in 1873 by Than Mór and Károly Lotz. The main images are symbolic representations of abstracts like Imagination, Inspiration and Enthusiasm for Beauty, while a frieze all round the top of the walls has scenes from Hungarian history, from St Stephen's conversion to Christianity up to the founding of the museum, a helpful prelude to the coming history lesson. A look at the family tree in Room 1 may help you with the convoluted dynasty of Hungary's early kings. It all begins with the turul-bird. You will probably get more out of the museum if you brush up on your Hungarian history beforehand (*see* pp.215–224), although there are explanations in English. The notes on individual exhibits are not given in English, on the other hand. On the positive side, dotted around are touch-screen information panels on 'History', 'Economy and Social Struggle', 'Science and Technological Development', 'Culture and Arts', and 'Who's Who in Hungarian History'. There is so much here of quality that it seems almost invidious to pick out individual examples of what is on show. It begins with a lot of weapons and religious relics and ends rather poignantly with a collection of Communist-flavoured street-signs, such as Leninváros, with red paint slashes across them.

Museum of Applied Arts

Üllöi út 33–7, t 456 5100, www.imm.hu; open daily 10–6; adm for temporary exhibitions only

Museum of Applied Arts (Iparművészeti Múzeum)

East of Kálvin tér on Üllöi út is one of Budapest's most interesting museums, worth visiting as much for the building as for the exhibitions. Designed by Ödön Lechner and Gyula Pártos, it is a significant example of Lechner's blending of traditional folk art with more eclectic elements and Art Nouveau to forge a national architecture. It features a wonderfully colourful patterned roof trimmed with yellow majolica, which also enlivens the beautiful dome. Tiles on the façade create flower and foliage patterns, markedly around the rose window above the porch. The steps up to the door are flanked by banisters of yellow ceramic curlicues. Inside, all white, it resembles the Taj Mahal. Originally it was highly decorated with colourful Hungarian folk motifs. The main permanent exhibition, 'Collectors and Treasures', is a disappointment: cramped, unattractively displayed and poorly labelled. However, the main attraction of the museum is its consistently superb temporary exhibitions, of which there are normally three or four.

Central Market Hall (Vamház)

Farther round the Kiskörút to the west of Kálvin tér is the magnificent Central Market Hall, resembling a grand old railway station, an impression maintained inside by the height of the ceiling and the iron staircases and walkways. Outside it is a particularly attractive, striking building with a fancy iron gate, lots of arches and a funky yellow, green and red roof. Inside it is incredibly clean and ordered, to the extent that one could almost think it existed just to impress tourists, yet thousands of Budapestians buy their groceries here every day. It is definitely worth looking inside, if only for the sausage stalls, where lumps of pork fat are sold by the kilo. Upstairs is food (including a good, rustic-style restaurant), souvenirs and lots of linen.

Next door is another notable building, the neo-Renaissance **University of Economic Sciences**, originally the Main Customs Office. The façade overlooking the river has 10 allegorical statues. It is worth going through the river-facing main entrance to check out the inner courtyard, once a customs hall, now an atrium, which contains a large bronze statue of Karl Marx. A bridge arches over the courtyard, commonly known as the 'Bridge of Sighs'.

Andrássy Út to City Park

⭐ Andrássy Út   Starting at one of Budapest's busiest junctions just north of Deák tér, Andrássy út runs northwest in a straight line for 2.5km, the central axis of Terézváros (Theresa Town), better known as District VI. In 2002, the street and its historical environs were granted UNESCO World Heritage status. It is worth a stroll along this most august of Budapest's boulevards just to admire the grandeur of the buildings, amongst them the State Opera House. But the main reason for coming here is the nightlife: the area around Andrássy út is easily the city's most lively quarter. The boulevard culminates in Heroes' Square (Hősök tere), a site of prime national importance flanked by two imposing edifices, including the excellent Museum of Fine Arts. Beyond lies City Park, a must for anyone with children, containing the fairytale Vajdahunyad Castle, the zoo, circus, amusement park and the most family-friendly spa complex in town.

Andrássy Út

Roads that just evolve rarely run straight, and sure enough Andrássy út was rigidly planned. Following the 1867 Compromise with Austria and birth of the Dual Monarchy, Budapest was reinvented as an imperial capital and for once had the luxury of wealth and peace with which to realize mighty ambitions. Heavily influenced by Haussmann's redevelopment of Paris, Andrássy út was conceived as a grand boulevard in the style of the Champs-Elysées. Inaugurated in 1884, the rather pompous result of these grandiose plans has carried a variety of names. First it was Sugár út (Radial Avenue), then it was named after the 19th-century statesman Count Gyula Andrássy, a name which natives upheld through the Communist designations Sztàlin út (1949–56) and the catchy Népköztársaság (Avenue of the People's Republic), and which officially returned in 1990.

The first part of Andrássy út as far as Oktogon is by far the liveliest, and should definitely be visited, preferably at night. The triangle bounded by Király út (south of Andrássy), Bajcsy-Zsilinsky and Teréz körút is a maze of small streets buzzing with restaurants, bars and clubs. This section is lined with closely built, eclectic but mainly neo-Renaissance buildings, as well as shops, offices and cafés.

State Opera House (Állami Operaház)

State Opera House
Andrássy út 22, t 332 8197, www.opera.hu; guided tour in several languages including English at 3pm and 4pm daily; adm;
box office
(t 353 0170) open Mon–Sat 11am until start of performance, Sun 4pm until start of performance

One of the most sumptuous buildings in Budapest, its interior is even more impressive than its outside, making a night at the opera a grand occasion at a comparatively good price. This neo-Renaissance building was the crowning achievement of Miklós Ybl, who designed the Basilica. He spent nine years overseeing the Opera House's construction and is said to have checked every cartload of bricks. Its first musical director was the acclaimed father of Hungarian opera Ferenc Erkel, who also took up the conductor's baton for the grand opening in 1884. Liszt had written a work for the occasion but it contained elements of the Hungarian rebel melody Rákóczi March, and so was not performed. After all, the Compromise had been reached, and the building's funding came mainly from Habsburg Emperor Franz Josef. Gustav

Mahler and Otto Klemperer have been musical directors here, and Puccini directed two of his operas. During the siege of Budapest in the winter of 1944–5, the vast cellars gave shelter to thousands, and the building survived relatively unscathed. In 1981 major renovations began and it reopened on its 100th anniversary on 27 October 1984 as brilliantly sparkling as new.

Either side of the entrance are statues of Liszt (right) and Erkel by Alajos Stróbl. Niches at the corners of the first floor contain statues of the four muses of opera, Terpsichore, Erato, Thalia and Melpomene (dance, love poetry, comedy and tragedy). On the stone balustrade around the second-floor terrace stand statues of the greatest opera composers (with the notable exception of Puccini). At the front (left to right): Rossini, Donizetti, Glinka, Wagner, Verdi, Gounod, Bizet. On the left side: Monteverdi, Alessandro Scarlatti, Gluck, Mozart, Beethoven. On the right side: Mussorgsky, Tchaikovsky, Moniuszko, Smetana. There is also an Egyptian motif, with the 'needles' on the corners of the balustrade and the sphinxes to left and right.

Even without buying a ticket or taking the tour, you can go into the lobby. The gilded vaulted ceiling is covered with wonderful murals by Bertalan Székely and Mór Than. The marble columns, mosaic floor and chandeliers are upstaged by the sweeping main staircase. Even this, however, is just a prelude to the bits you won't see: the auditorium where a bronze chandelier weighing three tons illuminates the 23-carat gold leaf and the fresco of *The Greek Gods on Mount Olympus* by the genre's master, Károly Lotz. The royal box in the centre of the circle has sculptures representing the four operatic voices: soprano, alto, tenor and bass.

Up Andrássy Út to Oktogon

The neo-Renaissance building opposite that so complements the Opera House is the **State Ballet Institute**. Behind it on Paulay Ede utca is one of Budapest's best buildings, the **New Theatre** (Új Színház), by local boy Béla Lajta (*see* Szervita tér, p.270). Designed in 1908–09 to house a music hall, its extraordinary façade combines elements of Art Nouveau, modernism, even Art Deco, which it pre-dates by some 15 years. Note the little monkeys above the 1950s-style doors, forlornly holding blue ceramic globes; the brass Egyptian-style figures lining the roof; and the chintzy blue letters carrying the theatre's name. Redesigned many times, it was mercifully returned to its original form in 1990.

Ernst Museum
t 413 1311, www. mucsarnok.hu; open Tues–Sun 11–7; adm

A block over at Nagymező 8 is the **Ernst Museum**, with avant-garde and small temporary international exhibitions. Inside are benches and banisters by Ödön Lechner and a wonderful 1911 post-impressionist stained-glass window by József Rippl-Rónai. Nearby is **Terézváros Parish Church**, with a graceful tapering tower that draws one's attention to the cross at its pinnacle. The simple, elegant interior has some good paintings and a fine neoclassical high altar but is usually locked. On the corner diagonally opposite is a run-down but still superb Romantic-Gothic building, **Pekáry House**. **Nagymező utca** north of Andrássy has been dubiously dubbed 'the Broadway of Pest'. It does contain a few theatres and clubs, such as the **Operetta**, **Moulin Rouge** and the beautiful **Thália Theatre**, along with a clutch of terrace cafés.

A little farther up Andrássy út, scrutinizing the traffic that passes it, is a **statue of romantic novelist Mór Jókai** on the square that bears his name. On the other side of the road is **Liszt Ferenc tér**, the most happening square in town. Pedestrianized, full of trees, benches, statues and terrace tables, it feels utterly Mediterranean and civilized. One statue is of journalist and poet Endre Ady, but the eye-catching one is the **statue of Ferenc (or Franz) Liszt**. Even sitting he looks like a crazed, dangerous maniac, which, if you listen to his music, is probably what he was. Erected to commemorate the centenary of his death, it contains a cameo of the sculptor (the bald man on Liszt's lapel). At the far end of the square is the **Franz Liszt Music Academy** (Ferenc Liszt Zeneakadémia), an extraordinary Art Nouveau building. A wealth of features adorns the façade, including a statue of Liszt, many strange mythological faces and musical motifs, and reliefs of children playing instruments. The interior is far grander. In the centre is a beautiful mosaic, while the walls above the entrances to the main auditorium carry a fresco by Hungarian Pre-Raphaelite Aladár Körösfői Kriesch entitled *Hungarian Wedding Procession in the 14th Century*.

Where the Nagykörút meets Andrássy út is **Oktogon**. Four enormous, very similar-looking buildings constructed in an eclectic mix of styles in 1873–4 face off against one another, their façades and the roads between them making a perfect octagon. Though surrounded by fast-food outlets and all-night restaurants, the effect is still impressive. This area never sleeps, largely because buses service the Nagykörút 24 hours a day. Like the boulevard on which it stands, Oktogon maintained its name while being officially subjected to others. It was Mussolini tér under the Horthy regime, and November 7 tér, recalling the date of the Bolshevik Revolution so important to Hungarians, under the Communists.

Oktogon to Heroes' Square

The section of Andrássy út running to Kodály körönd is noticeably wider, the thoroughfare flanked by secondary local-traffic roads separated off by pavements lined with trees, traditional lamp-posts and park benches. Though still close together, the buildings here are not so given over to commercial usage, so their self-important demeanour is more apparent.

Franz Liszt Museum
*t 322 9804,
www.lisztmuseum.hu;
open Mon–Fri 10–6,
Sat–Sun 9–5 (but check
Sunday opening hours,
as they are erratic); adm*

Budapest Puppet Theatre
*t 342 2702; shows
winter Mon–Thurs 3pm,
Fri and Sat 10.30am
and 4pm; closed
summer; adm*

House of Terror Museum
*t 374 2600,
www.terrorhaza.hu;
open Tues–Fri 10–6, Sat
and Sun 10–8; adm*

Kodály Memorial Museum
*t 764 81 518, www.
kodaly-inst.hu; open
Wed 10–4, Thurs–Sat
1–6, Sun 10–2; closed
Mon and Tues; adm*

Among them is the **Franz Liszt Museum** at Vörösmarty utca 35. A couple of rooms of the composer's former house lovingly display his belongings right down to nutcrackers and handkerchiefs. There are pianos and organs, portraits and busts of the master, and notes about his life that mainly focus on his friendships with Augusz and Zichy, not even touching upon his rampant womanizing. You'd have to be a real enthusiast to get much out of it. Close by is the **Academy of Fine Arts** containing the child-friendly **Budapest Puppet Theatre** at No.69.

The building at **No.60** has a notorious past. During the Horthy era, the ultra-right-wing regime made it their secret police headquarters, where they locked up, beat and tortured Communists. During the Second World War the Fascist Arrow Cross used it for the same purposes, the victims this time mainly Jews. After the war, the Communists kept the tradition alive, their secret police doing a fair amount of 'persuading' here, especially in the brutal 'dark 50s'. They probably used many of the same implements, though the legendary giant meat-grinder for disposing of bodies was never found. Today the building fittingly houses the **House of Terror Museum**, where photos, artefacts and daunting commentaries recall the victims of those two bitter pills so hard for the Hungarians to swallow: the Nazi Holocaust, and the Communist dictatorship.

Kodály körönd, like Oktogon, is defined by four massive buildings, but is much more sedate and elegant, and generally considered one of Budapest's most beautiful squares. The symmetrical neo-Renaissance edifices are near identical, though No.1 is better preserved and covered in attractive gilt *sgraffito*. It was once the home of composer, researcher and teacher Zoltán Kodály, who incorporated traditional folk melodies into his work and travelled the country to collect and preserve them. Now it houses his archives and the **Kodály Memorial Museum**. The house is in its original state, with furniture, manuscripts, and the composer's collection of folk art. At one point the square was named Hitler tér, which prompted Bartók to state that he didn't want his body to be buried in Hungary so long as anywhere was named after Hitler or Mussolini.

The boulevard gets more stately as it heads towards Heroes' Square, the buildings now detached mansions and villas, many containing embassies. Building buffs can veer left down **Bajza utca** for a look at Nos.42 and 44, then cut through to the parallel road **Munkácsy Mihály utca**, where Art Nouveau façades abound, particularly at Nos.19b, 21, 23 and 26. That Andrássy út was designed as a grand driveway leading to the Millenary Monument becomes clearer the closer you get. However, it is a long walk. The

M1 metro runs beneath the road, and the No.4 bus follows the same route.

Heroes' Square (Hősök Tere)

In concept akin to the Arc de Triomphe, in execution more like London's Trafalgar Square, this vast paved arena is distinct in one significant way: being far from the city centre, it is rarely full of people. Even the odd tourist bus makes hardly a dent on the acres of space. In the evening this emptiness, together with the smooth surface, makes it a paradise for skaters of all kinds, performing tricks and weaving past each other, oblivious to the stony faces of ancient ancestors. The square and its contents, like the boulevard that leads to them, represent a conscious act of Magyar nationalism, born of a short-lived era of prosperity. Coming at the end of the 19th century, it happened to coincide roughly with the millennial anniversary of the Magyars' conquest of the Carpathian Basin. Though nobody knew exactly when this occurred, a date for celebrations was fixed at 1895, then changed to 1896 when it became clear not everything would be ready. The date has been official ever since and dictated such details as the height of the Basilica and Parliament domes.

Approaching the square, the centre of attention is the **Millenary Monument**, with the Archangel Gabriel atop an imposing 120ft column. Legend has it that Gabriel appeared to King Stephen in a dream, instructing him to convert the pagan Magyars to Christianity and offering him the crown of Hungary, shortly after which a crown arrived from Pope Sylvester II. To augment the symbolism, the archangel is standing on a globe holding the Hungarian crown and an apostolic cross. Despite the setting back of celebrations, the column and statue were still a year late, and were deemed unstable. While a reinforced column was prepared, the statue was sent to the 1900 World Exhibition in Paris where it won the Grand Prix. At the column's base are equestrian statues of Prince Árpád and the chieftains who led the Magyar tribes into the region. In front is a block of stone traditionally used for wreath-laying ceremonies. This Heroes' Monument carries the inscription: 'To the memory of the heroes who have sacrificed their lives for the freedom of our people and national independence.'

At a respectful distance behind the column is a two-part semi-circular **colonnade**. On the top, four groups of symbolic figures represent, from left to right, Work and Wealth, War, Peace, and Knowledge and Glory. Between the columns are statues of Hungary's most important rulers, from King Stephen to Kossuth. The Transylvanian princes were only added after the Second World War, when they replaced statues of Habsburg rulers. Below, reliefs contain legendary scenes from their lives, though most of them are battle scenes. During the short-lived Council Republic period of 1919, the revolutionary Soviets had the whole square draped in red and the column covered by a huge red obelisk bearing a relief of Marx. Focal point of fervent sentiments that it is, many important gatherings have taken place here, most recently the ceremonial reburial on 16 June 1989 of Imre Nagy, which symbolized the beginning of a new democratic era. His coffin was accompanied by five others, four representing other leaders executed after 1956, the fifth representing unknown victims of the time.

The composition of the square is best taken as a whole, the column and Magyar chieftains flanked by the colonnades and, pulling back the focus, the colossal **galleries** on either side of the square. To the right is the neoclassical red brick **Palace of Arts** (Műcsarnok), whose steps were used for Nagy's reburial ceremony. The colourful mosaic that fills the tympanum represents St Stephen as patron of the arts. Behind the portico's six massive Corinthian columns, a three-part fresco depicts *The Beginning of Sculpture*, represented by figures of Vulcan and Athene, *The Source of Arts*, with Apollo and the Muses, and *The Origins of Painting*, with images from ancient mythology. Two smaller frescoes in between depict allegorical figures of Painting and Sculpture. Inside, the largest gallery in the country houses temporary exhibitions of chiefly modern art.

Palace of Arts
t 363 2671; open Tues–Sun 10–6; adm

Just off the square (to the right, on Felvonulási tér) is the location of the **1956 Monument**, unveiled in 2006 to mark the 50th anniversary of the Hungarian Uprising. Designed by creative group i-ypsilon, it features 2,006 metal columns which merge to form a wedge entering the ground. It has been placed on the exact spot where Stalin's statue was toppled by revolutionaries.

Museum of Fine Arts (Szépművéseti Múzeum)

Museum of Fine Arts
t 469 7100, www.museum.hu; open Tues–Sun 10–5.30; adm for temporary exhibitions only

On the north side of the square a neoclassical building with Italian-Renaissance, Romanesque and Baroque-revival influences is an appropriate building for the excellent Museum of Fine Arts, the European equivalent of the National Gallery. Eight gigantic Corinthian columns support a portico whose tympanum bears a relief with a completed copy of a fragment on the Temple of Zeus at Olympia, depicting the *Battle of the Centaurs and Lapiths*. The exhibitions have been made to conform to the gallery rather than vice versa, so the interior is just as grand, particularly the sweeping staircases and the Grand Hall. Most exhibits are labelled in English.

The **Egyptian collection** is interesting enough if you haven't been to a better one. Highlights include some good painted sarcophagi, the head of a statue of a New Kingdom young man, a young lady bearing the standard of Hathor, some Late Period bronze sculptures of Harpocrates, Osiris, a raven and a cat.

The **19th-century collection** focuses on French artists of that period. Here are all the big names: Monet, Manet, Renoir, Delacroix. There are some familiar works such as Cézanne's *The Cupboard*, Toulouse-Lautrec's *These Ladies in the Refectory* and Courbet's vast and wonderful *The Wrestlers*. With a few notable exceptions like Monet's *Plum Trees in Blossom*, Pissarro's *Le Pont Neuf* and Gauguin's exotic *Black Pigs*, however, the works of these famous artists are not their best, and the better art on display is the work of lesser names: Dagnan-Bouveret's *Landscape with Trees*, for instance, or Carrière's ethereal *Maternity*. There are some fine sculptures also, such as Carpeaux's *Laughing Girl with Roses* and Clésinger's *Lucretia*. Highlight of the collection, though, and on their own ample justification for a visit to this museum, are five sculptures by Rodin, including *Eternal Springtime* and *The Kiss*.

The **Old Masters Permanent Gallery** is the real *raison d'être* of the museum. The core of the collection was purchased from Count Miklós Eszterházy in 1871. Comprising 70 works, the **Spanish collection**, clustered around El Greco and his school, is probably the finest in the world outside Spain. It offers some vivid altarpieces, seven El Grecos, including *The Agony in the Garden* and *The Penitent Magdalene*, and five Goyas including two of the portrayals of common, humble folk for which he is famous, *The Knife-Grinder* and *The Water-Carrier*. There are also some excellent works such as Cerezo's powerful *Ecce Homo*, Ribera's plaintive *Martyrdom of St Andrew* and Velázquez' *Peasants at Table*. In the smaller **German collection** are Hans Baldung Grien's long, sumptuous, wonderfully stylized portraits, *Adam* and *Eve*. The three portraits by Christian Seybold are worthy of scrutiny, one of himself, one of his daughter, and the irrepressible *Laughing Man with Brawn*. Look out also for Dürer's *Portrait of a Young Man*, whose cheer is of a far subtler nature; the elder Jörg Breu's *Elevation of the Cross*; two works by Maulbertsch, *Scene with a Young Man* and *Christ on the Cross*; and Holbein's interesting *Dormition of the Virgin*. The **Italian collection** is more impressive and contains many stars, such as Raphael's so-called *Eszterházy Madonna* and Titian's *Portrait of the Doge Loredan*. Other first-class portraits include Giorgione's *Self-portrait* and *Young Girl*, and Bronzino's *Young Lady*. The latter was a favourite of late Canadian author Robertson Davies, who would have seen great depths in his allegorical *Venus, Cupid and Jealousy*. Other key players in the Italian dream-team are Tintoretto's *Supper at Emmaus*, Veronese's *The Crucifixion*, Bassano's *The Road to Calvary*, and Tiepolo's *St James Conquers the Moors*.

The **Dutch collection** is dominated by Brueghels. The younger Pieter provides the marvellous *Blind Hurdy-Gurdy Player* and *Affray between Peasants and Soldiers*, whereas the elder Pieter's quite different *St John the Baptist's Sermon* has the preacher addressing a group of Flanders peasants. The elder Jan's *Paradise Landscape* is another major work. Look out also for Rubens' *Mucius Scaevola before Porsenna*, and Sebastien Vrancx's *Outdoor Banquet*. Other exhibits include the **English collection**, which is a let-down, comprising a few mediocre portraits by Hogarth, Reynolds and Gainsborough. There is also some mainly very bad modern art, a selection of historical paintings, and some medieval Italian works. The **collection of antiquities** consists mostly of Greek ceramics that didn't fit in other collections, although there are some decent 5th-century BC Attic red-figure vases.

The museum also holds temporary exhibitions of 20th-century art, usually featuring major artists. The **shop** sells a decent selection of postcards, framed prints, posters, books, ceramics and jewellery. The **café** behind it is a good place to recover from sensory overload afterwards.

City Park (Városliget)

Heroes' Square is the gateway to the City Park, also created as part of the 1896 millenary celebrations. Over 200 halls and pavilions were erected here, displaying the agricultural, industrial and commercial life of the country. A bridge runs from the square over a lake that in winter is transformed into Europe's finest skating-rink, a marvellous scene when floodlit at night. Originally, skaters used the lake's frozen surface, but an artificial surface was added in 1926 that unfortunately uglifies this whole section of the water. The clubhouse down below operates a café and plays host to various events like live music or sporting competitions.

Across the water, hanging like a fairytale mirage, is the picturesque **Vajdahunyad Castle**. It is not an authentic castle but was designed by Ignác Alpár especially for the 1896 celebrations, intended to illustrate in one cohesive building all the different architectural styles found throughout Hungary. Erected as a temporary structure, it was so popular with the public that Alpár rebuilt it in more permanent brick. On the road to the castle is a statue of the architect dressed as a medieval guild-master. The building is arranged in chronological order, most of the sections using details copied from some of Hungary's most significant historic structures, or inspired more loosely by the work of a particular architect whose style reflects his age.

Vajdahunyad Castle
t 343 1345; open Tues–Sun 10–5; closed Mon; adm

To the left of the gate are towers copied from former castles in Upper Hungary, now Slovakia. To the right is a copy of the tower of Segesvár in today's Romania. The courtyard on the left contains the Romanesque wing, including a copy of the still-standing 1214 Benedictine Chapel of Ják in western Hungary. The portal, which is its finest feature, is also the part most true to the original, carrying statues of the 12 apostles. To the left is a chapel incorporating elements from the 11th to the 13th centuries. Opposite, to the right, the palace section mixes elements of the Romanesque and Gothic, while to the left the section based on the 15th-century Transylvanian Vajdahunyad Castle is pure Gothic. This is the finest part and most visible from across the lake. Farther left, Renaissance style is represented by a small building with a balcony based on Sárospatak Castle in eastern Hungary. Next door, the large yellow Baroque section is inspired by details from various 18th-century mansions. This part contains the **Agricultural Museum**, which traces the history of hunting and farming in Hungary, including the development of tools and some interesting varieties of livestock. Facing the entrance is the very popular **statue of Anonymous**, the first Hungarian chronicler, from whom much information about the Middle Ages has reached us. The words on the pedestal are those with which he signed his work, and translate as 'the notary of the most glorious King Béla'. Since there were four kings bearing that name in that era, the chronicler's identity remains a matter of speculation, thus the name Anonymous and the hood which shrouds the figure in wonderfully Gothic mystery. Behind him, a small lake surrounded by boardwalks and willows is a pleasant place for a picnic or a daydream.

Agricultural Museum
open Tues–Sun 10–5; closed Mon; adm

The bulk of the park stretches off to the south and west, encompassing the **Transport Museum** and the **Petőfi Hall**, both of which might hold some interest, especially for kids. The museum explains how transport expanded and flourished around the turn of the 20th century, and features vintage locomotives, scale models of trains, cars and steamboats, and posters and regalia covering a period of 100 years. The Petőfi Hall is a major venue for rock and pop events, as well as an informal youth centre that hosts films, theatre, parties and a roller-skating club for children, a decent weekend flea-market and occasional raves. Behind the building a stairway leads to the **Aviation and Space Flight Exhibition**, with more than 50 vintage aeroplanes on display, plus a new exhibition on space travel which opened in 2011 on the 50th anniversary of Man's first journey into space.

Transport Museum
XIV. Városligeti körút 11, t 273 3840, www.km. iif.hu; open Nov–Mar Tues–Fri 10–4, Sat–Sun 10–5; April–Oct Tues–Fri 10–5, Sat–Sun 10–5; closed Mon; adm

Aviation and Space Flight Exhibition
opening times and adm as for Transport Museum, above

To the north, on the other side of the busy road that bisects the park, stands a grandiose yellow neo-Baroque building containing not an embassy or summer palace but the **Széchenyi Baths**. At the entrance a statue depicts geologist Vilmos Zsigmond, who struck upon the hot spring while drilling a well in 1879. Apparently the water comes from deeper within the Earth's crust than any of the other baths, thus reaching the surface at a higher temperature (74–5°C). Inside the grand entrance hall is a series of mosaics, centred on the central dome, of a quality to rival anything in

✪ Széchenyi Baths
XIV. Állatkerti körút 11, t 321 0310; swimming pool and group thermal healing pool open daily 6am–10pm, earlier closing for other pools and medical and massage services; adm

Budapest, plus an extraordinary fountain. This is one of the nicest of the baths, and certainly the most accessible. Everything is here: indoor pools of different temperatures, steam room, sauna, a heated outdoor pool where bathers play chess on floating boards, a swimming pool and a children's pool with water jets and waves, plus plenty of room for sunbathing, and a restaurant. The masseurs here are recommended. The inside looks like a run-down Victorian sanatorium, though more atmospheric than ugly.

North of the baths, along Állatkerti körút, you'll find from east to west an amusement park, a circus and a zoo. The **amusement park** (Vidámpark) is not likely to impress you or your kids: the rides are old-fashioned and shabby, while the rickety roller-coaster is frightening for the wrong reasons and the ghost train not at all. There are a few newer, scarier rides, and you may find the lack of sophistication endearing. The gilded merry-go-round, dating from the park's opening before the war, is certainly appealing and a reminder of the fact that this was the setting for Ferenc Molnár's play *Liliom*, on which the musical *Carousel* was based. Next door is a funfair for toddlers.

The **Municipal Circus** (Fővárosi Nagycirkusz) next door has been housing shows year-round since it was built in 1971, but there has been a circus on the site since 70 years before that. Acts involving the exploitation of animals are still a feature. A circus festival is held every two years (the next will be held in 2012 and 2014).

Budapest's **Zoo** is an altogether more venerable establishment. Dating back to 1866, an initiative of the Academy of Sciences, it contains, as well as all the usual animals, some important examples of Art Nouveau. The very gateway, covered with fakirs and animals, is a good introduction. The same architect, Kornél Neuschloss-Knüsli, is responsible for the Elephant House, which resembles a large Moorish mosque decorated with majolica and ceramic animals. The Bird House designed by Károly Kós in a National Romantic style allows the birds to fly freely. There are also two greenhouses full of exotic plants and a garden of bonsai trees recently donated by the Japanese ambassador. For all that, it still retains the unpleasant flavour of an old-style zoo in which the comfort of the animals was never the highest priority; but renovations are under way to rectify that and to make it a more child-friendly environment, including special programmes such as snake-petting which are organised daily in summer. All the best animals are found around the big mountain to the right of the main entrance. A baby gorilla and a baby orangutan, both born in 2010, are the current stars of the zoo.

Amusement park
t 343 0996, www. vidampark.hu; check website for opening hours which vary each month; closed Nov–Feb

Municipal Circus
XIV Állatkerti körút 7, t 343 8300, ww.fnc.hu; check tourist office for show times

Budapest Zoo
Állat-és Növénykert, t 343 6075, www.zoobudapest.hu; check website for opening hours, which vary each month

The Old Jewish Quarter

District VII, or Erzsébetváros, is the slice of Budapest's pie south of the Andrássy út area. The old Jewish Quarter covers the innermost part of this district, traditionally located between the two circular roads, with Király to the north and Dohány to the south. From the outset it has been a testament to anti-Semitism, its very foundation dating from the 18th century when Jews were still prohibited from living within the city walls. Ironically, as a 3rd-century AD gravestone inscribed with a menorah proves, there were Jews living here at least six centuries before the Magyar founding fathers arrived. When the city outgrew its walls, new laws prevented Jews from buying property. The second half of the 19th century brought a relaxing of these property laws, leading to a rapid rise in the Jewish population in this quarter. In 1867 Jews gained formal emancipation, partly as a reward for enthusiastic support of Kossuth during the revolution. Jewish rights and assimilation crested towards the end of the century, some even rising to the ranks of nobility or gaining seats in the Chamber of Deputies. By 1939 there were about 200,000 Jews in Budapest, many of them living here in a thriving community that had its own kosher shops, restaurants, places of worship and clubs, while striving to assimilate itself and achieve acceptance in a city where anti-Semitism never really stopped being an issue (Mahler complained about it when he was director of the Opera House).

A community, yes, but the area was never a ghetto until 1944. Before that, the Hungarian government had avoided putting all the Jews in one place for fear that this would encourage the Allied forces to bomb the rest of the city. Such considerations were eventually abandoned when the Nazis and Fascist Arrow Cross walled off the whole area and herded the remaining Jews inside as a prelude to deportation. Since the men had already been taken away to do forced labour, which literally worked them to death, the 70,000 crammed into this small area were mainly women, children and pensioners. Owing to disease, malnutrition, random killings and the cold, many of them never made it through the winter (though they fared better than those outside the city, 90 per cent of whom perished in the Holocaust).

Today the city's remnant of 80,000 still constitutes the largest Jewish community in Central Europe. Despite Communist attempts to homogenize the area and a tendency of younger, wealthier Jews to move to quieter, more attractive districts, a sense of cultural identity has survived, fuelled by a resurgent interest in roots and religion, as well as increased contacts with the inter-national Jewish community. You can get a taste of this spirit by wandering around the shabby, decaying and bullet-pocked streets, but there's little to see apart from the magnificent Great Synagogue on Dohány út, which was one of the two entrances to the ghetto of 1944.

Great Synagogue

Great Synagogue
www.greatsynagogue.
hu; open Mar–Oct
Sun–Thurs 10.30–5.30,
Fri 10.30–3; Nov–Feb
Sun–Thurs 10–3.30, Fri
10.30–1.30; closed
Jewish High Holidays
and Sat; adm; details
of tours of the Jewish
Quarter are available on
the website and from
the tourist office

Situated on the edge of the Jewish Quarter, this enormous building is tucked discreetly up a side road off the Kiskörút so that, despite its size, you won't see it until the last moment. Before even arriving here, the corner building where Dohány utca meets the Kiskörút (No.3a) is worth attention. Its flattened corner holds a relief of a classical couple flanking an angel whose hands they hold, backed by a golden mosaic. Opposite this on the Kiskörút side is a fabulous Gothic building with much decoration, right-angled balconies jutting out point first, a central dome, and four gilded Art Nouveau mosaics across the fourth floor.

These are mere trifles, however, next to the Great Synagogue. Europe's largest synagogue, and the second largest in the world after Temple Emmanuel in New York, it can hold almost 3,000 people and has to be closed in winter because it's too big to heat. In the last decade, $40 million has been spent on its restoration, footed by the Hungarian State and an assortment of Jewish associations in the USA, chief among them the Emmanuel Foundation, fronted by Tony Curtis (né Bernard Schwartz), whose father was a Hungarian emigrant. It was money well spent, for this is truly one of Budapest's most outstanding constructions.

Built in a Romantic style in 1854–9 by Viennese architect Ludwig Förster, it incorporates many obvious Byzantine and particularly Moorish qualities. The patterns in the brickwork were inspired by ancient ruins in the Middle East, while the colours – yellow, red and blue – are representative of the Budapest coat of arms. This reflects other indications that the 19th-century Jews wished to assimilate with rather than distance themselves from their Gentile fellows. The twin towers, for instance, are reminiscent of church steeples, and the presence of an organ (which was played on many occasions by Liszt and Saint-Saëns) is not a very Jewish feature and was opposed by more Orthodox adherents. Its congregation was not and is not strictly Orthodox, espousing also certain Reformist elements in a uniquely Hungarian synthesis called Neolog. Thus the presence of the Ark of the Torah (*bimah*) is at one end rather than central, which is Reformist, but men and women sit separately (men on the ground floor, women in the gallery), which is Orthodox.

The outside of the synagogue avoids the brick-building trap of excessive squareness through its arched colonnade, doors and windows, the latter richly decorated with grilles and surrounds. Star-shaped motifs and curlicues abound, along with ceramic friezes at three levels. Two octagonal towers topped with gold-trimmed onion domes loom above a large rose window, below which a Hebrew inscription from the Book of Exodus reads, 'Make me a sanctuary and I will dwell among them' (25:8). The interior, designed by Vigadó architect Frigyes Feszl, is just as grand and clearly Eastern in its influences. The floor is inset with eight-pointed stars, the balconies surmounted by gilded arches, and the ceiling adorned with arabesques and Stars of David. Outside in the courtyard, a collection of humble headstones marks the mass grave of those 2,281 Jews who died here during that bitter winter of 1944. Part of the brick wall that surrounded the ghetto can still be seen, with a plaque commemorating its liberation by the Soviets on 18 January 1945.

Jewish Museum
open Mar–Oct Sun–Thurs 10.30–5.30, Fri 10.30–3; Nov–Feb Sun–Thurs 10–3.30, Fri 10.30–1.30; closed Jewish High Holidays and Sat; adm

The staircase up to the **Jewish Museum** bears a relief of Tivadar (Theodore) Herzl, the founder of the Zionist movement, who was born and educated here. It seems particularly appropriate that he should hail from a community continually struggling for emancipation within a country that has always faced the same struggle. The museum's foyer contains that highly significant 3rd-century AD gravestone inscribed with a menorah (seven-branched candlestick). The exhibition displays items from Hungary and abroad, mainly from the 18th and 19th centuries but some dating back to the Middle Ages, arranged according to the festival for which they were used. This includes some exquisitely crafted objects and books such as the Chevra book from Nagykanizsa, dating from 1792. The last room documents, through photos, clippings and examples of anti-Semitic propaganda, the nightmare of the Holocaust in Hungary.

Monuments and Memorials

Behind the courtyard is the **Heroes' Temple**, a squat, square building resembling a Moghul tomb, erected in 1931 to pay tribute to the 10,000 Jewish soldiers who died fighting for Hungary during the First World War. Since it is a working synagogue, it is not open to the public. Beyond it, farther down Wesselényi utca, a garden contains Imre Varga's 1991 **Holocaust Memorial**, which channels all that pain and sorrow into the poignant form of a metallic weeping willow in the shape of an inverted menorah. Each leaf bears the name of a family lost in the Holocaust. The broken marble slab in front contains the single word 'Remember'. The inscription from the Talmud on the plaque closer to the railings reads, 'Whose pain can be greater than mine?'

The **garden** is named in honour of Raoul Wallenberg, a Swedish consul who is believed to have saved as many as 20,000 Jews by placing them in safe houses or even rescuing them from Auschwitz-bound trains. The day before the liberating Red Army arrived, he went forward to meet them and was never seen again. After years of silence, a Soviet official announced in 1957 that Wallenberg had died in a Moscow prison 10 years earlier; they had believed him to be a spy. The Hungarian authorities were wary of the case. In April 1949, a sculpture of the hero depicting a male figure struggling with a snake disappeared on the eve of its unveiling and emerged years later, used for a different function, outside a factory in East Hungary. A copy appeared and remains in front of the Radiology Clinic on Üllői út, but was only acknowledged as Wallenberg in 1989. Even in 1987, a statue by Imre Varga (commissioned by the US Ambassador) was shoved miles away on an arterial road in Buda (at the junction of Szilágyi Erzsébet fasor with Nagyajtai utca, four stops on tram 56 from Moszkva tér). So the naming of this garden could be seen as a conscious political act on the part of the Jewish community, who begin their plaque, 'May this park commemorate as an exclamation mark for the post-Holocaust generations the name of the Swedish diplomat Raoul Wallenberg.'

From here, walk down Rumbach to Dob utca and look right. Opposite No.11 is a **memorial to Carl Lutz**, the Swiss diplomat who helped many Jews to survive by issuing them with Swiss or Swedish papers, a ploy later adopted by his colleague Wallenberg. A gold figure attached to the wall seems to be throwing down a sheet to a woman wrapped in bandages lying on the floor below. Locals know it as 'the figure jumping out of a window'. A quote from the Talmud on the easily missed plaque reads, 'He who has saved one life, it's as if he had saved the whole world.'

The 'Ghetto'

At the Dob/Rumbach junction are a few decent Art Nouveau buildings, while at No.11 Rumbach Sebestyén is a **synagogue** of the same name (also known as the 'Status Quo Synagogue'), built for worshippers of a more conservative persuasion. One of the only works in Hungary of the great Viennese architect Otto Wagner, its Moorish façade is similar to that of the Great Synagogue, with many fine features, finally being restored after decades of neglect. Inside, the Moorish theme is continued with arabesque arches, vivid colours and a lofty dome. There is still a lot of work to be done, but the synagogue's congregation has finally been re-established here.

Rumbach Sebestyén Synagogue
open Sun–Thurs 10–4.30, Fri 10–2.30; adm

For a hint of what this neighbourhood once looked like, seek out the amazing **Gozsdu Udvar**, a passageway linking seven courtyards between Dob utca 16 with Király utca 11. Abandoned and crumbling, this series of inelegant but enigmatic concrete squares with a dog-leg in the middle is eerie and atmospheric. Stand in the middle and look back towards the entrance and what you will see is a series of squares alternating light and shade, growing in size with perspective, thus illustrating what the Greeks called 'gnomonic expansion'. These days it is locked at the Király utca end, presumably for safety purposes. Run-down as it is, not much effort is required to imagine how it was at the beginning of the 20th century when this was the bustling heart of Jewish Budapest, filled with shops, artisans and immigrants. As a short building-lover's detour, Síp utca 11 is worth seeing for its Gothic arches, gargoyles and statue of a knight, and the Art Nouveau building on the corner of Síp and Dohány is wonderfully strange.

These days the community's central focus is on Kazinczy utca, a little farther down Dob utca, shortly after Hungary's best kosher *pâtisserie*, **Fröhlich Cukrászda**, whose appearance doesn't live up to its reputation. To the left of Dob utca, some decaying buildings at the Király end of Kazinczy have a certain nostalgic charm, especially No.51. Király utca 34 also has an interesting façade with Art Nouveau influences. The **Orthodox synagogue** is here, its Art Nouveau façade elegantly following the curve of the street. It is a plain building apart from the very top, whose undulating curves could be of Polynesian origin. Below this, amidst Stars of David and leaf patterns, big Hebrew letters read, 'This place is none other than the house of God and the gate to Heaven.' For Gentiles, entrance through the gate is unfortunately not allowed, but it's worth going through the doorway to the right, where a courtyard contains the back of the synagogue and an Orthodox complex including a Jewish school and the kosher Hanna restaurant. The buildings between here and Wesselényi utca are interesting if only for the radically differing architectural approaches they display. Note particularly the Wesselényi side of the corner building, with two giant topless angels spreading their wings. The building opposite is also worth a look, as is Wesselényi 17, which has nice Art Nouveau mosaics. There is also a beautiful Art Nouveau building farther down Dob utca at No.53.

If Kazinczy holds the local focus, the heart of activity is still centred on **Klauzál tér**, a block farther down Dob utca. It was the heart of the 1944–5 ghetto as well, when – as Wallenberg bravely complained to the Germans – 50,000 people were crammed into living space intended for 15,000. Nowadays, it is given over to one big playground, and the scene of so much suffering now echoes with the sound of children's laughter. In 2004, to mark the 60th anniversary of the Hungarian Holocaust, a **Holocaust Memorial Centre** was opened just south of the former Jewish ghetto. Among the exhibits is a memorial wall, which will eventually, it is hoped, features the names of all those who perished – Jews, Roma and other Hungarians.

Holocaust Memorial Centre
IX. Páva utca 39, www. hdke.hu; **t** *455 3333, metro to Ferenc Körút; open Tues–Sat 10–6; adm*

Outside the Centre

The Buda Hills

Forested countryside stretches to the west of Buda, perfect for walking and cycling. There are established trails with signs indicating distance, or duration in minutes (p) and hours (ó). Budapesters like to get back to nature too, so the tranquillity factor is reduced at weekends. Particularly popular, especially with children, are the Children's Railway and the Chairlift, which can be combined with the Cogwheel Railway to form a circuit.

Cogwheel Railway
a couple of stops west of Moszkva tér by bus 22, 56 and 156, or tram 18 and 56; trains leave every 15mins daily 5am–11pm; normal ticket required

The **Cogwheel Railway** starts in the Városmajor Park, opposite the cylindrical Budapest Hotel. The terminus at Széchenyi-hegy is a short walk from the start of the **Children's Railway**. This narrow-gauge railway (760mm) covers 11.1km in about 45mins, mostly through dense woodlands. Built by youth brigades in 1948, it is run by uniformed 10–14-year-olds (except the engineer), giving the whole experience a slightly magical feel. To visit the **Budakeszi Game Park**, alight at Szépjuhászné from the Children's Railway, catch the no.22 bus and ask the driver for the Vadaspark. The entrance is a 15min walk past the Hotel Tanne. Apart from the animals in enclosures (wild boar, deer, etc.), you're likely to see little but butterflies and flowers. It is a beautiful place to wander, however, and usually empty. A wooden lookout tower offers a nice view of the hills, forest and village.

Children's Railway
trains Mon–Fri every hour 8–5, Sat and Sun every 30–45mins 8.45– 5; Sept–May closed alternate Mon; adm

The terminus of the Children's Railway, **Hűvösvölgy**, is a large meadow equally good for tranquil meandering. Buses run from here day and night back to Moszkva tér. It is also worth leaving the Children's Railway at **János-hegy** and following the trail across to the **Chairlift**. From here it is a short but steep walk up to the four-tiered neo-Romanesque **Erzsébet Lookout Tower**, designed by Frigyes Schulek, who built the Matthias Church. On the highest spot in the Buda Hills, it offers superb views. The Chairlift descends 235 metres in its 1km journey, taking about 15mins. Its Hungarian name, Libegő, means 'floater', and this is exactly what it does, about 8 metres above the ground, enough to bother those scared of heights and excite children who relish gentle doses of danger. Bus 158 runs from Zugliget at the bottom back to Moszkva tér.

Chairlift
runs May–Sept 9.30–5; Oct–April 9.30–4, closed alternate Mon; adm

Caves in the Buda Hills

Since Buda's caves were created by the action of hot thermal waters from below rather than cold rainwater from above, their appearance is unique, consisting of strangely beautiful rock sculptures. The two that are open to visitors are in the Buda Hills not far from Óbuda. They are reached from **Kolosy tér** (itself reached by bus 86 from Batthyány tér, M2 or Flórián tér in Óbuda, or bus 6 from Nyugati station, M3).

Pál-Völgyi

II. Szépvölgyi utca 162, t 388 9537; open Tues–Sun 10–4; bus 65 from Kolosy tér

The larger and more impressive is **Pál-Völgyi**. This is the longest labyrinth discovered in the Buda Hills. The 30-minute tour involves narrow passages, steep climbs and some 600 steps. The stalagmites and stalactites are awesome, and many formations protruding from the rock face resemble animals.

Szemlő-hegy Cave

II. Pusztaszeri utca 35, t 315 8849; open Wed–Fri 9–3, Sat–Sun 9–4, closed Tues; adm; bus 29 from Kolosy tér

About a 10-minute walk away is the **Szemlő-hegy Cave**. Not as big, impressive or convoluted, this system is maybe more striking. Instead of stalactites the walls are covered with bulbous, cauliflower-like mineral formations called 'cave pearls'. The air is so clean and pure that the lowest level (not on the 25min tour) contains a therapy centre for respiratory illnesses. A small museum displays cave finds from all over Hungary.

Béla Bartók Memorial House (Bartók Béla Emlékház)

Béla Bartók Memorial House

II. Csalán utca 29; t 394 2100, www.bartok museum.hu; open Tues–Sun 10–5; closed Mon; adm; bus 5 from Moszkva tér

Set in beautiful grounds, this Art Nouveau villa was Bartók's last Hungarian home before he left in disgust at the country's increasing Fascism. The concert hall, often used for chamber concerts on Fridays, features the painted wooden panels of a 1740 church, plus artworks and portraits. His study, personal objects and folklore collection are all displayed, along with the Edison phonograph he used for collecting old folk tunes.

Ludwig Museum of Contemporary Art (Kortárs Müvészeti)

Ludwig Museum of Contemporary Art

t 555 3444, www. ludwigmuseum.hu; open Tues–Sun 10–8; closed Mon; adm

Way south on the Pest embankment by Lágymányosi Bridge is the unlikely site for the Millenium City, planned to emulate London's South Bank. Recently constructed are the National Theatre, and the Palace of Culture (Művészetek Palotája), home to the National Philharmonic Orchestra and the Ludwig Museum of Contemporary Art. Much of the stuff here is really modern, so much so that no accepted views of what to think of it have yet been laid down. The core of the collection was donated by the German billionaire and art patron Peter Ludwig, who is reputed to have bought at least one painting every day, largely according to his own enthusiasm rather than for investment purposes. Here you will find works of famous 1960s and '70s pop-artists such as Warhol, Lichtenstein, Rauschenberg, Hockney, Jasper Johns and Claes Oldenburg, as well as some lesser-known Europeans and even the odd Hungarian such as Miklós Erdély (*War Secrets*).

Cemeteries

Kerepesi Cemetery

next to Keleti station (M2)

Kerepesi Cemetery was declared a 'decorative' cemetery in 1885, meaning it is where the establishment of each age buried those it chose to honour, be they poets, politicians, artists, architects or war heroes. It thus provides an interesting perspective from which to view Hungary's turbulent recent history. All the big names are here, often easily reached by the wide avenues that criss-cross the vast, orderly area. The main mausoleums, at key junctions, are those of Kossuth (by Alajos Stróbl), Batthyány and Deák, but look out also for the particularly beautiful tomb of popular singer Lujza Blaha.

Farkasréti Cemetery *tram 59 from Moszkva tér*

Farkasréti Cemetery on Németvölgyi utca in the Buda Hills is mainly visited for the extraordinary Mortuary Chapel built by Imre Makovecz, situated just to the right of the main entrance. A prime example of his 'organic architecture', the whole wooden structure resembles a giant oesophagus of some exotic creature. Another delightful spot for a stroll, the cemetery is overcrowded with graves and trees, and contains a rich and varied assortment of tombstones, some of them bearing famous names. Béla Bartók is buried here, with Georg Solti alongside him. Visit the information building to the left of the main gate for a map showing the locations of the cemetery's inmates.

Újköztemető Cemetery *Kozma utca 8–10; tram 28 or 37*

One grave in particular attracts people – almost exclusively Hungarians – to the other major burial ground, **Újköztemető Cemetery**, way out at the edge of District X. It is here that Imre Nagy was secretly buried in 1958, along with other key figures from the 1956 Uprising, and a large number of civilians dumped in a mass grave. After the ceremonial funeral of 1989 in Heroes' Square, they were reburied in the same plot (301), which is right in the farthest corner, about 30 minutes' walk from the main gate – not far enough to stop Hungarians from secretly placing flowers on the anonymous grave before 1989, which were duly removed by Soviet policemen. At the beginning of one of the paths leading into plot 300, which contains the mass graves, is a Transylvanian Gate inscribed with the words, 'Only a Hungarian soul may pass through this gate.' In the middle of the plot stands a wooden campanile, a type of decoration traditionally found in old Hungarian cemeteries, in front of panels listing the names of over 400 victims of the Uprising. Adjacent to Nagy's simple grave is György Jovánovics' *Monument to the Martyrs of the 1956 Revolution*, which could be seen as a 'deconstructed' early Christian basilica or as a symbolic passage through Purgatory.

Statue Park *XXII. Balatoni út, t 227 7446, www.szoborpark. hu; take Volán bus nos.710, 720, 721, or 722 from Volanbusz bus station (behind Kelenfoldi pu train station), get off after 15mins at 'Memento Park' stop (Volán buses not included on Budapest Card); or take a direct bus from Deák tér, 4,500Ft incl. park entrance or 3,500Ft with Budapest Card: leaves daily 11am, July and Aug also 3pm; open daily 10–dusk; adm*

Alongside this cemetery lies Hungary's largest **Jewish burial ground**. There are many grand tombs here, but the most striking, not far from the entrance, to the right of the main path, is that of the Schmidel family designed by Ödön Lechner and Béla Lajta. A central mosaic in green and gold tiles, representing the Tree of Life, is surrounded by flamboyant turquoise ceramics and floral motifs.

Statue Park (Szoborpark)

After the fall of Communism in 1989, instead of destroying all those Socialist monuments, the Hungarians consigned them to a kind of retirement home on the edge of the city, far from impressionable young eyes and tormented older eyes, but close enough so that Hungarians can visit them and jeer, laugh or curse in catharsis. It's also a pretty unique tourist attraction. Here you will find all the old favourites like Marx, Lenin and Engels, plus idealized happy workers, victorious soldiers and martyrs galore. Many of them are frighteningly massive, like the Red Army soldier that stood at the foot of the Liberty Statue on Gellért Hill. Aesthetically most interesting are Imre Varga's statue of Béla Kún, and the giant charging sailor based on a 1919 call-to-arms poster. Each of the 43 monuments represents a facet of Hungarian history. You're given most of the information you need with the ticket, but for those with a special interest the guide book is a worthy investment. The half-hearted should be warned, however, that it's a long way to go and many people find the site small.

(i) **Budapest >**
TOURINFORM:
V. Süto u. 2 (Deák tér),
t (01) 438 8080, suto@
budapestinfo.hu;
open 8–8
I. Szentháromság tér
(Castle Hill),
t (01) 488 0475,
open daily 10–6
VI. Liszt Ferenc tér
9–11, t (01) 322 4098,
open daily 10–6
www.budapestinfo.hu

Ferihegy Airport
Terminal 1, t 438 8080,
ferihegy1@
budapestinfo.hu;
open daily 8am–1pm
Terminal 2A, arrivals,
t 438 8080,
ferihegy2a@
budapestinfo.hu;
open daily 8am–11pm
Terminal 2B, arrivals,
t 438 8080,
ferihegy2b@
budapestinfo.hu;
open daily 8am–10pm

Hungarian National
Tourist Office:
II. Margit körút 85,
t (01) 355 1133,
www.hungary
tourism.hu

Tourist Information in Budapest

TOURINFORM, *www.hungary tourism.hu*, is the very helpful state-run tourist office. It can be found at several addresses throughout the city, and there are also information booths in each terminal at the airport.

If you want information about trips outside the city, you will need to contact the **Hungarian National Tourist Office**.

TOURINFORM run **a 24-hour information line, t** 438 8080, or t +36 30 30 30 600 from abroad; *hungary@tourinform.hu*.

Budapest Card

The Budapest Card, *www.budapest-card.hu*, costs 6,300Ft (2 days) or 7,500Ft (3 days). It covers unlimited free use of public transport, free or discounted entry to most sights, and discounts in many shops, spas, etc. Nonetheless, you would need to pack in a lot of sightseeing and travelling to make it a good deal. Children under 14 accompanied by the card-holder receive the same benefits. The card is available from big metro stations, TOURINFORM offices, travel agencies and hotels.

There is also a **Hungary Card**, *www.hungarycard.hu*, 4,500Ft, which is only useful if you plan to explore extensively outside the city.

Guided Tours

By Boat
Legenda, t (01) 266 4190, *www.legenda.hu*. City cruises, including hour-long sightseeing ones along the Danube and candle-lit dinner cruises, from the dock at Vigado tér.

Mahart, t (01) 484 4013, *www.mahartpassnave.hu*, run several sightseeing tours daily from the dock at Vigadó tér. These include 1hr sightseeing cruises (*April–Oct*) with audio commentary in several languages, and evening cruises with a three-course dinner and gypsy music and dancing (*weekends in April; daily May–Sept; Sat only Oct–mid-Dec*).

RiverRide, t (01) 332 2555, *www.riverride.com*. An amphibian bus that plunges into the river, this comes with an audio commentary (if you can hear it above the squeals). Departures from Roosevelt tér.

By Bus
Budatours, t (01) 374 7070, reservations **t** (01) 353 0558, *www.budatours.hu, www.citytour.hu*, run a range of bus tours, including the hop-on, hop-off City Tour. They also run a hop-on, hop-off boat cruise along the Danube. You can get a 24-hour pass which allows you to combine the bus and boat options. They also offer special interest tours, including an opera tour and a Jewish Budapest tour.

IBUSZ, t (01) 485 2700. Organize 'live' English tours from Erzsébet tér at 10.30am year-round and 3pm May–Sept, as well as lots of other tours.

By Car/Trabant/Barkas

Cityrama, t (01) 302 4382, *www. cityrama.hu,* run a whole host of different tours, including a Communist Tour either in a Trabant, or a Barkas van (the Hungarian answer to a VW), plus combined walking/car tours of the city centre, cruises and concert tours.

Rent a Trabant, t 309 890 531 (mobile), *www.rentatrabantbudapest. com.* Tours in a classic Trabant, plus rental if you fancy driving one yourself.

On Foot

Absolute Walking Tours, *www. absolutetours.com,* host tours in English daily. Themes include Absolute Budapest, Communist Budapest and even a pub crawl tour. Private tours can be arranged, and it is easy to book online.

Jewish Heritage walking tours, *www.greatsynagogue.hu,* start at the Great Synagogue every day but Sat. At the end there is a chance to taste traditional non-kosher Central European Jewish food (except Sun).

Pál Street Tours, t 06 20 9335 240 (**t** 0036 20 9335 240 from outside Hungary), *www.palstreettours.com,* offer guided tours to small groups. They also provide audioguides for self-guided tours (two can be downloaded for free on its website).

Services in Budapest

Internet Cafés and WiFI

Most hotels and guesthouses now offer WiFi (curiously, the most luxurious hotels tend to charge a steep daily fee, while moderate and budget establishments offer it for free) and a few have computer terminals available to guests.

For those travelling with laptops and smartphones, there's a full list of WiFi hot spots around the city at *www.hotspotter.hu.*

Fougou, VII. Wesselenyi utca 57, **t** (01) 787 4888. Internet café and call centre, with printing and photocopying services. *Open 7am–2am.*

Yellow Zebra, VI. Lázár utca 2, **t** (01) 269 8843, *www.yellowzebra bikes.com.* The bike rental company has a sideline in offering internet access, and also provides printing, copying and fax facilities, but it doesn't offer coffee. Handily located near the opera house.

Post Offices

The main post office (*posta*) is at Petőfi Sándor utca 13, *open Mon–Fri 8–8,* near Deák tér.

There are also post offices at Keleti and Nyugati stations, *open Mon–Sat 7–7.*

Emergencies and Medical

Police: t 107 or **t** 112.

Tourist police: V. Vigadó utca 6, **t** (01) 438 8080.

Ambulance: t 104.

Fire: t 105.

Hospitals with 24-hour emergency departments include:

FirstMed Centers, I. Hattyú utca 14, **t** 224 9090; *www.firstmedcenters.com.* A private clinic.

Bethesda Gyermekkórház (Children's Hospital), XIV. Bethesda utca, **t** 364 9020, *www.bethesda.hu.* Children's hospital, with an emergency department.

MÁV Kórház, VI. Rippl-Rónai utca 37, **t** 475 1800. General hospital, with emergency room.

SOS Dental Services, VI. Király utca 14, **t** 269 6010, *www.nonstopdentist.com.* 24-hour emergency dentistry.

A notice on the door of **pharmacies** indicates the address of the closest 24hr pharmacy. Those with a permanent 24-hour service include the following:

Teréz Patika, VI. Teréz korút 41, **t** (01) 311 4439.

Déli Gyógyszertár XII. Alkotás utca 1b, **t** (01) 355 4691.

Elefánt Gyógyszertár, X. Pongrácz út 1a, **t** (01) 431 9940.

Festivals in Budapest

An asterisk denotes a public holiday when shops and businesses are closed. *See also* 'National Holidays', p.209.

6 Jan–Ash Wed: *Farsang*. Celebrates the end of winter and fattening up before the fasting of Lent. Open-air music, carnivals and balls, culminating in a fancy-dress parade.

15 Mar: *Revolution Day. Commemorates Petőfi's recital of his National Song outside the National Museum in 1848. Events there and around his statue in Március 15 tér.

Late Mar/early April: Budapest Spring Festival. The major annual arts event. Classical music, opera, jazz and folk; dance, including folk dance; painting and sculpture; theatre and cinema, often subtitled in English. Information at *www.fesztivalvaros.hu*.

Easter: Mainly passes off quietly with church processions and egg painting. Arts and crafts fairs, e.g. in the Ethnography Museum; free performances of Bach's St John Passion in the Lutheran Church. *Easter Monday is a rowdy drunken occasion, when men douse women in cheap perfume in exchange for shots of *pálinka*. It can start as early as 6am, gets ugly by about 10am, and by the afternoon it is better to be off the streets.

1 May: *Labour Day. No longer involving compulsory homage to Communist bigwigs, this is still a big event organized by trade unions in the parks, especially City Park.

Nearest weekend to 21 June: World Music Day. Most venues participate in this French innovation, and stages are set up in open places.

30 June: *Budapesti Bucsú*. A celebration of the withdrawal of Soviet troops in 1991. Music, theatre and dance in squares and parks.

One weekend in Aug: Hungarian Grand Prix (at Hungaroring). A major event; all the hotels are full and jack up their prices, restaurants are often fully booked, and every bar and café sets up its TV or screen. Check dates in advance.

Mid-Aug: Sziget Festival. One of Europe's biggest rock and pop festivals, transforming Óbuda Island into a giant open-air party with big-name international acts, beer tents, rave-marquees and every type of music, plus dance, theatre, films, etcetera.

Budafest. Opera and ballet festival in the State Opera House. Information at *www.sziget.hu*.

Mid-Aug: Budapest Folk Arts Festival. Held in Buda castle, with traditional singing and dancing and displays of historic crafts and skils.

20 Aug: *St Stephen's Day. Rites at the Basilica, craft fair and folk dancing in Castle Hill, and the procession through the streets with the Holy Right Hand leads up to a firework display from the Citadella.

Sept: Budapest international Film Festival. A new event beginning 2012 highlighting the best Hungarian and international cinema.

Early Sept: Budapest Wine Festival.

Mid–late Sept: Budapest International Music Competition, Budapest Jazz Festival and Museum Festival.

Late Sept: European Heritage Days. Public buildings open up for a weekend.

Late Sept–mid-Oct: Budapest Autumn Festival. Like the Spring Festival but more contemporary arts.

Late Sept–Oct: Budapest Music Weeks. The classical music season kicks off as close to the anniversary of Bartók's death as possible (25 Sept), with events at venues across the city.

Around 1 Oct: Budapest Marathon and Running Festival.

23 Oct: *Remembrance Day. Commemorates the 1956 Uprising. Wreath-laying at Imre Nagy's statue, at his grave in the New Cemetery, and in Kossuth tér.

1 Nov: All Souls' Day. Make an evening trip to the cemeteries, which stay open late for people to light candles to their departed.

6 Dec: *Mikulás*. The night before, children put cleaned shoes out on the windowsill, expecting the national Santa Claus to fill them. If they've been bad, Krampusz the bogeyman might turn up instead.

Shopping in Budapest

Like most formerly Communist cities, Budapest has gone consumer-mad, opening its doors to all the major brand names from the West, and embarking on a passionate love affair with shopping malls, the bigger the better. The best are the **West End Mall** behind Nyugati station and the **Budapest Europeum**, which opened in 2011 on Blaha Lujza tér. High-street fashions are still a few steps behind but a number of talented young native designers are producing original, quality garments. Visit the monthly **WAMP** market to see the best in contemporary Hungarian fashion and design (details of venue at *www.wamp.hu*).

WAMP market

Getting clothes made is an affordable option, and trawling the second-hand shops and flea markets for a quirky retro bargain can be fun. The specialist local products most suitable as gifts include folk art (although much of it is mass-produced), hand-made porcelain and ceramics from the world-famous factories of Herend and Zsolnay.

Budapest excels in the range and quality of art and artefacts. A staggering quantity of galleries carry works from Hungary's past, as well as showcasing the talents of today's artistic community. The many antique shops around **V. Falk Miksa utca** and the southern end of **Váci utca** will let you know what you are legally entitled to take from the country. For real bargains, junk and kitsch head to a flea market and haggle. The best window-shopping is on **Váci utca** and its many side streets and courtyards, the north end over-flowing with souvenirs, folk art and Western clothes shops, the south lined with antiques, jewellers, boutiques and cafés.

Department Stores and Malls

Budapest Europeum, VIII. József körút 5. Designer fashion, international chains like H&M. Opened in 2011.

Mammut, II. Széna tér, **t** (01) 345 8020. Mammoth indeed, with two giant wings, one with designer label outlets, the other holding onto older names. Huge food store in the basement.

West End City Center, VI. Váci út 1–3. A giant postmodern mall next to Nyugati station, with a large food court, all the major designer stores, bars and cafés.

Flea Markets

These can be great fun, though you'll have to turn up early to get the bargains among the junk: things that haven't yet come back into fashion in Budapest or kitsch memorabilia. Even the inflated tourist prices can be extremely low, though haggling is essential. Decide on your maximum, start haggling at a third or half of what you're willing to pay, and don't ask the price unless you're willing to buy.

Ecseri Piac, XIX. Nagykőrösi út 156 (bus 54 from Boráros tér). The biggest and best flea market. In a vast lot in an industrial area: follow the crowds, or ask the bus driver. Cross the pedestrian overpass when you get off the bus. *Mon–Sat 8–4.*

Gouba, Gozsdu Udvar, entrances at VII. Király utca 13 and VII. Dob utca 16, *www.gouba.hu*. Atmospheric Sunday bazaar held at the beautifully restored Gozsdu courtyard in the Jewish Quarter, with local crafts and food stalls. *Sundays from spring to summer, 10am–7pm.*

Józsefvárosi Piac, VII. Kőbányai út 21–3 (tram 28 or 37). There are no used goods or antiques here, just regular goods, such as clothes, of dubious provenance. It's known locally as the Chinese market: most of the phoney brand-name goods were probably made there. There are bargains to be found, but be careful of pick-pockets and of being cheated. *Daily 6–4.*

Városligeti Bolhapiac, in the Petőfi Csarnok in City Park (Széchenyi fürdő, M1). A Hungarian garage sale full of old books, records, toys and Communist relics. *Sat and Sun 7–2.*

Folklore and Souvenirs

Anna Antikvitás, V. Falk Miksa utca 18–20. Good selection of beautiful embroidered linens.

Folkart Centrum, V. Váci utca 14, *www.folkartcentrum.hu*. The first stop for all kinds of Hungarian souvenirs.

Great Market Hall, entrance on Fővám tér, near Kálvin tér. Colourful costumes and linens: first floor.

Herend Porcelain, V. József Attila utca 7, t (01) 317 2622, *www.herend.com*. Hungary's finest porcelain since 1826.

Manier, V. Váci utca 68. Gorgeous, theatrical and original women's clothes and accessories in this jewel-box of a store. Styles range from the eminently wearable to full-on diva.

Zsolnay Porcelain, V. Kigyó utca 4, t (01) 318 3712. Bolder, more modern styles than Herend, but equally respected.

Where to Stay in Budapest

Budapest t (01) –

Private rooms and apartments represent a growing business in Budapest, and offer better value than hotels. Rooms often have a bath and kitchen shared with other guests or with the owner. The apartments are self-contained and can be very nice, if small. Good website-based accommodation agencies include *www.apartmentsapart.com*, *www.budapestapartments.org*, and *www.flatinbudapest.com*.

Breakfast-lovers will be horrified to learn that the morning meal doesn't really fit into the Hungarian scheme of things. Few places bother with it at all.

Buda

*****Budapest Hilton, I. Hess András tér 1–3, t 889 6600, *www.hilton.com* (€€€€). Luxury in the heart of the Castle district. Described by the Hilton president as the most beautiful pearl in the whole string, the modern building incorporates medieval remains, its wings linked by corridors running through a Gothic church tower. *Várbusz from Moszkva tér (M2)*.

art'otel >

****art'otel, I. Bem rakpart 16–19, t 487 9487, *www.artotels.com* (€€€€). This well-located boutique hotel is refreshingly innovative, with a stylish, modern interior and an enormous collection of works by US artist Donald Sultan. The west wing consists of four renovated Baroque houses on Fő utca, whose high vaulted ceilings and old doors retain a genuine sense of history. The rooms are a good size and very attractive, with nice bathrooms. Those on the west side have views of the Matthias Church. Parking and sauna. *Batthyány tér (M2)*.

****Racz Hotel & Thermal Spa, I Hadnagy utca 8–10, t 266 0666, *www.raczhotel.com* (€€€€). Part of the 'Leading Small Hotels of the World' group, this offers opulent rooms and state-of-the-art amenities. The complex contains the famous Turkish baths of the Racz complex.

****Danubius Hotel Gellért, XI. Gellért tér 1, t 889 5501, *www.danubiushotels.com* (€€€). A sumptuous and historic Art Nouveau building, as much tourist attraction and thermal bath as hotel; old-fashioned rooms of a good size, with decent bathrooms and large windows, though renovation is long overdue. First-floor rooms have balconies. Baths are free to guests, a major bonus. *Tram 47 and 49 from Deák tér.*

****Buda Castle Fashion Hotel, I. Úri utca 39, t 224 8100, *www.budacastlehotelboutique.hu* (€€). This modern hotel tucked within a 15th-century shell is a good option for a romantic weekend, with a perfect location near the castle, and bright, contemporary rooms overlooking a courtyard,. Buffet breakfast included. There's no restaurant, but several are within easy walking distance. *Várbusz from Moszkva tér (M2)*.

****Danubius Grand Hotel, XIII. Margitsziget, t 329 2300, *www.danubiushotels.com* (€€). Situated at the northern end of Margaret Island, this mansion-like building and its 19th-century period furnishings offer the comfort and grandeur of a bygone age. Rooms are decorated in fine taste, and those on the park side have balconies. You can take the waters for free in the attractive bathing complex of the Thermal Hotel, reached by an underground tunnel. *Bus 26 from Nyugati station.*

****Hotel Regnum Residenz,
Ganz utca 8, t 265 5090, *www.
regnumresidenz.com* (€€). A modern,
elegant hotel, which opened in 2010,
this offers spacious rooms and suites
some of which have balconies.
Thoughtful details include tea- and
coffee-making facilities, and
reasonably priced parking. Good
central location, with easy access to
public transport. *Batthyány tér (M2).*

⭐ Uhu Panzió > Uhu Panzió, II. Keselyű utca 1a, t 394
3876, *www.uhuvilla.hu* (€€). Hard work
to get to, but this lovely turn-of-the-
century villa is situated in a quiet
⭐ Gresham Palace >> forested valley in the Buda Hills. A
dozen simple but tasteful rooms, a
small pool and sauna, and a lovely
flower garden with views. 10pm
curfew. There's a fabulous restaurant
too. *Tram 56 from Moszkva tér (M2)
and a 1km walk, mostly uphill.*

***Victoria, I. Bem Rakpart 11, t 457
8080, *www.victoria.hu* (€€). Simple,
tastefully decorated rooms with big
beds. Front rooms offer river views,
while garden rooms have nice patios.
Buffet breakfast. Polite and friendly
English-speaking staff. *Bus 86 from
Batthyány tér (M2), or walk.*

⭐ Abel Panzió > Ábel Panzió, XI. Ábel Jenő utca 9,
t 209 2537, *www.abelpanzio.hu* (€). A
beautiful ivy-covered villa set on a
quiet street away from the centre.
⭐ Palazzo Zichy >> The common areas are exquisitely
decorated with antique furniture and
the owner's fabulous paintings; the
veranda overlooks a tree-filled garden.
Highly recommended. Breakfast
included. *Tram 61 from Moszkva tér
(M2) or Móricz Zsigmond Körtér.*

Beatrix Panzió Hotel, II. Széher utca 3,
t 394 3730, *www.beatrixhotel.hu* (€).
This friendly B&B has good-sized
rooms with decent bathrooms. Lovely
front garden with terraces and pond.
Apartments also available. Sauna,
safes, and a helpful owner with good
English. *Bus or tram 56 from Moszkva
tér (M2), then 200m walk.*

Helios Panzió, XII. Lidérc utca 5a,
t 246 4658, *www.heliospanzio.hu* (€).
Traditionally decorated rooms, some
with balconies. Excellent views. Big,
beautiful garden at back, and a
terrace at the front. Apartments also
available. Parking, and helpful staff.
Bus 8 from Ferenciek tere (M3).

Central Pest

*****Kempinski Hotel Corvinus,
V. Erzsébet tér 7–8, t 429 3777, *www.
kempinski-budapest.com* (€€€€). A
postmodern extravaganza: glass,
granite and steel put together with
taste and imagination. The interior is
equally well executed. The rooms are
nicer and larger than most, with many
distinctive touches, and the best
bathrooms in town. Facilities include
parking, pool, and a luxury spa. Its
Corvinus restaurant is one of
Budapest's finest.

*****Gresham Palace, V. Roosevelt tér
5–6, t 268 6000, *ww.fourseasons.com*
(€€€€). Spacious and stylish, a Four
Seasons hotel decked out in marble,
granite and polished wood, the rooms
in this handsomely restored historic
gem adhere to its exquisite Art
Nouveau mood (*see* p.254) and
breathtaking grandeur.

*****Sofitel Atrium, V. Roosevelt tér 2,
t 266 1234, *www.sofitel.com* (€€€€).
The exterior may be ugly, but the
Sofitel's inside really is an atrium: a
glass-roofed courtyard with palm
trees, plants hanging from the balconies, and a glider plane suspended
in mid-air. Even the lift is beautiful.
The rooms are decent enough, but
you'll be drawn back to the lobby.

****Palazzo Zichy, VIII. Lorinc pap tér
2, t 235 4000, *www.hotel-palazzo-
zichy.com* (€€€). A sumptuous 19th-
century mansion has been converted
into the city's most fashionable hotel.
Sleek contemporary design contrasts
with original details, including
ravishing stuccowork. But it's not the
design or the amenities which make
this hotel stand out: it's the truly
excellent service. They even provide a
pre-arrival concierge service, ensuring
that spa visits, concerts and
restaurants are booked even before
you check in.

***City Panzió Mátyás, V. Március 15
tér 8, t 338 4711; City Panzió Pilvax, V.
Pilvax köz 1–3, t 266 7660; City Panzió
Ring, V. Szent István körút 22, t 340
5450. All *www.taverna.hu* and (€€).
This small chain of hotels offers
modern, clean no-nonsense rooms
with no real personality but handy
locations. The Mátyás is best for both
location and exterior.

Gerlóczy Rooms de Lux, V. Gerloczy utca 1, **t** 510 4000, *www.gerloczy.hu* (€€). A very charming little hotel, with chic individually decorated rooms and friendly staff. The food in the café below is a little hit-and-miss, and the buffet breakfast costs a hefty €12, but it's well located for all the main sites and some rooms look out over a delightful square.

Kálvin Ház, IX. Gönczy Pál utca 6, **t** 216 4365, *www.kalvinhouse.hu* (€). Simple, white, huge rooms with high ceilings and wooden floors in a handsome building nicely located near the National Museum and Market Hall. TVs and bathtubs. Breakfast included. Great value.

Peregrinus Elte Hotel, V. Szerb utca 3, **t** 266 4911 (€). Small gem of a hotel in a quiet but central location. Good-sized plain rooms with high ceilings. Good value.

Around Andrássy Út

*****Mamaison Andrássy Hotel, VI. Andrássy út. 111, **t** 462 2100, *www.andrassyhotel.com* (€€€€). Part of the 'Small Luxury Hotel' group. Attractive Bauhaus building with a striking, chic interior, but certainly overpriced (although amazing deals can be found on the website). Deluxe rooms are bigger, with balconies.

*****K & K Hotel Opera, VI. Révay utca 24, **t** 269 0222, *www.kkhotels.com* (€€€). This large chain-hotel feels smaller and more friendly than most, thanks to its bright, upbeat décor. Rooms are modern and tastefully furnished with big windows. Health club, sauna and buffet breakfast.

★ **New York Palace >>**

****Bohem Art Hotel, IX. Molnar utca 24, **t** 269 0222, *www.bohemart hotel.com* (€€€). A hip hotel in a handsome 19th-century building, this is designed, furnished and decorated by local artists. Check out the website for deals: rack rates are a tad high.

★ **Kapital Inn >**

Kapital Inn, VI. Aradi utca 19, **t** 915 2029 (€€). You'll need to book well in advance to grab one of the four rooms (two share a bathroom) at the city's most sought-after B&B. Exquisitely furnished, charmingly staffed, and centrally located.

****Hotel Liget, VI. Dózsa György utca 106, **t** 269 5300, *www.liget.hu* (€€).

Situated near Heroes' Square (*M1*), this building is a mish-mash of shapes, colours and textures. The lobby is bright and shiny, centred on a long, curving bar. Rooms are small but agreeable. Well run with professional staff. Breakfast included.

***Hotel Pest, VI. Paulay Ede utca 3, **t** 343 1198, *www.hotelpest.hu* (€€). Plain outside, but a wonderful classical building inside, with a pleasant courtyard. Rooms are simple with big windows. Buffet breakfast included. A great budget option.

***Radio Inn, VI. Benczúr utca 19, **t** 342 8347 (€). Close to Kodály körönd (*M1*), the institutional and dated feel of this large hotel is made up for by the huge apartments with big windows, separate toilets and bathrooms, and small kitchens. At the back are gardens surrounded by trees.

Elsewhere in Pest

*****Corinthia Hotel (formerly Grand Royal), VII. Erzsébet körút 43–9, **t** 479 4000, *www. corinthiahotels.com* (€€€€). The views as you enter this magnificent, beautifully restored, palace from 1896 are breathtaking: an atrium courtyard crossed by a glass bridge with perspective-hugging staircases and gorgeous chandeliers. A vast labyrinth, it boasts five restaurants and more than 400 rooms, which are plush and comfortable.

*****New York Palace, VI. Erzsébet körút 9–11, **t** 8866 111, *www.boscolo hotels.com* (€€€€). This is located in a stunning 19th-century building which once housed the legendary pre-war New York Café (now restored, *see* p.303). The magnificent original details have been preserved, but the chic 21st-century luxuries include a spa and wellness centre with indoor pool. *Near Blaha Lujza tér metro (M2)*.

*****Adina Apartment Hotel, XIII. Hegedus Gyula utca 52–4, **t** 236 8888, *www. adina.eu.com* (€€€). These spacious flats come with a bedroom, lounge, kitchen and bathroom, with all the accessories you could want: indoor pool, Jacuzzi, sauna, steam room, gym, in-house masseur, laundry facilities, car park, and terrace. *A 5min walk from Lehel tér (M3)*.

****Hotel Ambra**, VII. Kis Diófa utca 13, t 321 1533, *www.hotelambra.hu* (€€). A large, modern hotel, with spacious rooms and apartments decorated in pastel shades. Buffet breakfast. It doesn't ooze charm, but it's clean, functional and prices are very reasonable. *Metro to Opera (M1)*.

***Corvin Hotel**, IX. Angyal utca 31, t 218 6566, *www.corvinhotel budapest.hu* (€€). In a building with lots of character, this modern little hotel has small but clean, pleasant rooms, five apartments, a car park, a good restaurant and a big, attractive garden at the back. *Close to Ferenc körút (M3)*.

***Ibis Centrum**, IX. Ráday utca 6, t 456 4100, *www.ibis-centrum.hu* (€€). This pleasant, professional hotel gives value for money. Rooms are modern, clean, simple and quiet. Windows are a bit small, and bathrooms are small with showers but no tub. Three no-smoking floors. There's an open-air 'garden' on the first floor.

***Sissi Hotel**, IX. Angyal utca 33, t 215 0082, *www.hotelsissi.hu* (€€). A good value, old-fashioned little hotel in an eclectic building with a terraced façade. The decor is dated, but the rooms are immaculate. There's a garden too.

***Unio Hotel**, VII. Dob utca 73, t 479 0400, *www.uniohotel.hu* (€€). Very spacious rooms with high ceilings, big windows, and wood furnishings. Good value. *Walk from Oktogon (M1), or tram 4 or 6*.

Marco Polo Hostel, VII. Nyár utca 6, t 413 2555, *www.marcopolohostel.com* (€). An attractive building, with a courtyard and cavernous cellar bar-restaurant that has TV, pool tables, computers, and live music. Shared bath and kitchenette. *Free bus service from Keleti station. Astoria is the nearest metro (M2)*.

Eating Out in Budapest

Budapest t (01) –

In Budapest, there is often a fine line between a restaurant, café and bar, so see the Cafés and Bars categories (below) for more options. Restaurants in expensive hotels are almost always excellent, and only mentioned here if exceptional.

Traditionally, culinary class barriers have not existed, so menus in the cheapest and most expensive restaurants can be virtually identical. The food in the more expensive place will normally be superior, as will the surroundings, but the greatest difference will be in the service. However, you can generally expect even the cheapest place to have a menu in English and a waiter who knows enough English to take your order. Check to see if service is included: that the menu says it won't be doesn't mean a thing. And check the price of drinks.

In bars and some restaurants, wine, juices and soft drinks are often sold by the *deci*, which is a tenth of a litre (100ml). A glass of wine usually costs twice the number on the menu, which is the cost per *deci*.

Buda: Castle Hill

Alabárdos, I. Országház utca 2, t 356 0851, *www.alabardos.hu* (€€€€). In a 15th-century Gothic building, this feels like a banquet hall, with paintings of knights, swords and shields. Specialities of ancient Hungarian cuisine are put together with an expertise that explains the prices. The service is impeccable, the selection of drinks vast. *Closed Sun*.

Arany Kaviar, I. Ostrom utca 19, t 201 6737, *www.aranykaviar.hu* (€€€). Good portions of authentic Russian dishes in a lavish *fin-de-siècle* style dining room, including some reasonably priced caviar, smoked salmon and beef. A good range of vodkas and wines.

Pest Buda Vendéglő, I. Fortuna utca 3, t 212 5880 (€€€). Intimate and old-fashioned, with a pianist playing schmoozy favourites. Gourmet meat-based food, excellent wine list. Lunch is more affordable.

Rivalda, I. Színház utca 5–9, t 489 0236, *www.rivalda.net* (€€€). By the Castle Theatre, decorated with classy but over-the-top theatre regalia. There's also an expansive cobbled courtyard and live music every night. Co-owned by an ex-Gundel chef, with a European-Hungarian menu.

21 Restaurant/ Hungarian Kitchen

Náncsi Néni >>

21 Restaurant, I. 21 Fortuny utca, t 202 21 13, *www.21restaurant.hu* (€€). A relaxed and stylish 'Hungarian Kitchen', this offers exquisitely updated versions of classic local cuisine accompaned by well-chosen local wines. Charming little pavement terrace in summer.

Víziváros

Csalogány 26, II. Csalogány utca 26, *www.csalogany26.hu* (€€€). Excellent Hungarian cuisine, prepared with rigorously sourced ingredients, and plenty of contemporary flair. The decor is restrained but elegant, and the service a little cool.

Café Kör >>

Belgian Brasserie (Belga Söröző), I. Bem Rakpart 12, t 201 5082, *www. belgasorozo.com* (€€). Popular Belgian-style bar-restaurant, stylishly fitted out, with a pleasant Hungarian crowd. A staggering range of beers, including Belle Vue Kriek and Leffe (light and dark) on tap. Starters include brioche, snails and frogs' legs, followed by mussels or meat with a French slant. Tasty, plentiful food, good service, and a riverside terrace. *Batthyány tér (M2), then tram 19 or walk.*

Horgásztanya Vendéglő, I. Fő utca 27, t 212 3780 (€€). Famous for their spicy fish soup, with décor to match, including an upside-down boat complete with plastic fisherman stuck to the ceiling. They also rustle up marjoram veal steak with brains, mushroom and bacon, or dishes fried on lava stone.

Mák Bistro >>

San Remo, II. Török utca 6–8, t 212 1991 (€€). Simple, clean Italian-style cellar close to Margaret Bridge. Lots of pizzas and seafood, a good range for vegetarians. *Closed Mon. Batthyány tér (M2), tram 4 or 6.*

Marxism, II. Kisrokus utca, t 316 0231 (€). A smoky, cavernous tavern, wildly decorated with kitsch Communist memorabilia (including fake barbed wire between the booths and plenty of red stars everywhere), this serves good, cheap pizzas with names like Gorbi-Gorbi and the Anti-Vegetarian.

Elsewhere in Buda

Remíz, II. Budakeszi utca 5, t 275 1396, *www.remiz.hu* (€€€). In the Buda Hills next to a tram depot. Highly

recommended for the best of traditional Hungarian cuisine. Barbecues in the wonderful garden are particularly popular in summer. *Bus 22 from Moszkva tér (M2).*

Náncsi Néni, II. Ördögárok utca 80, t 397 2742, *www.nancsineni.hu* (€€). The most famous place in town for home-cooked Hungarian cuisine. Top marks for quality and quantity, and a thoroughly authentic experience. Try the braised wild boar cutlets. *Booking is essential. Bus 56 from Moszkva tér (M2), or Children's Railway then walk.*

Marcello, XI. Bartók Béla utca 40, t 466 6231 (€). Popular and intimate Italian: an incredible range of pizzas, a good salad bar and a no-smoking policy. One of the few options in Gellért. *Closed Sun.*

Pest: City (Lipótváros)

Café Kör, V. Sas utca 17, t 311 0053 (€€). Wonderful little bistro near the Basilica, with a simple, tastefully trendy interior and a miniature pavement terrace. The menu is small yet more diverse and exciting than most places in town, and the food is pretty good. Reserve well in advance. *Breakfast until 11.30am. Closed Sun.*

Lugas Étterem, V. Bajcsy-Zsilinszky 15, t 302 5393, *http://lugas-etterem.hu/* (€€). Best views of the back of the Basilica from this terrace across the main road. Laid-back and friendly, offering good portions of well-cooked Hungarian fare. There are a few veggie choices, like grilled courgette (zucchini) with dill and cheese sauce.

Mák Bistro, V. Vigyázó Ferenc utca 4, t 307 239 383, *www.makbistrot.com* (€€). Very fashionable, this relaxed, whitewashed cellar bistro produces imaginative modern Hungarian dishes like calf´s foot with chard along with amazing desserts. Everything is beautifully presented. *Closed Sun and Mon.*

Café Alibi, V. Egyetem ter, t 317 4209, *www.cafealibi.hu* (€). A pretty café with wooden tables and white linen, this serves everything from great breakfasts to light snacks, and a selection of pasta, meat and fish dishes. The staff are very friendly, and in the evenings it is candle-lit. Very good value.

Govinda, V. Vigyázó Ferenc utca 4,
t 269 1625, *http://govinda.hu* (€).
Vegetarian set meal changing daily
but basically an Indian thali: dal, two
vegetable dishes, puri, rice, chutney.
Healthy, filling and tasty, not
necessarily spicy. Drinks are good,
especially the lassis.

Iguana Bar&Grilla, V. Zoltán utca 5,
t 331 4352 (€). For a break from
Hungarian food, try this lively
Mexican *cantina* for quesadillas, tacos,
burritos and more. Good for families,
with a kid's menu and toys available.

Kisharang Étkesde, V. Október 6 utca
17, **t** 269 3861, *www.kisharang.hu* (€).
Typical small Hungarian diner.
Chequered tablecloths, the whole bit.
One of the survivors round here,
which says a lot. Daily specials, tasty
food, very cheap.

Szeraj, V. Szent István körút 13 (€). Self-
service Turkish place near Margaret
Bridge, whose food is fast but far from
junk. Great if you're in a rush, hungry,
or have kids. *Open 9am–4am, until
5am on Fri and Sat, and always packed.*

Via Luna, V. Nagysándor József utca 1,
t 312 8058, *www.vialuna.hu* (€). The
dining room resembles an Italian
country villa. Pastas, risottos, lots of
fish and pizzas, salads and steaks.

Pest: Belváros

Onyx, VI. Vorosmarty tér 7 (entrance
on Harmincad utca), **t** 429 9023,
www.onyxrestaurant.hu (€€€€).
Currently one of the most talked-
about restaurants in town, with
sumptuous modern décor, award-
winning cuisine (with a Michelin star),
and a stellar wine list. Go for the
'Hungarian Evolution' set menu
(19,900Ft), which can be served with
wine pairings (9,900Ft). Set lunch
menus are considerably more
affordable, starting at 3,490Ft for two
courses. *Reservations essential. Closed
Sun and Mon.*

Kárpátia, V. Ferenciek tere 7–8, **t** 317
3596, *www.karpatia.hu* (€€€). An
extraordinary interior, bold, busy and
very medieval, the walls covered in
heavy patterns, much like the
Matthias Church. There is a pleasant
covered area outside. The food is
traditional Hungarian cuisine, and
there's gipsy music in the evenings.

Múzeum Kávéház Étterem, VIII.
Múzeum körút 12, **t** 267 0375,
www.muzeumkavehaz.hu (€€€).
Established in 1885, still with much of
the original décor, including Károly
Lotz frescoes. Good food in
sumptuous surroundings. The menu
is enormous. Very good wine list.
Booking essential. Closed Sun.

Cyrano, V. Kristóf tér 7–8, **t** 266 4747
(€€€–€€). Modern European cuisine,
plus gourmet salads and sandwiches.
Just off Váci utca, the terrace is
wonderful for people-watching, while
the interior is stylish and cavernous.

Vapiano V. Bécsi utca 5, **t** 411 0864 (€).
A trendy spin on fast food, this big,
colourful restaurant has different bars
serving delicious, made-to-order pizza,
pasta, salads made with outstanding
produce at very decent prices.

Pest: Around Andrássy Út

Fausto's, VII. Székely Mihály utca 2,
t 877 6210, *www.fausto.hu* (€€€€).
High-quality, genuine Italian food in
elegant new surroundings just off
Andrassy út. The pasta is home-made,
the sauces exquisite. A gastronomic
delight with service to match. The
restaurant has been replaced at its
former address by the slightly less
expensive **Fausto's Osteria** at Dohány
utca 5, **t** (01) 269 6806. *Closed Sat
lunch and Sun.*

Cactus Juice, VI. Jókai tér 5, **t** 302 2116,
www.cactusjuice.hu (€€). Basement
pub with an unfortunate Wild West
theme and speakeasy feel but
excellent food. Well-prepared
Hungarian and international fare with
imaginative twists, and portions so
big, some dishes require two plates.
Try the Giant Pork BBQ with pickles.
Some choices for veggies, and a good
selection of beers.

Chez Daniel, VI. Szív utca 32, **t** 302
4039, *www.chezdaniel.hu* (€€). Real
French food cooked by a real French
chef using the freshest ingredients.
The menu is small and select, with an
ever-changing specials board. The
bright little courtyard is delightful.
Booking essential.

Fészek Művész Klub Étterem,
VII. Kertész utca 36, **t** 322 6043,
www.feszek-muveszklub.hu (€€). The
best of meaty Hungarian cuisine

served in a leafy interior courtyard surrounded by arcades and old street-lamps, or in the expansive, sophisticated interior, with live music. Large portions at surprisingly reasonable prices, popular with locals and tourists alike. *Tram 4 or 6 or walk from Oktogon (M1)*.

Karma Café, VI. Liszt Ferenc tér 11, **t** 413 6764, *www.karmabudapest.com* (€€). A stunning interior that doesn't overplay the Eastern angle, with subdued lighting, plenty of brick and wood, and multiple layers. The very eclectic international menu features tandoori oven specialities. Equally suitable for drinks. Live jazz and soul.

Elsewhere in Pest

Costes Restaurant, IX. Ráday utca 4, **t** 219 0696, *www.costes.hu* (€€€€). International fusion food involving some imaginative combinations, served in a plush, intimate environment. This was the first restaurant in Hungary to earn a Michelin star. It's the fanciest of several good options on this happening street.

 Gundel >

 Angelika >>

Gundel, XIV. Állatkerti út. 2, **t** 468 4040, *www.gundel.hu* (€€€€). Founded in 1894, Gundel is a legend: the most famous restaurant in Hungary, it has won high praise around the world. The interior is exquisite, the garden a delight and the menu adds refinement to traditional Hungarian dishes. Of course it is expensive, and a little stiff and formal. The Sunday lunch buffet, served 11.30–3, is a bit less so. *Hősök tere (M1)*.

Robinson, XIV. Városligeti tó 5, **t** 422 0222, *www.robinsonrestaurant.hu* (€€€). An island restaurant (about 4m from the shore) in City Park, bravely placed opposite Gundel. A friendly, laid-back atmosphere in beautiful surroundings. The French-inspired menu changes regularly. Huge summer terrace. *Hősök tere (M1)*.

Bagolyvár (The Owl's Castle), XIV. Állatkerti út. 2, **t** 468 3110, *www.baholyvar.com* (€€). Gundel's sister restaurant is in a rustic Transylvanian building with wooden beams. The emphasis is on traditional cooking. They also serve a children's menu. *Hősök tere (M1)*.

Soul Café and Restaurant, IX. Ráday utca 11–13, **t** 217 6986, *www.soulcafe.hu* (€€). Large, trendy but comfortable interior with high vaulted ceilings, leather armchairs and soft lighting. The fireplace is a draw in winter. There's a small but interesting menu of international dishes. Free WiFi. *Open daily till 1am*.

Fecske Presszó, VIII. Baross utca 10, **t** 318 0091, *http://fecsketerasz.hu* (€). Arty, unassuming café-bar, where you can eat cheap but tasty food (the menu is on the vaulted ceiling), or simply drink a beer with friends, or even watch a movie during the special film screenings on Sunday evenings.

Kádár Étkezde, VII. Klauzal tér 9, **t** 321 3622 (€). Small, very authentic Hungarian eatery with a nice atmosphere and a great menu of well-balanced meat dishes. Arrive early to grab a table, particularly at weekends. *Open Tues–Sat 11.30–3.30*.

Cafés in Budapest

Buda

Angelika, I. Batthyány tér 7, **t** 212 3784. On the river side of St Anne's Church, this is a chic, much-loved café with a wonderful summer terrace offering views of Parliament. Inside, curvy white sofas make it a comfortable place to sprawl. Good selection of coffees, cakes, juices, teas, wines, spirits, cocktails, ice creams, beers and breakfast.

Café Miró, I. Úri utca 30, **t** 375 5458. The most successfully stylish modern spot in Castle Hill, decked out to resemble a large-scale piece of art by Miró, and with a terrace offering views of Matthias Church. Mixed clientele in the day, buzzing with locals in the evening. Good drinks, but if you're hungry, eat elsewhere. Staff may be young, but are still old school when it comes to service – surliness is *de rigueur*.

Pierrot Café, I. Fortuna utca 14, **t** 375 6971. At the Béksi Kapu tér end of the street, this comfortable little café is bursting with eclectic charm. It is halfway to being a restaurant, with crêpes, seasonal specials like asparagus, vegetarian dishes and lunch deals (€€). The bar has a good range of beer and wine as well as speciality coffees and cocktails. Live piano after 7pm.

Ruszwurm Cukrászda, I. Szentháromság tér 7. Budapest's oldest *pâtisserie*, open since 1827, its interior featuring some fine *chaises-longues* and an old stove. Lovely views of Matthias Church, but it's always staggeringly busy. There's a tiny café attached. *Closed eves.*

Pest

Amstel River Café, V. Párizsi utca 6. On a quiet side street, with an atmosphere like a small French café, the perfect place to escape the bustle of nearby Váci utca. Meals also (€€).

Auguszt Cukrászda, V. Kossuth Lajos utca 14–16, t 337 6379, *www.auguszt cukraszda.hu*. Delightful little old-style coffee shop hidden away in the corner of a courtyard near Astoria. Good coffee and cakes, and an oasis of sophistication away from the down-town bustle.

Aztec Chocolat, V. Károly körút 22/ Semmelweis utca 19. Tiny and incredibly popular, this is a must for chocaholics. Tuck into a spicy hot chocolate flavoured with chilli, or one of more than 20 other varieties on offer. *Closed Sun.*

Café Eckermann, VI. Andrássy út 24, t 374 4076. A calm, modern place with great art, a nice terrace, a couple of Internet terminals, and a decent selection of coffees, teas, snacks, juices, wine and beer. *Closed Sun.*

Café Mediterrán, VI. Liszt Ferenc tér 10, t 344 4615. The selection of drinks here is inexplicably poor, but the atmos-phere is great and the clientele cheer-ful. Its summer terrace is one of the town's busiest. The action goes on till late then moves downstairs.

Café Miró Grande, VI. Liszt Ferenc tér 9. The comfy armchairs, funky furnishings, aquarium and stylish bar make this yet another satisfying spot on the square for any kind of drink. Stick with drinks and eat elsewhere.

Café Picard, V. Falk Miksa utca 10, t 311 8273, *www.cafepicard.hu*. Tiny, stylish continental café near Parliament. Excellent strong coffee, tasty tapas, plus beer, wines and juices.

Café Vian, VI. Liszt Ferenc tér 9, t 268 1154. With its big, bright, comfortable interior decorated with wonderful art, and a small, elegant terrace, this still stands out despite the stiff competition. Excellent selection of bottled beer and wines, plus coffees, juices and cocktails. The food includes omelettes, salads, croissants and desserts. The clientele is sophisticated and not necessarily young.

Central Kávéház, V. Károlyi Mihály utca 9, *www.centralkavehaz.hu*. Vast old-style coffee house on Ferenciek tere with extremely high ceilings. Leather upholstery, marble tables and the gold, green and orange colour scheme add to the grandeur. Reasonable prices; intimate seating upstairs. The food is surprisingly good.

Gerbeaud, V. Vörösmarty tér 7, t 429 9000. The place to sit and enjoy coffee and (fabulous) cake at the social heart of Belváros. Sit out on the terrace to watch the crowds. Inside is replete with turn-of-the-century antique furniture and fittings. They also do breakfast, cold food and beer, but at a price. Round the corner is a slightly cheaper stand-up version and an expensive restaurant. The whole affair is quite touristy, and service is rushed.

Komédiás Kávéház, VI. Nagymező utca 26, t 302 0901. Small, old-style theatrical café, all wood, mirrors, brass and plush seating.

Mai Manó Café, VI. Nagymező utca 20. Trendy little café on the ground floor of the sumptuous Mai Mano House (now a photography gallery), this is decorated with cushions and cosy corners. The food is limited to simple toasted sandwiches and a few cakes. The crowd is young and arty. Tiny terrace too.

New York Kávéház, VII. Erzsébet körút 9–11. Budapest's last remaining genuine coffee house from the pre-war era has been magnificently refurbished and is now part of a stunning five-star hotel. The atmosphere has suffered, but the glorious neo-Renaissance/Art Nouveau building overflows with sumptuous details.

Entertainment in Budapest

The monthly magazine *Funzine* (*www.funzine.hu*) has good listings for music and English-language shows. *Pesti Est* and its sister *Pesti Súgó* are more comprehensive but published in Hungarian. They are all available in bars and restaurants across town, as well as tourist offices. Or look in one of the ticket agencies on Váci utca.

Ticket Express, t 303 030 999, *www.tex.hu*, has an office at Andrassy út 19. You can buy tickets for most major events at *www.ticketpro.hu*, *www.kulturinfo.hu* or *www.jegy.hu*. Note that nearly all the theatres close for the summer (*June–Sept*), although there are often outdoor performances during those months.

Theatre

International Buda Stage, II. Tárogató utca 2–4, t 391 2525, *www.ibs-b.hu*. This theatre hosts English and Hungarian theatre, music, dance and concerts. Simultaneous translation into English during Hungarian shows. *Box office open daily 10–6. Tram 56 from Moszkva tér (M2).*

Katona József, V. Petőfi Sándor utca 6, t 318 6599, *www.katonajozsef szinhaz.hu*. The best-reputed mainstream theatre company. *Box office at Kossuth Lajos utca 3 open daily 2–7. Ferenciek tere (M3).*

Kolibri, VI. Jókai tér 10, t 312 0622, plus two other venues. Specialising in children's theatre and puppetry, with a special children's festival in summer. Some shows are in English. *Box office open Mon–Fri 9–5. Oktogon (M1).*

Merlin International Theatre, V. Gerlóczy utca 4, t 317 9338, *www. merlinszinhaz.hu*. This offers theatre and dance, with several English-language events including dinner performances on Mon and Wed. *Box office open Mon–Fri 11–7. Deák tér metro.*

Palace of Arts/Culture (Művészetek Palotája), IX. Komor Marcelli sétány 1, t 555 3000, *http://mupa.hu*. This is one of the city's biggest venues, used for everything from theatre to ballet to rock concerts. It's next door to the

National Theatre in the Millenium City. *Tram 2 or 24.*

Thália Szinház, VI. Nagymező utca 22–4, t 312 4230, *www.thalia.hu*. Very attractive venue hosting theatre (often in English), dance, and musicals. *Box office open Mon–Fri 10–9, weekends 2–7. Oktogon (M1).*

Trafó, IX. Liliom utca 41, t 456 2040, *www.trafo.hu*. The best contemporary arts venue, with all sorts of events, often crossing over between art forms: art, poetry, music, theatre, exhibitions, dance, comedy, etc. See below for the club venue. *Box office open daily 4–8, until 10 on performance days. Ferenc krt. (M3).*

Vígszínház (Comedy Theatre), XIII. Szent István krt. 14, t 329 2340, *www.vigszinhaz.hu*. Wonderful gilded 19th-century theatre focusing on comedy; some big musicals. *Box office open Mon–Fri 1–7, Sat and Sun 1hr before curtain. Nyugati pu (M3).*

Classical Music and Opera

The classical scene in Budapest is booming, and audiences are well known for their enthusiasm. Yehudi Menuhin called this 'the town of Bartók, Kodály, Doráti and the very responsive concert public'. It is thanks to these first two, who scoured the country for folk melodies which they incorporated into their own works, that Hungary found its own true classical voice. The best orchestras are the **Budapesti Fesztivál Zenekar**, the **Nemzeti Filharmónia**, the MRT **Szimfónikus Zenekara**, and the **Liszt Ferenc Chamber Orchestra**. Choirs are generally even better, the **Nemzeti Énekkar** and **MRT Gyermek Kórusa** (a children's choir) are among those rated very highly. The **Bartók String Quartet** (Bartók Vonósnégyes) is also always worth seeing. The **Hungarian State Opera** company puts on a wonderful show, and a night spent at the magnificent Opera House is one of the most truly memorable experiences Budapest has to offer. They publish their own monthly schedule, available at the Opera House or at ticket agencies.

As well as the venues listed below, look out for events at **St Stephen's Basilica**, the **Lutheran Church**, the

Great Synagogue, Kiscelli Museum and the Old Music Academy in the Liszt Museum. Note that most venues close for summer, when open-air venues are set up for music of all kinds, the main ones being Budai Park Stage, XI. Kosztolányi Dezső tér (tram 49 from Deák tér/ Kiskörút); Vajdahunyad Castle in City Park (Hősök tere, M1); Városmajor, just east of Moszkva tér (M2), and the Millenaris Park (behind the Mammut shopping centre), Kis Rókus utca 16–20.

Bartók Béla Memorial House, II. Csalán utca 29, t 394 2100, www.bartokmuseum.hu. Chamber concerts, usually on Fridays. Bus 5 from Moszkva tér (M2).

Hungarian State Opera House (Magyar Állami Operaház), VI. Andrássy út. 22, t 353 0170, www.opera.hu. Everything you could want from an opera house. Productions are lavish and dramatic. Tickets available online through their website. Box office open Tues–Sat 11–7 (or showtime). Opera (M1).

Magyar Nemzeti Hangversenyterem (Hungarian National Concert Hall), IX. Komor Marcell utca 1, t 555 3000, http://mupa.hu. The city's modern national concert hall (part of the major arts complex in south Pest) attracts top international orchestras and is home to the renowned Hungarian National Philharmonic.

Mátyás Templom, I. Szentháromság tér 2, t 355 5657. The beautiful church (see p.241) makes a striking concert venue, usually used for organ recitals. The audience cannot see the player. The poor acoustics are unsuitable for the choir and orchestra works also performed here. Tickets from the door of the church. Várbusz from Moszkva tér (M2).

Zeneakadémia (Franz Liszt Music Academy), VI. Liszt Ferenc tér 8, t 462 4600, www.musicacademy.hu. One of the city's top venues: closed for refurbishment until at least 2012 but check the website for updates. Oktogon (M1).

Jazz and Blues

Birdland, VI. Liszt Ferenc tér 7, t 413 7983, www.birdlandcafe.hu. Classic interior with plain walls and B&W jazz prints. Live jazz Thurs–Sat. Small meat-based menu (€€€).

Budapest Jazz Club, VIII. Muzeum utca 7, www.bjc.hu. Easily the city's best jazz venue, with jam sessions and concerts by students from the Franz Liszt academy on Mondays and Tuesdays, Hungarian and inter-national bands at weekends, and usually big band-style orchestras on Sundays. The programme is posted on the website.

Fat Mo's, V. Nyári Pál utca 11, t 267 3199, www.fatmo.hu. Open till 2 or 4am nightly. Done up as a speakeasy, with one very long bar and B&W gangster prints; always staggeringly full. The restaurant is Tex-Mex (€€€), with live music or DJs nightly.

Jazz Garden, V. Veres Pálné utca 44a, t 266 7364. With plastic trees and a black ceiling dotted with stars, the sensation of being in a garden is a little eerie. Jazz nightly. The pastel-coloured restaurant offers the regular fare plus some veggie choices (€€€). Reasonably priced drinks. Cover charge. Open daily 6pm–1am. Kálvin tér (M3).

Folk Music and Dance

Dance houses (táncház) were formed during the Transylvania-inspired folk-tradition revival in the 1970s. A few places around town have weekly gatherings, at which outsiders are welcome, usually with the chance to learn the steps beforehand. The three longest established ensembles put on shows several times a week at the Budai Vigadó (Hungarian Historic House, I. Corvin tér 8), which is home to the Hungarian State Folk Ensemble, and at the Duna Palota (V. Zrínyi utca 5) or the Bábszinház (VI. Andrássy utca 69). You can find out about dance clubs showing less polished but possibly more authentic performances, as well as details of Hungarian dance classes and courses from Tánchez, http://tanchaz.hu.

Cinema

There are plenty of English-language cinemas. Pesti Est often has an English-language film listing. Many old movie houses survive, a few showing art-house films. The best multiplex, in a graceful old building, is **Corvin**, VIII. Corvin köz 1, **t** 459 5050, www.corvin.hu, Ferenc krt. (M3). Arthouse venues include: **Cirko-gejzír**, VIII. Balassi Bálint utca 15–17, **t** 269 1915, www.cirkogejzir.hu, tram 2; **Hunnia**, VII. Erzsébet krt. 26, **t** 322 3471, Blaha Lujza tér (M2); **Művész**, VI. Teréz krt 30, **t** 459 5050, www.artmozi.hu, Oktogon (M1); **Odeon-Lloyd**, XIII. Hollán Ernő utca 7, **t** 329 2065, http://odeonlloyd.com, tram 2, 4 or 6; **Örökmozgó Filmmúzeum**, VII. Erzsébet krt., **t** 342 2167, www.filmarchiv.hu, tram 4 or 6 to Wesselényi utca; and **Tabán Art Mozi**, I. Krisztina krt. 87–9, **t** 356 8162, www.tabanmozi.hu, tram 18 from Moszkva tér.

Dance

There are a host of modern Hungarian dance groups. The **National Dance Theatre**, I. Színház utca 1–3, **t** 375 8649, www.nemzetitanc szinhaz.hu, is located in a beautiful 18th-century building on Castle Hill and showcases a wide range of dance, from ballet to folk to contemporary dance. The **Hungarian National Ballet Company** (Magyar Nemzeti Balett) performs at the National Dance Theatre and the State Opera House. For contemporary dance, try the **Sin Culture Centre**, XIII. Gyutacs utca 10–18, www.sinarts.org, and the **Trafó Contemporary Arts Centre** (see above).

Nightlife in Budapest

It is hard to identify a typically Hungarian bar culture, unless you mean the many dark, rather desperate-looking places filled almost exclusively with unsteady men: the borozó, a cheap wine cellar, usually full of early drinkers; the söröző, a beer-cellar, but not like those found in Prague; the presszó, a dingy style of café-bar. You won't find many of these listed below, though they're certainly of cultural interest. Budapest's bar scene is vivacious, and too eclectic to classify. Many of the best bars are also cafés, venues or even restaurants, so see above. For the best taste of what's on offer, head to Liszt Ferenc tér or Raday utca.

A38 Ship, moored at Petőfi Bridge, Buda side, **t** 464 3940, www.a38.hu.

One of Budapest's busiest venues, for all genres of music, is also a dance hall, restaurant and bar, whose door prices deter the younger partiers. Open daily 11–4.

Corvintentő, VI.Blaha Lujza tér 1–2, http://corvinteto.hu/. This alternative club occupies the rooftop of the run-down Corvin shopping centre dating from the 1920s. There's a fabulous terrace garden on the roof; chill out over drinks and the views early in the evening, or stay to watch the action heating up around midnight. Metro to Blaha Lujza.

Crazy Café, VI. Jókai utca 30, **t** 302 4003. This long cellar bar has an astounding selection of draught and bottled beers. Live music and karaoke. The restaurant is done out like a jungle, with plastic vegetation and stuffed animals. Imaginative menu (€€). Open daily 12pm–1am.

Fregatt Pub, V. Molnár utca 26, **t** 318 9997. English-style laid-back cellar pub, with live music most evenings. Open Mon–Fri, Sun 4pm–1am, Sat 5pm–1am. Ferenciek tere (M3).

Kis Erkel Café, IX. Erkel utca 14, **t** 210 7351, http://kiserkelcafe.hu. Step off busy Raday utca to find this mellow bar, which has sofa-style seating for lounging about, and changing art on the walls to ponder over a beer or two. It get busier and livelier as the night wears on.

Leroy Café, VI. Liszt Ferenc tér 10, www.leroycafeobuda.hu. An extraordinary interior featuring arched stone ceilings, chandeliers and a spectacular bar. There's a menu, with lots of steaks (€€), but this place is better used for drinks.

Negro, V. Szent István tér 11, **t** 302 0136. A chic, fashionable cocktail bar with a panoramic terrace facing the Basilica, this attracts a mixed crowd of well-heeled locals and footsore tourists.

Old Man's Music Pub, VII. Akácfa utca 13, **t** 322 7645. Probably the most fun, popular and crowded nightspot in town. Mainly disco, with live blues, jazz or funk earlier in the evening. Book a table if you want to see the stage. The menu is surprisingly good (€€). Open daily 3–3. Blaha Lujza tér (M2).

Day and Overnight Trips from Budapest

Óbuda

Situated on the Buda side, level with the northern tip of Margaret Island, today's suburb of Óbuda was actually the first settlement of any significance in this area. Using the Danube as the northern boundary of their province Pannonia, the Romans established a legionary camp and fortifications here as defence against the barbarians beyond. By the 2nd century BC a thriving civilian settlement had grown around the camp, centred on Aquincum 3km to the north. In the Middle Ages, Árpád and his successors built their royal residence here and the town flourished, but when Béla IV moved the royal seat to the more strategic location of Castle Hill, this original Buda (the ancient Hungarian word Ó means old) lost its importance along with its name. After the Turkish occupation, it enjoyed a renaissance as a market town, producer of wines, and somewhat bohemian gastronomic centre. Today's Óbuda, plagued by an ugly rash of tower blocks and housing estates, is the sort of area many people go on holiday to get away from, but its main attractions – mostly galleries and Roman ruins – can be seen simply and easily, and make a well-rounded day-trip when combined with Szentendre (*see* p.309).

Opposite the HÉV exit on Szentlélek tér, a splendid old white building contains the **Vasarely Museum**, with an exhaustive collection of Op Art by one of the fathers of the genre, Victor Vasarely, endlessly exploring spatial distortions and optical illusions with geometric patterns. It's a bit tedious if you're not a fan. In the square to the left stands a fine **Holy Trinity column**. On the right, where Szentlélek and Fő squares merge, the Baroque Zichy mansion (Zichy Kúria) holds the **Kassák Museum** and a local history exhibition. Lajos Kassák was a radical constructionist and publisher whose left-wing but anti-authoritarian stance led him into conflict with almost everyone. The museum contains works of avant-garde painting, sculpture, literature and typography.

Literally meaning Main Square, **Fő tér** remains to this day the focal point of the town. With its pedestrianized cobbled streets, old buildings like the lovely **theatre** (Városháza), antique lamp-posts and traditional restaurants that still make a living from Óbuda's *bon-vivant* reputation, it almost single-handedly retains the fragile ambience of a medieval village. The 18th-century Copf-style house at No.4 contains the **Zsigmond Kun Folk Art Museum**, a collection of mainly 19th-century folk art: pottery, textiles, carvings and

Vasarely Museum
open Tues–Sun 10–5;
closed Mon; adm

Kassák Museum
open Tues–Sun 10–6;
closed Mon; adm

Zsigmond Kun Folk Art Museum
open Tues–Fri 2–6, Sat and Sun 10–6; closed Mon; adm

Getting to Óbuda

HÉV train to Árpád híd from Batthyány tér.
Bus 6 from Nyugati station, or 86 from any stop on the Buda promenade.

---

furniture, presented in the former home of this connoisseur who gathered them from all over greater (pre-Trianon) Hungary.

At the northeast corner of the square is the strange sight of three metallic and miserable-looking women beneath umbrellas. This is the start of Laktanya utca, and the statue composition a prelude to Óbuda's only essential attraction, the **Imre Varga Gallery** at No.7. Within is a substantial collection by this striking and versatile artist, who is responsible for the Holocaust Monument and the statue of Károlyi Mihály close to Parliament. As well as copies and photos of these and other major works, such as his *St Stephen* and composition of *Our Lady of Hungary* which stand in the Hungarian Chapel of St Peter's in Rome, there are many excellent sculptures.

Imre Varga Gallery
open Tues–Sun 10–6; closed Mon; adm

A number of **Roman ruins** pay testament to Óbuda's ancient history, but you have to be a real aficionado to find them worth seeking out. **Flórián tér**, Óbuda's largest square and an unpleasant junction of major roads and flyovers, was built over the nucleus of the Roman military camp. Various remains, including some elegant columns, stand in the grassy centre, while the underpass is dotted with display cabinets and relics, and holds the **Roman Baths Museum**, a series of badly reconstructed low walls. South from here on Pacsirtamező utca, the limited remains of a large **amphitheatre** (at the junction with Nagyszombat utca, a 30min walk), are still quite impressive. Built in the 2nd century AD with an arena larger than that of the Colosseum in Rome, it could seat up to 15,000 spectators.

Roman Baths Museum
open mid–end April and Oct Tues–Sun 9–5; May–Sept Tues–Sun 9–6; closed Mon and Nov–14 April; adm

North of Flórián tér (northwest up Vörösvári utca then right on Vihar utca as far as Meggyfa utca) is the **Hercules Villa**. A series of mosaics are preserved where they were found. Under the first canopy an almost complete mosaic portrays Hercules shooting the centaur Nessos. The third canopy contains a mosaic of Alexandrian origin once composed of 60,000 stones and depicting Hercules about to vomit at a wine festival. It would be spectacular if complete, but sadly the three central figures are cut off just above the waist.

Hercules Villa
same opening hours as Roman Baths Museum; adm

About 1km southwest of Flórián tér on a forested hilltop at Kiscelli utca 108, and well worth the walk, is the **Kiscelli Museum**. This 1745 Baroque Trinitarian monastery contains a selection of major Hungarian artworks from about 1880 to 1990, including Rippl-Rónai's *My Parents after 40 Years of Marriage* and János Kmetty's Cubist *Városliget*. There are some fine 18th–19th-century engravings of Budapest, with the brand-new Chain Bridge and the

Kiscelli Museum
t 388 7817, www. btmfk.iif.hu; open April–Oct Tues–Sun 10–6; Nov–Mar Tues–Sun 10–4; closed Mon; adm

Eating Out in Óbuda

Óbuda t (01) –

Kéhli, III. Mókus utca 22, **t** 368 0613, www.kehli.hu (€€€). First-class home-made food based on traditional 19th-century cuisine. In a pretty inn, with live music from 8pm. Their classic dish is the hotpot with marrowbone. *Closed Mon–Fri lunch.*

Kisbuda Gyöngye, III. Kenyeres utca 34, **t** 368 6402 (€€€). An intimate little place with a plush, old-style interior and an excellent reputation. Expertly prepared cuisine. Attentive service, and a fine selection of wine, whisky and *pálinka. Closed Sun.*

Uj Sipos halászkert, III. Fő tér 6, **t** 388 8745, http://ujsipos.hu (€€). Elegant interior resembling a country manor, and outdoor tables in a round cobbled courtyard. The menu is old-style traditional.

Gigler, III. Föld utca 50c, **t** 368 6078 (€). The cheap and cheerful option. The interior and courtyard are basic but the food is authentic home-cooked Hungarian, tasty, plentiful and cheap. *Closed Sun eve and Mon.*

Great Synagogue. The bombed-out shell of a Gothic church is now an eerie gallery, providing a striking setting for spectacles such as operas and fashion shows, permanent exhibitions of the urban history and fine art collections of Budapest, and temporary exhibitions of contemporary art. From here you're not far from the caves in the Buda Hills (*see* p.289).

Aquincum

Aquincum
*t 250 1650,
www.aquincum.hu;
open mid–end April and
Oct Tues–Sun 9–5,
May–Sept Tues–Sun
9–6; closed Dec–mid-
April; adm; HÉV to
Aquincum from
Óbuda's Árpád híd, or
from Batthány Tér with
the Szentendre HÉV, or
bus 34, 42 and 106
from Óbuda*

Roughly 3km north of Óbuda is Budapest's major Roman archaeological site, the former town of Aquincum. Starting life as a military camp and growing to become provincial capital of Pannonia Inferior, Aquincum was a buzzing civilian town of 40,000 inhabitants. No buildings survive, but the arrangement of the foundation walls and the underground piping give a fair idea of the scale and layout of the town, including the remains of public baths, houses, a market place, a forum, law courts, an old Christian church, and a shrine to the Persian sun-god Mithras. The neoclassical **Aquincum Museum** contains locally found relics such as statues, pottery, tools, mosaics and jewellery, as well as a reconstructed 3rd-century Roman water organ. Across the road by the side of the HÉV station are the ruins of the civilian town **amphitheatre**, which could seat 8,000, considerably smaller than the military one in Óbuda. No ticket required; just walk around the surrounding bank peering through the vegetation.

Szentendre

Situated just 20km north of Budapest, the picturesque town of Szentendre is easily the most rewarding day trip from Budapest thanks to two very different types of historical migration. At the end of the 17th century, a mixture of Slav ethnic groups including Bulgarians and Dalmatians, but predominantly Greek Orthodox

Getting to Szentendre

HÉV from Óbuda's Árpád híd or Budapest's Batthyány tér (45mins).
Boat from Budapest's Vigadó tér from April–Oct (*weekends only April and October, Tues–Sun May–Sept*).
Check fares and timetables at *www.mahartpassnave.hu*.

Serbians, arrived here in several waves, fleeing from the advancing Turks. Hard workers in trade and viniculture, they soon began building grand houses and churches with a characteristically Balkan flavour. Over two centuries later, after a series of floods and epidemics had all but emptied the town, this marvellous architecture, combined with the bucolic ambience and Danube setting, began to attract a stream of artists, whose numbers have swollen ever since, filling the streets with galleries and studios. Today this combination of art and history, together with the undeniably quaint cobble-stoned streets, has led to a third wave of visitors: the tourists whose excessive volume represent Szentendre's only down side.

Following Kossuth Lajos utca north from the HÉV station, the first site is **Pozharevachka Church**, with the oldest iconostasis in town. Stop to pick up a map at the TOURINFORM office, then head to the focal **Fő tér**, a picturesque cobblestoned square centred on a memorial cross and lined with restaurant terraces. To its west on **Városház tér** is **Art'éria**, Hungary's first private, post-Communist gallery; on its east side is the **Art Gallery of Szentendre**; at No. 20 is **Erdész Gáleria**, a commercial gallery with an impressive collection of 20th-century masters; to the north is **Blagovestenska Church** (*adm*) with a dark, atmospheric incense-scented interior and a wonderful iconostasis. Round the corner is the **Museum of Margit Kovács**, which contains an extensive collection from this prolific, much-beloved ceramic artist. Frequently dismissed as mere kitsch, the beguiling simplicity and naïveté of her work draws attention away from the intense and complex emotions it often captures and evokes.

Museum of Margit Kovács
Vastagh György utca 1; open Tues–Sun 10–6; adm

Heading north, Bogdányi utca, too quaint for its own good, is lined with restaurants, souvenir stalls, and a few more worthwhile galleries, including the **Museum of Painters Anna Margit and Amos Imre**, and, at No.32, the **Art Mill** (Művészet Malom). This ruined sawmill, featuring a dramatic half-empty shell used for festivals and shows, exhibits works by Hungarian and international artists, as well as the local community.

Art Mill
t (26) 301 701; adm

Serbian Orthodox Art Museum
Pátriáka utca; open May–Sept Tues–Sun 10–5; Oct–April Tues–Sun 10–4; adm, inc church

The best thing to do from here is to wander the maze of cobbled streets that range over the hillside above, lined with handsome, colourful, well-preserved houses and churches. You can't miss the large and impressive terracotta-coloured **Serbian Orthodox cathedral**, whose grounds also contain the **Serbian Orthodox Art Museum**. Nearby is a **museum** dedicated to pre-war surrealist

Vajda Lajos Museum
Hunyadi utca 1; adm

Eating Out in Szentendre

ⓘ Szentendre >
*TOURINFORM,
Dumtsa Jenő utca 22,
t (26) 317 965,
www.szentendre.hu;
open Nov–Feb Mon–Fri
9–4.30; Mar–Oct
Mon–Fri 9–4.30, Sat
and Sun 10–2*

Szentendre t (26) –

Aranysárkány, Alkotmány utca 1a, **t** 301 479, *www.aranysarkany.hu* (€€€). Probably the best restaurant in town, with an interesting menu that includes sour cherry soup followed by goose liver with brandy, or lamb with rosemary.

Labirintus Etterem, Bogdányi 10, **t** 317 054, *www.bor-kor.hu* (€€€). Situated in the Wine Museum, with an interesting, extensive menu of traditional Hungarian cuisine such as larded venison with cranberries. It also organizes wine-tastings.

Chez Nicolas, Kigyó utca 10, **t** 311 288 (€€). Less crowded than those down the hill. Good if predictable food at reasonable prices. Small terrace upstairs.

Szentendrei Corner Kisvendéglő, Duna Korzó 4, **t** 300 027 (€€). The usual menu, but with some Serbian specialities also. Small courtyard, but no views.

Városháza Étterem, Rákóczi Ferenc utca 1, **t** 505 755 (€€). Smart and elegant turn-of-the-20th-century interior with a beautiful garden courtyard. The food is standard Hungarian fare.

painter Vajda Lajos. Further south is Szentendre's oldest structure, the **Roman Catholic parish church**, constructed between 1241–80. The nave, chancel and sacristy are original, but most of it was rebuilt in the early 14th century. There are nice views from up here of church spires, the town's red-tiled roofs, and the Danube.

Open Air Village Museum (Szabadtéri Néprajzi Múzeum/Skanzen)

Open Air Village
Museum
*t (26) 502 500,
www.skanzen.hu; open
April–Oct Tues–Sun
9–5; closed Mon; adm,
free Tues and Wed;
Skanzen bus from stand
7 in Szentendre, every
40mins–1hr*

Covering an area of 115 acres, 5km north of Szentendre, this museum's goal is to represent traditional types of settlement and architecture from 10 regions considered to be Hungary's most characteristic. The buildings and their interiors elaborately recreate those inhabited by the various social strata and groups in villages and towns from the late 18th–mid-20th centuries. From Thursday to Sunday, handicraft masters perform traditional labours in a working environment: the baker makes bread, the farmer tends his animals, etc. You can play traditional games, eat traditional food, see ancient breeds of livestock, and so on. Every second Sunday, craft workshops are held, offering the visitor hands-on experience of such skills as basket-weaving or pottery, and festivals are celebrated with dancing and other folkloric merry-making.

Esztergom

A further 20km north of Szentendre on the scenic 'Danube Bend' is Esztergom, Hungary's second most historically important town. Another former Roman settlement, where Marcus Aurelius wrote his *Meditations*, this was Hungary's first real capital, home of Prince Géza and reputed birthplace of his son Vajk, who was crowned here by the pope on Christmas Day AD 1000 to become

Getting to Esztergom

Buses from Budapest's Árpád híd station run every half-hour. Those via Dorog take 75mins. The **train** from Nyugati Stn leaves up to 13 times daily and takes 90mins. The last one returns at 10.10pm (check timetables at *www.mav-start.hu*). Esztergom's train station is about 1km from the centre, linked by local buses. **Boats** run 2–3 times daily June–Sept. One speedy **hydrofoil** runs daily June–Aug, leaving at 9.30am (journey time 90mins), returning at 5pm. By car, follow Route 11 north.

Hungary's first king, István I (Stephen). Stephen executed the pagan rebel Koppány here and hung his quartered remains on the city walls. He built a royal palace (excavated in 1934) that his descendants retained as royal seat and centre of the Hungarian Church until the Tatar Invasion of 1241, after which King Béla IV moved his capital to Buda and gave the castle to the archbishopric. It was razed again in 1543 by Sultan Suleiman II, and most of the town's remaining medieval buildings were destroyed 50 years later when the Habsburgs took it back. In 1761 the archbishopric recovered the castle and set about planning the biggest cathedral in the country.

Esztergom Basilica
*t (33) 402 354;
www.bazilika-esztergom.hu; church open April–Oct daily 8–6; Nov–Mar daily 8–4; cupola open April–Oct daily 9.30–5*

Completed in the 1860s on the site of a destroyed 12th-century church, **Esztergom Basilica** took three architects and 40 years to complete. Situated high up on Castle Hill, surrounded by manicured grounds and extensive fortifications, and fronted by a pompous set of mighty pillars and portico, it really is a monumental example of neoclassical architecture. Ferenc Liszt composed his famous *Esztergom Mass* (1856) for its consecration. The marble-heavy interior focuses on an impressive cupola that rises 71.5m above the floor, but its real highlight is the red marble **Bakócz Chapel**, originally built in 1510 by Florentine craftsmen, then dismantled during the Turkish occupation, and reassembled in 1823. The lookout point at the top of the **cupola** offers magnificent views over the attractive Baroque townscape. The **treasury**

Treasury and crypt
open daily 9–4.30; adm; adm

contains an impressive collection of priceless ecclesiastical artefacts, including the 13th-century Hungarian coronation cross. The large **crypt** is best known for the tomb of controversial Cardinal Mindszenty (*see* Szabadság tér, pp.258–9).

Castle Museum
t (33) 415 986; open April–Oct Tues–Sun 10–6; Nov–Mar Tues–Sun 9–4.30; adm

South of the cathedral is the **Castle Museum**, displaying remnants of the medieval royal palace and other local finds.

The town below is a regular, nitty-gritty place, barely affected by tourism, but full of Baroque and neoclassical buildings dating chiefly from the 18th century. Stretching along the banks of the Little Danube southwest of Castle Hill is the attractive Víziváros district centred on the pretty white **Víziváros parish church** (1738) on Mindszenty tere. The nearby **Primate's Palace** contains a **Christian Museum** that holds Hungary's finest collection of medieval religious art. South of here, **Maria Valeria Bridge** connects with the city of Štúrovo in Slovakia.

Christian Museum
Berényi Zsigmond utca 2, t (33) 413 880, www.kereszteny muzeum.hu; open Jan–Feb Tues–Sun 11–3; Mar daily 10–5; April–Oct daily 10–6; Nov–Dec daily 11–3; adm

Tourist Information in Esztergom

There is no official tourist office, and the tourism section of the town website, *www.esztergom.hu*, is rather out of date. Your best bet is to pick up some local information from TOURINFORM in Budapest before leaving (*see* p.292).

Eating Out in Esztergom

Esztergom t (33) –

Anonim, Berényi Zsigmond utca 4, t 411 880, *www.anonim-vendeglo.hu* (€€). Perfectly prepared Hungarian dishes served in a 300-year-old town house close to the river in Víziváros. Local specialities include the catfish soup and Hungarian pork fillet with creamy mushroom sauce.

Csülök Csárda, Batthyány Lajos utca 9, t 412 420 (€). Serving ñarge helpings of good home-cooked food, this friendly spot is handy for the Basilica, and popular with locals.

Hotel Esztergom Restaurant, Prímás sziget, t 412 555, *www.hotel-esztergom.hu* (€). European-style cuisine in surroundings that are striving to be upmarket.

Mélytányér, Pázmány Péter utca 1, t 412 534 (€). A charmingly old-fashioned inn, with red gingham tablecloths and local specialities.

Prímás Pince Restaurant, Szent István tér 4, t 313 495 (€). A great location, a gorgeous vaulted interior, and a pleasant, relaxed patio. Typical Hungarian food. Very popular.

Eger

Hungarians revere Eger as the site of one of their history's most glorious events. During a siege in 1552, a group of some 2,000 Magyars led by István Dobó kept an army of 10,000 Turks at bay here for over a month. Legends abound: apparently, Dobó opened the wine caskets so that his men would greet their attackers with red liquid dripping from their mouths. These days, the wine itself is what the town is more famous for, in particular the red blend Egri Bikavér, better known abroad as Bull's Blood. For the casual visitor, however, Eger is simply a gorgeous little town full of attractive Baroque buildings, that represents the most satisfying overnight trip from Budapest, 128km away.

The **castle** itself is Eger's most obvious sight, but there hasn't been too much to see since the Habsburgs blew it up in 1702. Within its rebuilt 15th-century Gothic Palace, however, is the **Castle Museum** with exhibitions on the history of castle and city, and tours of the underground fortress (Kazamaták). In the southeastern part of the castle is the **tomb of Géza Gárdonyi**, whose novel about that famous siege, *Egri csillagok* (*Stars of Eger*), remains a perennial favourite. More enticing is a walk along the **castle walls** for great views of Eger's picturesque townscape.

Castle Museum
t (36) 312 744, www.egrivar.hu; open 8–dusk; museum closed Mon, but you can still explore the rest of the castle; see website for exact times and tours available; adm

A lovely place for aimless strolling, the pedestrianized centre revolves around **Dobó tér**, which contains a **Minorite Church** from 1771. Towering over nearby Eszterházy tér is Hungary's second biggest church, **Eger Basilica**, designed by József Hild, also

Getting to Eger

Trains depart approximately hourly from Keleti pu station, taking 2hrs, but the train station in Eger is on the outskirts of town and some trains may require a change at Füzesabony. Check timetables at *www.mav-start.hu*. More convenient is the Volán **bus**, which departs from the bus station behind Keleti pu train station, which will bring you directly to the town centre.

Astronomical Museum
t (36) 520 400; open Tues–Sun 9.30–3; adm

Turkish minaret
open April–Nov Tues–Sun 10–6; adm

responsible for the one in Budapest. Its impressive façade is topped by statues of Faith, Hope and Charity by Italian sculptor Marco Casagrande, who also produced the statues of kings and apostles that line the lengthy flight of stairs down to the square. Opposite, the **Lyceum** contains an **astronomical museum** full of 18th-century instruments, including a *camera obscura* (the 'Eye of Eger') which projects a view of the whole town. At the corner of Knézich and Markó Ferenc streets is a **Turkish minaret** from 1596 believed to be the northernmost in Europe. There are great views from the top, if you can stand the claustrophobia-inducing ascent.

A mere 25-minute walk from town is the horseshoe-shaped **Szépasszonyvölgy**, or 'Valley of Beautiful Women', the perfect place to sample local wines. Dozens of small, private wine cellars cater to the revellers who come to sample their cheap wares, eat, dance, listen to the spontaneous musical happenings, and make exceeding merry. Many places are closed by evening, so arrive early.

ⓘ **Eger >**
TOURINFORM, Dobó tér 2, t (36) 517 715; open June–Sept Mon– Fri 9–8, Sat and Sun 9–5; April and Oct Mon–Fri 9–5, Sat 9–1

★ **Hotel Romantik >>**

Tourist Information in Eger

Information from TOURINFORM. The city website *www.eger.hu* is exclusively in Hungarian. More useful for visitors is *www.egercity.hu*, which is also in English, and provides a good list of concerts, events and festivals.

Where to Stay in Eger

Eger t (36) –
****/***Hotel Villa Völgy, Tulipánkert utca 5, t 321 664, *www.hotelvilla volgy.hu* (€€–€). Set amid extensive gardens, with a wellness centre, good restaurant and indoor and outdoor pools, plus another for children.
***Hotel Korona, Tündérpart utca 5, t 313 670, *www.koronahotel.hu* (€). A large, well-equipped hotel with decent rooms, a pool, Jacuzzi, sauna, fitness room and its own wine cellar. The hotel has a spectacular cellar restaurant and a lovely garden terrace. Breakfast included.

***Hotel Senator-Ház, Dobó tér 11, t 411 711, *www.senatorhaz.hu* (€). A handsome 18th-century townhouse (the Senator's House) right on the main square, very comfortable and popular. Service is erratic, sadly. Breakfast included.
***Panorama Panzió, Joó János utca 9, t 420 531, *www.panoramapanzio.hu* (€). A beautiful building with bright, attractive common areas, and rooms equipped with antique furniture. Sauna, Jacuzzi, and a delightful garden. Breakfast included.
***Hotel Romantik, Csíky Sándor utca 26, t 310 456, *www.romantikhotel.hu* (€). A charming little place close to the centre, with bright, pleasant rooms and a garden.

Eating Out in Eger

Eger t (36) –
Two of the best places to eat are the **Hotel Korona** and **Hotel Senator-Ház** (*see* above).

Arany Oroszlán étterem (Golden Lion), Dobó tér 5, **t** 518 210 (€€). A decent, central spot for Hungarian classics.

Imola Udvarház, Dózsa Gy. tér, **t** 516 180 (€€). A little more fancy, but with the emphasis still on home-cooked food.

Fehérszarvas Vadásztanya (White Deer Hunter's Camp), Klapka utca 8, **t** 411 129 (€). Close to Dobó tér, but with the feel of a country lodge, decked out with silly hunting regalia. The hearty fare features wild game. It's very popular with locals, with live music most evenings.

There are a number of places to eat scattered among the wine cellars of Szépasszonyvölgy. Two of the best are **Talizmán étterem** in the lovely Tulip Garden (Tulipánkert), **t** 412 533; and **Kulacs Csárda és Borozó** ('Canteen' Inn and Tavern), **t** 311 375.

Language

German/Austrian

German is a complex language. There are three, rather than two, genders; nouns and adjectives decline; it is full of irregular verbs and deceptive conjugations; and the syntax is ornate, and often littered with parentheses. The verb often comes only at the end.

But there are some advantages. Nouns are capitalized and easy to spot. Spelling is phonetic, so once you have grasped the basics of pronunciation there are few surprises.

Austrians speak German with a softer accent and many of their own colloquialisms; the most important to remember is that the usual greeting is not *Guten Tag* but *Grüss Gott* – which you should use whenever you encounter someone, to be polite.

Pronunciation

Consonants

Most are the same as in English. There are no silent letters. **G**s are hard, as in English 'good', but **ch** is a guttural sound, as in the Scottish 'loch' – though **sch** is said as 'sh'. **S** is also pronounced 'sh', when it appears before a consonant (especially at the beginning of a word), as in *stein*, pronounced 'shtine'. Otherwise the sound is closer to 'z'. **Z** is pronounced 'ts', and **d** at the end of the word becomes 't'. **R**s are rolled at the back of the throat, as in French. **V** is pronounced somewhere between the English 'f' and 'v', and **w** is said as the English 'v'.

Vowels

A can be long (as in 'father') or short, like the 'u' in 'hut'. Similarly **u** can be short, as in 'put', or long, as in 'boot'. **E** is pronounced at the end of words, and is slightly longer than in English. Say **er** as in 'hair' and **ee** as in 'hay'.

Say **ai** as in 'pie'; **au** as in 'house'; **ie** as in 'glee'; **ei** like 'eye' and **eu** as in 'oil'.

An **umlaut** (¨) changes the pronunciation of a word. Say **ä** like the 'e' in 'bet', or like the 'a' in 'label'. Say **ö** like the vowel sound in 'fur'. **ü** is a very short version of the vowel sound in 'true'. Sometimes an umlaut is replaced by an e after the vowel. The printed symbol **ß** is sometimes seen instead of **ss**, though this guide uses 'ss'.

Useful Words and Phrases

yes/no/maybe *ja/nein/vielleicht*
excuse me *Entschuldigung, bitte*
I am sorry *es tut mir leid*
please *bitte*
thank you *danke (schön)*
it's a pleasure *bitte (schön)*
hello *guten Tag; hallo;*
  Grüss Gott (in Austria)
goodbye; bye *auf Wiedersehen; tschüss*
good morning *guten Morgen*
good evening *guten Abend*
goodnight *gute Nacht*
how are you? (formal) *wie geht es Ihnen?*
  (informal) *wie geht es dir?* or *wie geht's?*
I'm very well *mir geht's gut*
I don't speak German *ich spreche kein Deutsch*
do you speak English? *sprechen Sie Englisch?*
I don't know *ich weiss nicht*
I don't understand *ich verstehe nicht*
my name is... *mein Name ist...; ich heisse...*
I am English (m) *ich bin Engländer*
I am English (f) *ich bin Engländerin*
  American *Amerikaner(in)*
leave me alone *lass mich in Ruhe*
with/without *mit/ohne*
and/but *und/aber*
I would like... *ich möchte...*
a little bit *a bissel* (Austria)

how much is this? *wieviel kostet dies?*
where is/are...? *wo ist/sind...?*
how far is it to...? *wie weit ist es nach...?*
near/far *nah/weit*
left/right/straight on *links/rechts/ gerade aus*
can you help me? *konnen Sie mir bitte helfen?*
I am lost *ich weiss nicht wo ich bin*

Notices and Signs

open/closed *geöffnet/geschlossen*
no entry *eingang verboten*
(emergency) exit *(Not)ausgang*
entrance *Eingang*
toilet *Toilette*
Ladies/Gents *Damen/Herren*
push/pull *drücken/ziehen*
bank *Bank*
police *Polizei*
rural police *Gendarmerie* (Austria)
hospital *Krankenhaus*
pharmacy *Apotheke*
post office *Post*
airport *Flughafen*
railway station *Bahnhof*
train *Zug*
platform *Gleis*
reserved *besetzt*

Days and Months

Monday *Montag*
Tuesday *Dienstag*
Wednesday *Mittwoch*
Thursday *Donnerstag*
Friday *Freitag*
Saturday *Samstag*
Sunday *Sonntag*

January *Januar; Jännar* (Austria)
February *Februar; Feber* (Austria)
March *März*
April *April*
May *Mai*
June *Juni*
July *Juli*
August *August*
September *September*
October *Oktober*
November *November*
December *Dezember*

Numbers

one/two *eins/zwei*
three *drei*
four/five *vier/fünf*
six/seven *sechs/sieben*
eight/nine *acht/neun*
ten *zehn*
eleven *elf*
twelve *zwölf*
thirteen *dreizehn*
fourteen *vierzehn*
seventeen *siebzehn*
twenty *zwanzig*
twenty-one *einundzwanzig*
thirty *dreissig*
forty *vierzig*
fifty *fünfzig*
sixty *sechszig*
seventy *siebzig*
eighty *achtzig*
ninety *neunzig*
hundred *hundert*
two hundred *zweihundert*
thousand *tausend*
three thousand *dreitausend*
million *eine Million*

Time

morning *Morgen; Vormittag*
in the morning *in der Früh* (Austria)
afternoon *Nachmittag*
evening *Abend*
night *Nacht*
week *Woche*
month *Monat*
year *Jahr*
today/yesterday *heute/gestern*
tomorrow *morgen*

Food and Drink

the menu, please *die Speisekarte bitte*
the bill, please *die Rechnung bitte*
I am vegetarian *ich bin Vegetarier(in)*
breakfast *Frühstuck; Brotzeit*
lunch *Mittagessen*
dinner *Abendessen*
supper *Abendbrot*
snack *Jause* (Austria)
cup *Tasse*
pot (e.g. of coffee) *Kännchen*
glass *Glas*
bottle *Flasche*

salt/pepper *Salz/Pfeffer*
milk/sugar *Milch/Zucker*
bread/butter *Brot/Butter*
boiled *gekocht*
steamed *gedämpft*
baked *gebacken*
roasted *gebraten*
smoked *geräuchert*
stuffed *gefüllt*
starters *Vorspeise*
main course *Hauptgericht*

Meat and Poultry *Fleisch und Geflügel*
roast beef *Beiried* (Austria)
meatball *Boulette*
duck *Ente*
minced meat *Hackfleisch*
chicken *Huhn; Hähnchen*
goose *Gans*
veal *Kalbfleisch*
chop *Kotelett; Schnitzel*
lamb *Lammfleisch*
liver *Leber*
oxtail *Ochsenschwanz*
beef *Rindfleisch*
ham *Schinken*
pork *Schweinefleisch*
bacon *Speck*
steak *Steak*
turkey *Truthahn; Puter*
sausage *Wurst*

Fish *Fische*
trout *Forelle*
prawns *Garnalen*
herring *Hering; Matjes*
cod *Kabeljau*
salmon *Lachs*
haddock *Schellfisch*
plaice *Scholle*
sole *Seezunge*
tuna *Thunfisch*
squid *Tintenfisch*

Vegetables *Gemüse*
aubergine *Aubergine; Melanzani* (Austria)
beans *Bohnen*
cauliflower *Blumenkohl; Karfiol* (Austria)
peas *Erbsen*
potatoes *Erdäpfel* (Austria)

green beans *Fisolen* (Austria)
cucumber *Gurke*
garlic *Knoblauch*
cabbage/red cabbage *Kohl/Rotkohl*
leeks *Lauch*
maize *Mais; Kukuruz* (Austria)
noodles *Nockerl* (Austria)
peppers/capsicums *Paprika*
mushrooms *Pilzen; Champignons; Schwammerl* (Austria)
asparagus *Spargel*
spinach *Spinat*
tomato *Tomate; Paradeiser* (Austria)
onions *Zwiebeln*

Fruit *Obst*
pineapple *Ananas*
apple *Apfel*
orange *Apfelsine; Orange*
banana *Banane*
pear *Birne*
strawberry *Erdbeere*
raspberry *Himbeere*
cherry *Kirsche*
apricot *Marille* (Austria)
grapefruit *Pampelmuse*
peach *Pfirsich*
grapes *Trauben*
sour cherries *Weichseln* (Austria)
lemon *Zitrone*

Desserts/Cheese *Nachtisch/Käse*
ice cream *Eis*
almonds *Mandeln*
jam *Marmelade* (Austria)
nuts *Nüsse*
(whipped) cream *Sahne/Schlagsahne; Obers* (Austria)
chocolate *Schokolade*
cheese *Käse*
curd cheese *Topfen* (Austria)
tart/cake *Torte/Kuchen*
sweets *Zuckerl* (Austria)

Drinks *Getränke*
(mineral) water *(Mineral)wasser*
fruit juice *Saft*
tea (with milk) *Tee (mit Milch)*
coffee *Kaffee*
beer *Bier*
red wine/white wine *Rotwein/ Weisswein*

Czech

It is difficult to imagine how Czech could be more alien to English-speakers. The language is Slavonic, with Latin influences, and in its modern form it dates from the 19th century, when, after 200 years of Germanization, it was re-established by scholars, with the help of peasants, a few old texts, and Polish, Serbo-Croat, Bulgarian and Russian dictionaries.

If you try to speak a few words of Czech it's appreciated by most people. Until the 1989 revolution German was the city's second language, but it has now been firmly overtaken by English. That linguistic shift – which seemed far from inevitable even fifteen years ago – has reasonable claim to be the most significant cultural change to hit Prague since the Thirty Years War.

Pronunciation

Czech is a phonetic language (pronounced consistently according to its spelling) with none of the shenanigans of silent letters and the like. That's simple enough – the problem is learning how to pronounce the letters. If the language of the English southern middle class is used as a benchmark, the main differences are that c is spoken as 'ts', j is a vowel sound like the English 'y', and r is rolled at the front of the mouth. Ch is a consonant in itself – it's pronounced as in the Scottish 'loch', and you'll find it after 'h' in the dictionary.

A háček (ˇ) above a consonant softens it: thus č is pronounced 'ch' as in 'chill', š is 'sh', and ž is the 'zh' sound in 'pleasure'. With ř, you venture into territory uncharted by the English language, and every other known language in the world. Even Czech children have to be taught how to say it; the closest you're likely to get is by rolling an 'r' behind your teeth and then expelling a rapid 'zh'.

Vowels are less complicated – a is the 'u' in 'up', e is as in 'met', i and y are both as in 'sip', o as in 'hot', and u as in 'pull'. The sounds are lengthened if the vowel is topped with an accent (´), or in the case of 'u', also the symbol (°) – they're pronounced like the vowels in, respectively, 'bar', 'bear', 'feed', 'poor' and 'oooooh!'. The letter ě is pronounced as

though it were 'ye' as in 'yet' and softens the consonant that comes before it. Accents affect only the sound of a vowel; and when pronouncing a word, it's always the first syllable that's stressed.

You don't use a subject (I, you, etc.) with a verb, since the ending in itself makes it clear who's doing the deed. The English pronoun 'you' has two forms, as in many European languages: 'vy' is polite and is used in most everyday situations (and where more than one person is being addressed); 'ty' is widespread among young people, and can be used to address anyone whom you could call your friend (you can also use it to be contemptuous to someone you've never met before). Beware also of the bewildering number of endings any ordinary word can have, depending on which of the seven cases, three-and-a-half genders and two categories it belongs to; if you're looking something up in a dictionary, plump for whatever looks closest. Finally, be alert to the fact that Czechs generally say 'no' or 'ano', when they're agreeing to something that's in doubt.

Useful Words and Phrases

yes/no *ano/ne*
I don't understand *nerozumím*
I don't know *nevím*
Do you speak English? *mluvíte anglicky?*
I am English *jsem angličan(ka)*
Please *prosím*
Please speak slowly *mluvte prosím pomalu*
Thanks (very much) *děkuji (moc)*
You're welcome *prosím*
Not at all *není zač*
I'm sorry *promiňte*
Good morning *dobré ráno*
Good day *dobrý den*
Good evening *dobrý večer*
Goodbye *na shledanou*
My name is... *jmenuji se...*
Pleased to meet you *těší mě, že vás*
Call a doctor *zavolejte lékaře*
Let me through *pučte mě*
Who? *kdo?*
What? *co?*
Where (is)...? *kde (je)...?*

When? *kdy?*
How much/many? *kolik?*
Do you have...? *máte...?*
post office *pošta*
stamp *známka*
How are you? *jak se máte?*
When are you open? *jak máte otevřeno?*

Travel

How can I get to ... ? *jak se dostanu na...?*
Where is...? *kde je...?*
Let me out *půtte mě ven*
airport *letigtě*
bus/tram-stop *zastávka*
metro station *stanice*
(railway) station *nádraží*
taxi-rank *stanoviště taxi*
aeroplane *letadlo*
bus *autobus*
tram *tramvaj*
train *vlak*
ticket *lístek*

Days and Months

Monday *pondělí*
Tuesday *úterý*
Wednesday *středa*
Thursday *čtvrtek*
Friday *pátek*
Saturday *sobota*
Sunday *neděle*

January *leden*
February *únor*
March *březen*
April *duben*
May *květen*
June *červen*
July *červenec*
August *srpen*
September *září*
October *říjen*
November *listopad*
December *prosinec*

Numbers

zero *nula*
one *jedna*
two *dva*
three *tři*
four *čtyři*

five *pět*
six *šest*
seven *sedm*
eight *osm*
nine *devět*
ten *deset*
eleven *jedenáct*
twelve *dvanáct*
thirteen *třináct*
fourteen *čtrnáct*
fifteen *patnáct*
sixteen *šestnáct*
seventeen *sedmnáct*
eighteen *osmnáct*
nineteen *devatenáct*
twenty *dvacet*
twenty-one *dvacet-jedna*
twenty-two *dvacet-dva*
thirty *třicet*
thirty-one *třicet-jedna*
forty *čtyřicet*
fifty *padesát*
sixty *šedesát*
seventy *sedmdesát*
eighty *osmdesát*
ninety *devadesát*
one hundred *sto*
one hundred and one *sto-jedna*
two hundred *dvě stě*
three hundred *tři sta*
four hundred *čtyři sta*
five hundred *pět set*
six hundred *šest set*
one thousand *tisíc*
two thousand *dva tisíce*
million *milión*

Time

What time is it? *kolik je hodin?*
morning *ráno, dopoledne*
afternoon *odpoledne*
evening *večer*
night *noc*
minute *minuta*
hour *hodina*
(to)day *dnes*
week *týden*
tomorrow *zítra*
yesterday *včera*

Food and Drink

Do you have a table? *máte volný stůl?*
vegetarian *vegetarián*
Do you have vegetarian dishes?
  máte bezmasé jídlo?
Enjoy your meal *dobrou chut'!*
breakfast *snídaně*
lunch *oběd*
dinner *večeře*
soup *polévka*
appetizer *předkrm*
braised *dušené*
grilled *na rožni*
roast *pečené*
fried *smažené*
boiled *vařené*
pasta *těstoviny*

Meat/Poultry *Maso/Drůbež*
pheasant *bažant*
steak *biftek*
wild boar *divočák*
  (also used to mean potent man)
ham *šunka*
beef *hovězí*
goose *husa*
liver *játra*
stag *jelení*
duck *kachna*
sausage *klobás(a)*
rabbit *králík*
turkey *krocan*
chicken *kuře*
kidneys *ledvinka*
stewed meat (beef) *roštěná*
minced meat *sekaná*
kebab *špíz*
venison *srnčí*
sirloin *svíčková*
veal *telecí*
sausage *uzeniny*
pork *vepřové*

Fish *Ryby*
carp *kapr*
crab *krab*
lobster *humr*
plaice *platýz*
trout *pstruh*
anchovy *sardelka*
sardine *sardinka*
pike *štika*
tuna *tuňák*
eel *úhoř*
whale *velryba*
shark *žralok*

Fruit/Vegetables *Ovoce/Zelenina*
pineapple *ananas*
banana *banán*
potatoes *brambory*
peach *broskev*
pear *hruška*
apple *jablko*
strawberry *jahoda*
apricot *meruňka*
nuts *ořechy*
orange *pomeranč*
cherries *třešně*
garlic *česnek*
asparagus *chřest*
onion *cibule*
mushrooms *houby*
french fries *hranolky*
carrots *mrkev*
cucumber *okurka*
tomato *rajčata*
rice *rýže*
salad *salát*
mushroom *žampion*
cabbage *zelí*

Desserts/Cheese *Moučnicky/Sýr*
cake *koláč*
pancake *palačinka*
ice-cream sundae *pohár*
whipped cream *šlehačka*
cream *smetana*
ice cream *zmrzlina*
sheep cheese *ovčí sýr*

Drinks *Napoje*
coffee *káva*
tea *čaj*
with lemon *s citrónem*
with milk *s mlékem*
without milk *bez mléka*
milk *mléko*
juice *džus*
mineral water *minerálka*
beer *pivo*
wine (white, red) *víno (bílé, červené)*

Hungarian

No other language that uses Latin script is as baffling as Hungarian. Normally in a European country you would expect to be able to understand a few written words – the basics, the essentials. Come to Hungary with such expectations and they are soon dashed against the harsh rocks of impossible letter combinations, absurdly long words, and endless accents. The easy explanation for this is that Hungarian is one of the few languages in Europe that is not of Indo-European origin. During the course of trying to work out where the Magyars originally came from, linguistics experts were called upon, and found that the core vocabulary of Hungarian, the basic words that have descended through millennia, is related to languages in the Finno-Ugric family, though far too distantly for Finns and Hungarians to understand one another. This places Hungarians' origins in Western Siberia and the northern part of the Ural mountains.

The problem is compounded by the fact that the Hungarians, who have managed to avoid the usual fate of small countries surrounded by large predatory empires – that of having their language carefully eradicated – love their language and are reluctant to learn anybody else's. In tourist situations like hotels and restaurants, there is usually someone who speaks some English, but in shops, museums or at the baths, even rudimentary communication has to be conducted in sign language. If they do have a few words of something, it is likely to be German. Latin languages will gain no glimmer of recognition. In desperate circumstances, seek out a young person.

There's no point trying to learn to speak the language, whose grammar is as difficult as its vocabulary. What follows is a glossary of words and expressions that might make life easier for you and the Hungarians you encounter. If you do make the effort, they may find it hard to hide their amusement at your pronunciation, but they will love you for it.

Pronunciation

Hungarian pronunciation is fairly straight-forward and consistent. Letters and combinations are always pronounced in the same way; there is no nonsense with silent letters and the like. The stress pattern is regular, with the first syllable slightly emphasized and each following syllable clearly and evenly pronounced. Accents denote a longer vowel (except for é and á). Double consonants are pronounced longer.

In dictionaries and listings, words beginning with ö and ő count as separate letters, with their own listings after 'o'. Sz also counts as a separate consonant.

a	like *o* in hot	á	like *a* in far
e	like *e* in send	é	like *a* in day
i	like *i* in hit	í	like *ee* in feet
o	like *o* in open	ó	same but longer
ö	the sound that starts earth		
ő	like the *u* in fur	u	like *u* in put
ú	like *u* in rule	ü	like *u* in French tu
ű	the same but longer		
c	like *ts* in hats	s	like *sh* in cash
cs	like *ch* in touch	sz	like *s* in sit
zs	like *s* in pleasure		
j	like *y* in yes	ly	like *y* in yes
gy	like *d* at the start of dune		
ny	like *n* in new	ty	like *t* in tulip

Useful Words and Phrases

yes/no/maybe *igen/nem/talán*
please *kérem*
thank you/thanks *köszönöm/kösz*
OK/very good *jó/nagyon jó*
good/nice *szép*
bad/ugly *csúnya*
hello (to one person) *szervusz*
hello (to more than one) *szervusztok*
hello (familiar) *szia*
goodbye/bye *viszontlátásra/viszlát*
excuse me (to get past) *szabad?*
excuse me (for attention) *bocsánat, uram*
I beg your pardon? *Tessék?*
Can you help me? *Kérhetem a segítségét?*
Do you speak English? *Beszél angolul?*
I am English/American *Angol/amerikai vagyok*
I don't speak Hungarian *Nem beszélek Magyarul*

I (don't) understand *(Nem) értem*
What is your name? *Mi a neve?*
My name is... *A nevem...*
Nice to meet you *Örvendek*
police *rendőrség*
doctor *orvos*
ambulance *mentőautó*
I feel ill *Rosszul vagyok*
I would like... *Kérek...*
How much is this? *Ez mennyibe kerül?*
expensive *drága*
cheap *olcsó*
big *nagy*
small *kicsi*
open *nyitva*
closed *zárva*
entrance *bejárat*
exit *kijárat*
this one *ez*
that one *az*
push *tolni*
pull *húzni*
men's *férfi*
women's *női*
bookshop *könyvesbolt*
chemist *patika; gyógyszertár*
department store *aruház*
market *piac*
post office *postahivatal*
art gallery *képcsarnok*
bridge *híd*
castle *vár*
cinema *mozi*
hill *hegy; domb*
palace *palota*
tower *torony*
wood or park *liget*
left *bal*
right *jobb*
straight on *egyenesen*
where *hol*
Where is the...? *Hol van a...?*
How far is...? *Milyen messze van...?*
address *cím*
floor *emelet*
street/avenue *utca/út*
square *tér/tere*
boulevard *körút*
walk/promenade *sétány*
bus *autóbusz*
tram *villamos*

trolleybus *troli(busz)*
train *vonat*
underground *metró*
bus stop *buszmegálló*
railway station *pályaudvar*
station *állomás*
platform *vágány*
boat *hajó*
aeroplane *repülőgép*
airport *repülőtér*
departure *indulás*
arrival *érkezés*
ticket *jegy*
seat (place) *hely*

Days and Months
Monday *hétfő*
Tuesday *kedd*
Wednesday *szerda*
Thursday *csütörtök*
Friday *péntek*
Saturday *szombat*
Sunday *vasárnap*

January *január*
February *február*
March *március*
April *április*
May *május*
June *június*
July *július*
August *augusztus*
September *szeptember*
October *október*
November *november*
December *december*

Numbers
one *egy*
two *kettő/két*
three *három*
four *négy*
five *öt*
six *hat*
seven *hét*
eight *nyolc*
nine *kilenc*
ten *tíz*
eleven *tizenegy*
twelve *tizenkettő*
twenty *húsz*
twenty-one *huszonegy*

thirty *harminc*
forty *negyven*
fifty *ötven*
sixty *hatvan*
seventy *hetven*
eighty *nyolcvan*
ninety *kilencven*
one hundred *száz*
one hundred and ten *száztíz*
two hundred *kétszáz*
one thousand *ezer*
one million *millió*

Time

minute *perc*
hour/half an hour *óra/félóra*
day/week *nap/hét*
month/year *hónap/év*
morning/afternoon *reggel/délután*
evening *este*
today/tomorrow *ma/holnap*
yesterday *tegnap*
now *most*

Food and Drink

I'd like... *Szeretnék egy...*
I am a vegetarian *Vegetáriánus vagyok*
The bill please *Számla, kérem*
menu *étlap*
wine list *itallap*
breakfast *reggeli*
lunch *ebéd*
dinner *vacsora*
restaurant *étterem; vendéglő*
salt *só*
pepper *bors*
glass *pohár*
bottle *üveg*
cheers *egészségedre*
starters *előételek*
main courses *főételek*
vegetables *zöldség*
desserts *édességek*
soup *leves*
egg *tojás*

Meat *Hús*

lamb *bárány*
chicken *csirke*
sausage *kolbász*
beef *marha*

liver *máj*
pork *sertéshúst*

Fish *Halételek*

trout *pisztráng*
carp *ponty*
pike-perch *süllő*

Vegetables *Zöldségek*

beans *bab*
boiled potatoes *főttburgonya*
mushroom *gomba*
onion *hagyma*
chips/fries *hasábbburgonya*
cabbage *káposta*
tomato *paradicsom*
rice *rizs*
peas *zölborsó*
dumplings *zsemlegombóc*

Fruit *Gyümölcsök*

apple *alma*
banana *banán*
lemon *citrom*
orange *narancs*
plum *szilva*
strawberry *eper*

Drinks *Italok*

mineral water *ásvány-víz*
fruit juice *gyümölcslé*
coffee *kávé*
tea *tea*
sugar *cukor*
milk *tej*
red wine *vörösbor*
white wine *fehérbor*
beer *sör*

Hungarian Dishes

jókai bableves bean soup with vegetables, smoked pork and small dumplings
libamáj zsirjában roast goose liver
hortobágyi palacsinta pancakes stuffed with minced pork, covered with sauce made from pork gravy, mushrooms and sour cream
bakonyi sertéshús pork in mushroom and sour cream sauce
kacsasült roast duck
töltött paprika stuffed peppers
pörkölt stew, usually meat
paprikás pörkölt with sour cream

paprikás csirke paprika chicken
halászlé hot and sour fish soup
gombafejek rántva breaded and fried
mushrooms
saláta salad (often pickled cabbage, gherkin
or pepper)

rántott sajt cheese fried in batter
rétes (almás/cseresznyés/túrós)
(apple/cherry/curd cheese) strudels
túrógombóc curd cheese balls
Gundel palacsinta pancakes stuffed with
walnuts and topped with chocolate sauce

Index

Main page references are in **bold**. Page references to maps are in *italics*.

3rd American edition published 2012 by

CADOGAN GUIDES USA
An imprint of Interlink Publishing Group, Inc
46 Crosby Street, Northampton, Massachusetts 01060
www.interlinkbooks.com
www.cadoganguidesusa.com

Text Copyright © Mary-Ann Gallagher, Sadakat Kadri, Matthew Gardner 2005, 2007, 2011
Copyright © 2011 New Holland Publishers (UK) Ltd

Cover photographs: front cover Kohlmarkt, Vienna © Martin Painhart/istockphoto.com; back cover Charles Bridge, Prague © Courtyardpix/istockphoto.com
Photo essay photographs: © istockphoto.com, except p.5 © Viennaslide / Alamy, and p.14 (top)© Guy Hobbs
Maps © Cadogan Guides, drawn by Maidenhead Cartographic Services Ltd
Publisher: Guy Hobbs
Cover design: Jason Hopper
Photo essay design: Ben Cracknell Studios
Editor: Mary-Ann Gallagher
Proofreading: Elspeth Anderson
Indexing: Isobel McLean

Printed in Italy by Legoprint

Library of Congress Cataloging-in-Publication Data available
ISBN: 978-1-56656-871-5

Budapest: Metro

M3
Újpest-Központ
Újpest-Városkapu
Gyöngyösi u.
Forgách u.
Árpád híd
Dózsa Gy. út
Lehel tér
Nyugati pu.
Arany J. u.
DEÁK F. TÉR

Danube

M4
Bosnyàk ter
Róna utca
Széchenyi fürdő   Mexikói út   **M1**
Hősök tere
Bajza u.   Hungária Körut
Kodály körönd
Vörösmarty u.
Oktogon
Opera   Dózsca György út
Bajcsy-Zs. út   **M2/ HÉV**

BATTHYÁNY TÉR
Moszkva tér
Déli pu.
Kossuth tér
Vörösmarty tér
M1
Ferenciek tere

Astoria
Blaha L. tér
Népszinház utca
Rákoczi tér
Keleti pu.
Népstadion
Pillangó u.
ÖRS VEZÉR TERE

M4   **M2**
Kelenföld pályaudvar
Tétényi út
Bocskai út
Moriez Zsigmond Kor tér
Szert Géllert tér
Danube
Fővám tér
Kálvin tér
Ferenc krt.
Klinikák
Nagyvárad tér
Népliget
Ecseri út
Pöttyös u.
Határ út
Kőbánya-Kispest
M3

M1/M2/M3: metro lines
M4: opening 2012
M5: slated for 2015

Vienna: U-Bahn

U6 FLORIDSDORF

U1 LEOPOLDAU
Gorssfeldsiedlur
Aderklaaer Strass
Rennbahnweg
Kagraner Platz
Kagran
Alte Donau
Kaisermühlen-
Vienna Int.Centre
Donauinsel
Vorgartenstrasse

U4 HEILIGENSTADT
Jägerstrasse
Neue Donau
Dresdner Strasse
HANDELSKAI

SPITTELAU
Nussdorfer Strasse
Währinger Strasse-Volksoper
Michelbeuern-Allg. Krankenhaus
Alser Strasse
Friedensbrücke
Rossauer Lände

PRATERSTERN (WIEN NORD)
Messe-Prater
SCHOTTENRING
Schottentor
U2
Krieau
Stadion
Hardeggasse
ASPERNSTRASS
Donauspital

U3 OTTAKRING
Kendlerstrasse
Hütteldorfer Strasse
Schweglerstrasse
Josefstädter Strasse
Thaliastrasse
Rathaus
Burggasse-Stadthalle
Johnstrasse

Nestroyplatz
Donaumarina
SCHWEDENPLATZ
Stadiau

HÜTTELDORF
U4
Ober St. Veit
Unter St. Veit
Braunschweiggasse
Hietzing
Schönbrunn
Meidling Hauptstrasse
LÄNGENFELDGASSE
Niederhofstrasse
WESTBAHNHOF
Gumpendorfer Strasse
Zieglergasse
Neubaugasse
Museums-Quartier
Margaretengürtel
Pilgramgasse
Kettenbrückengasse
VOLKSTHEATER
Herrengasse
STEPHANSPLATZ
Stubentor
LANDSTRASSE (WIEN MITTE)
Donaustadtbrücke
Rochusgasse
Kardinal-Nagl-Platz
Schlachthausgasse
Erdberg
Gasometer
Zippererstrasse
Enkplatz
SIMMERING
U3

U2
KARLSPLATZ
Stadtpark
Taubstummengasse

MEIDLING PHILADELPHIABRÜCKE
SÜDTIROLER PLATZ

Tscherttegasse
Am Schöpfwerk
Alterlaa
Erlaaer Strasse
Perfektastrasse
Siebenhirten
U6

Keplerplatz
Reumannplatz
U1